VIZ GRAPHIC NOVEL

EL-HAZARD

THE MAGNIFICENT WORLD

volume 3

Story and Art by Hidetomo Tsubura

Based on El-Hazard
Created by Hiroki Hayashi and Ryoe Tsukimura

CONTENTS

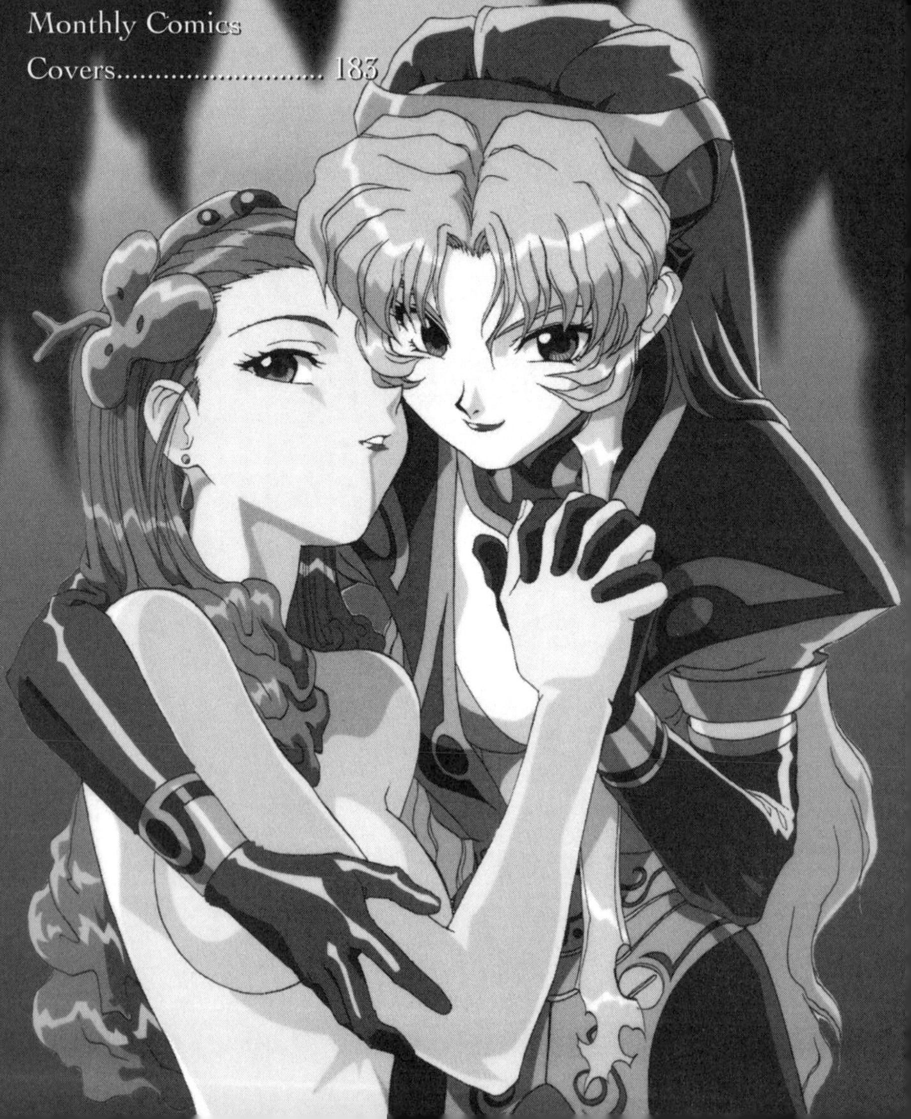

EL-HAZARD

THE MAGNIFICENT WORLD

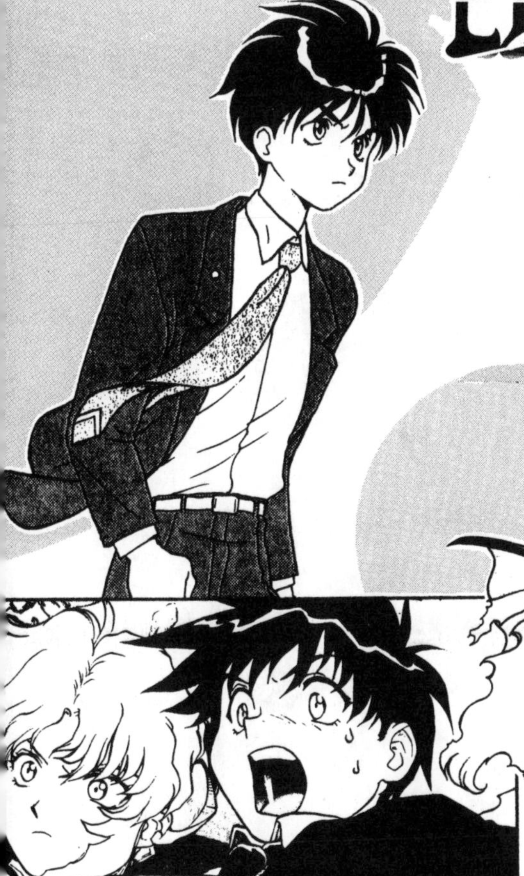

Makoto Mizuhara ▲

The main character of our story, Makoto is a kind-hearted science geek. Through the process of being transported to El-Hazard, Makoto somehow gained the same special powers as the royal family of El-Hazard.

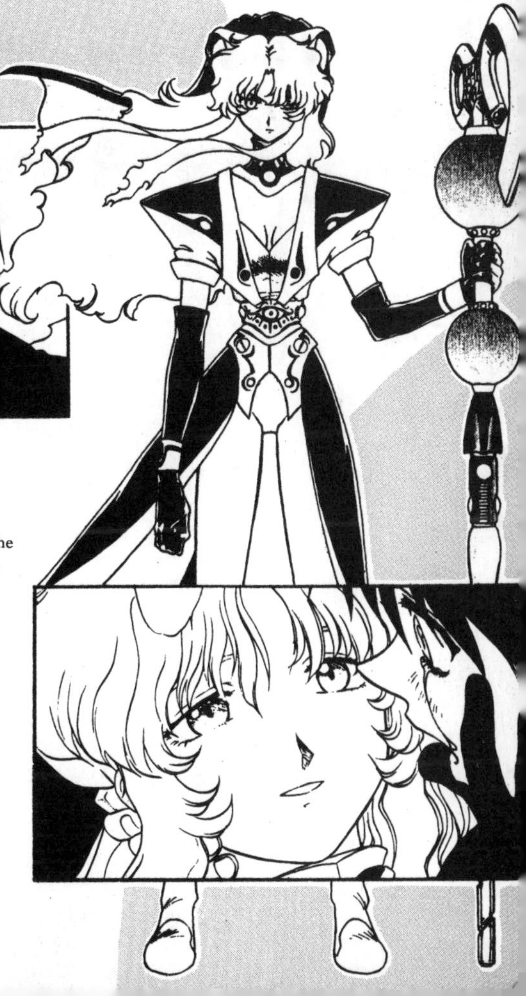

Ifurita ▶

A weapon (Demon God) left over from the ancient civilization of El-Hazard. Because of her devastating power, she is misunderstood and feared by all. Her interactions with Makoto have somehow unlocked her previously emotionless demeanor. The mystery still remains: what was she doing underneath Makoto's school? Why and how did she send Makoto and the others to El-Hazard?

The Allied Kingdoms

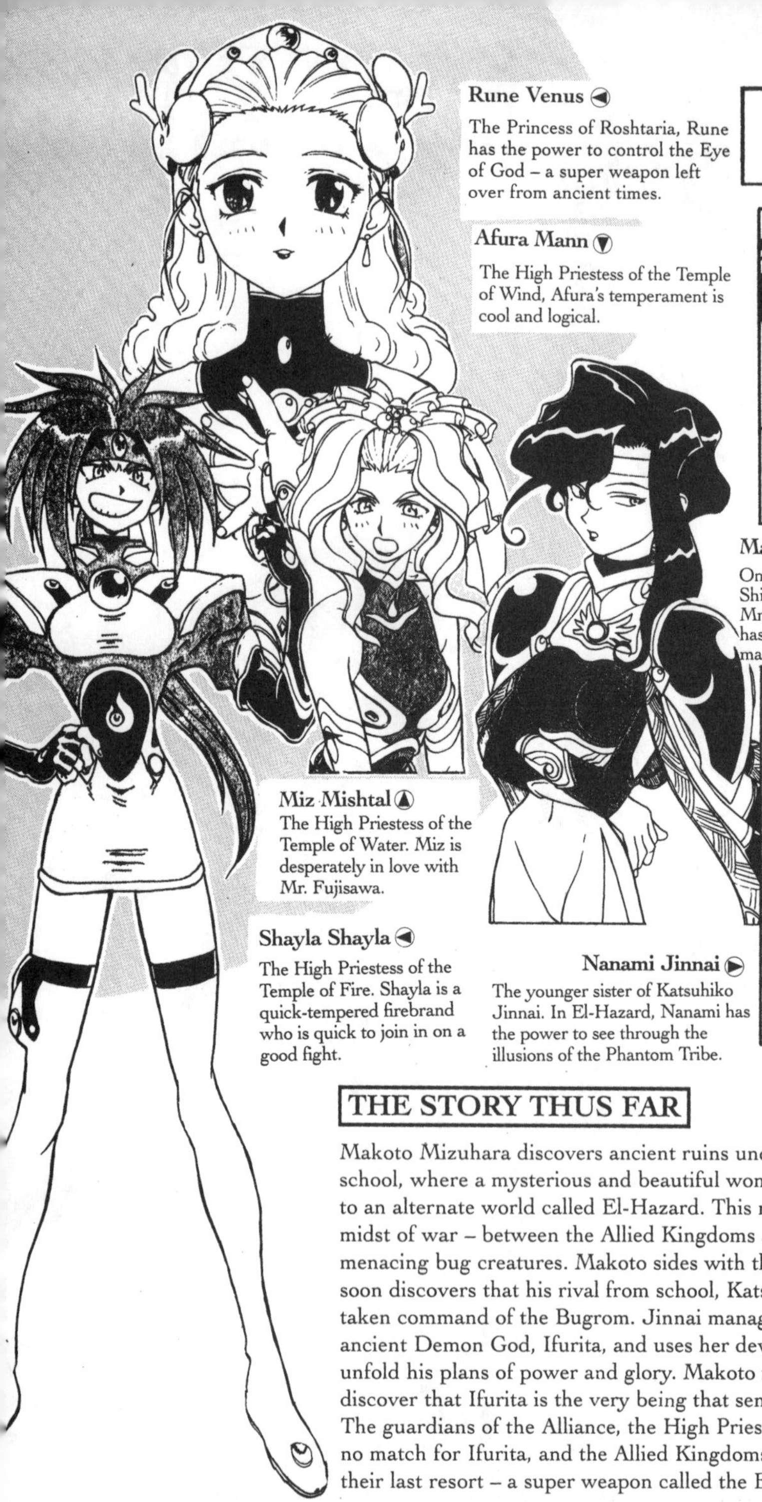

Rune Venus ◀
The Princess of Roshtaria, Rune has the power to control the Eye of God – a super weapon left over from ancient times.

Afura Mann ▼
The High Priestess of the Temple of Wind, Afura's temperament is cool and logical.

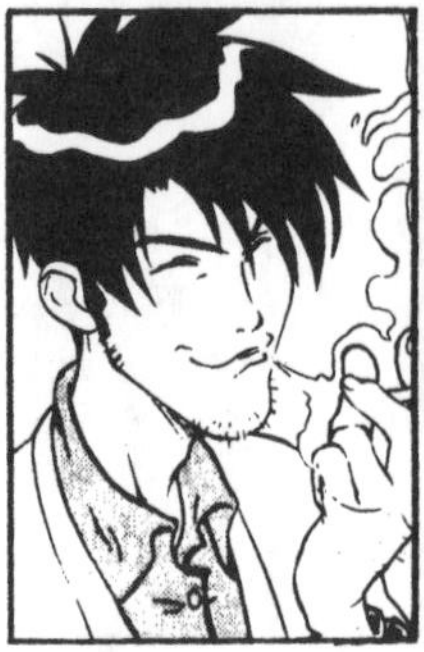

Masamichi Fujisawa ▲
One of Makoto's teachers from Shinonome High. In El-Hazard Mr. Fujisawa discovers that he has somehow gained superhuman strength.

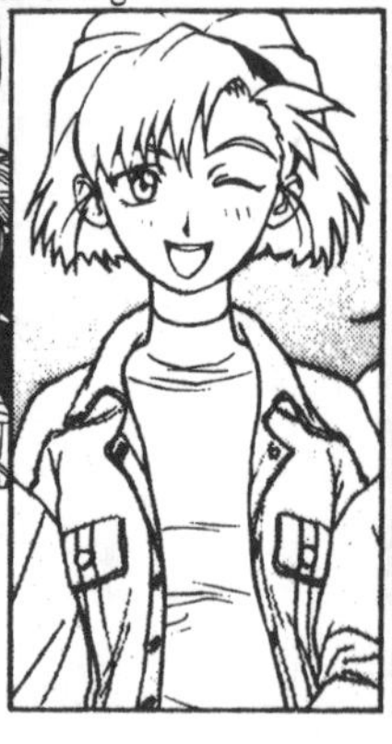

Miz Mishtal ▲
The High Priestess of the Temple of Water. Miz is desperately in love with Mr. Fujisawa.

Shayla Shayla ◀
The High Priestess of the Temple of Fire. Shayla is a quick-tempered firebrand who is quick to join in on a good fight.

Nanami Jinnai ▶
The younger sister of Katsuhiko Jinnai. In El-Hazard, Nanami has the power to see through the illusions of the Phantom Tribe.

THE STORY THUS FAR

Makoto Mizuhara discovers ancient ruins underneath his high school, where a mysterious and beautiful woman transports him to an alternate world called El-Hazard. This magical land is in the midst of war – between the Allied Kingdoms and a race of menacing bug creatures. Makoto sides with the Alliance and he soon discovers that his rival from school, Katsuhiko Jinnai, has taken command of the Bugrom. Jinnai manages to revive the ancient Demon God, Ifurita, and uses her devastating power to unfold his plans of power and glory. Makoto is alarmed to discover that Ifurita is the very being that sent him to El-Hazard. The guardians of the Alliance, the High Priestesses, turn out to be no match for Ifurita, and the Allied Kingdoms decide to turn to their last resort – a super weapon called the Eye of God.

However, a race of illusionists, called the Phantom Tribe, have kidnapped Rune Venus – the only person in El-Hazard who has the ability to control the Eye of God. The Phantom Tribe also control two Demon Gods, who together, prove to be even more powerful than Ifurita.

With all the trump cards in the hands of the Phantom Tribe, Makoto and Ifurita team up to get the Princess back. Ifurita acquires an increasing fondness for Makoto – who is the only person who seems to understand her plight. Will this weakness prove to be Ifurita's downfall or her salvation?

The Bugrom

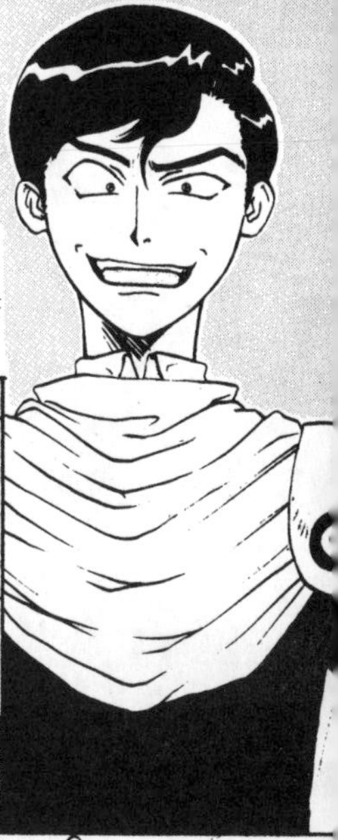

Katsuhiko Jinnai ▶

Makoto's self-proclaimed arch rival. Jinnai will stop at nothing to gain power and glory and most important of all to beat Makoto.

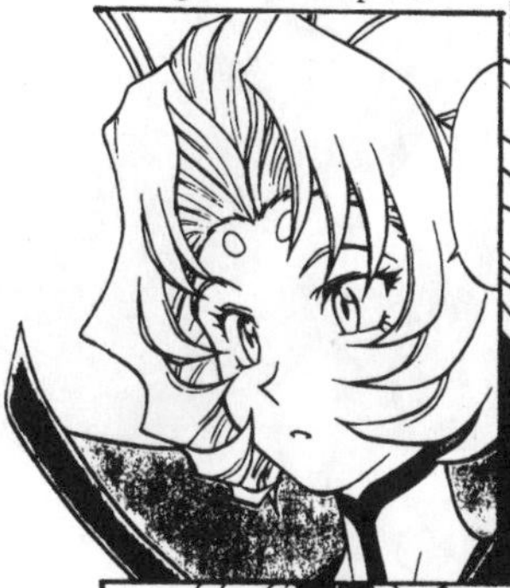

Diva ▶

The Queen of the Bugrom Empire. Diva has the utmost confidence in Jinnai and his megalomaniacal plans.

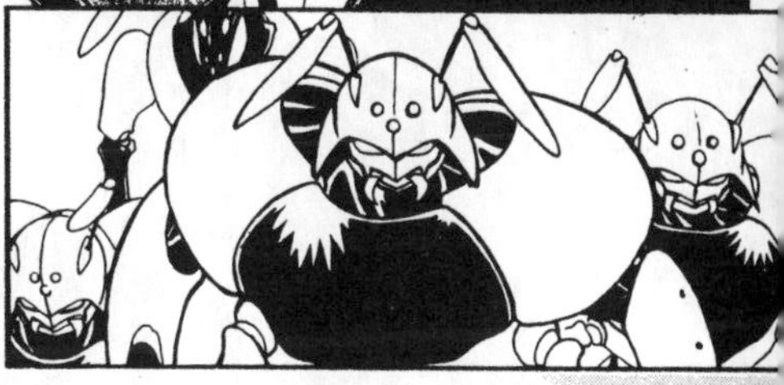

The Bugrom ▲

Plenty strong but not too bright.

The Phantom Tribe

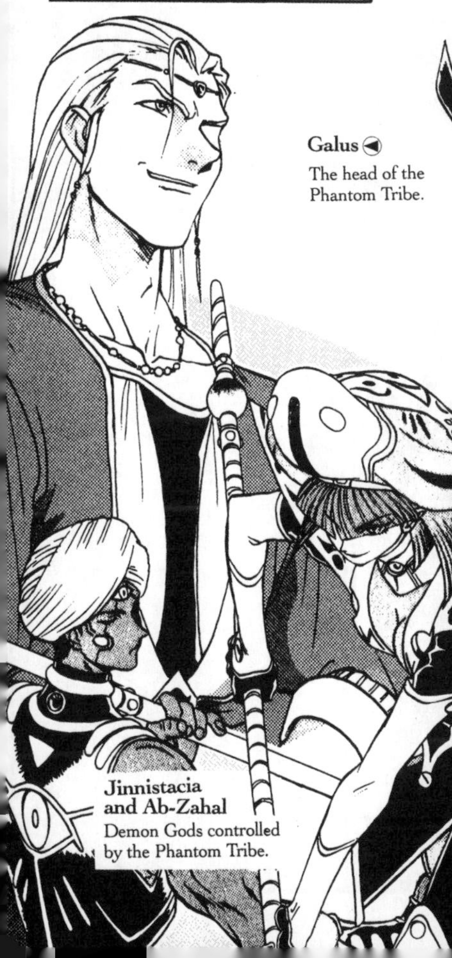

Galus ◀

The head of the Phantom Tribe.

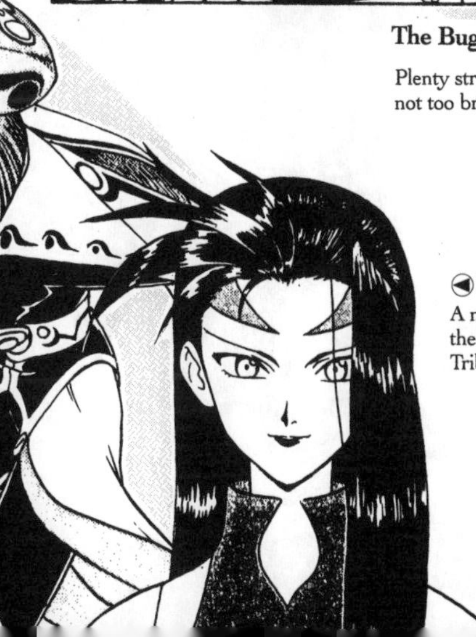

◀ Kiriya

A member of the Phantom Tribe.

Jinnistacia and Ab-Zahal

Demon Gods controlled by the Phantom Tribe.

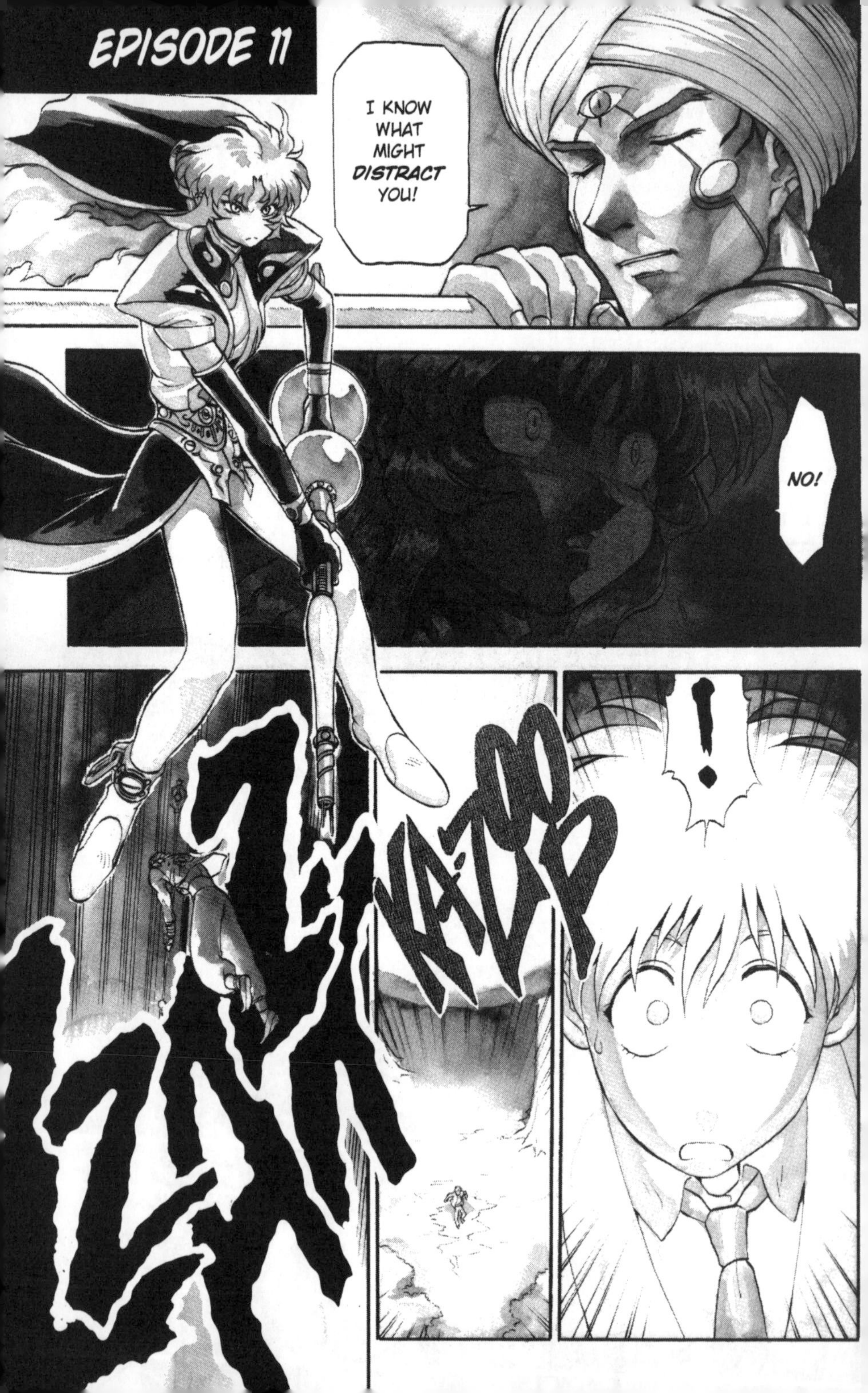
EPISODE 11
I KNOW WHAT MIGHT DISTRACT YOU!
NO!
!
KA-ZOOP

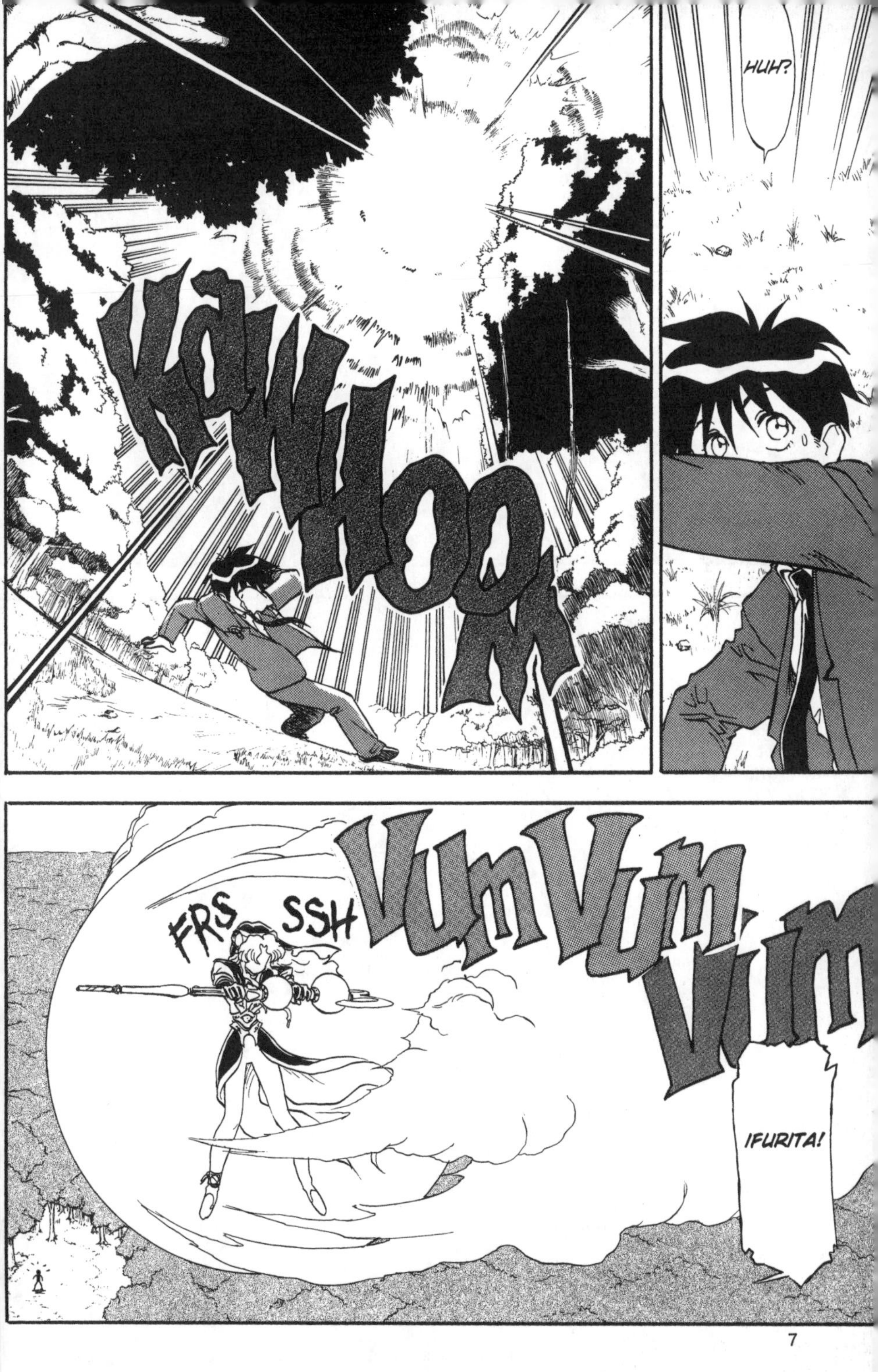
HUH?
KAWHOOM
FRS SSH
VUMVUM
VUM
IFURITA!

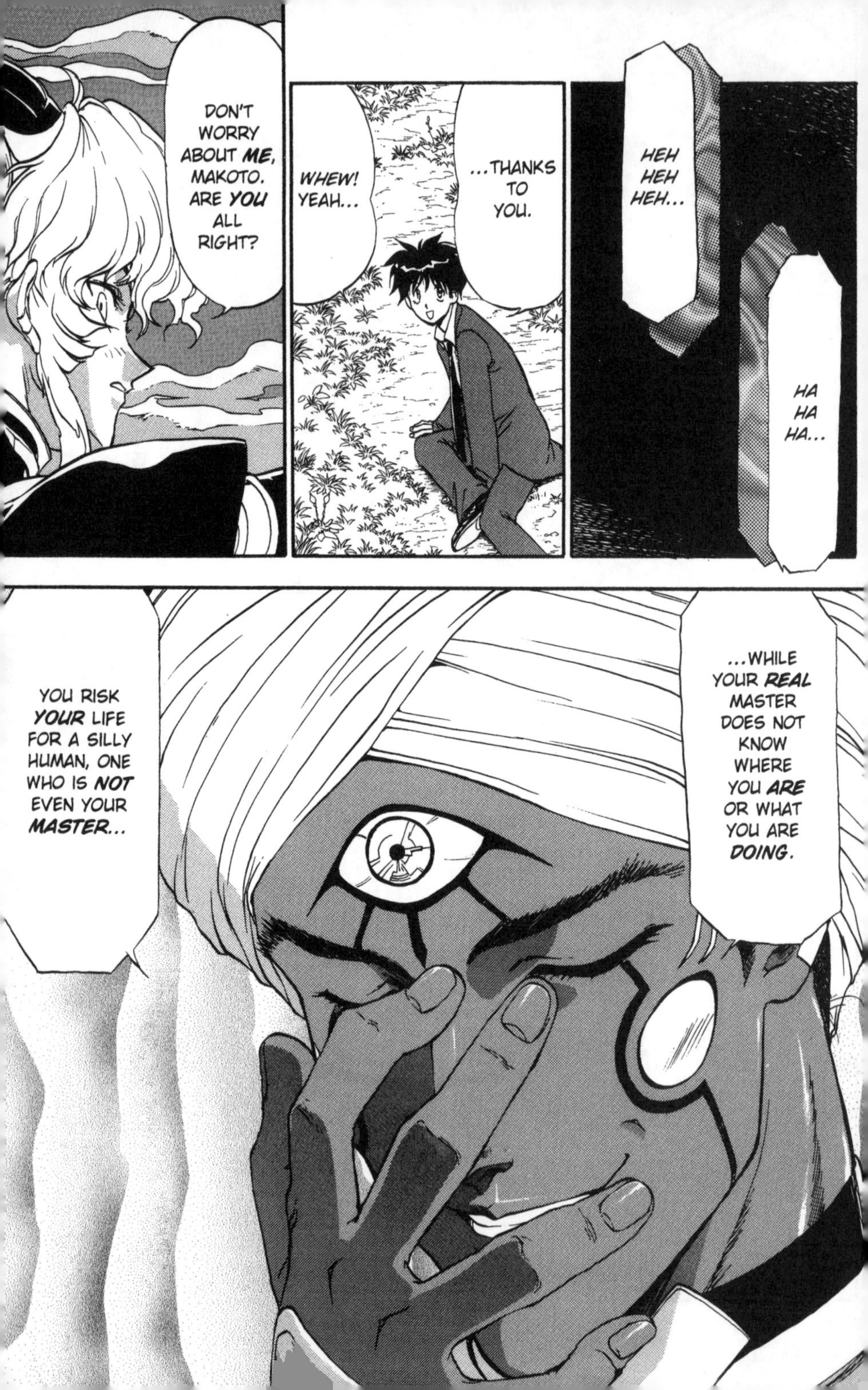
DON'T WORRY ABOUT ME, MAKOTO. ARE YOU ALL RIGHT?
WHEW! YEAH...
...THANKS TO YOU.
HEH HEH HEH...
HA HA HA...
YOU RISK YOUR LIFE FOR A SILLY HUMAN, ONE WHO IS NOT EVEN YOUR MASTER...
...WHILE YOUR REAL MASTER DOES NOT KNOW WHERE YOU ARE OR WHAT YOU ARE DOING.

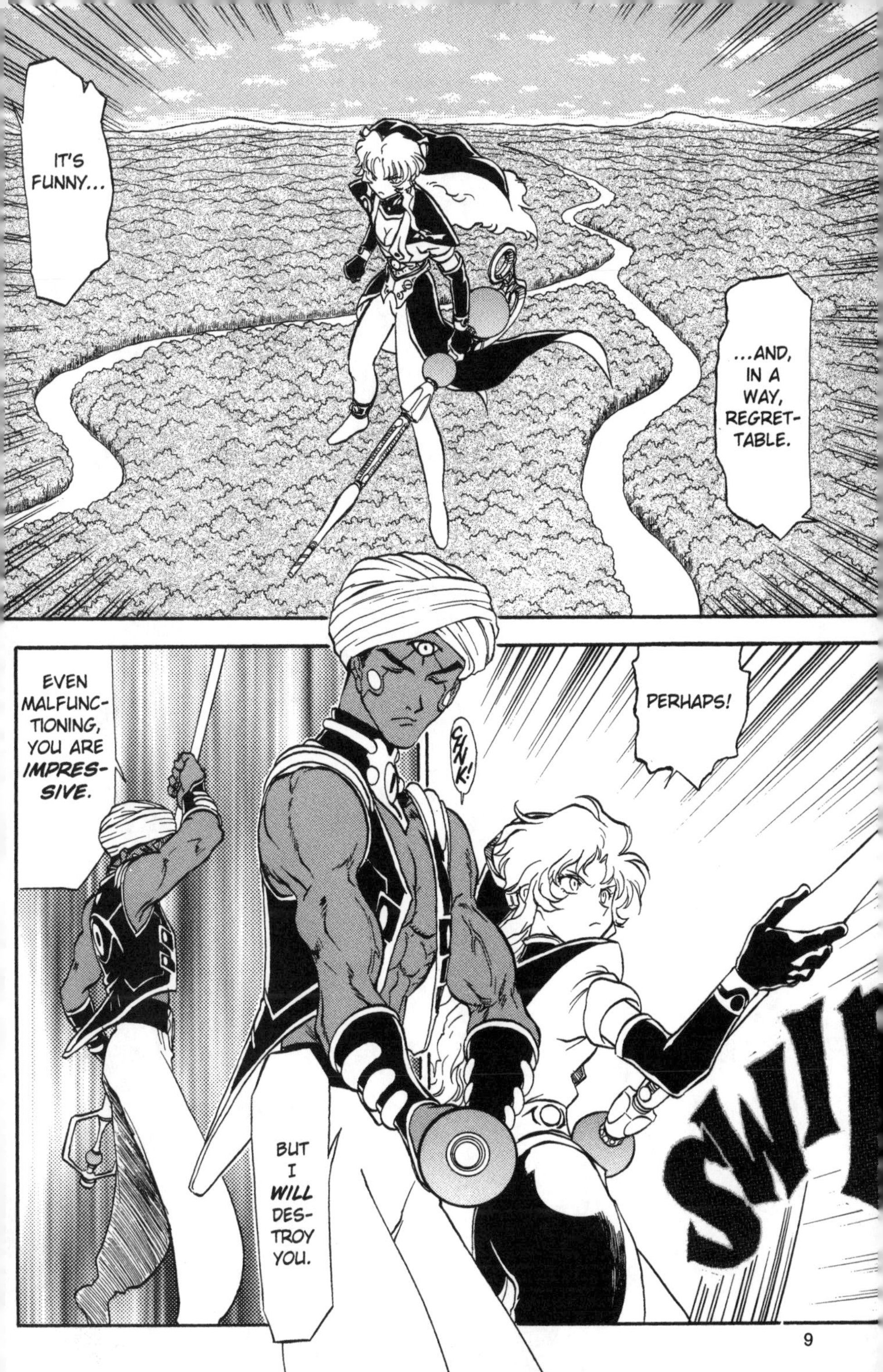

IT'S FUNNY...
...AND, IN A WAY, REGRETTABLE.
EVEN MALFUNCTIONING, YOU ARE *IMPRESSIVE*.
CHINK!
PERHAPS!
BUT I *WILL* DESTROY YOU.

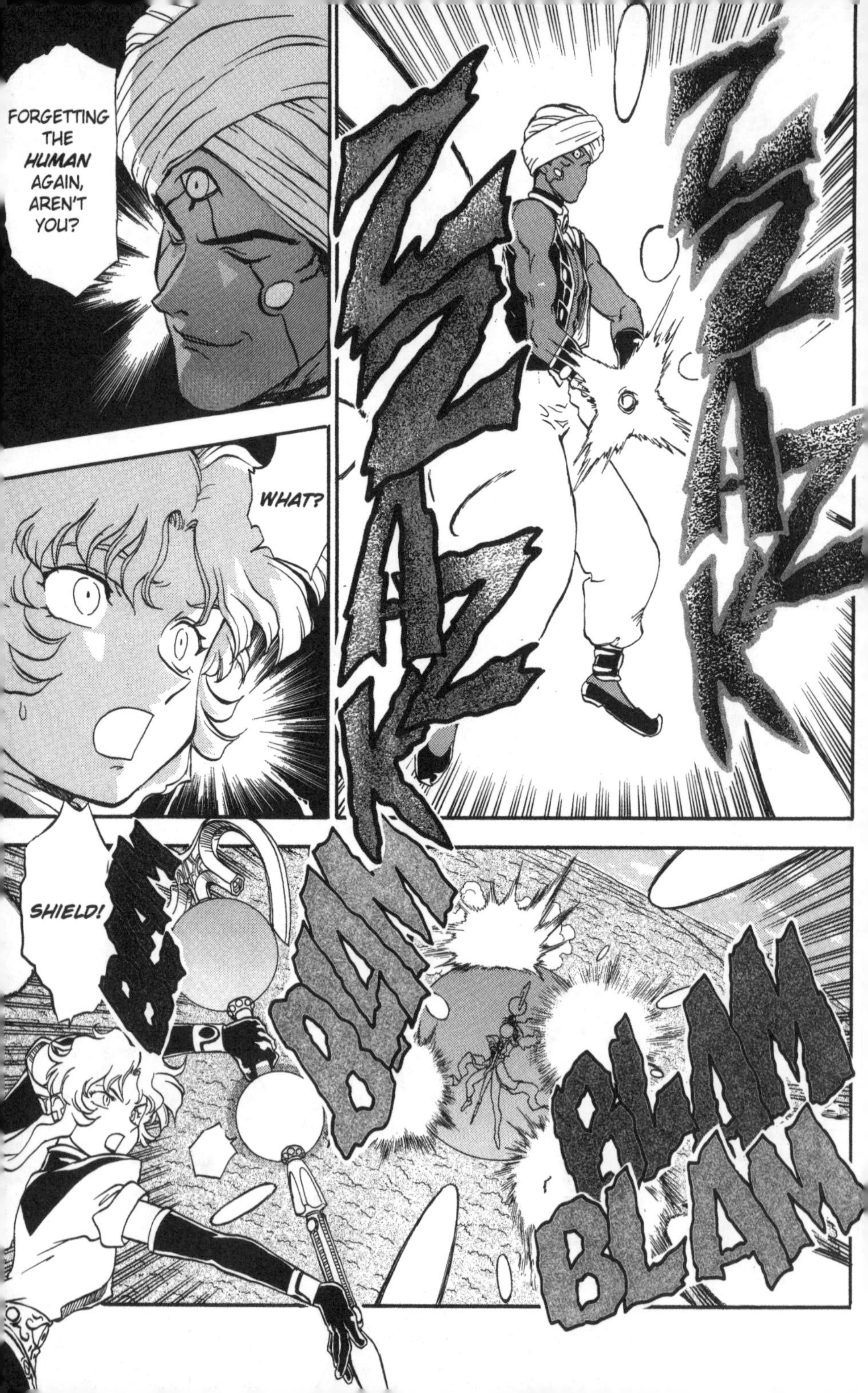
FORGETTING THE *HUMAN* AGAIN, AREN'T YOU?
WHAT?
SHIELD!
BOOM
BLAM BLAM

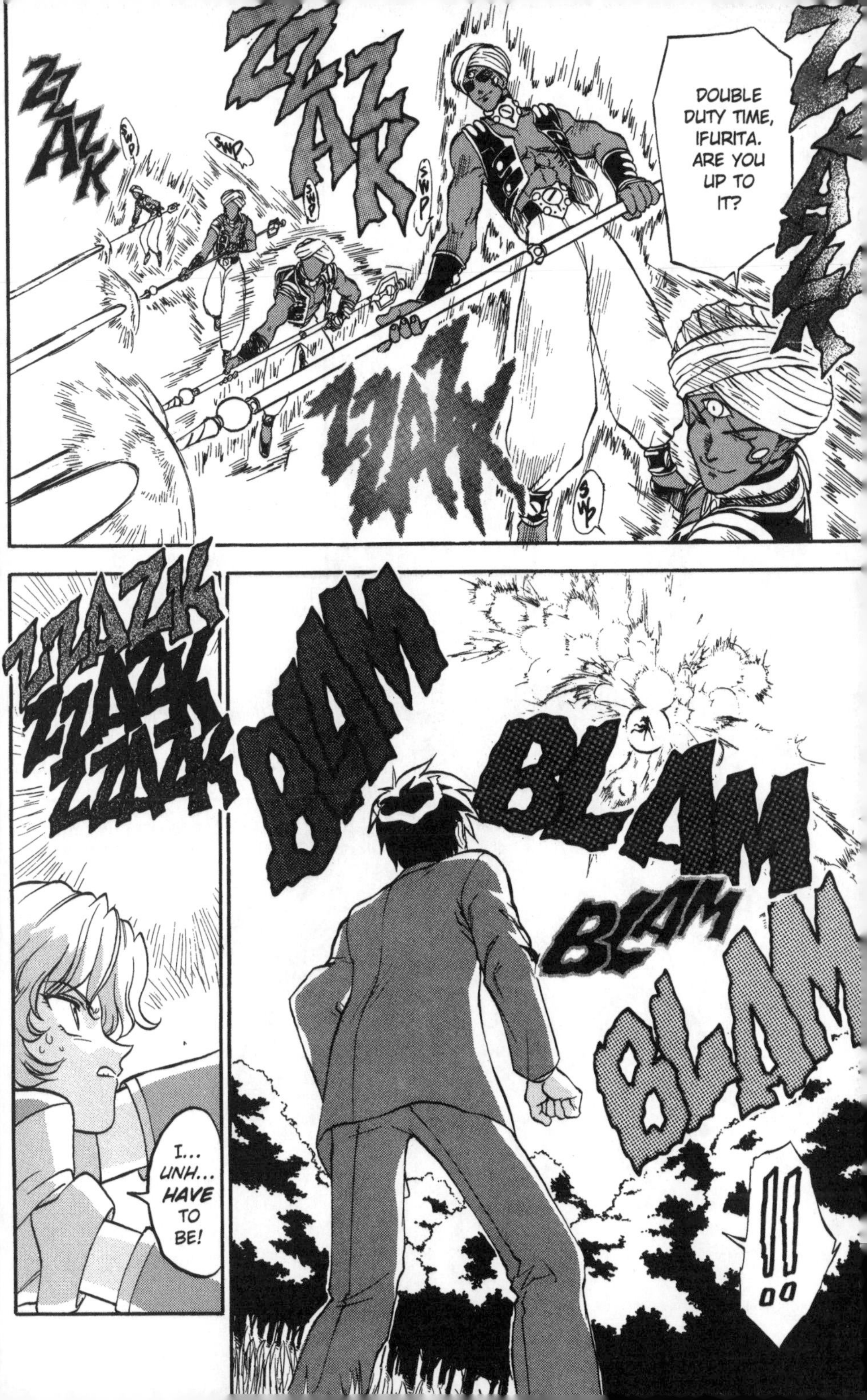
DOUBLE DUTY TIME, IFURITA. ARE YOU UP TO IT?
ZZAZK
ZZZAZK
ZZZAZK
SWP
BLAM
BLAM
BLAM
BLAM
ZZAZK ZZAZK ZZAZK
!!
I... UNH... HAVE TO BE!

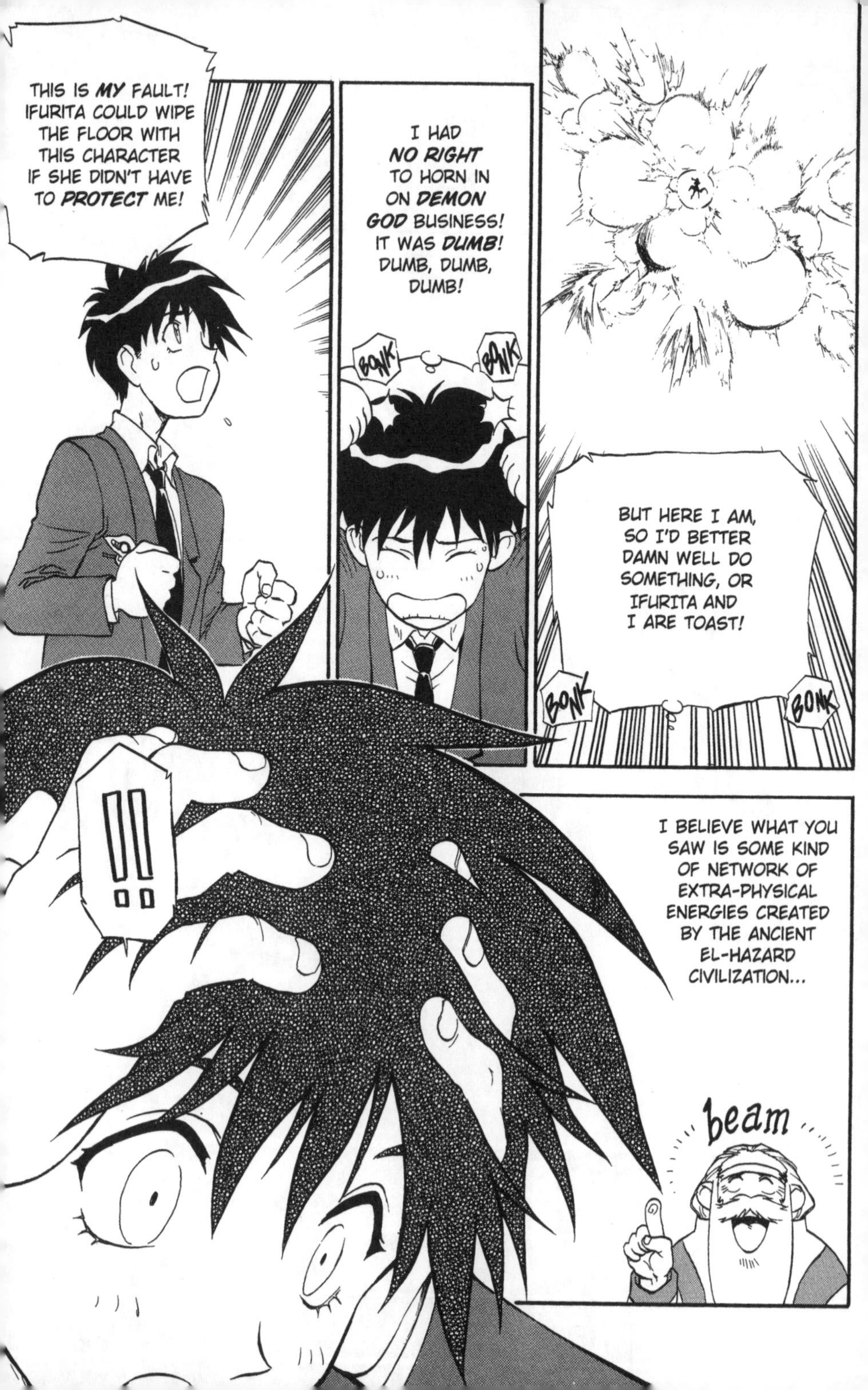
THIS IS MY FAULT! IFURITA COULD WIPE THE FLOOR WITH THIS CHARACTER IF SHE DIDN'T HAVE TO PROTECT ME!
I HAD NO RIGHT TO HORN IN ON DEMON GOD BUSINESS! IT WAS DUMB! DUMB, DUMB, DUMB!
BONK
BONK
BUT HERE I AM, SO I'D BETTER DAMN WELL DO SOMETHING, OR IFURITA AND I ARE TOAST!
BONK
BONK
!!
I BELIEVE WHAT YOU SAW IS SOME KIND OF NETWORK OF EXTRA-PHYSICAL ENERGIES CREATED BY THE ANCIENT EL-HAZARD CIVILIZATION...
beam

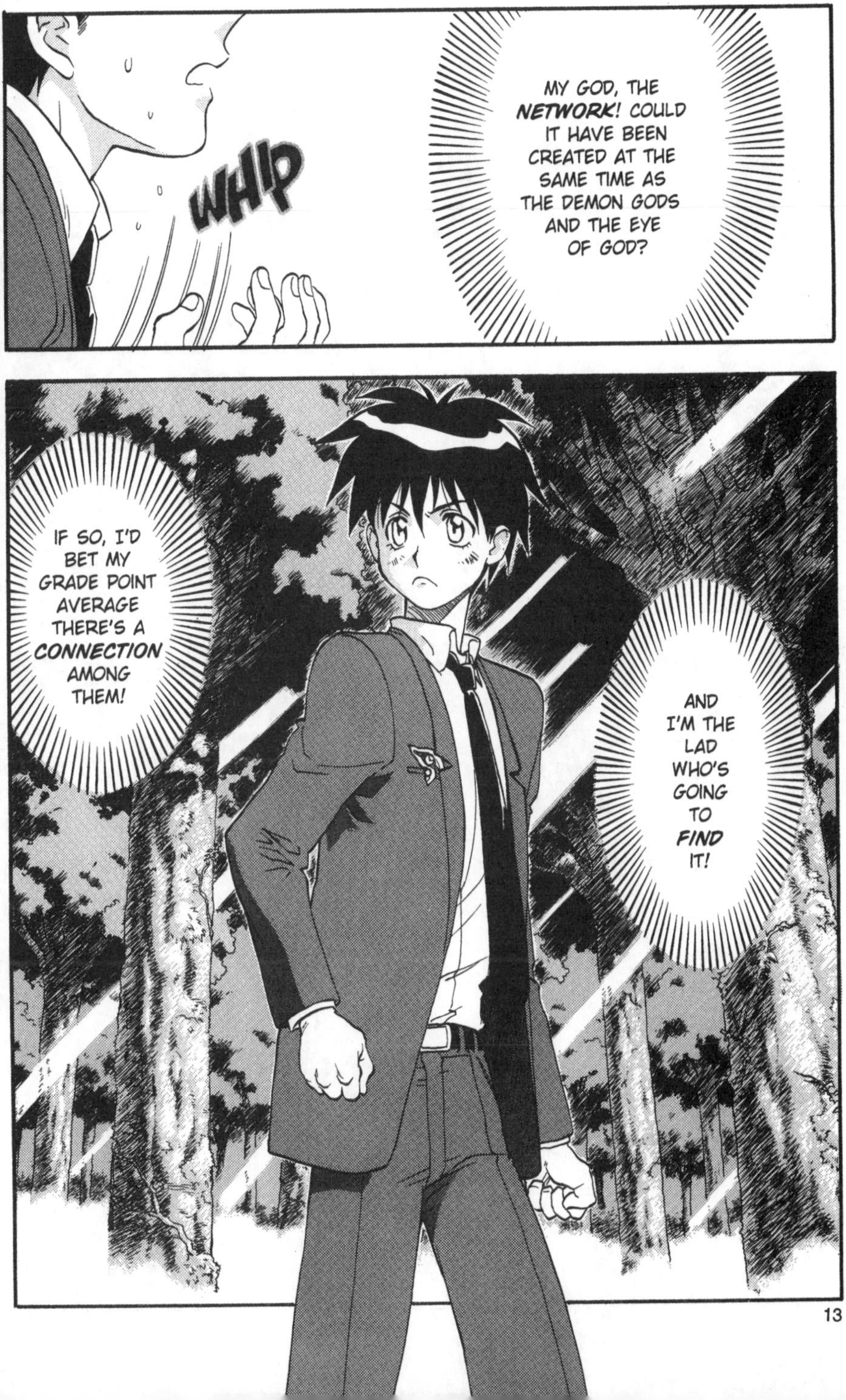
MY GOD, THE NETWORK! COULD IT HAVE BEEN CREATED AT THE SAME TIME AS THE DEMON GODS AND THE EYE OF GOD?
WHIP
IF SO, I'D BET MY GRADE POINT AVERAGE THERE'S A CONNECTION AMONG THEM!
AND I'M THE LAD WHO'S GOING TO FIND IT!

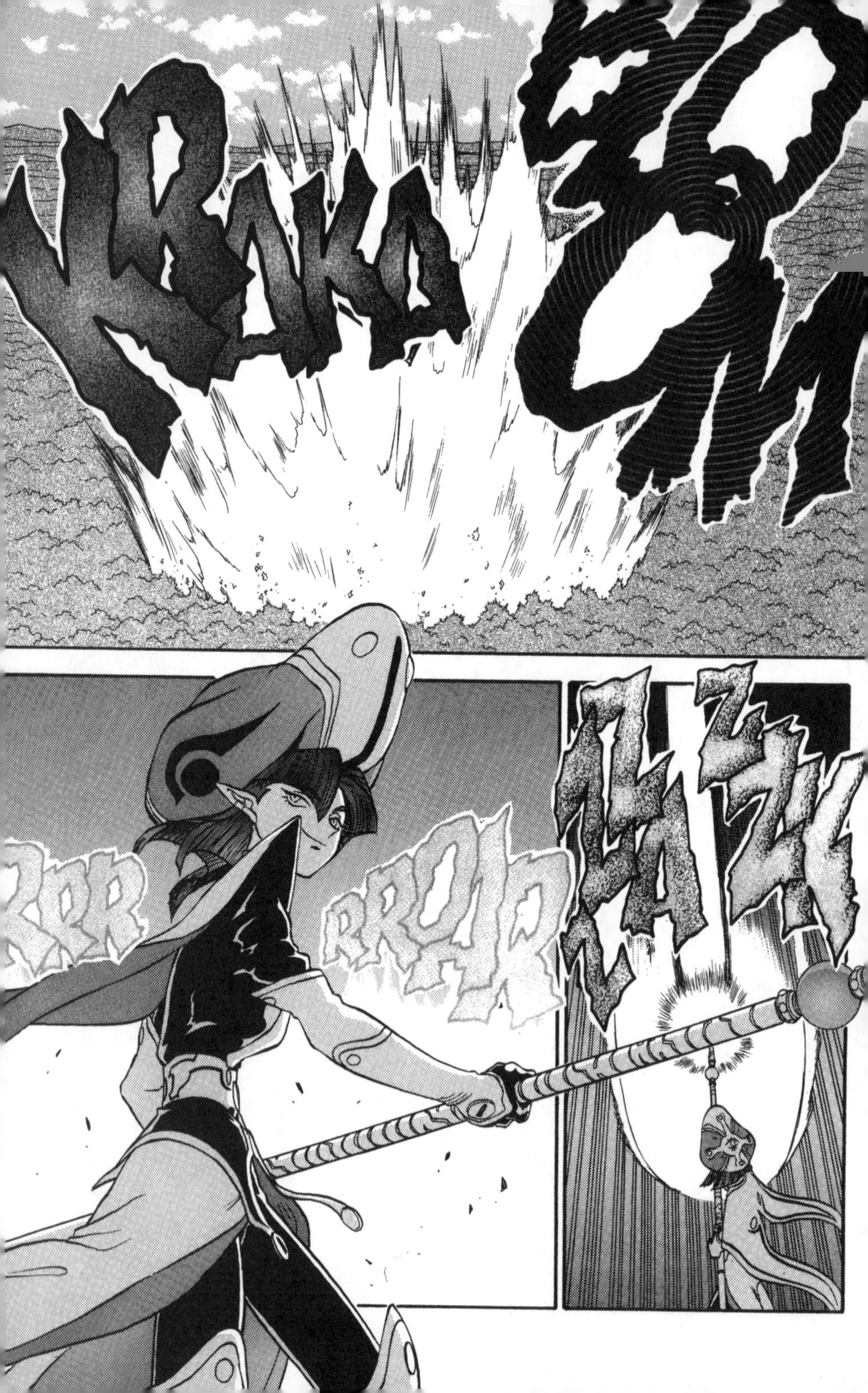

KRAKA
BOOM
RROAR

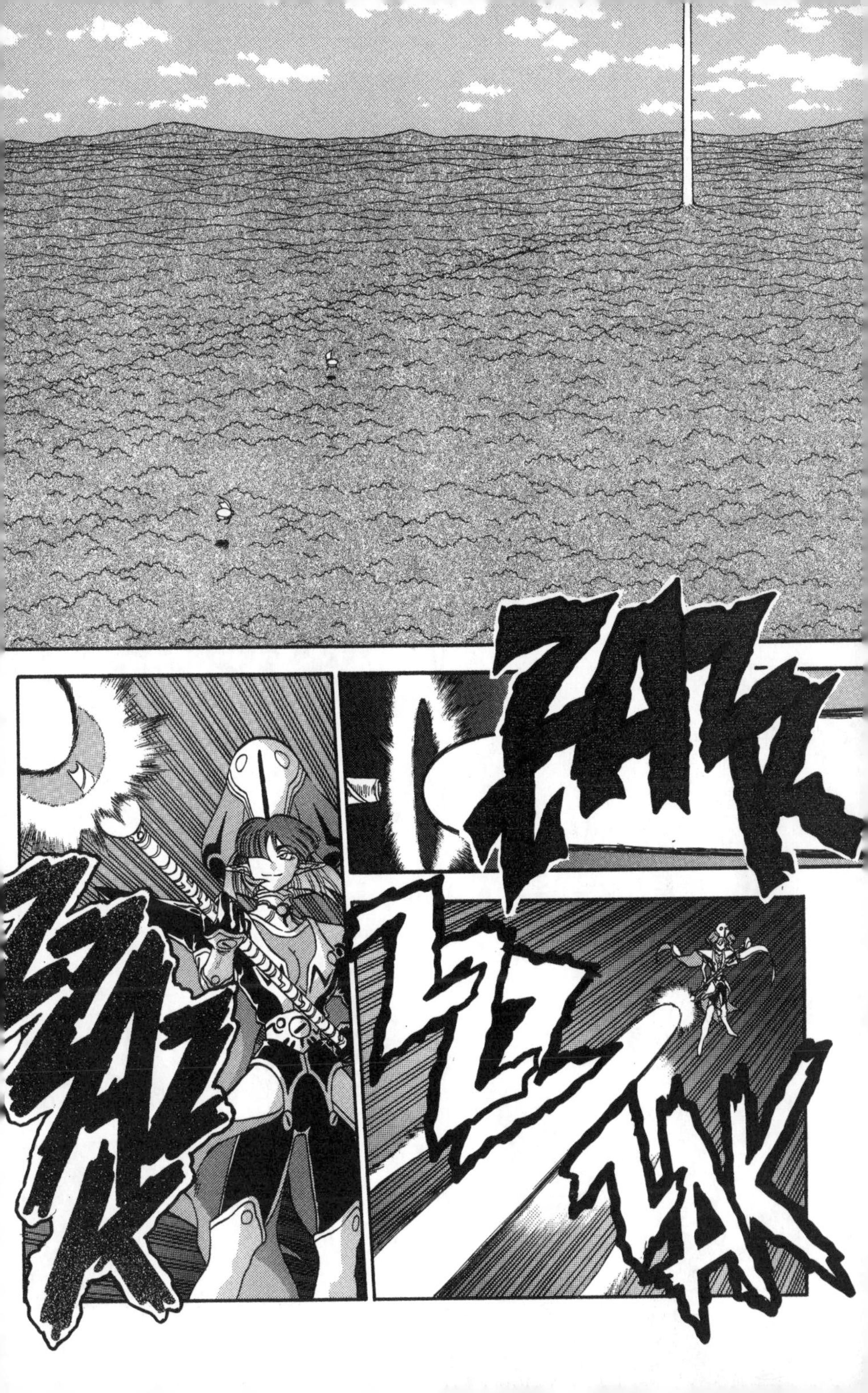
ZAK
ZAK

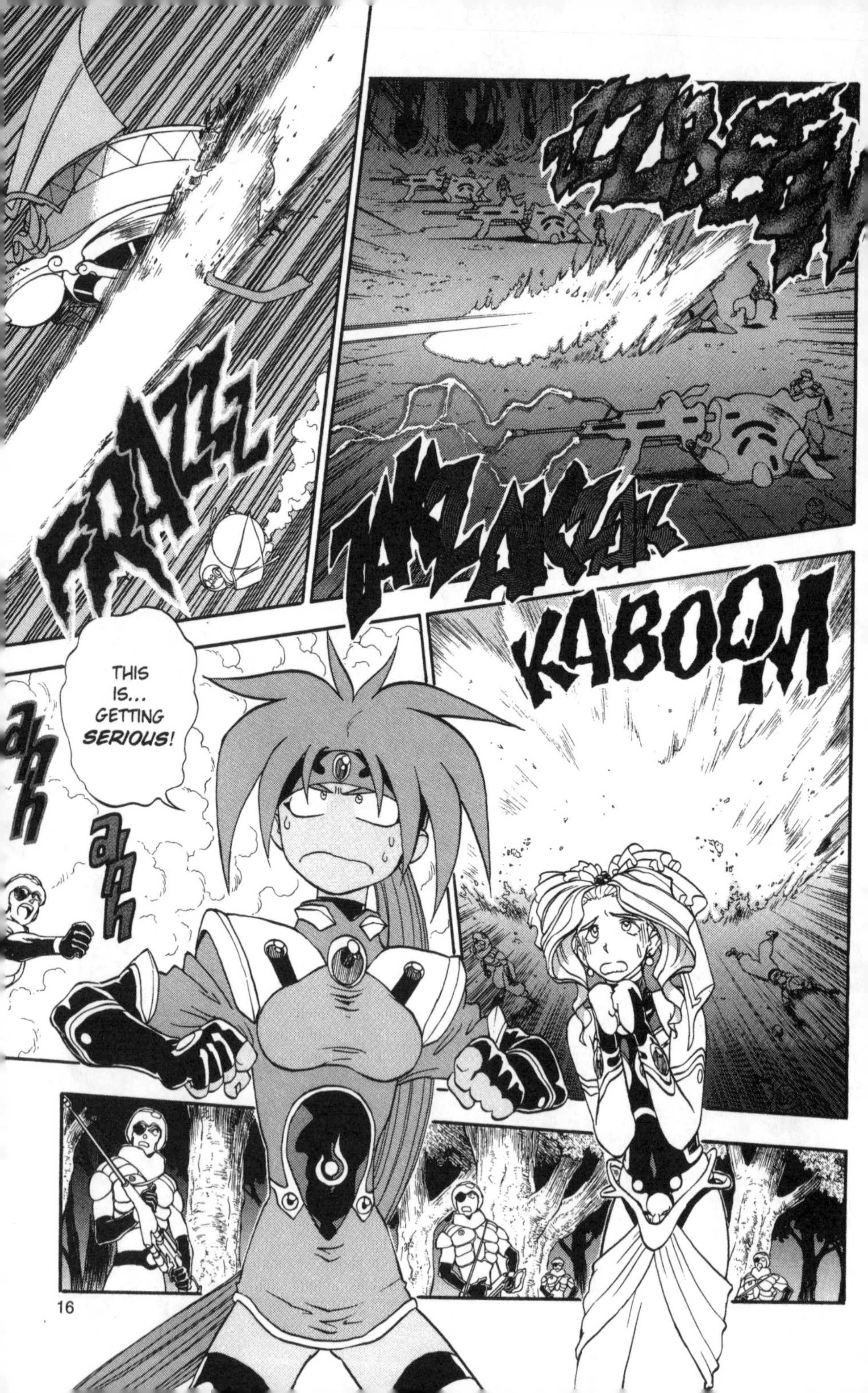
FRAZZZ
TAKZAKZAK
KABOOM
THIS IS... GETTING SERIOUS!
ahh
ahh

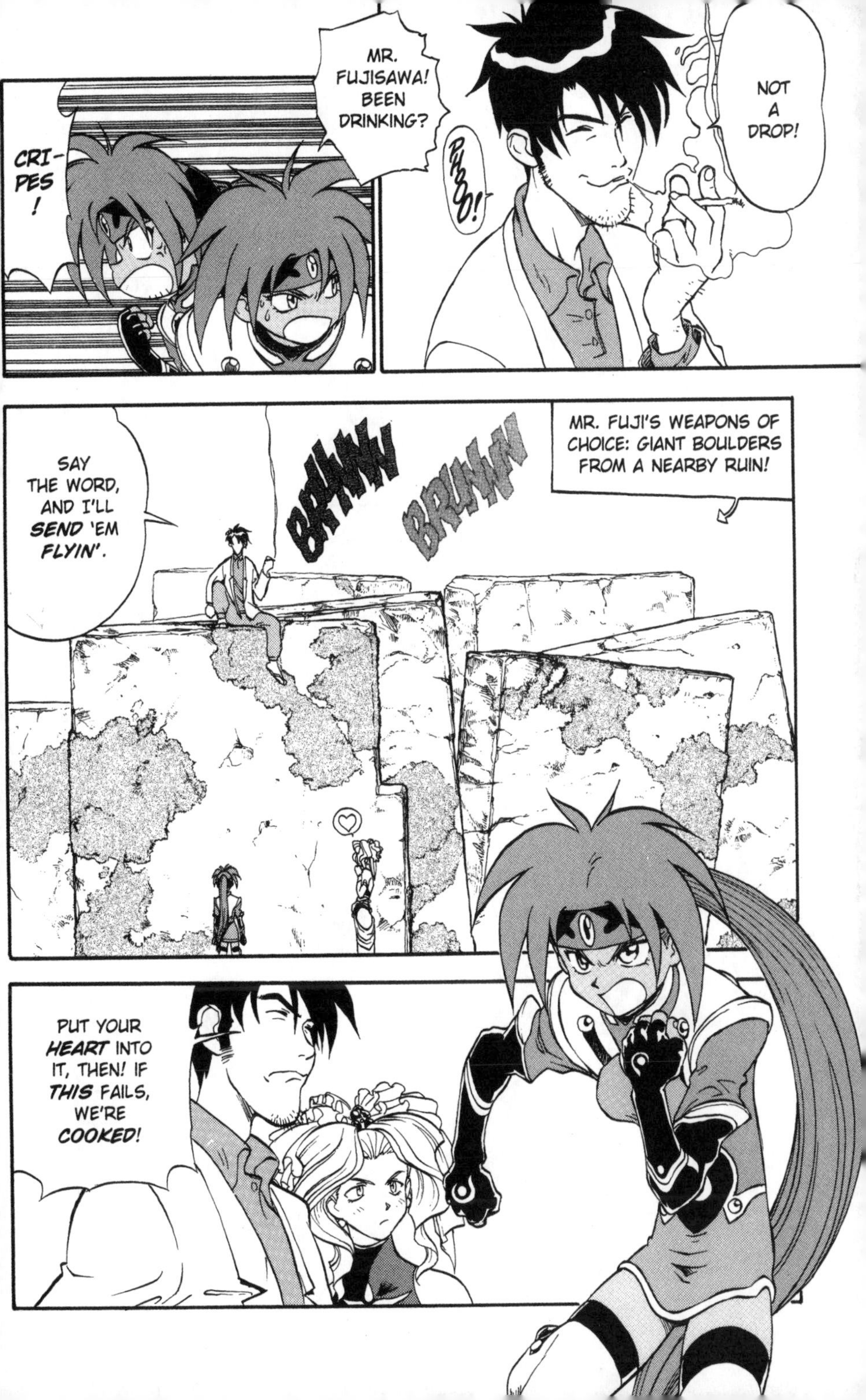
CRI-PES!
MR. FUJISAWA! BEEN DRINKING?
PHOOO!
NOT A DROP!
MR. FUJI'S WEAPONS OF CHOICE: GIANT BOULDERS FROM A NEARBY RUIN!
BRUMM
BRMMM
SAY THE WORD, AND I'LL *SEND* 'EM *FLYIN'*.
PUT YOUR *HEART* INTO IT, THEN! IF *THIS* FAILS, WE'RE *COOKED*!

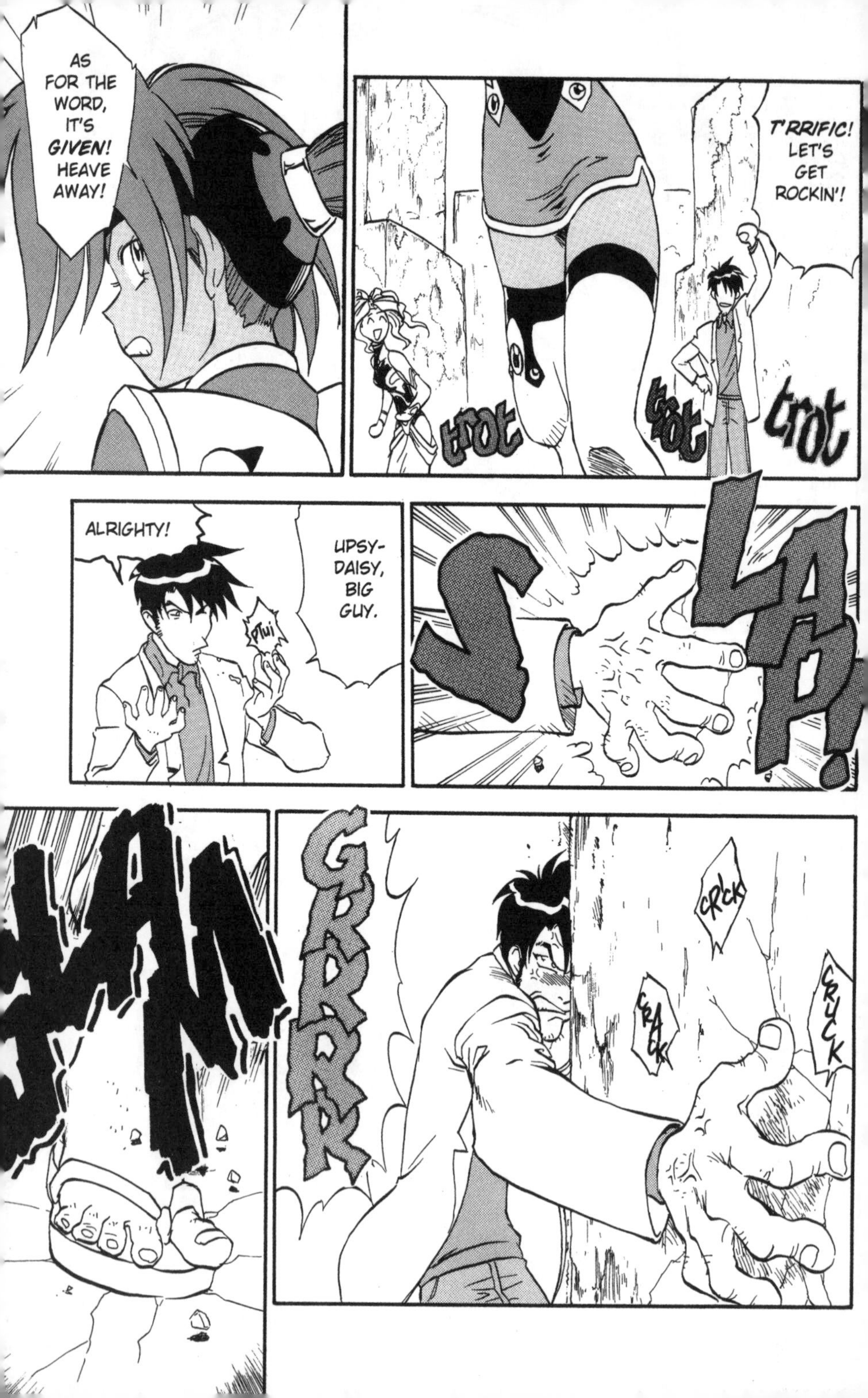
AS FOR THE WORD, IT'S GIVEN! HEAVE AWAY!
T'RRIFIC! LET'S GET ROCKIN'!
trot
trot
trot
ALRIGHTY!
UPSY-DAISY, BIG GUY.
PTUI
SLAP!
GRRRR
CRICK
CRACK
CRUCK

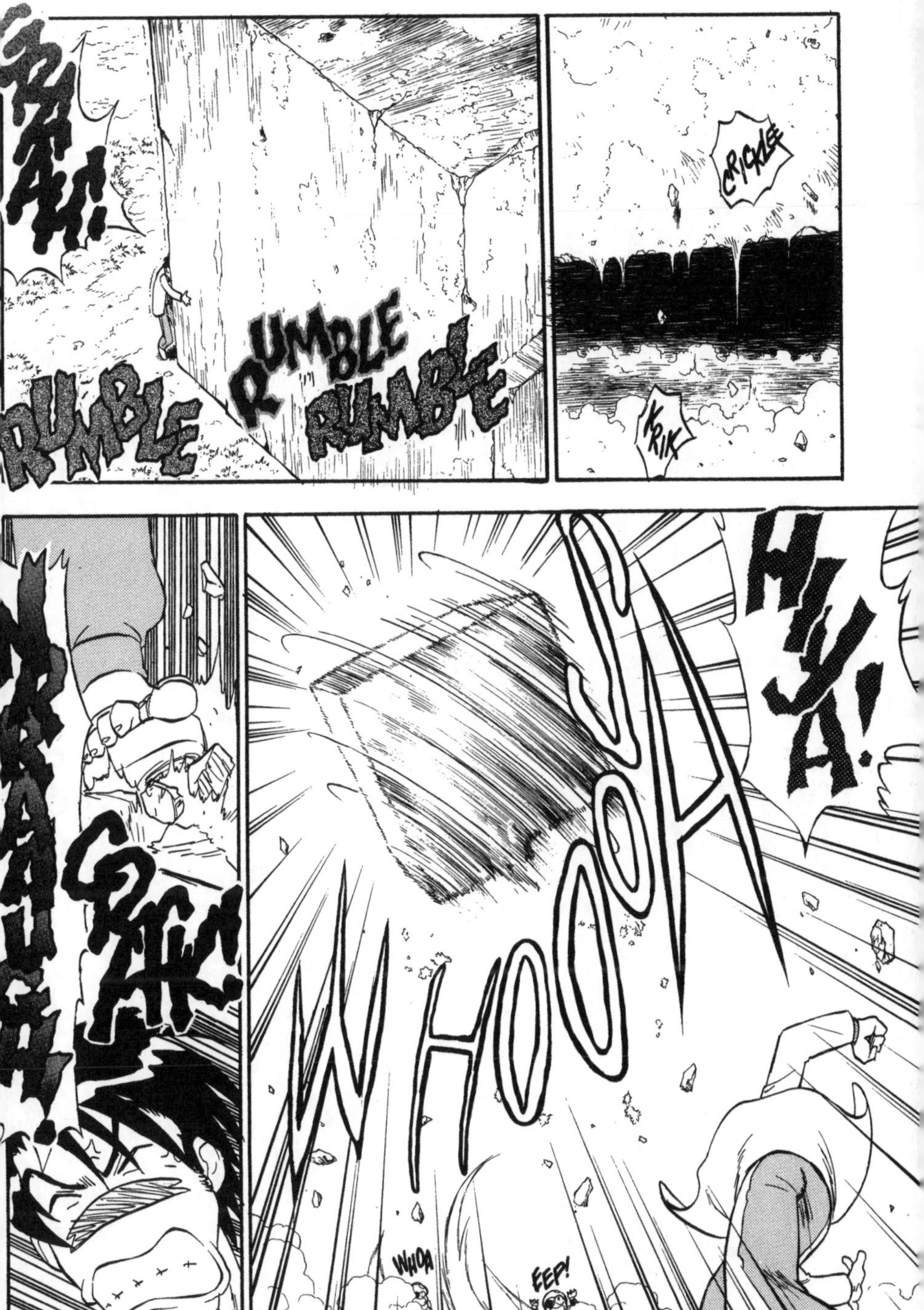
CRICKLE
KRIK
RUMBLE
RUMBLE
RUMBLE
HIYA!
WHOA
EEP!

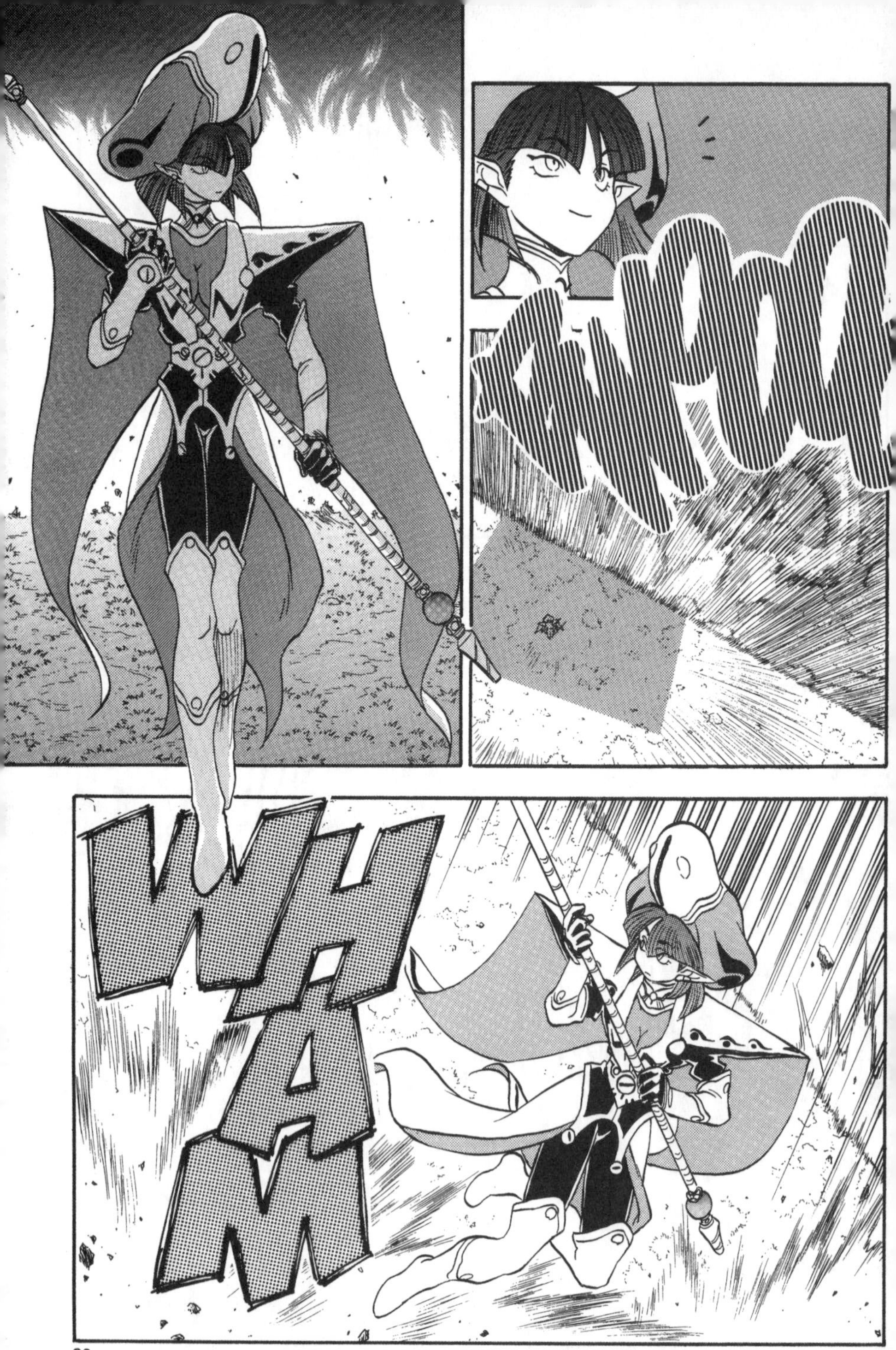
WHAM

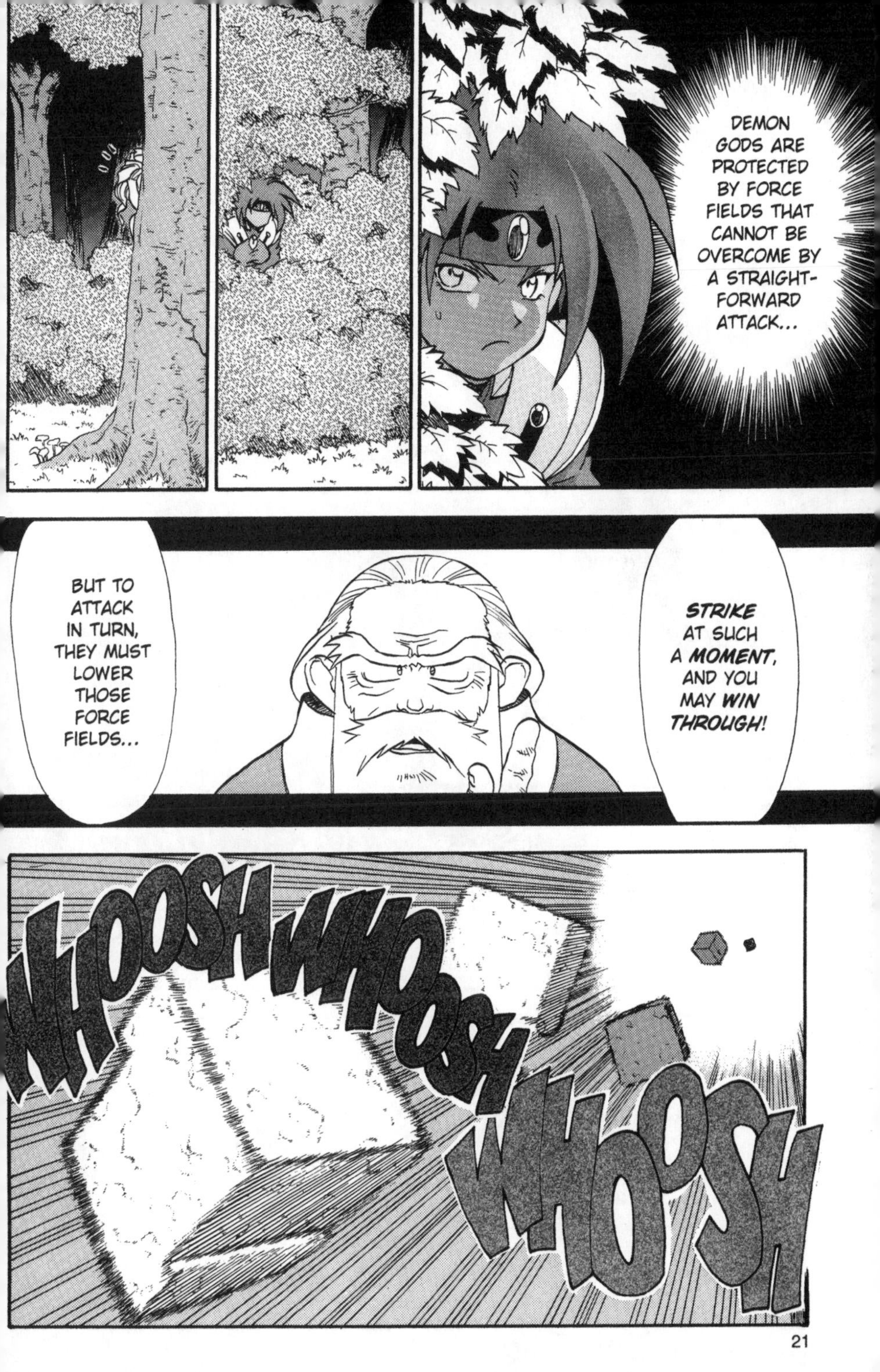
DEMON GODS ARE PROTECTED BY FORCE FIELDS THAT CANNOT BE OVERCOME BY A STRAIGHT-FORWARD ATTACK...
BUT TO ATTACK IN TURN, THEY MUST LOWER THOSE FORCE FIELDS...
STRIKE AT SUCH A MOMENT, AND YOU MAY WIN THROUGH!
WHOOSH WHOOSH
WHOOSH

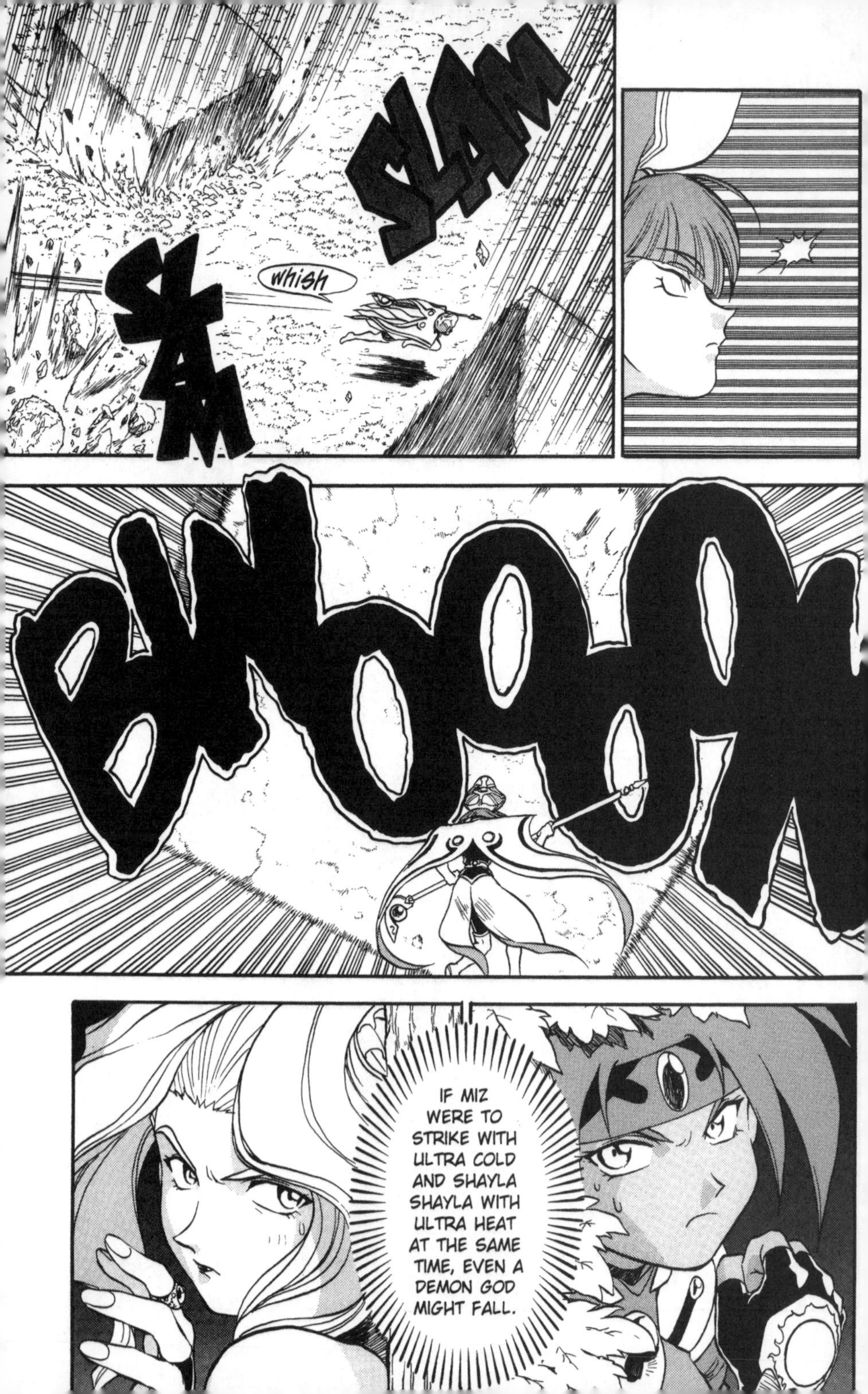
SLAM
whish
SLAM
BWOOOOM
IF MIZ WERE TO STRIKE WITH ULTRA COLD AND SHAYLA SHAYLA WITH ULTRA HEAT AT THE SAME TIME, EVEN A DEMON GOD MIGHT FALL.

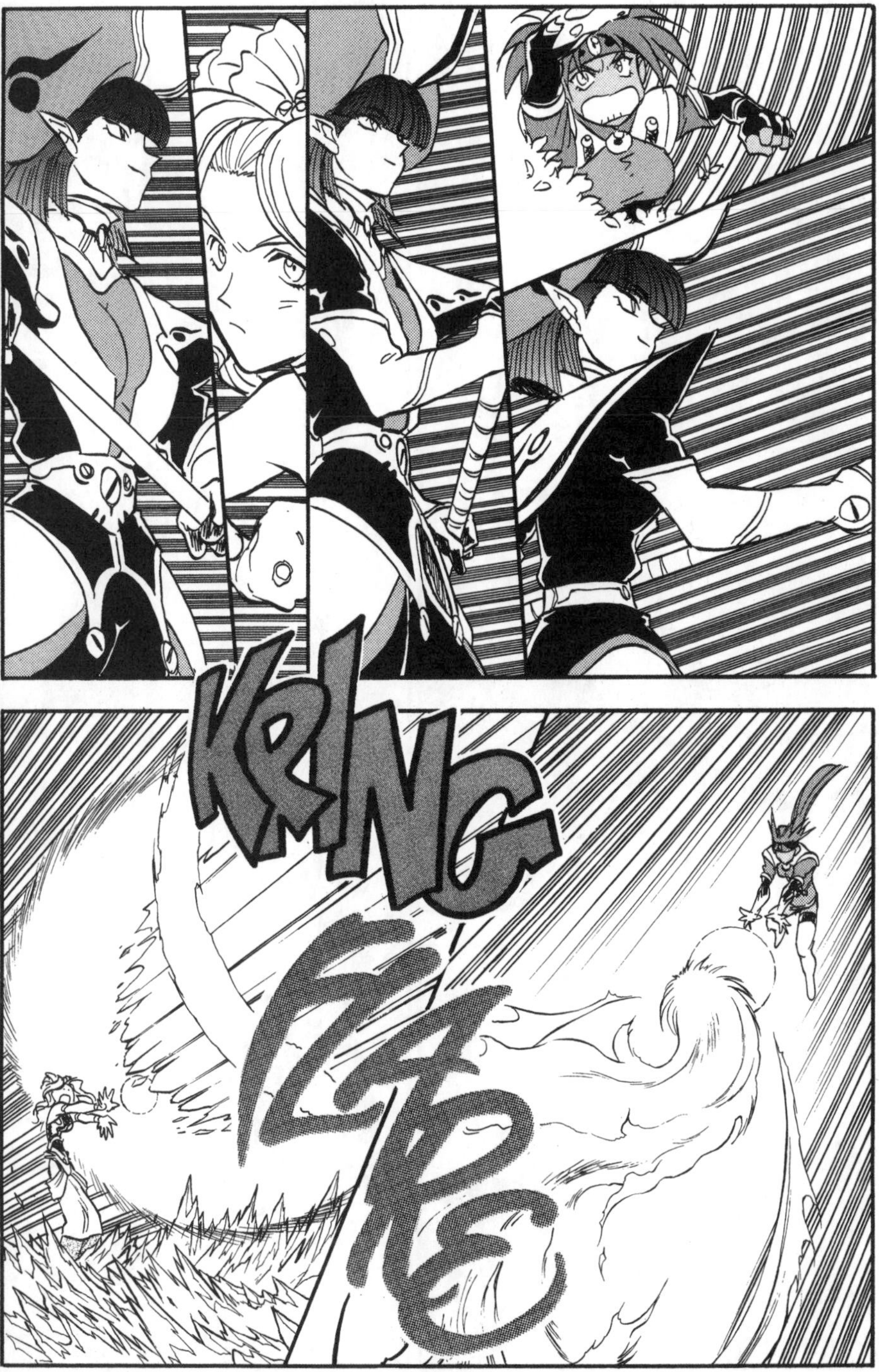
KRING

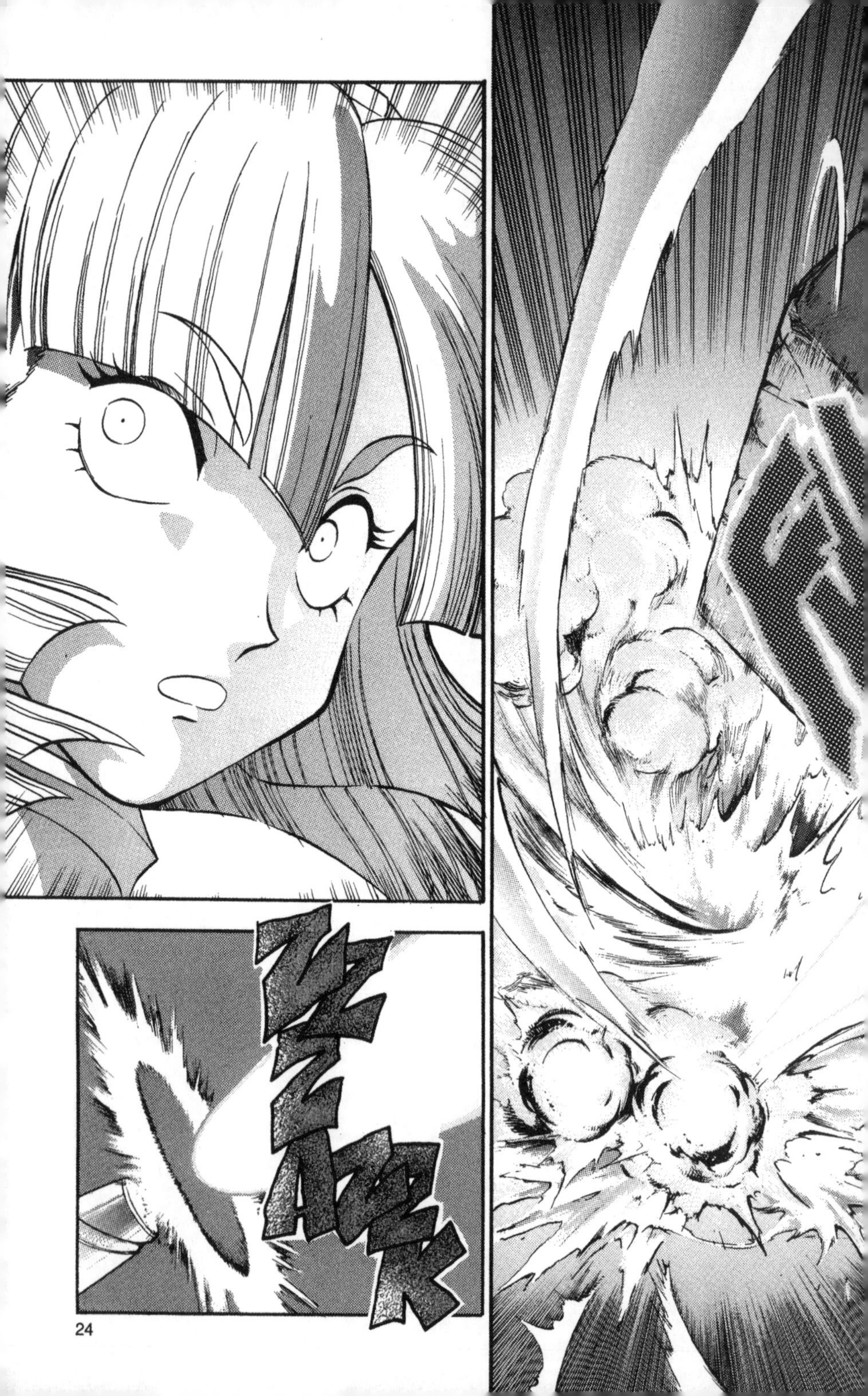
ZZZACK

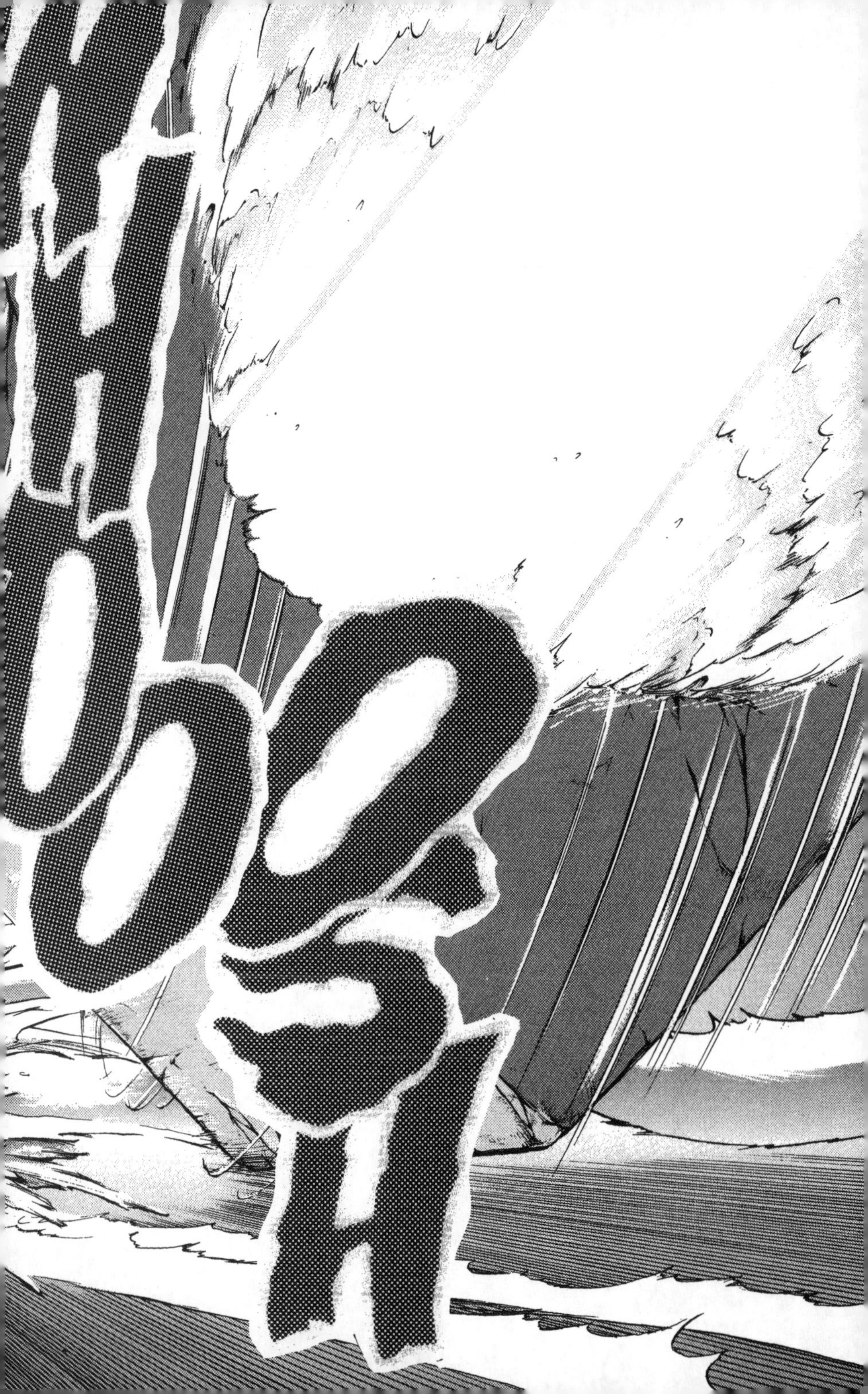
HOOSH

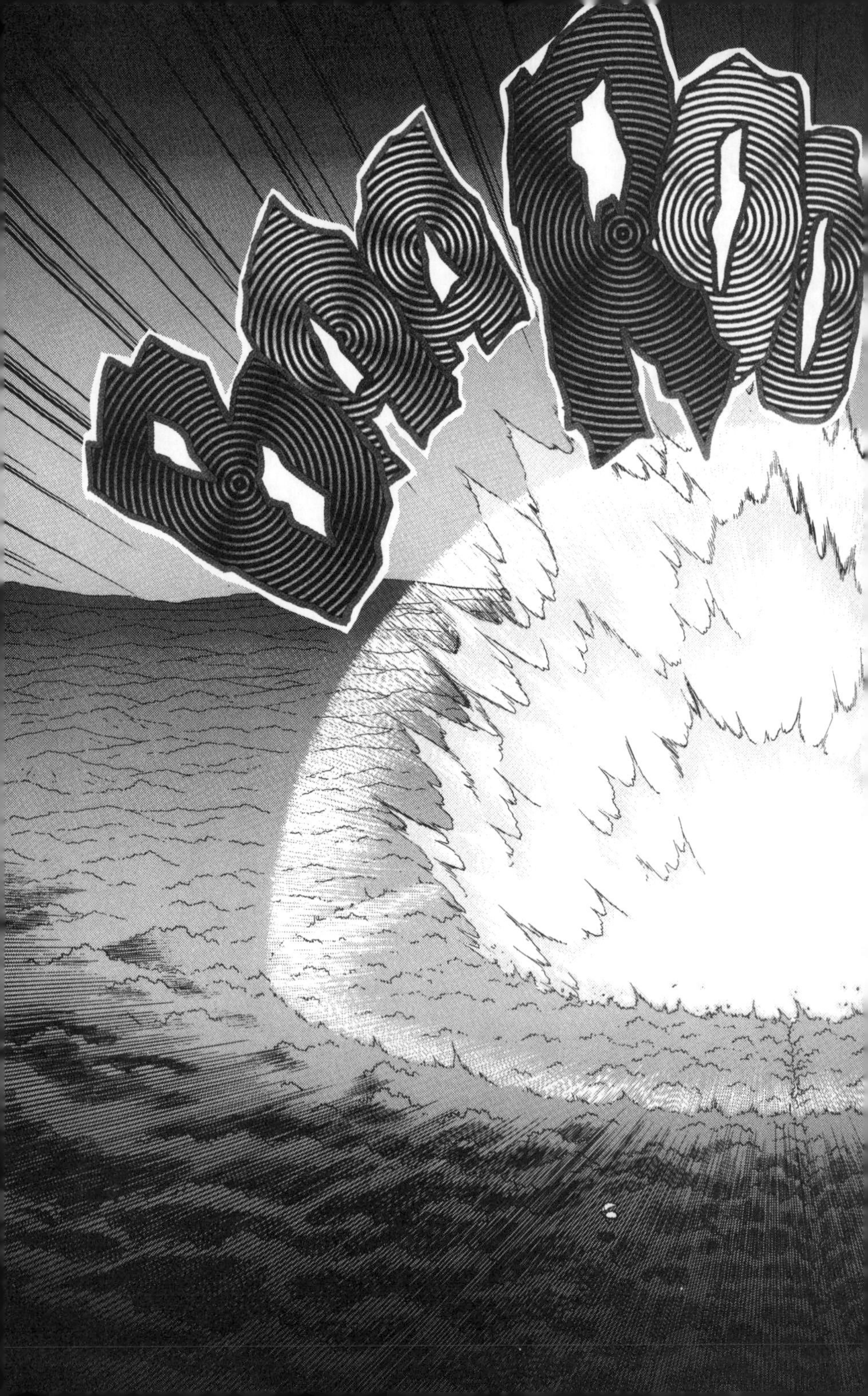

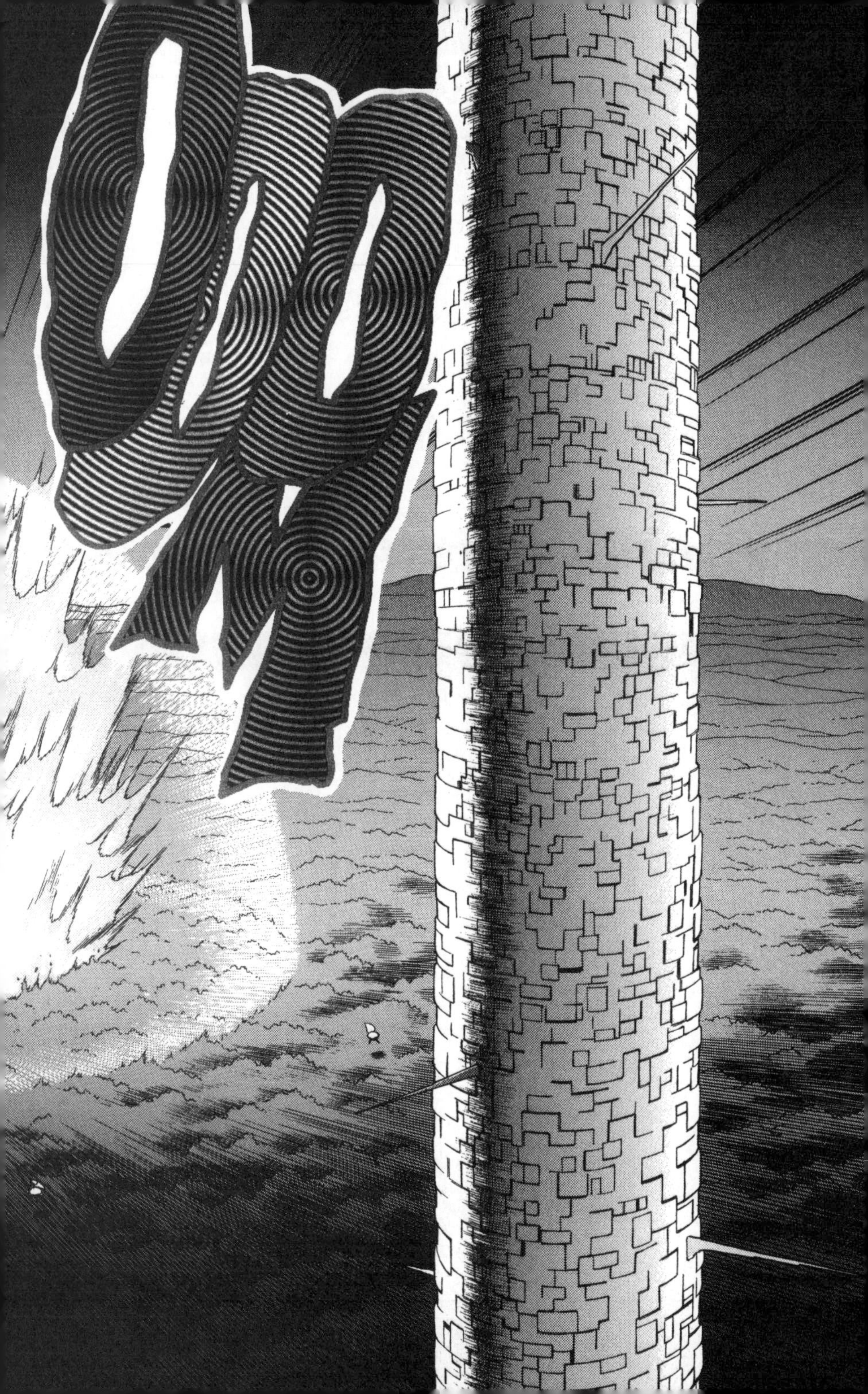

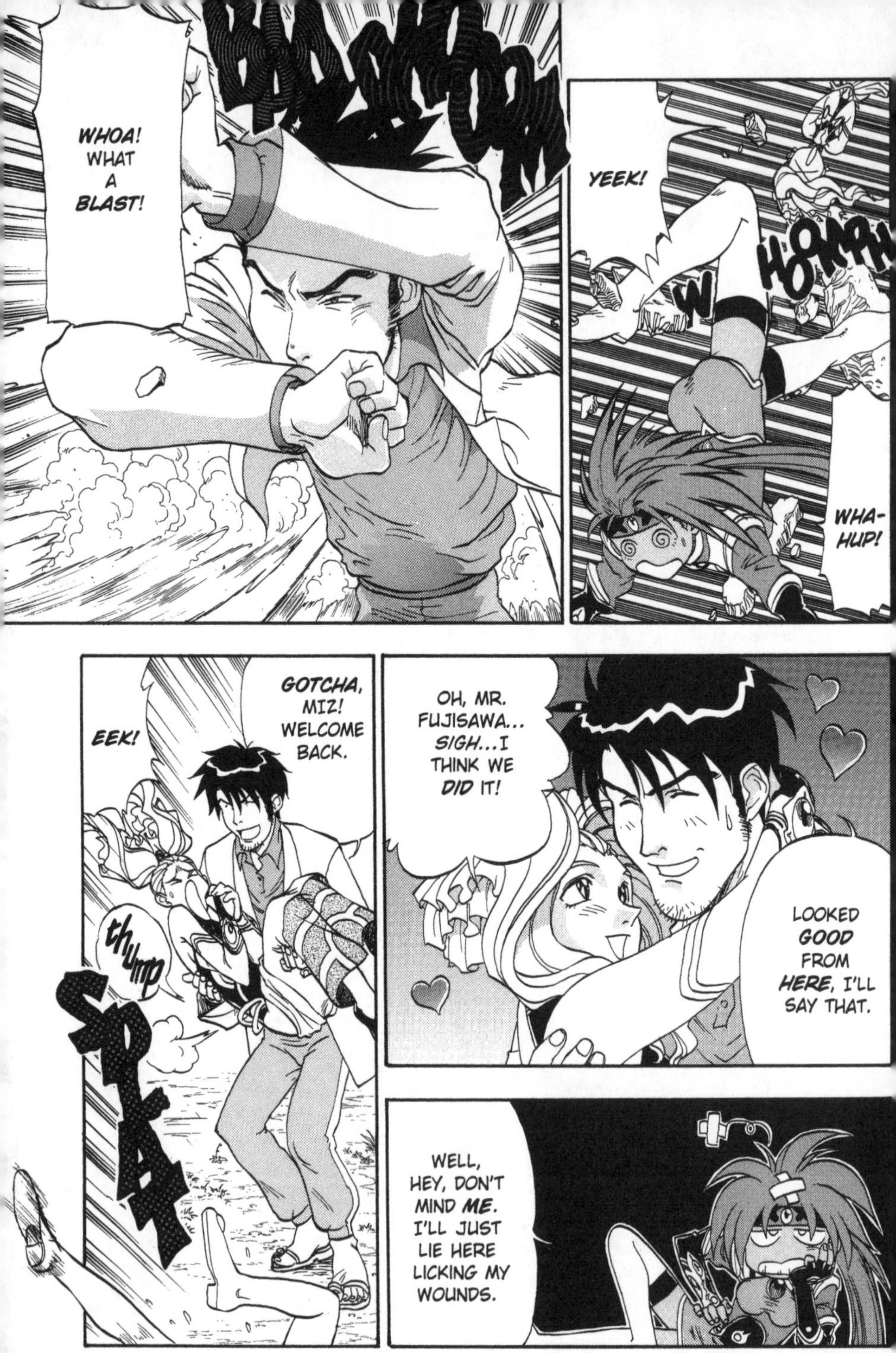
WHOA! WHAT A BLAST!
YEEK!
WHA-HUP!
EEK!
GOTCHA, MIZ! WELCOME BACK.
thump
OH, MR. FUJISAWA... SIGH...I THINK WE DID IT!
LOOKED GOOD FROM HERE, I'LL SAY THAT.
WELL, HEY, DON'T MIND ME. I'LL JUST LIE HERE LICKING MY WOUNDS.

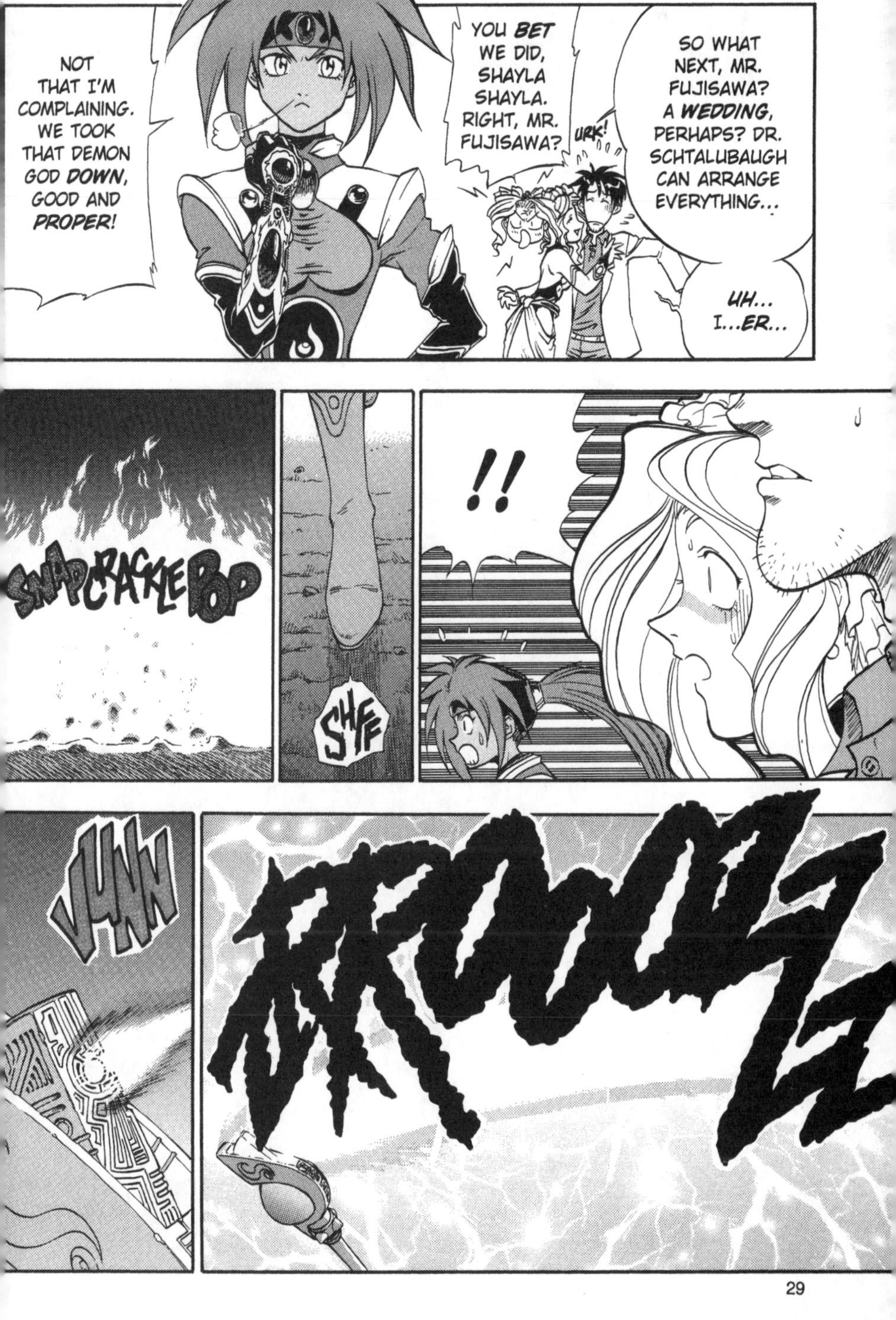
NOT THAT I'M COMPLAINING. WE TOOK THAT DEMON GOD DOWN, GOOD AND PROPER!
YOU BET WE DID, SHAYLA SHAYLA. RIGHT, MR. FUJISAWA?
URK!
SO WHAT NEXT, MR. FUJISAWA? A WEDDING, PERHAPS? DR. SCHTALUBAUGH CAN ARRANGE EVERYTHING...
UH... I...ER...
SNAP CRACKLE POP
SHFF
!!
JUNN

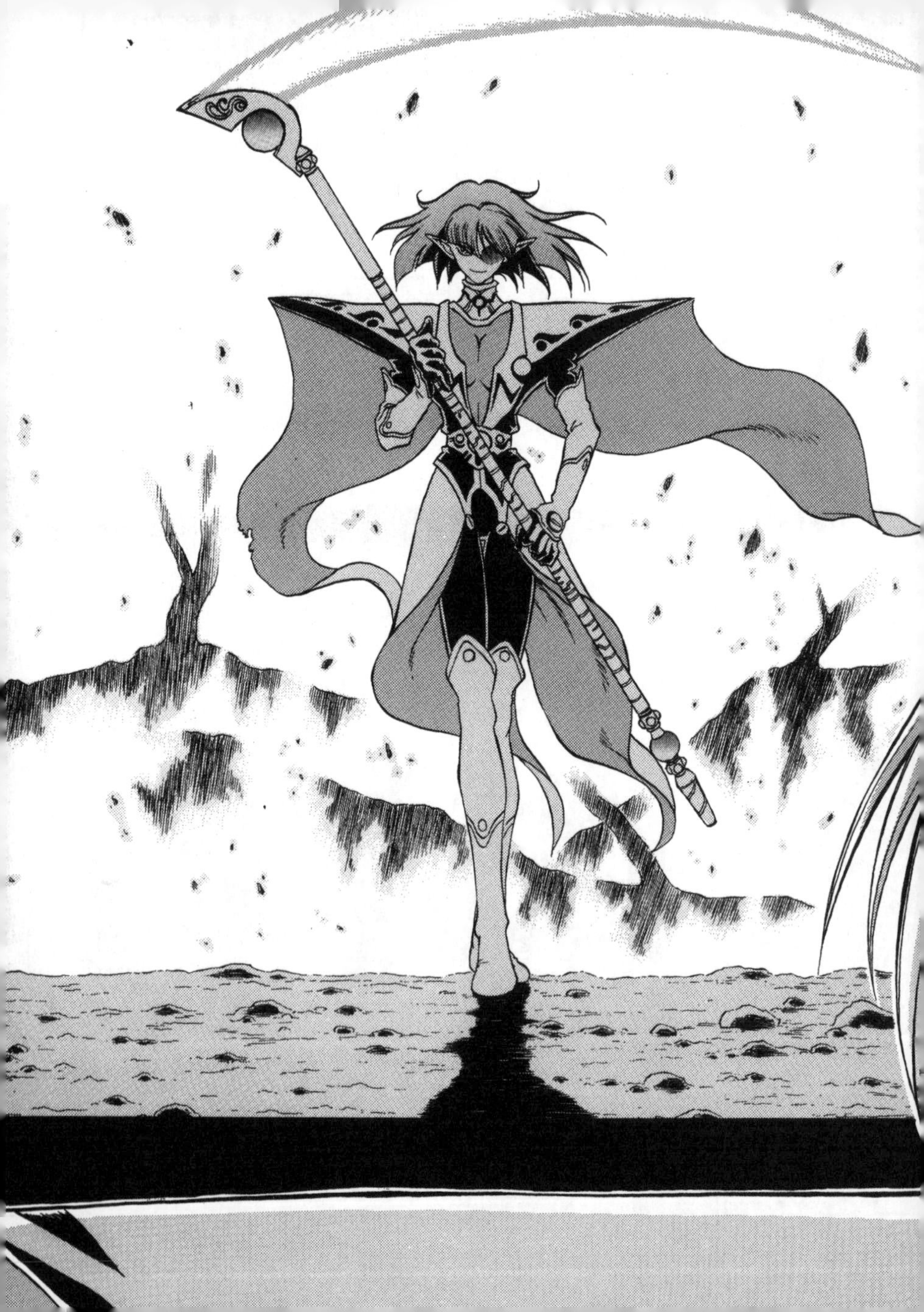

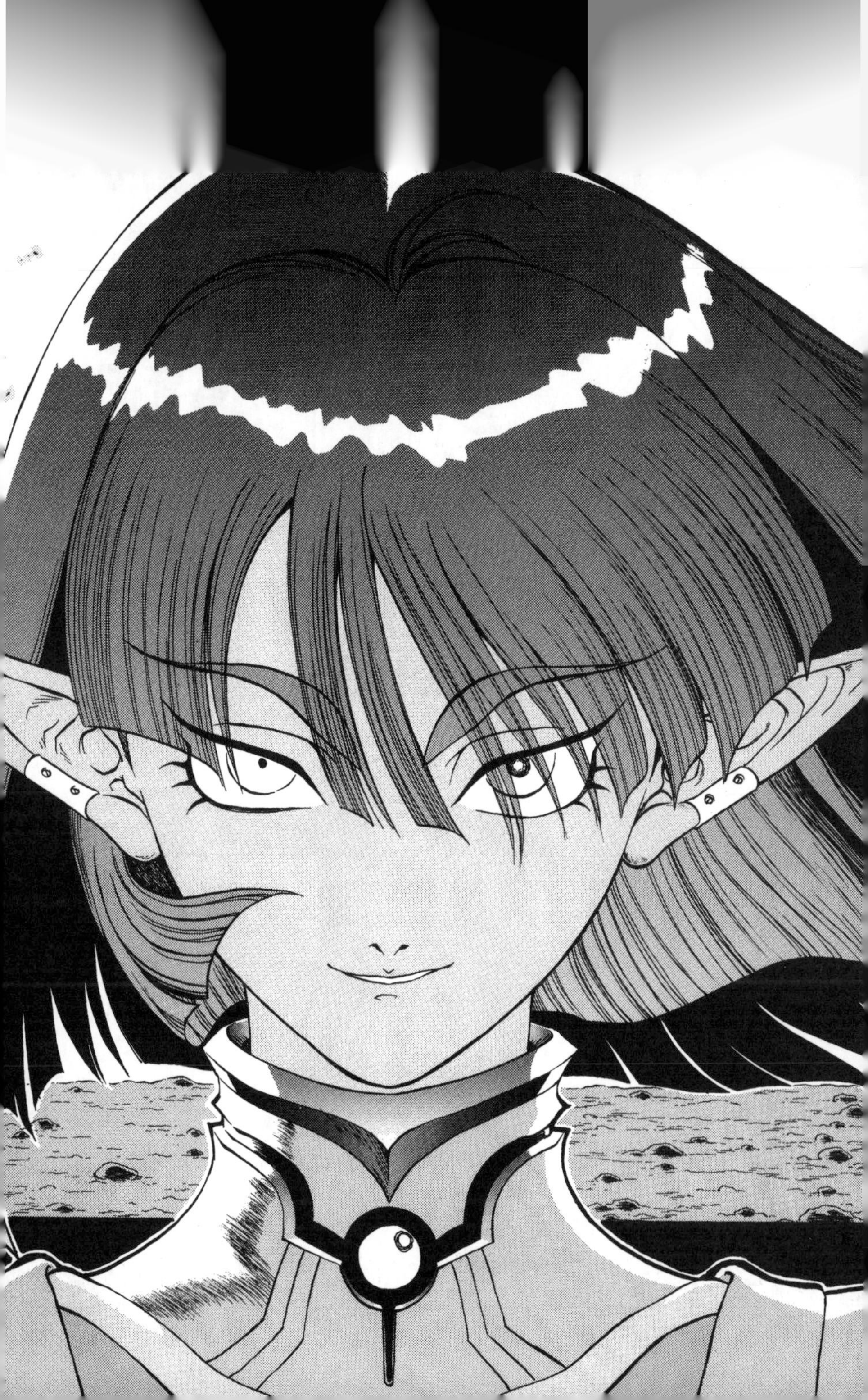

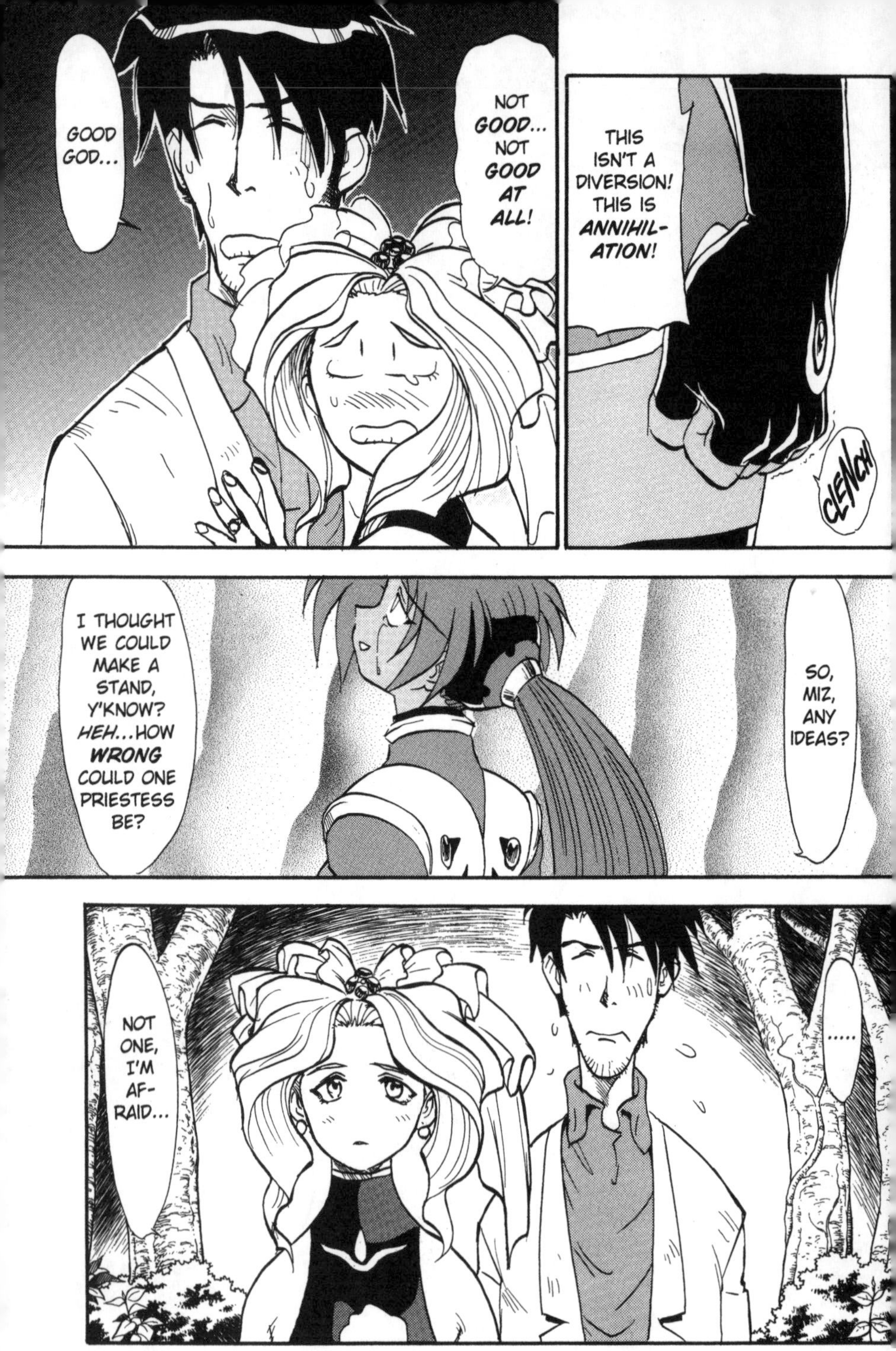
GOOD GOD...
NOT GOOD... NOT GOOD AT ALL!
THIS ISN'T A DIVERSION! THIS IS ANNIHIL-ATION!
CLENCH
I THOUGHT WE COULD MAKE A STAND, Y'KNOW? HEH...HOW WRONG COULD ONE PRIESTESS BE?
SO, MIZ, ANY IDEAS?
NOT ONE, I'M AF-RAID...
.....

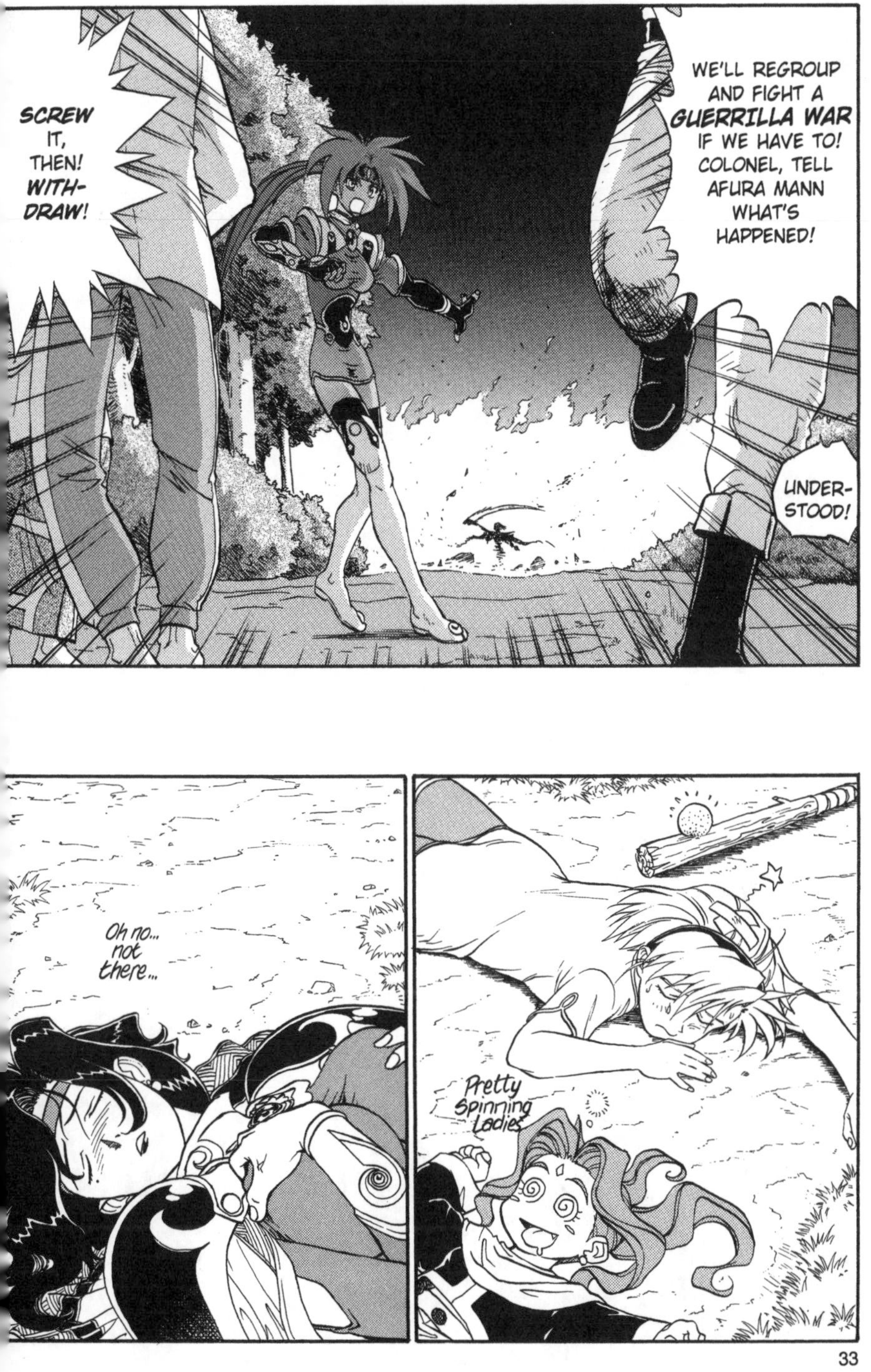
SCREW IT, THEN! WITH-DRAW!
WE'LL REGROUP AND FIGHT A GUERRILLA WAR IF WE HAVE TO! COLONEL, TELL AFURA MANN WHAT'S HAPPENED!
UNDER-STOOD!
Oh no... not there...
Pretty Spinning Ladies

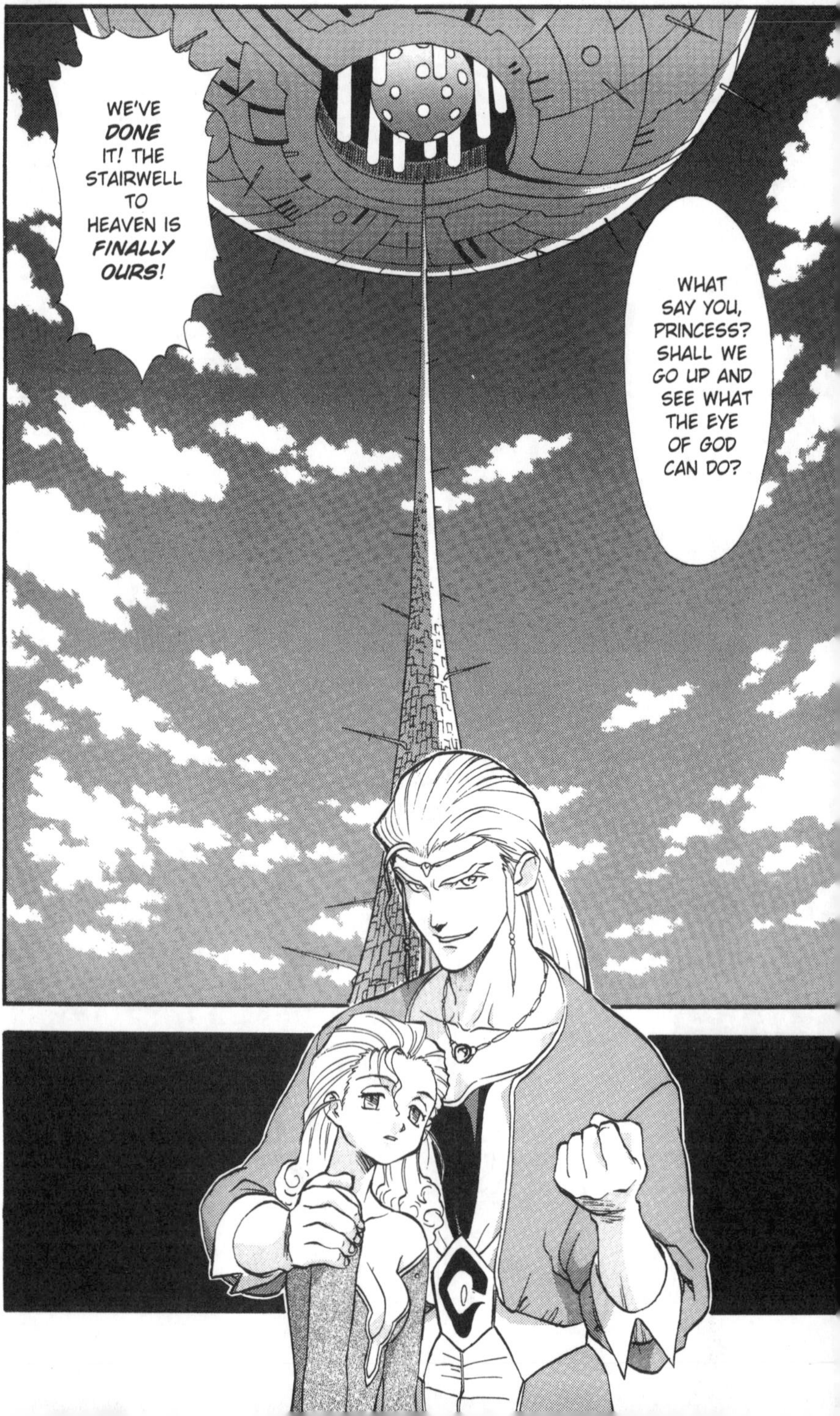
WE'VE DONE IT! THE STAIRWELL TO HEAVEN IS FINALLY OURS!
WHAT SAY YOU, PRINCESS? SHALL WE GO UP AND SEE WHAT THE EYE OF GOD CAN DO?

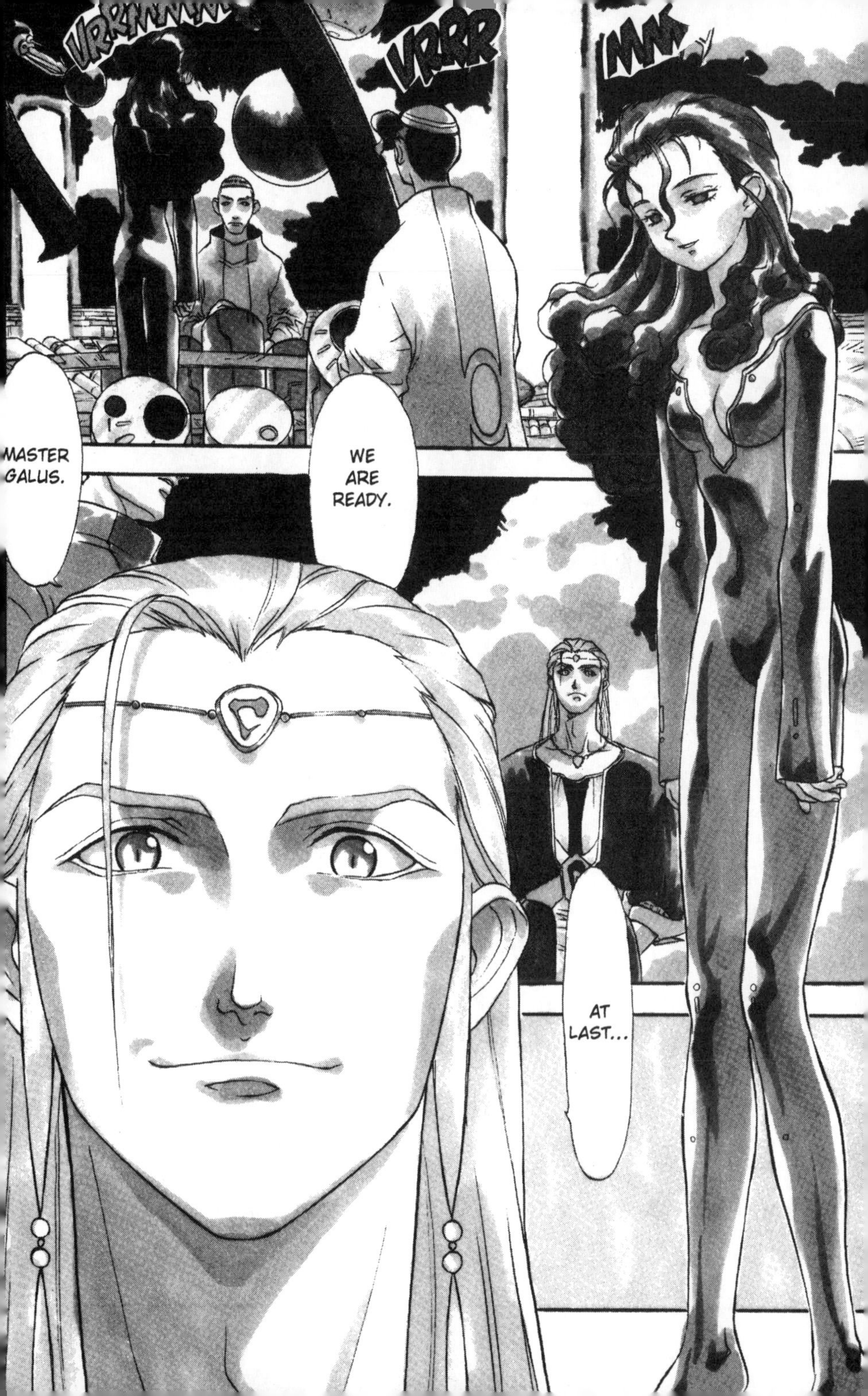
VRRMMMMM
VRRR
MMM
MASTER GALUS.
WE ARE READY.
AT LAST...

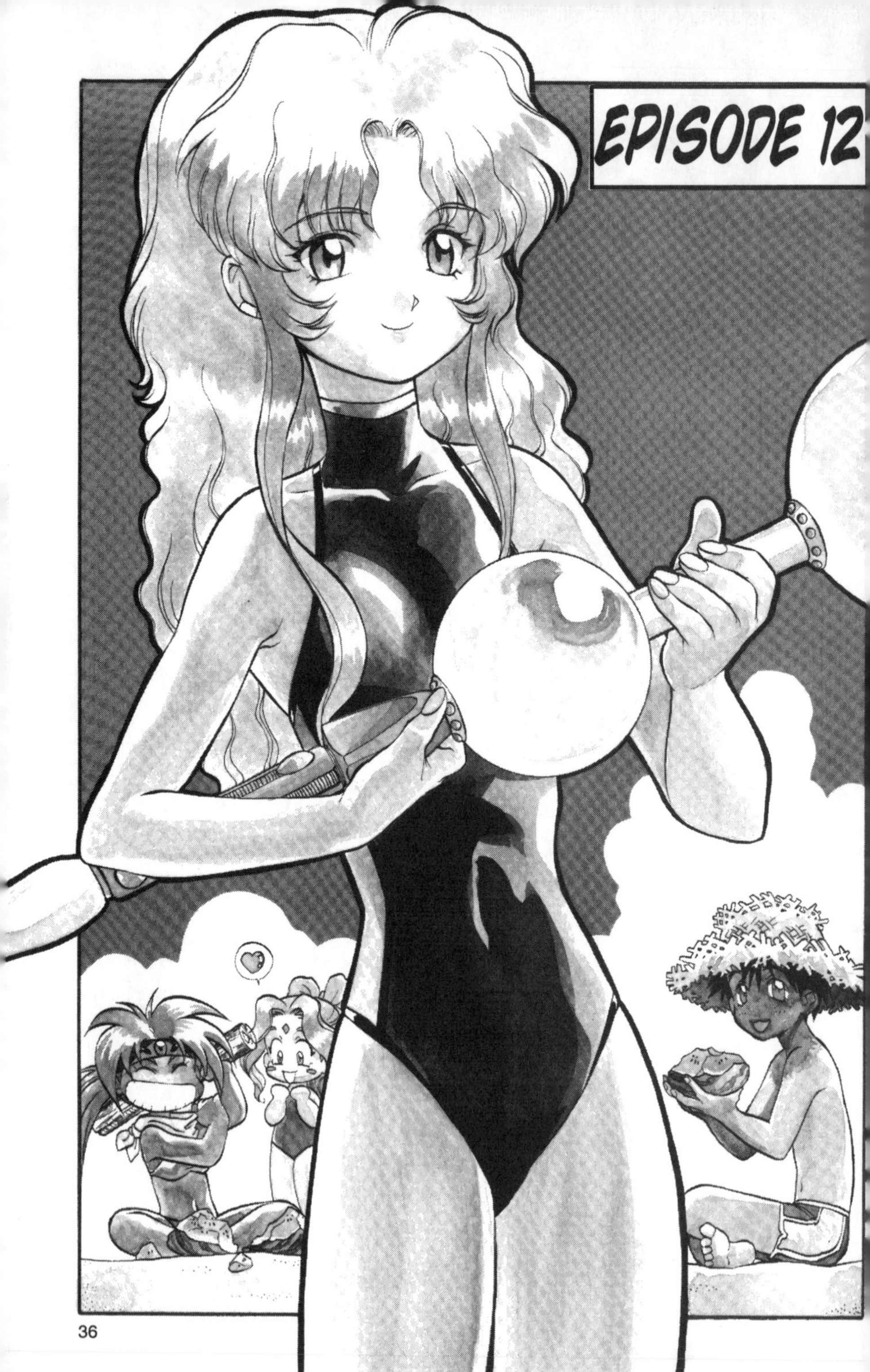
EPISODE 12

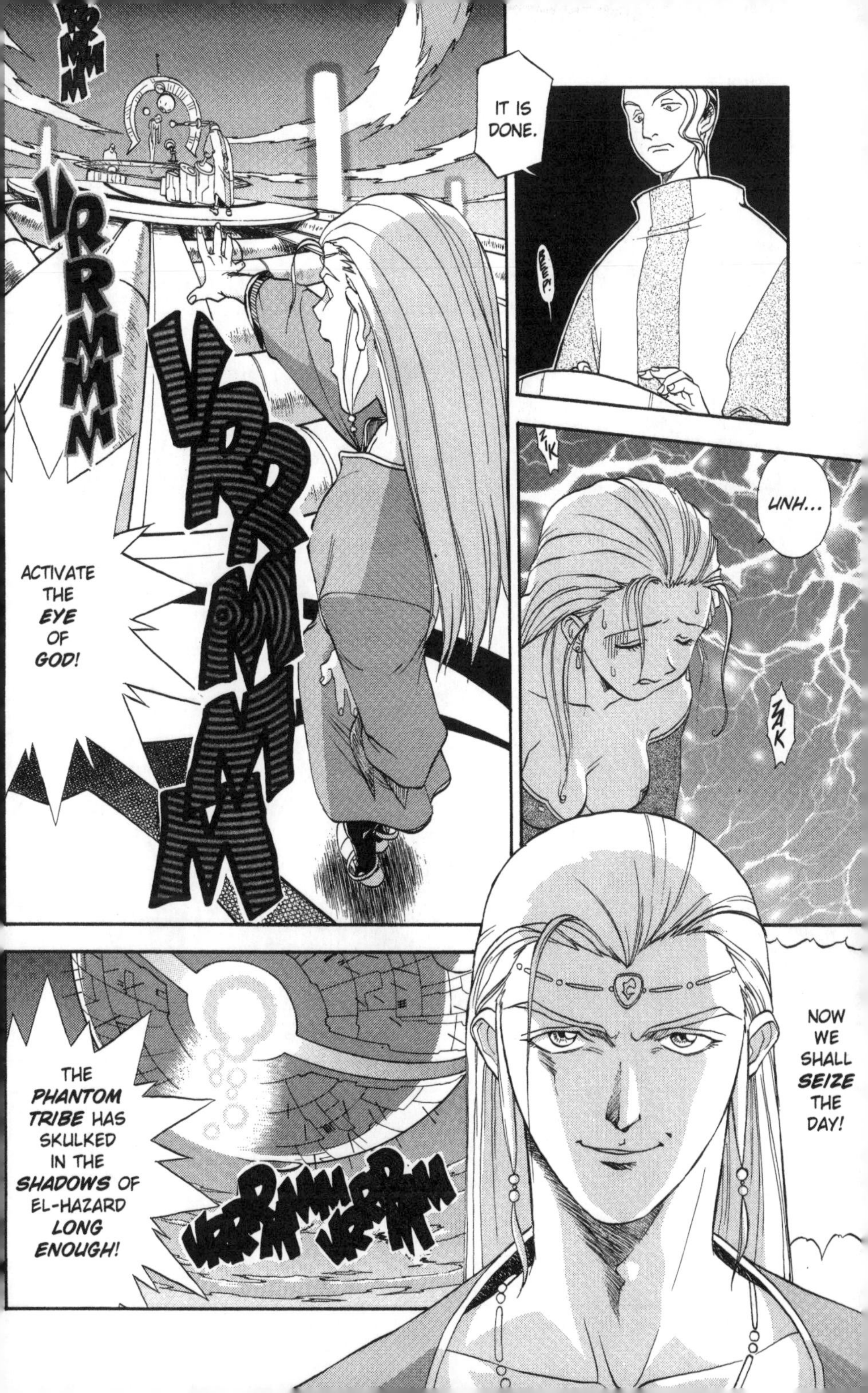

IT IS DONE.
UNH...
ZAK
VRRMMM
ACTIVATE THE EYE OF GOD!
NOW WE SHALL SEIZE THE DAY!
THE PHANTOM TRIBE HAS SKULKED IN THE SHADOWS OF EL-HAZARD LONG ENOUGH!

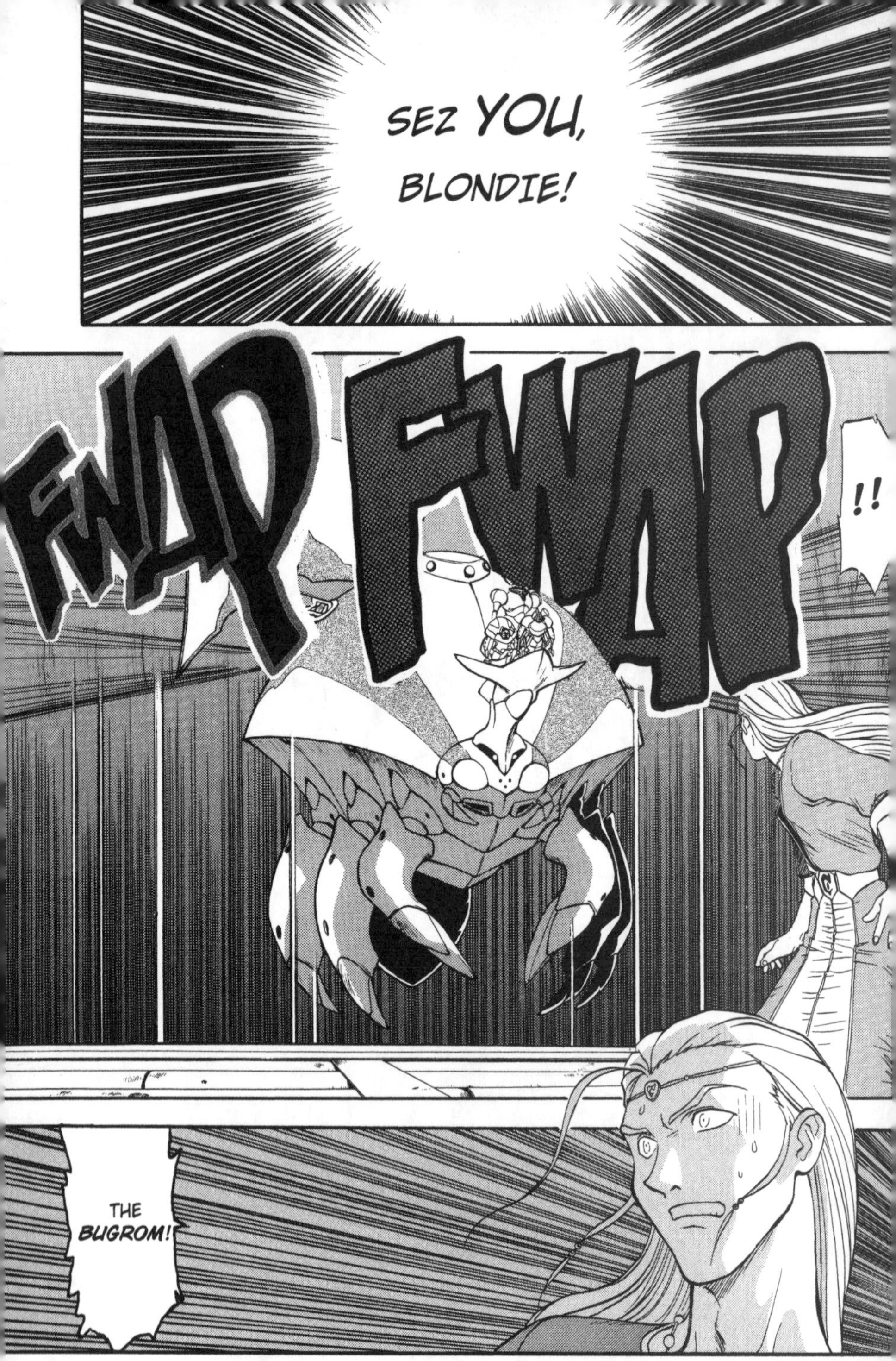

SEZ YOU, BLONDIE!
FWAP FWAP
!!
THE BUGROM!

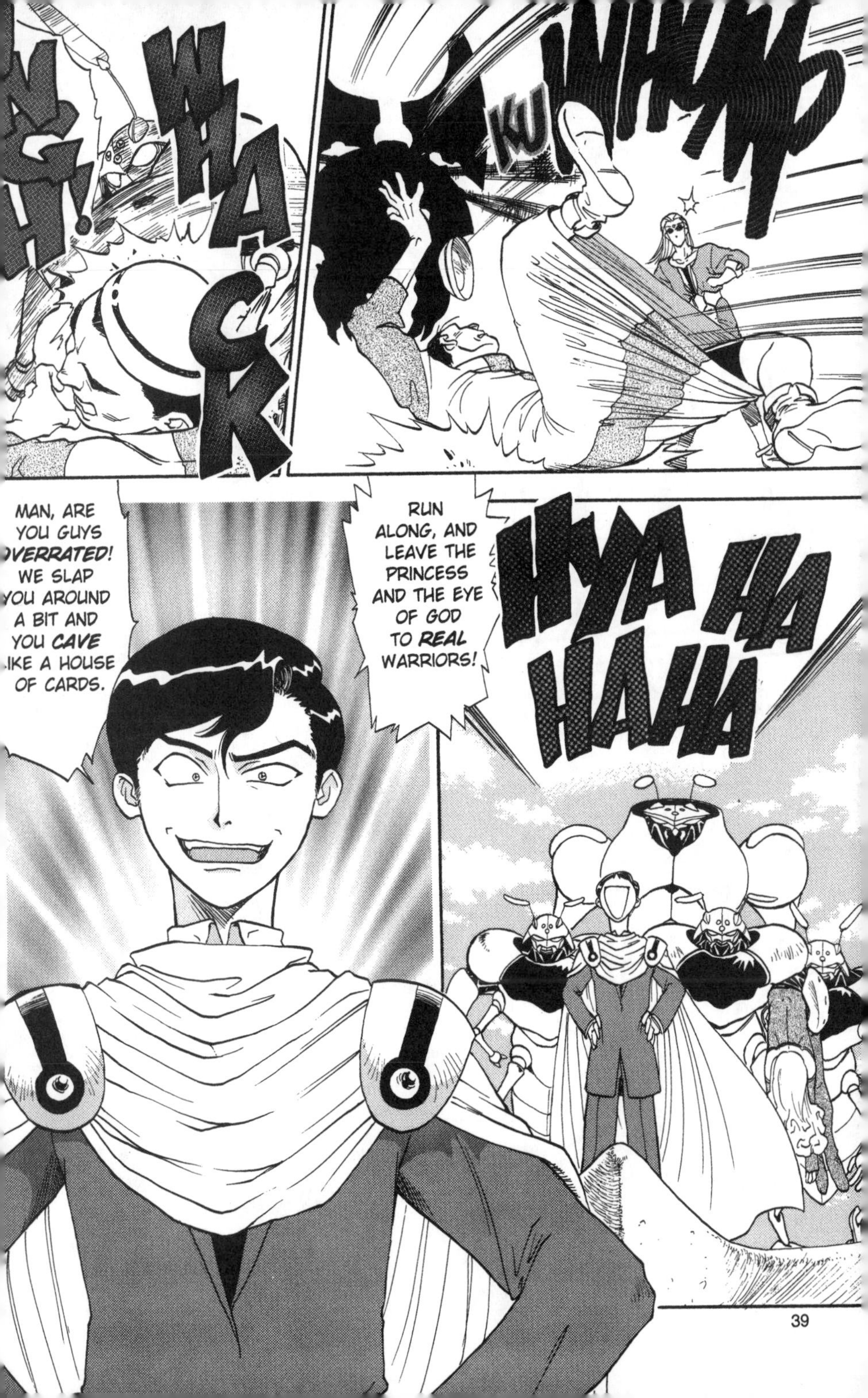
WHACK
KU
WHUMP
MAN, ARE YOU GUYS OVERRATED! WE SLAP YOU AROUND A BIT AND YOU CAVE LIKE A HOUSE OF CARDS.
RUN ALONG, AND LEAVE THE PRINCESS AND THE EYE OF GOD TO REAL WARRIORS!
HYA HA HAHA

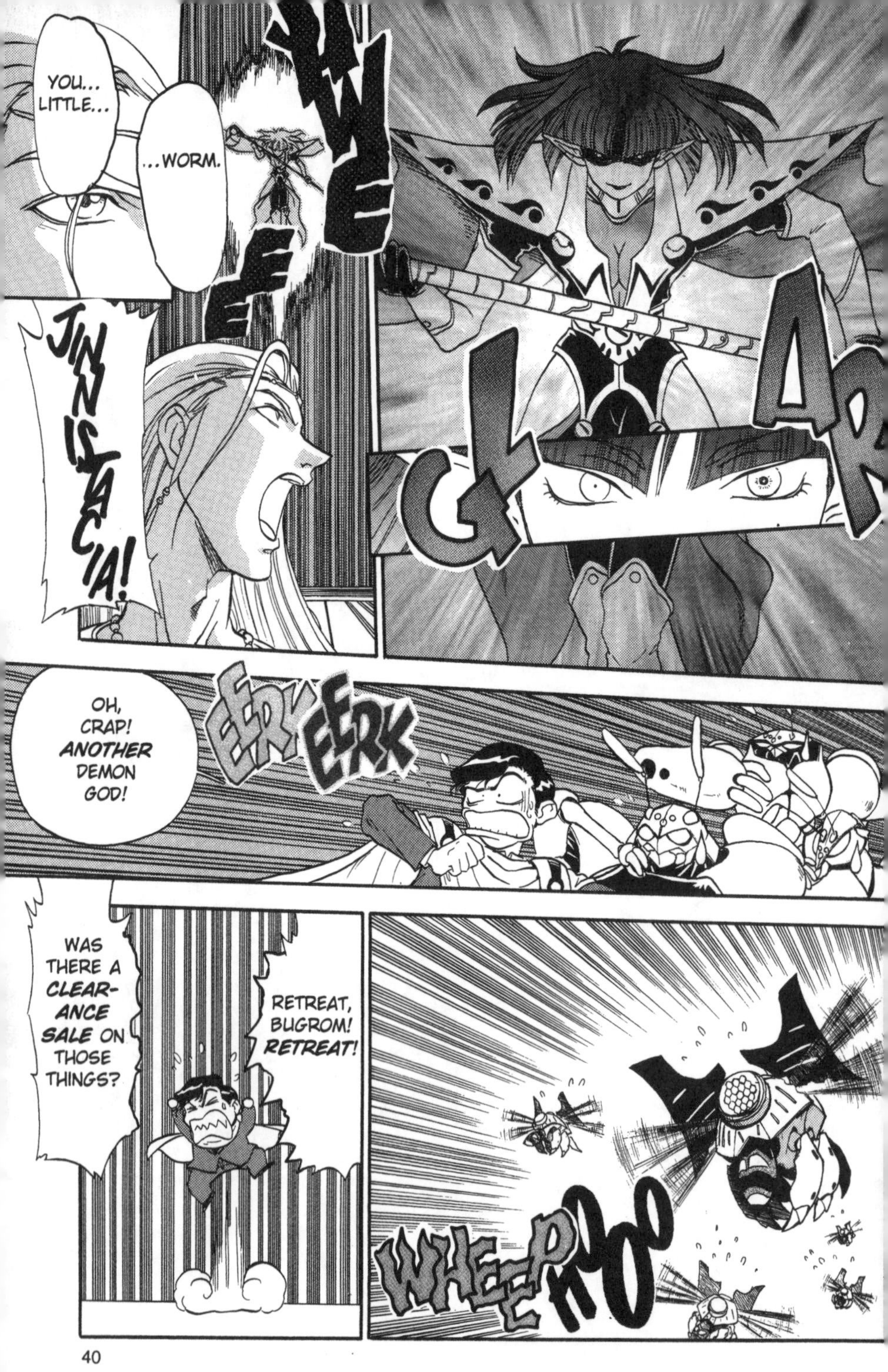
YOU... LITTLE...
...WORM.
JINNISTACIA!
OH, CRAP! ANOTHER DEMON GOD!
EERK EERK
WAS THERE A CLEARANCE SALE ON THOSE THINGS?
RETREAT, BUGROM! RETREAT!

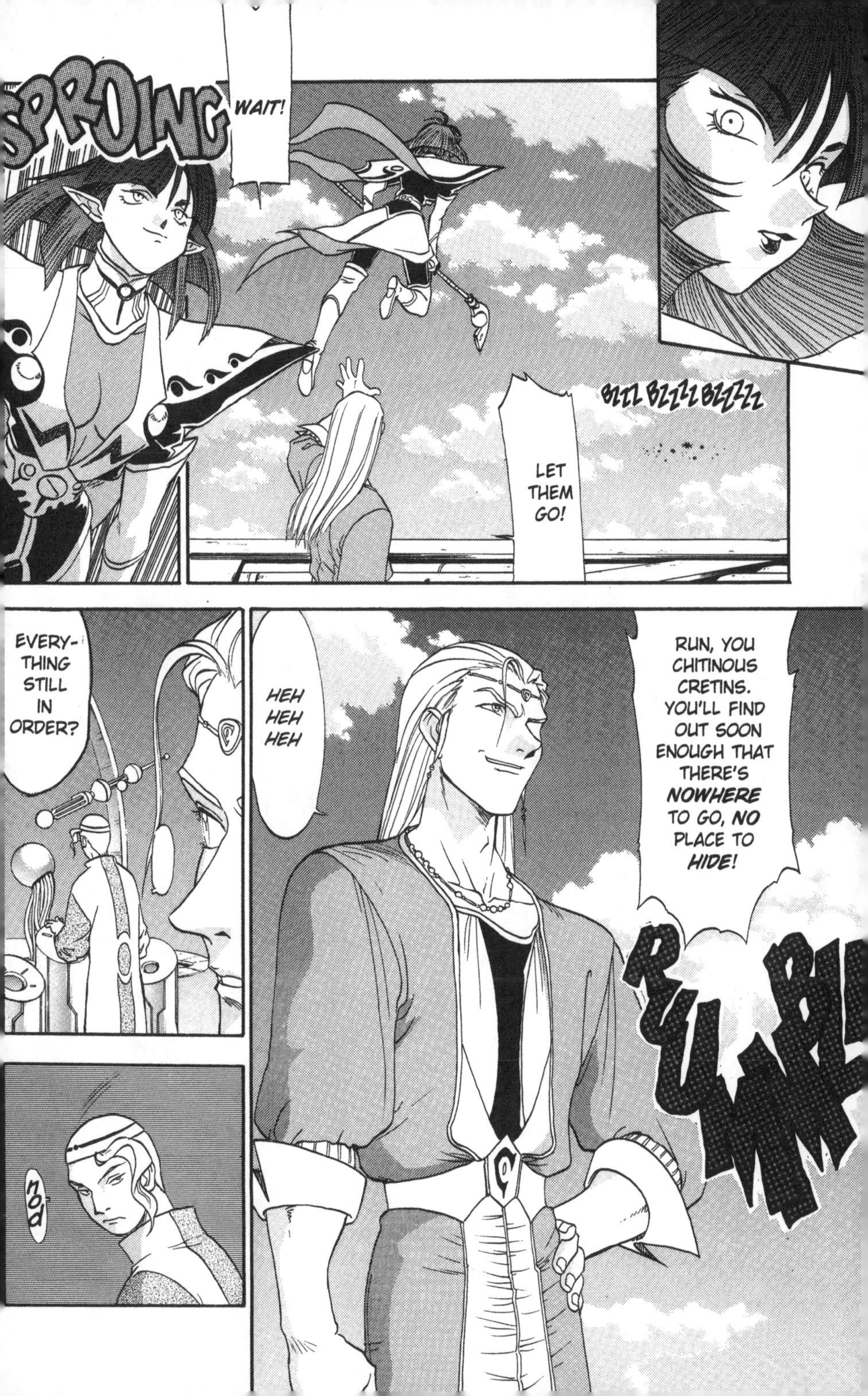
SPROING
WAIT!
BZZZ BZZZZ BZZZZZ
LET THEM GO!
EVERY-THING STILL IN ORDER?
HEH HEH HEH
RUN, YOU CHITINOUS CRETINS. YOU'LL FIND OUT SOON ENOUGH THAT THERE'S ***NOWHERE*** TO GO, ***NO*** PLACE TO ***HIDE***!
RUMBLE
nod

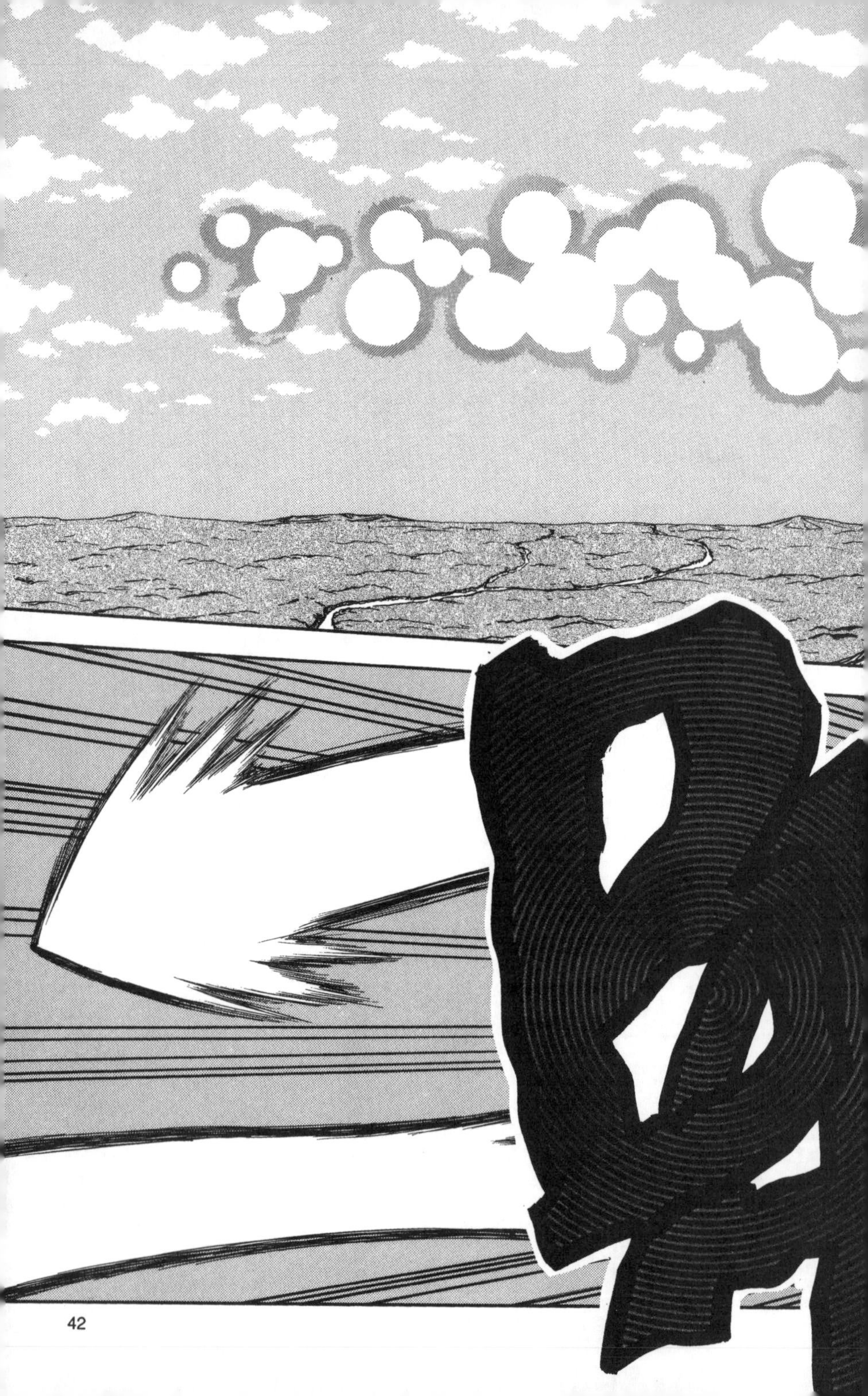

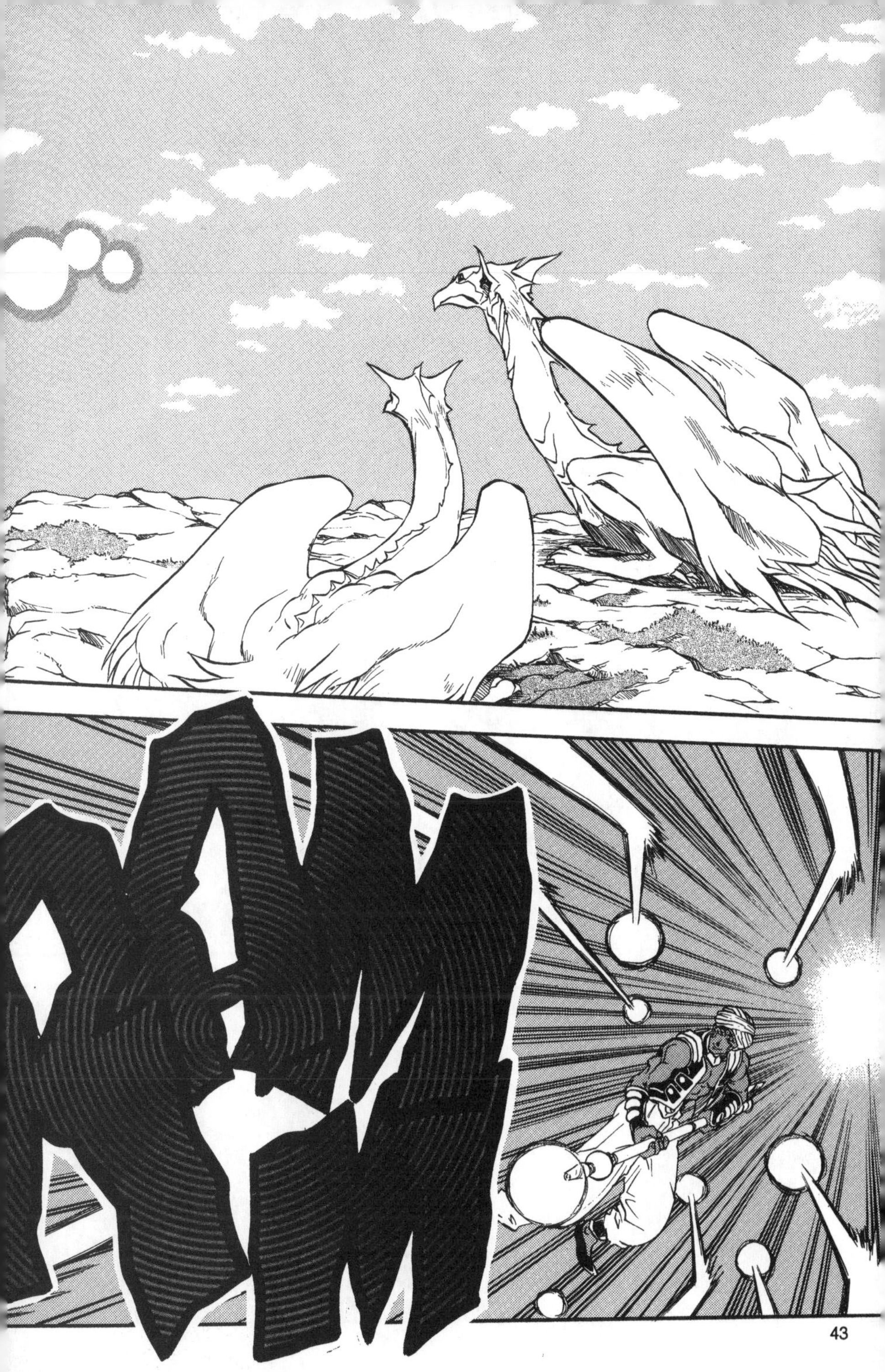

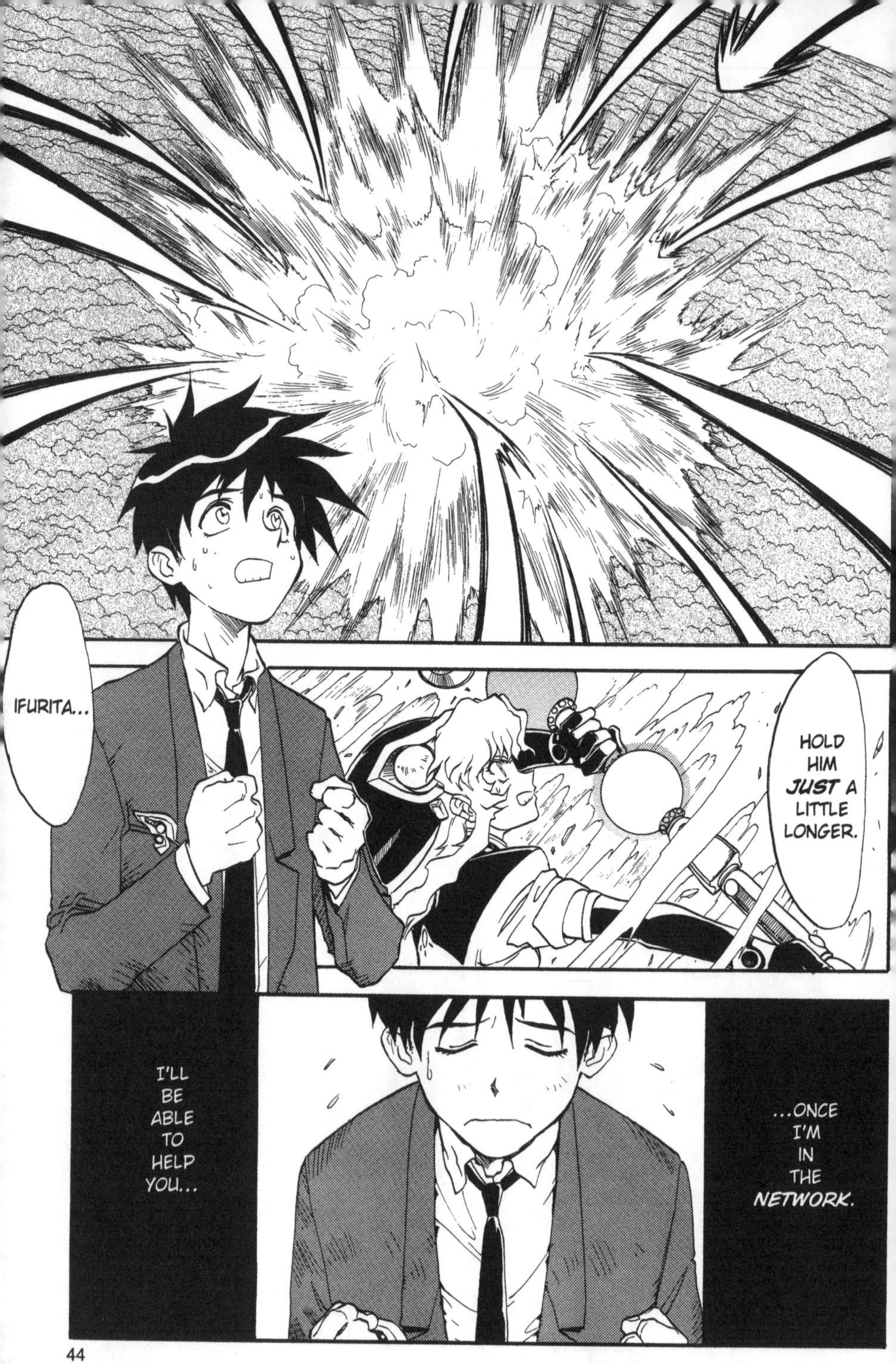
HOLD HIM JUST A LITTLE LONGER.
IFURITA...
...ONCE I'M IN THE NETWORK.
I'LL BE ABLE TO HELP YOU...

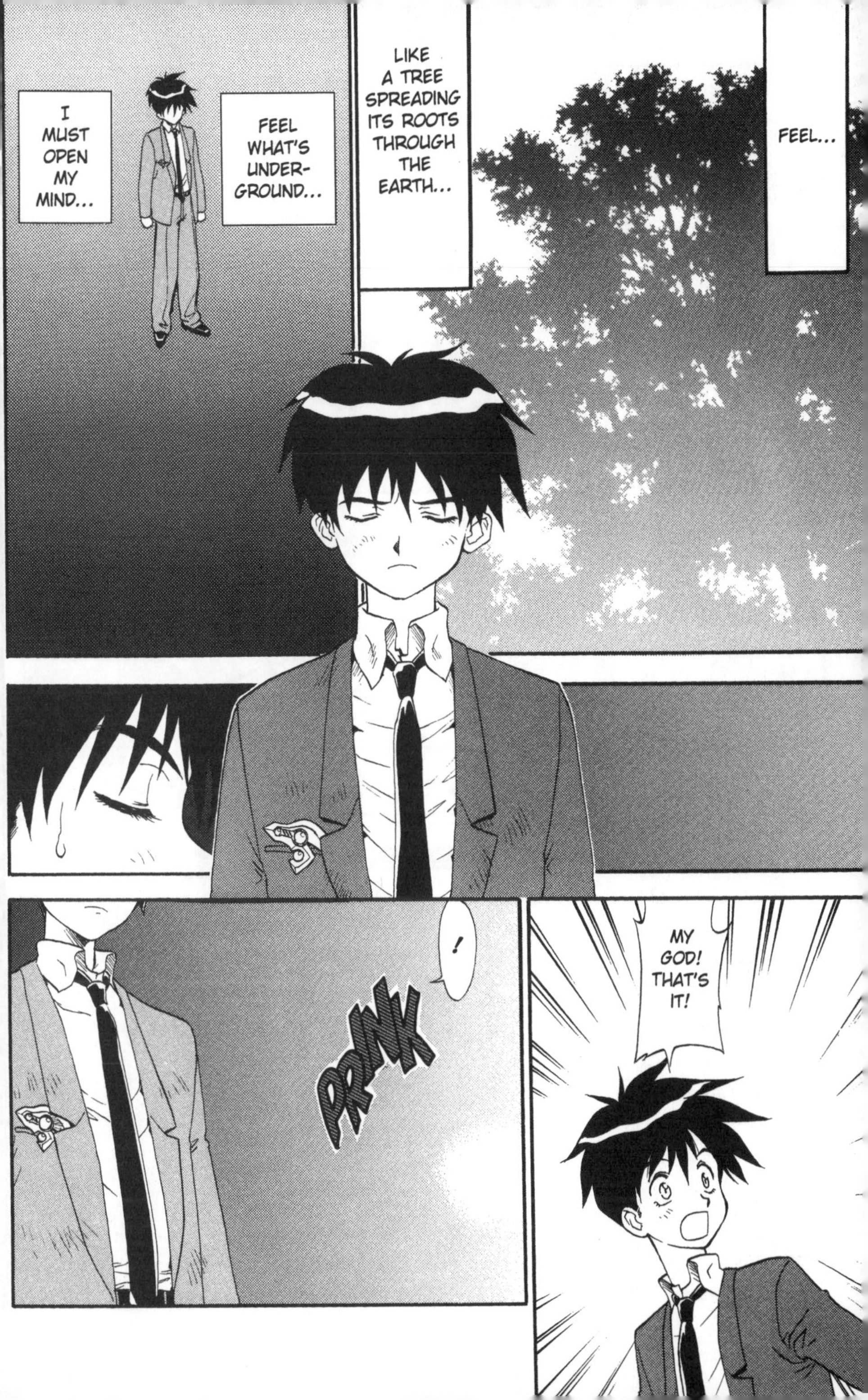
I MUST OPEN MY MIND...
FEEL WHAT'S UNDER-GROUND...
LIKE A TREE SPREADING ITS ROOTS THROUGH THE EARTH...
FEEL...
!
PRINK
MY GOD! THAT'S IT!

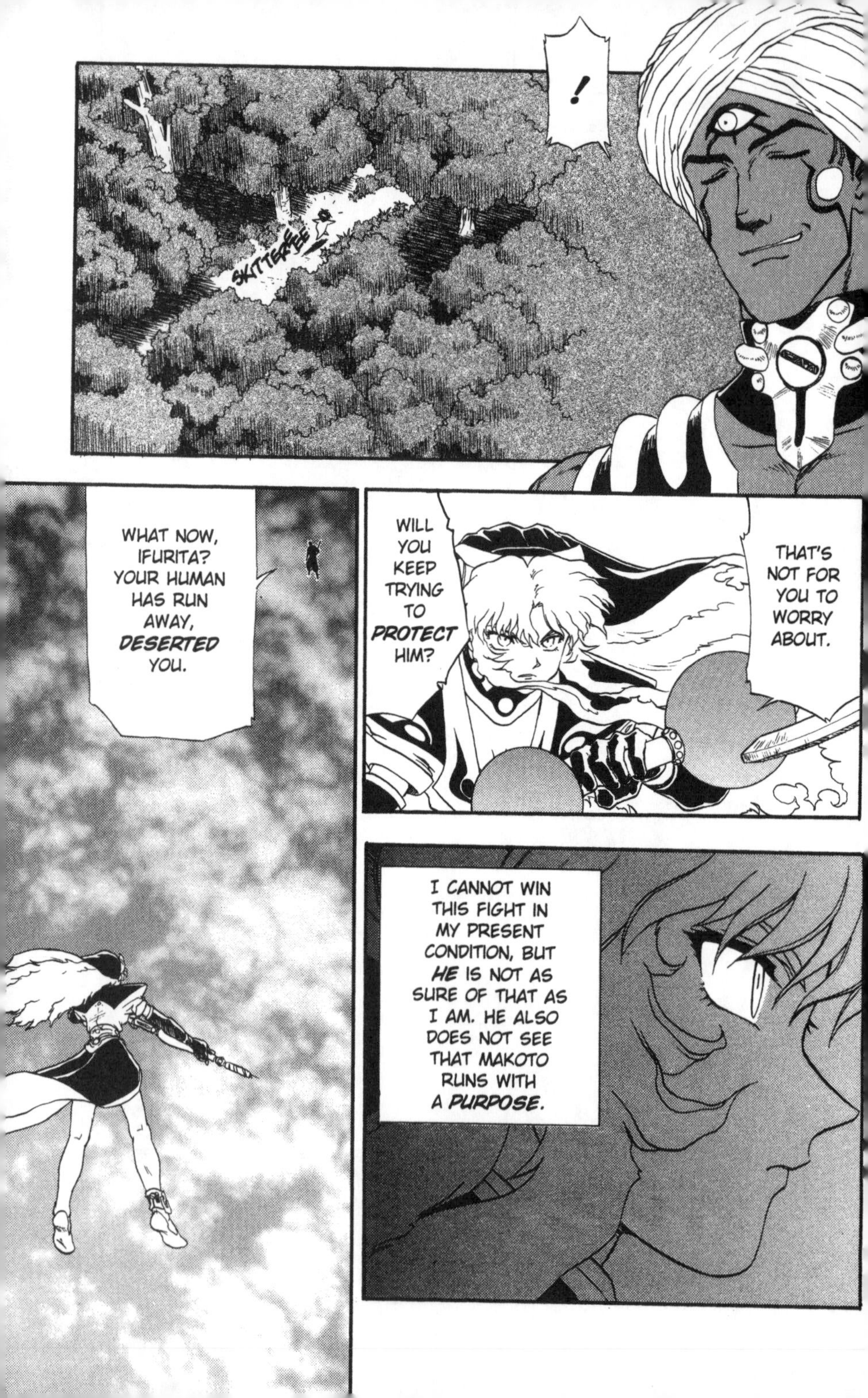

!
SKITTERRR
WHAT NOW, IFURITA? YOUR HUMAN HAS RUN AWAY, DESERTED YOU.
WILL YOU KEEP TRYING TO PROTECT HIM?
THAT'S NOT FOR YOU TO WORRY ABOUT.
I CANNOT WIN THIS FIGHT IN MY PRESENT CONDITION, BUT HE IS NOT AS SURE OF THAT AS I AM. HE ALSO DOES NOT SEE THAT MAKOTO RUNS WITH A PURPOSE.

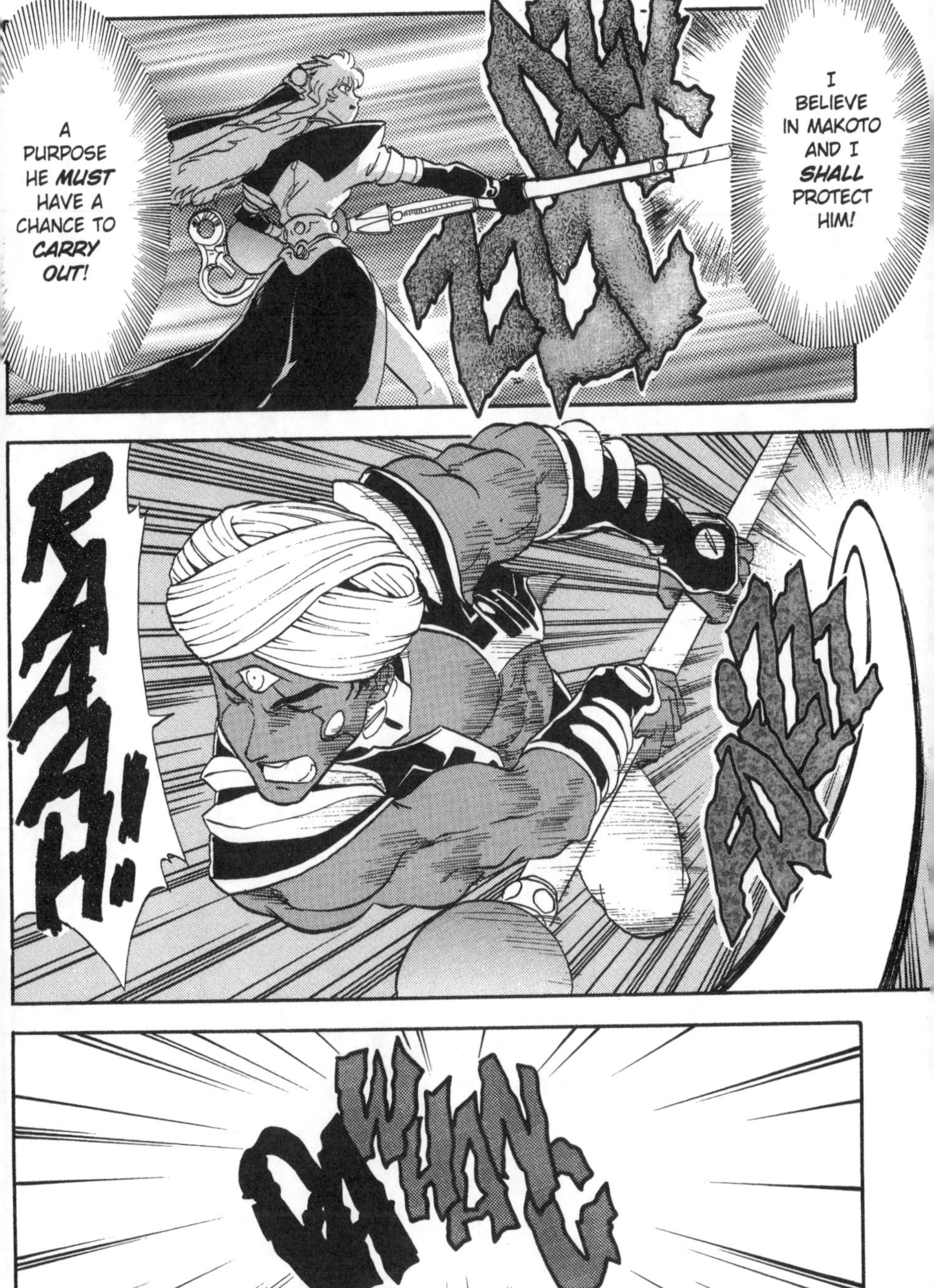
I BELIEVE IN MAKOTO AND I **SHALL** PROTECT HIM!
A PURPOSE HE **MUST** HAVE A CHANCE TO **CARRY OUT!**
RAAH!!

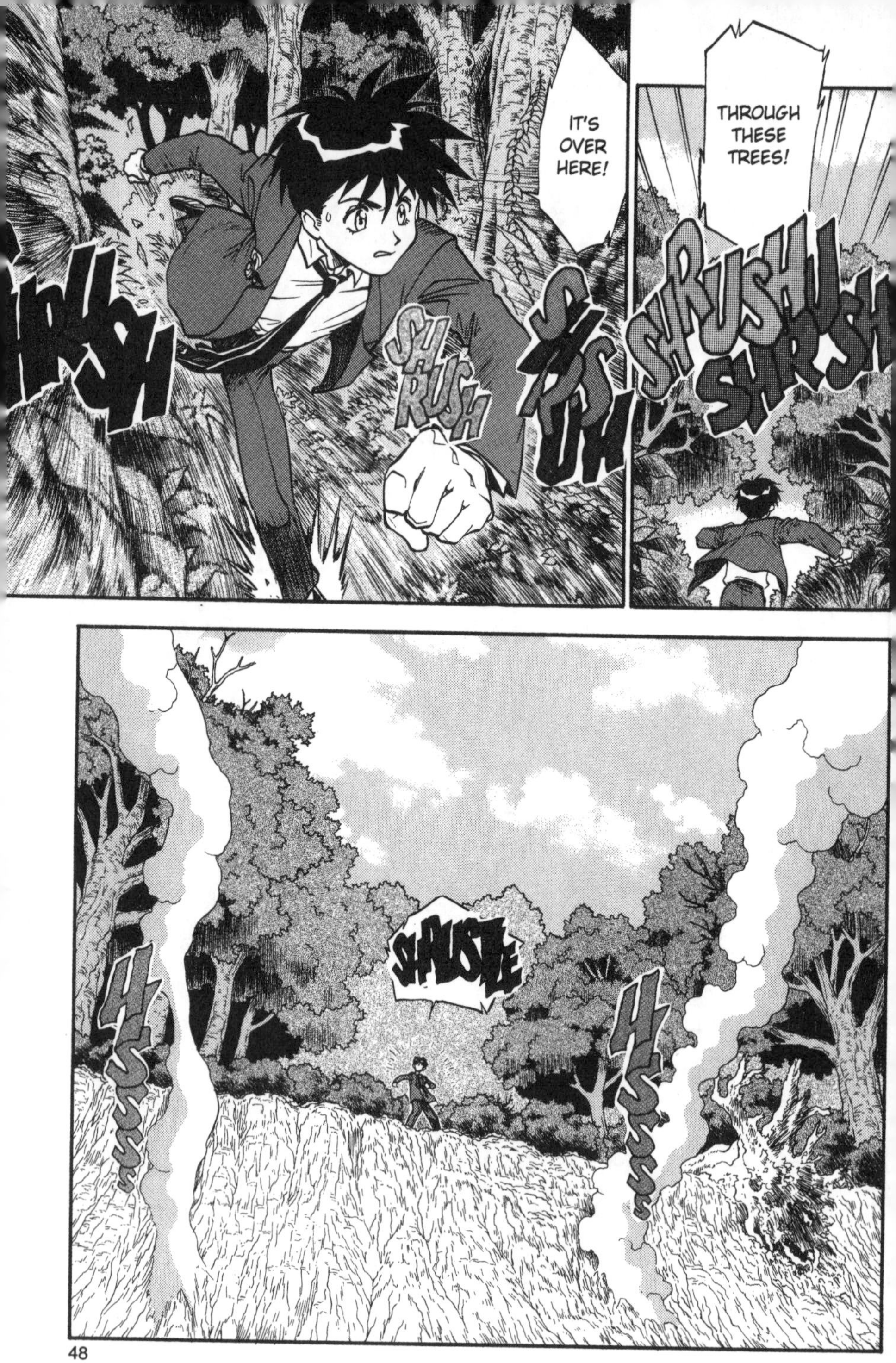
THROUGH THESE TREES!
SHRUSH SHRUSH
IT'S OVER HERE!
SHRUSH
HSSS
HSSS

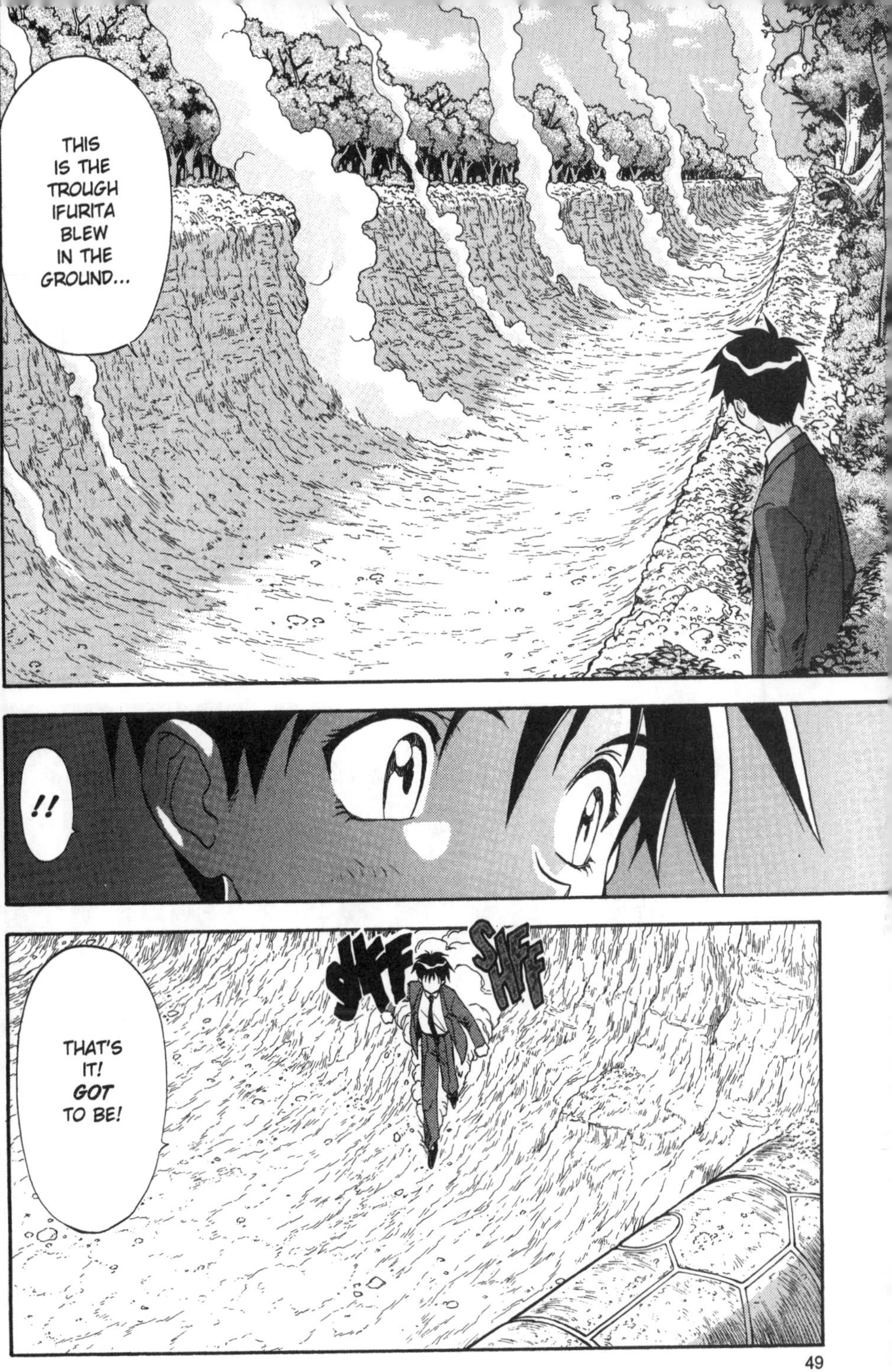

THIS IS THE TROUGH IFURITA BLEW IN THE GROUND...
!!
SHFF SHFF
THAT'S IT! GOT TO BE!

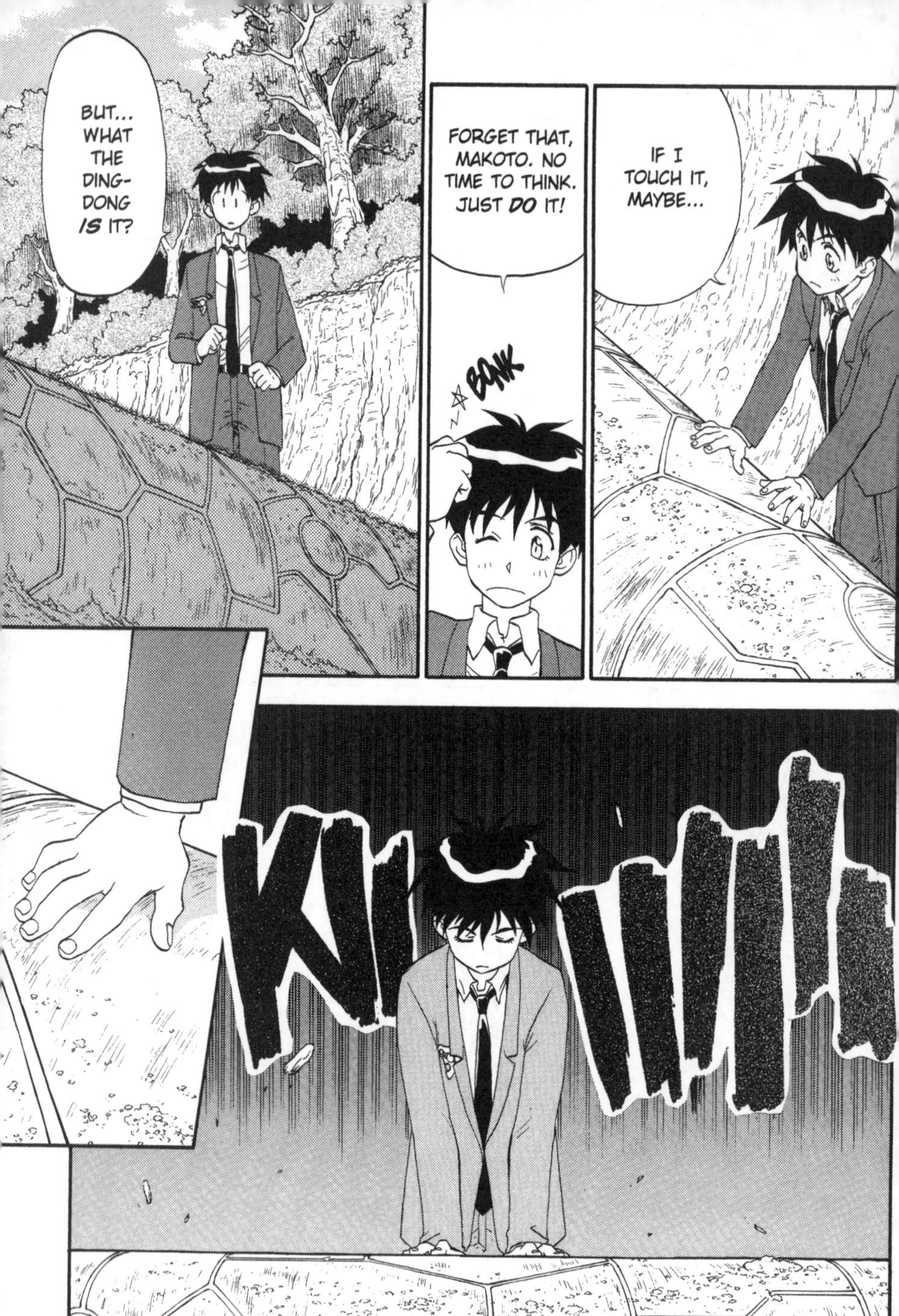
IF I TOUCH IT, MAYBE...
FORGET THAT, MAKOTO. NO TIME TO THINK. JUST DO IT!
BONK
BUT... WHAT THE DING-DONG IS IT?

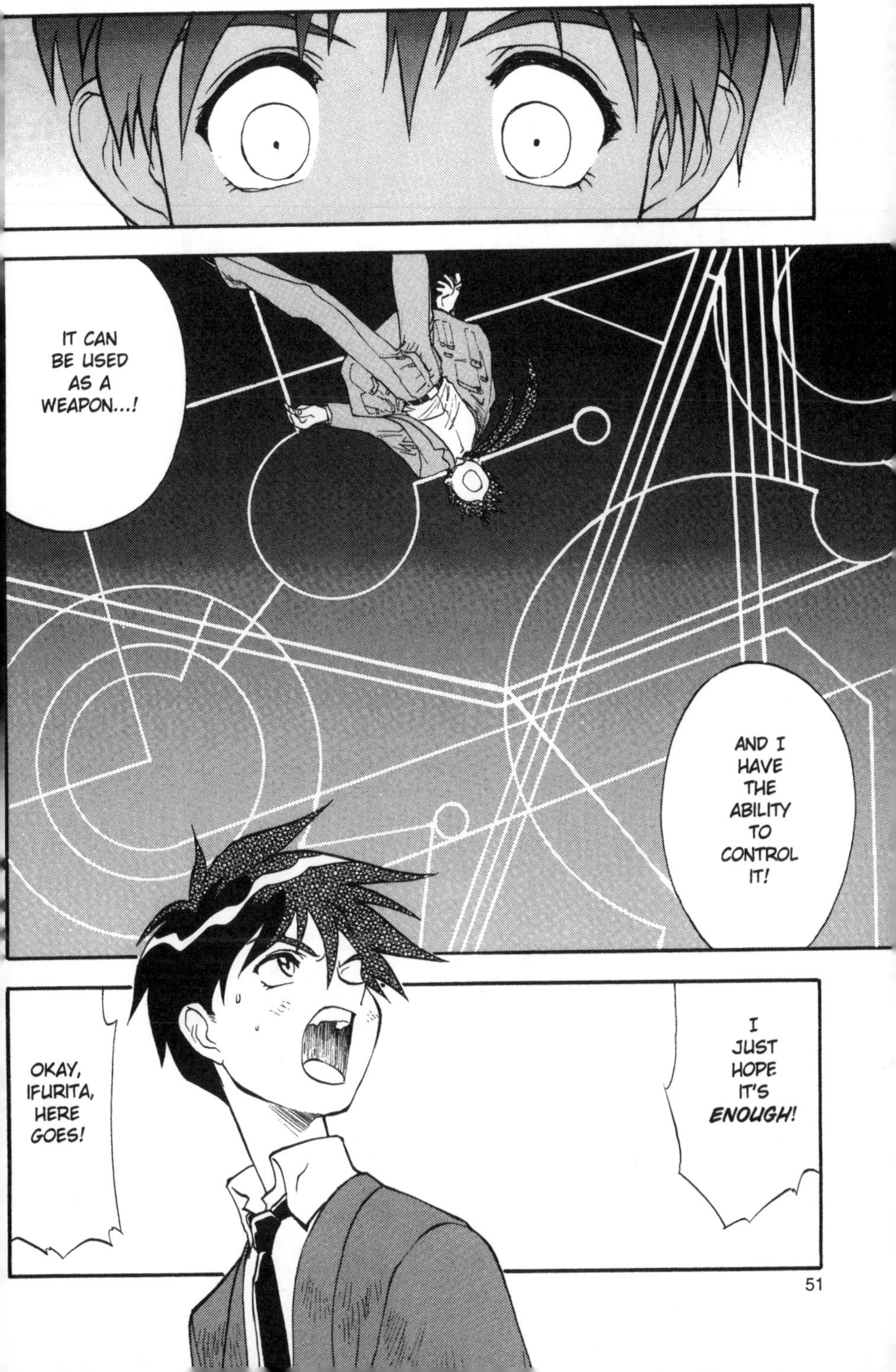
IT CAN BE USED AS A WEAPON...!
AND I HAVE THE ABILITY TO CONTROL IT!
I JUST HOPE IT'S *ENOUGH*!
OKAY, IFURITA, HERE GOES!

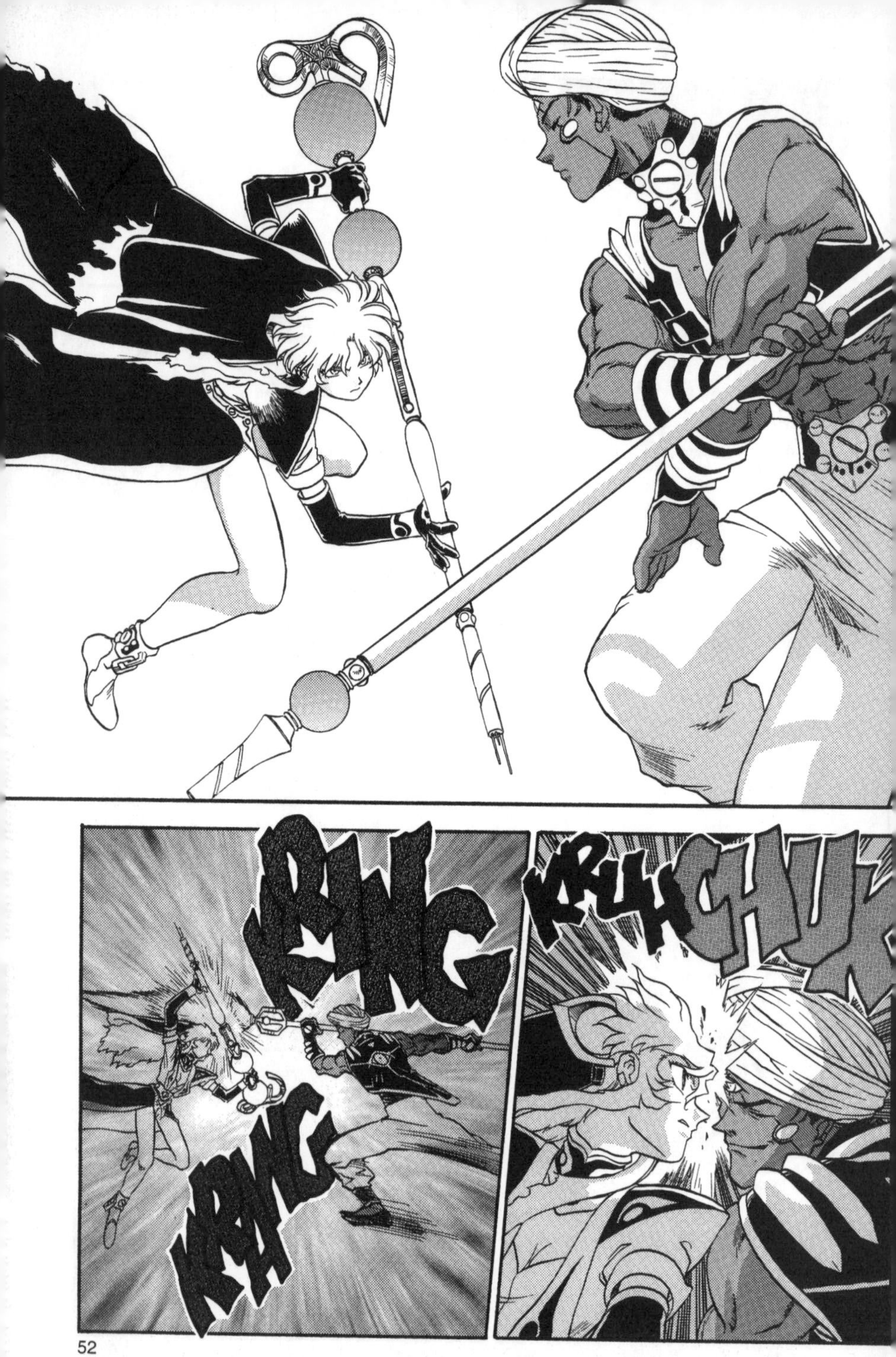
KRANG
KRANG
KRUHCHUK

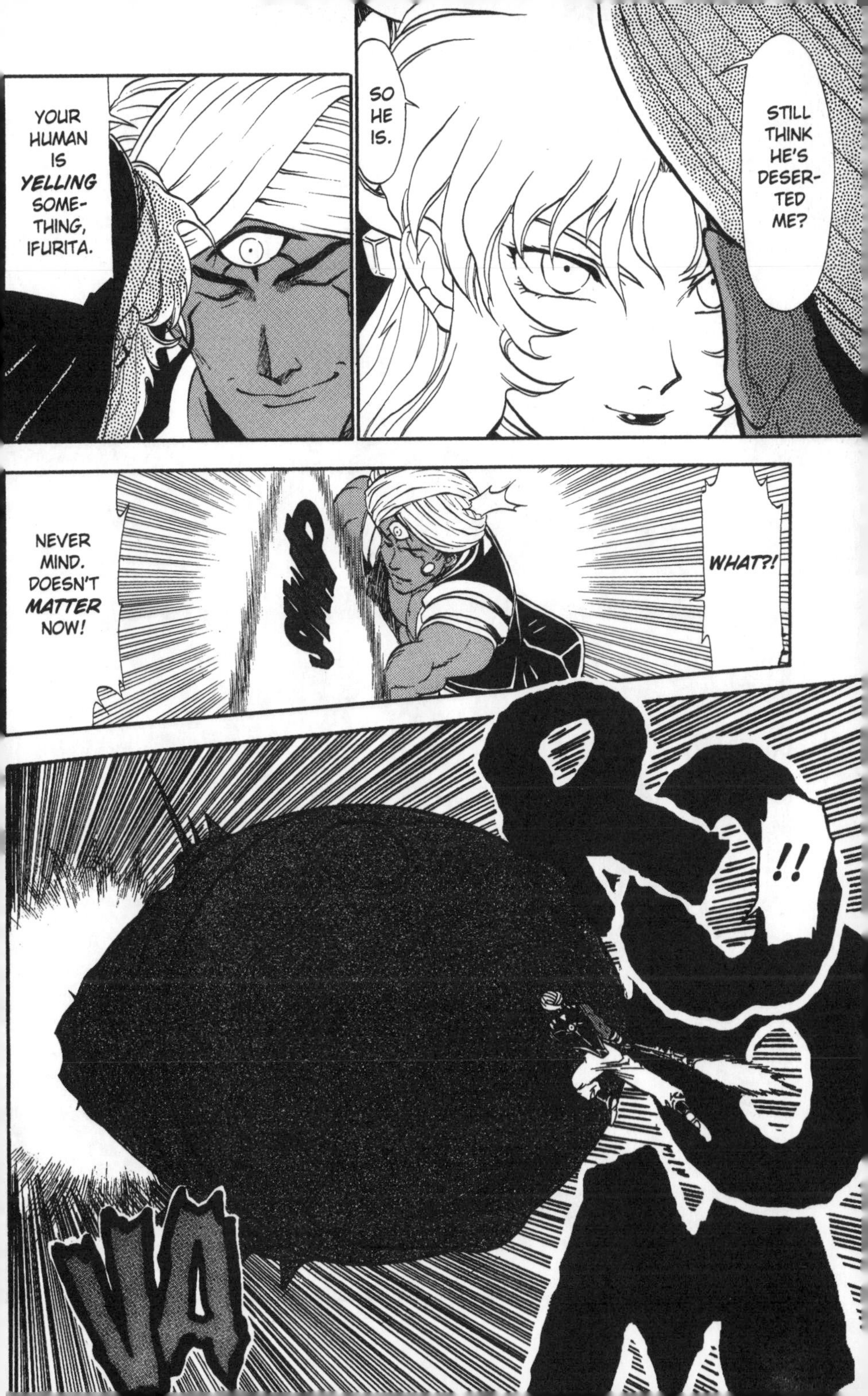

YOUR HUMAN IS *YELLING* SOMETHING, IFURITA.
SO HE IS.
STILL THINK HE'S DESERTED ME?
NEVER MIND. DOESN'T *MATTER* NOW!
WHAT?!
!!

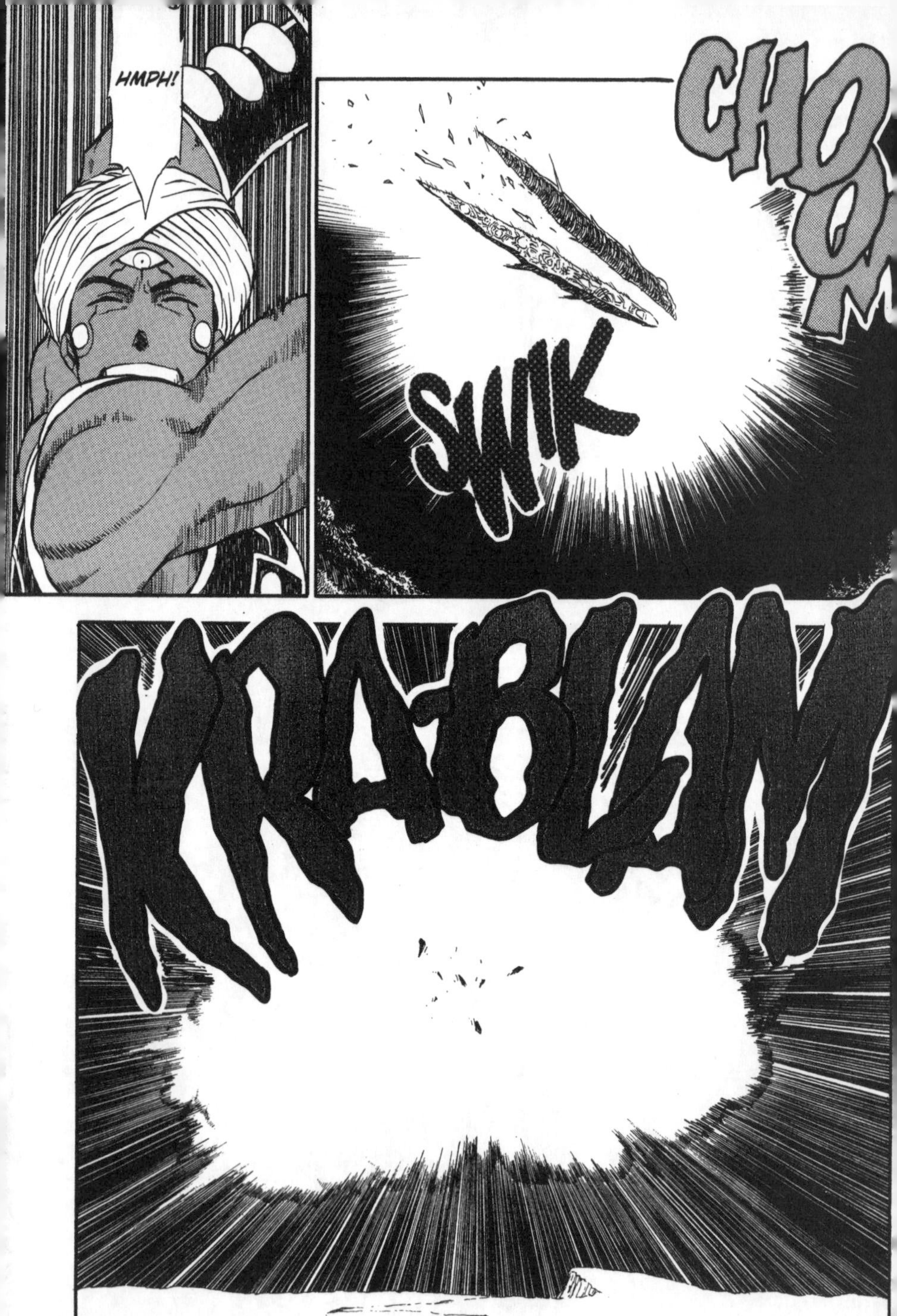
HMPH!
CHOOM
SWIK
KRA-BLAM

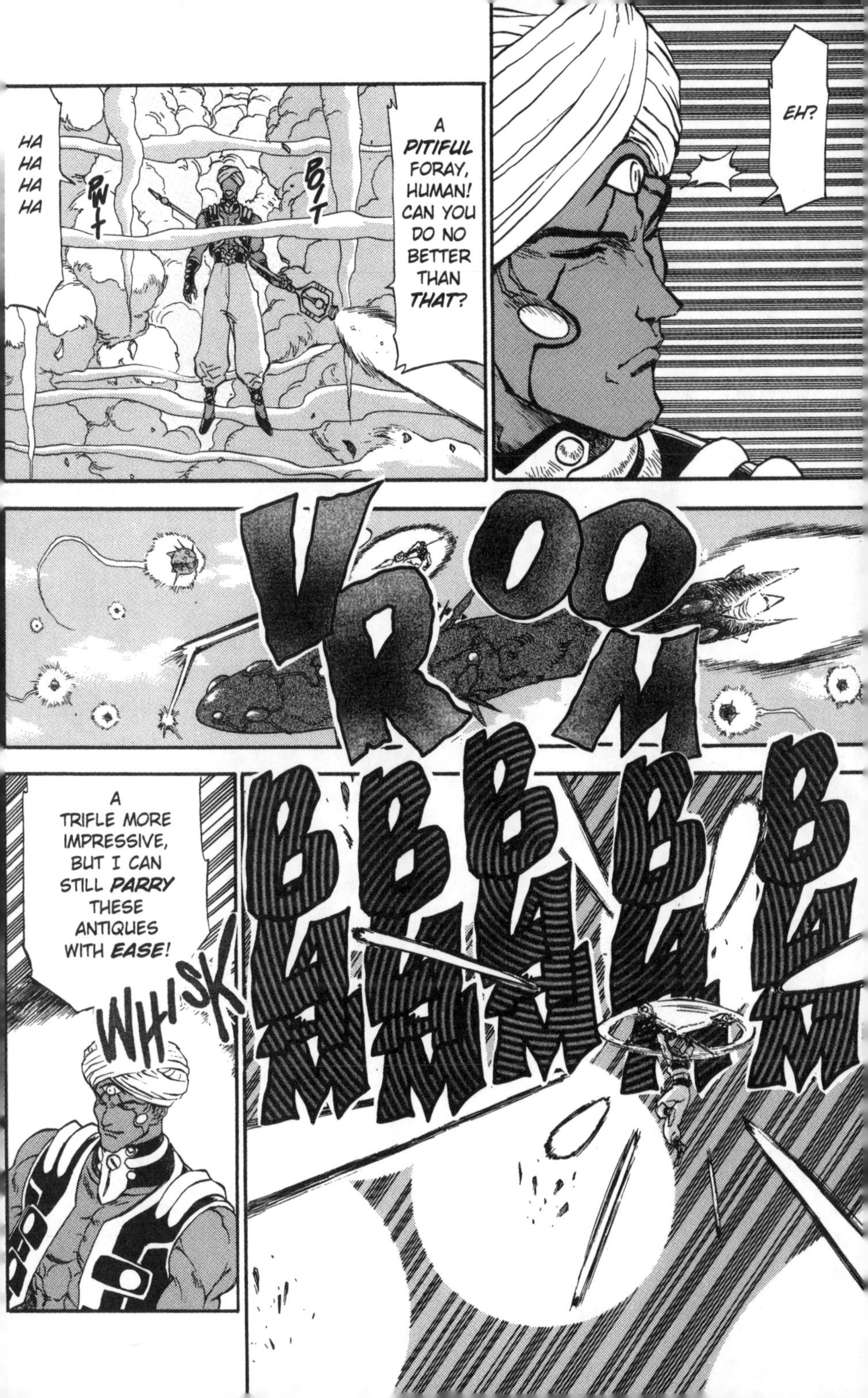

A PITIFUL FORAY, HUMAN! CAN YOU DO NO BETTER THAN THAT?
HA HA HA HA
PWT
BOIT
EH?
VROOOM
A TRIFLE MORE IMPRESSIVE, BUT I CAN STILL PARRY THESE ANTIQUES WITH EASE!
WHISK
BBBBBLAM

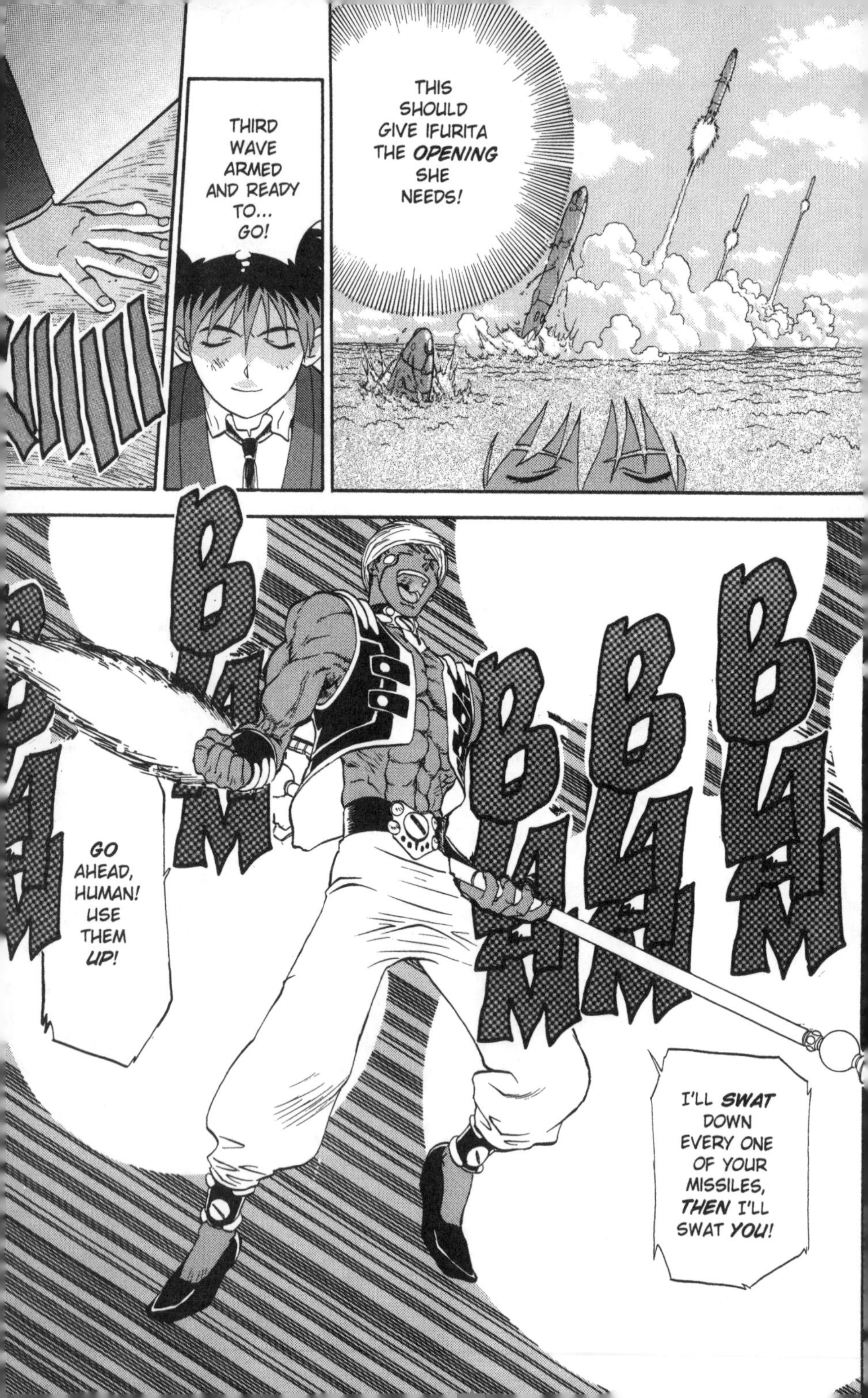
THIRD WAVE ARMED AND READY TO... GO!
THIS SHOULD GIVE IFURITA THE *OPENING* SHE NEEDS!
BLAM
BLAM
BLAM
BLAM
GO AHEAD, HUMAN! USE THEM UP!
I'LL *SWAT* DOWN EVERY ONE OF YOUR MISSILES, *THEN* I'LL SWAT *YOU!*

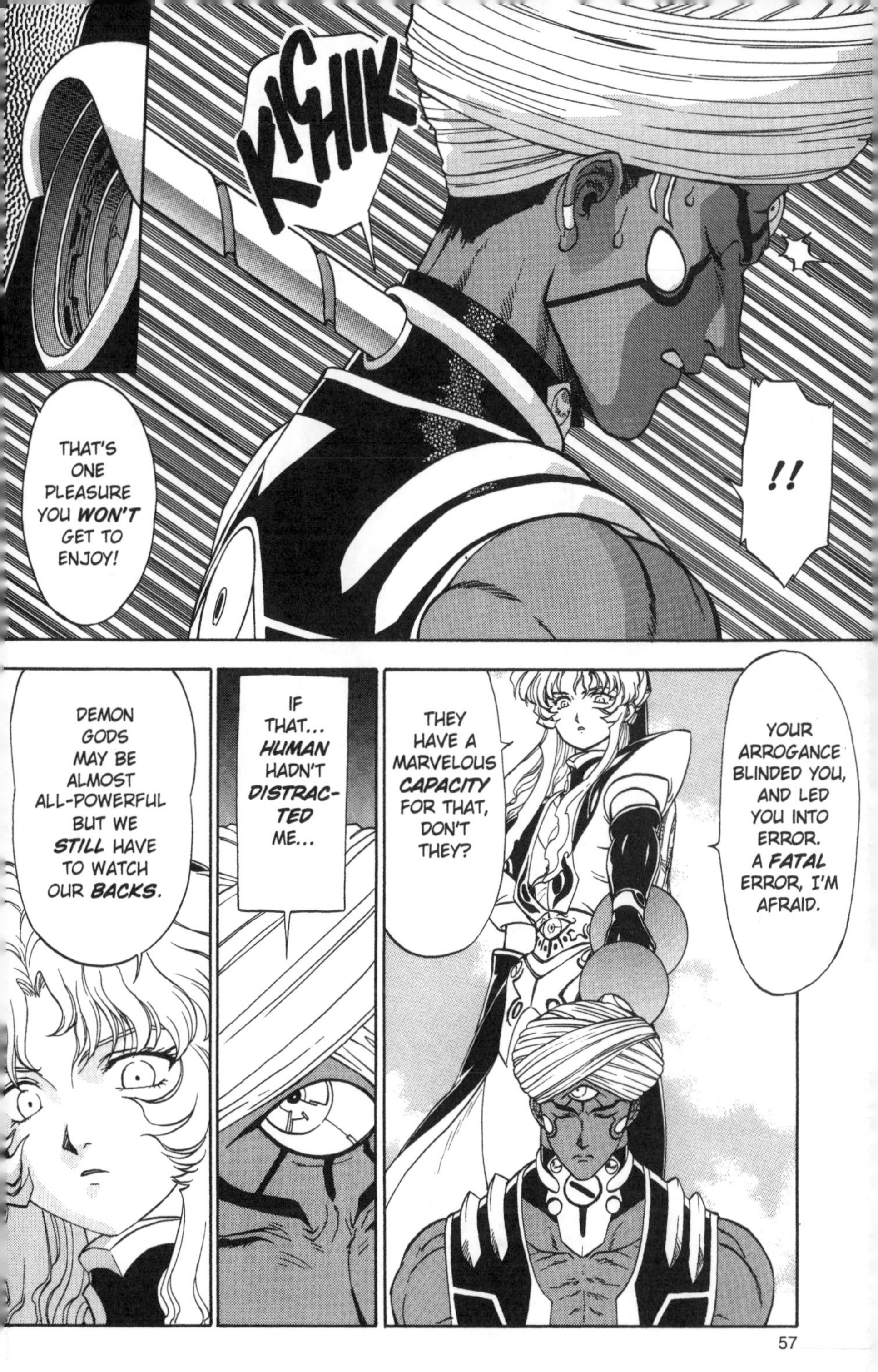
KICHIK
!!
THAT'S ONE PLEASURE YOU **WON'T** GET TO ENJOY!
YOUR ARROGANCE BLINDED YOU, AND LED YOU INTO ERROR. A **FATAL** ERROR, I'M AFRAID.
THEY HAVE A MARVELOUS **CAPACITY** FOR THAT, DON'T THEY?
IF THAT... **HUMAN** HADN'T **DISTRACTED** ME...
DEMON GODS MAY BE ALMOST ALL-POWERFUL BUT WE **STILL** HAVE TO WATCH OUR **BACKS**.

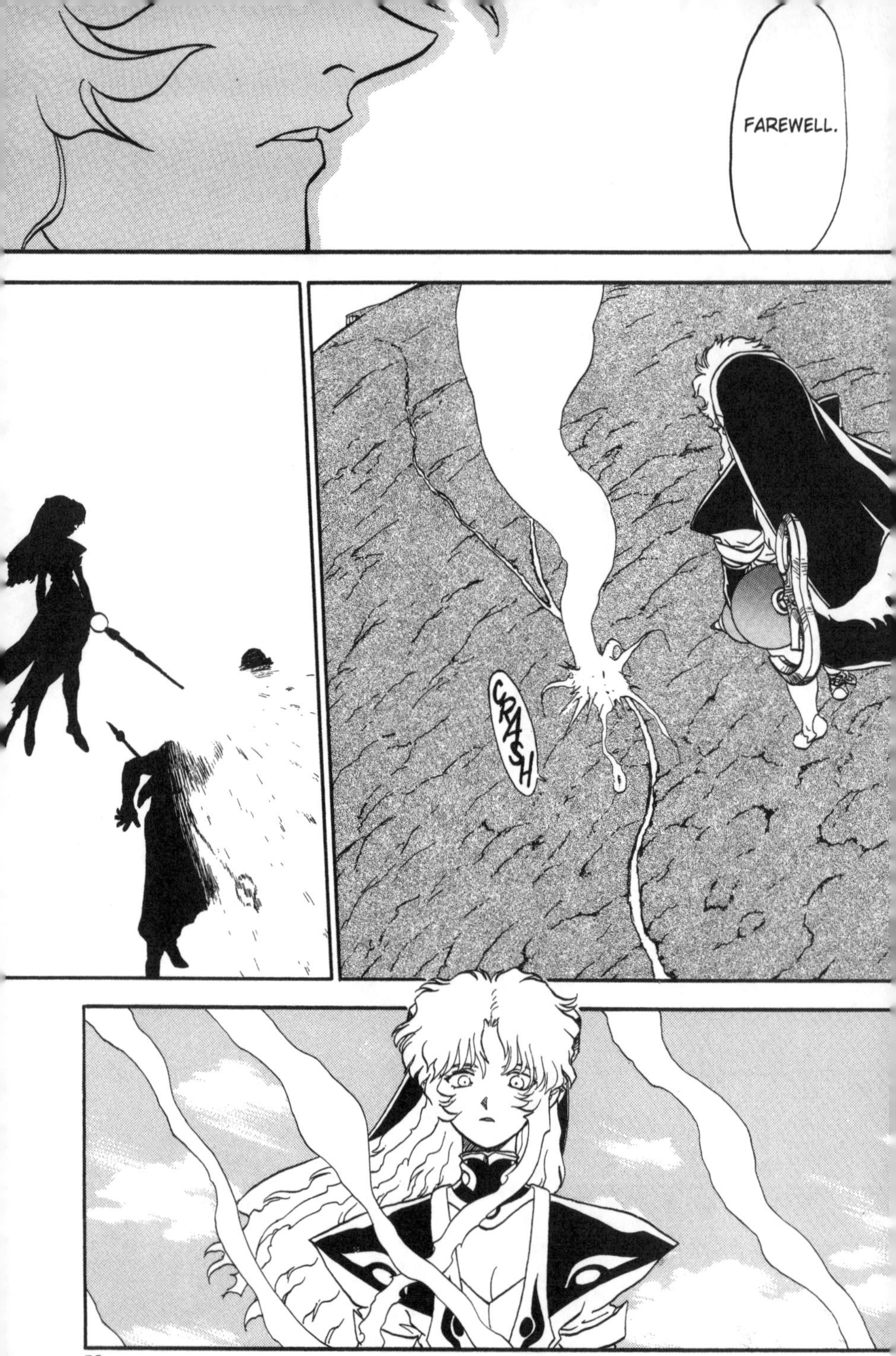
FAREWELL.
CRASH

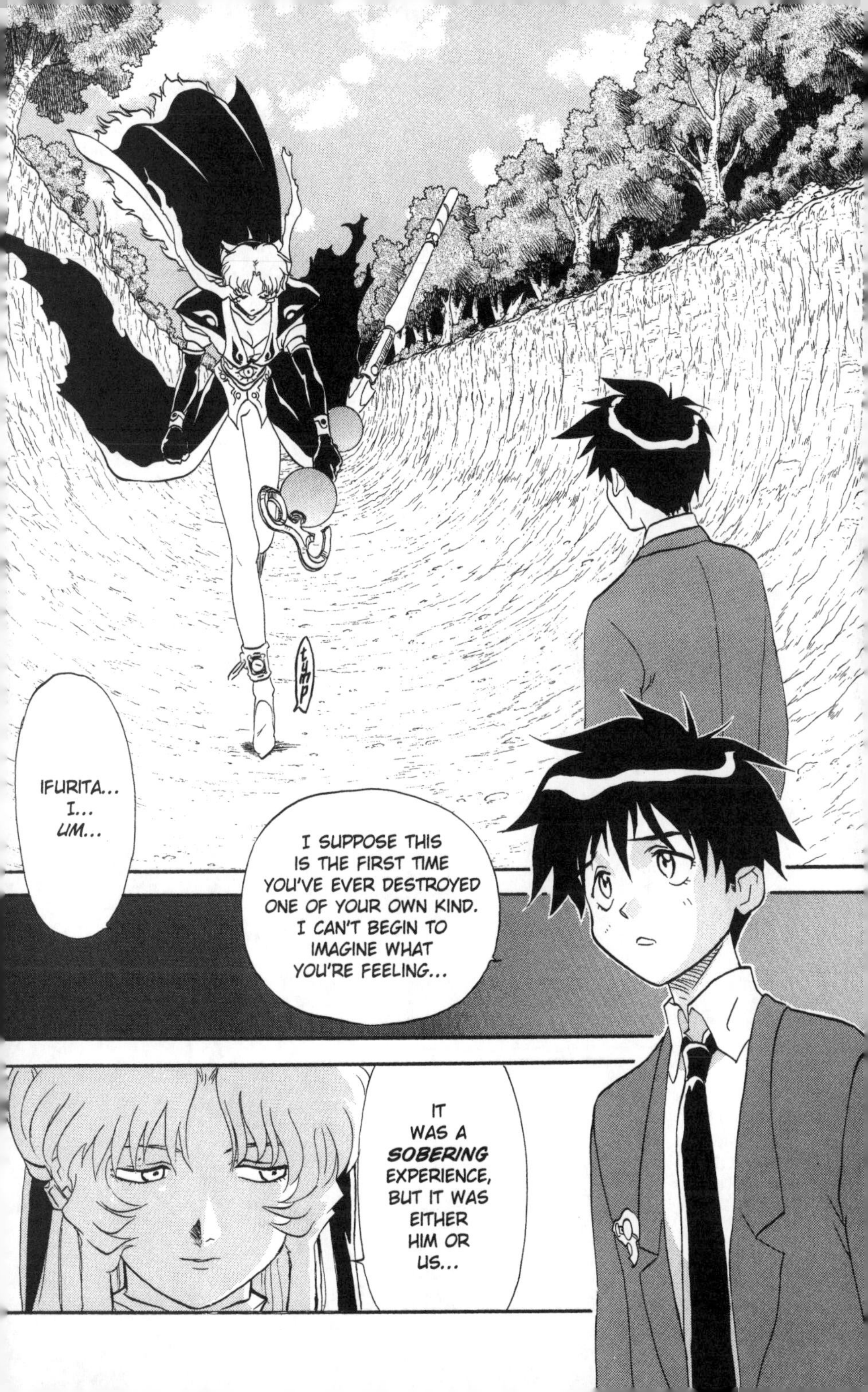
TUMP
IFURITA... I... UM...
I SUPPOSE THIS IS THE FIRST TIME YOU'VE EVER DESTROYED ONE OF YOUR OWN KIND. I CAN'T BEGIN TO IMAGINE WHAT YOU'RE FEELING...
IT WAS A *SOBERING* EXPERIENCE, BUT IT WAS EITHER HIM OR US...

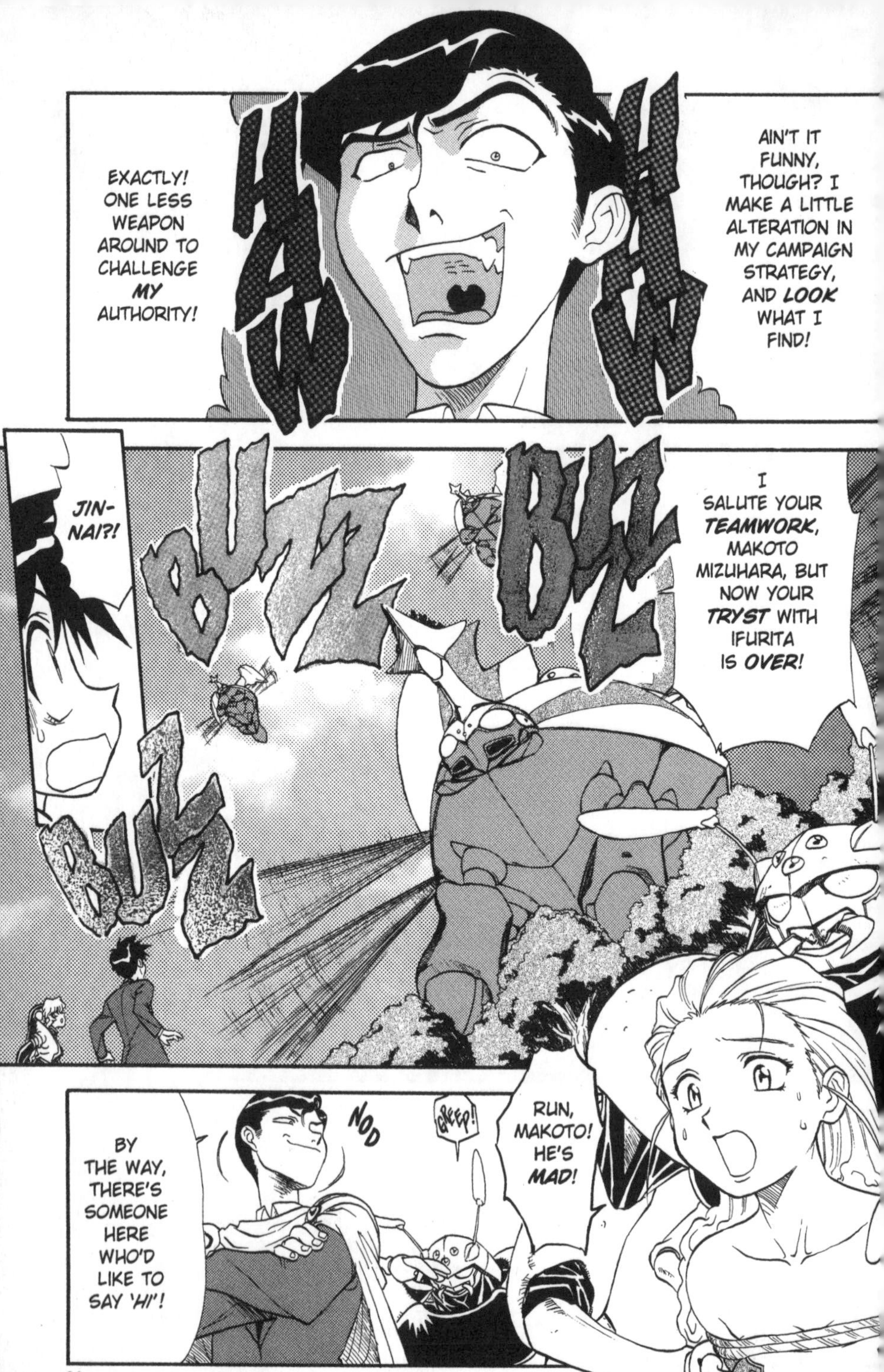
AIN'T IT FUNNY, THOUGH? I MAKE A LITTLE ALTERATION IN MY CAMPAIGN STRATEGY, AND LOOK WHAT I FIND!
EXACTLY! ONE LESS WEAPON AROUND TO CHALLENGE MY AUTHORITY!
I SALUTE YOUR TEAMWORK, MAKOTO MIZUHARA, BUT NOW YOUR TRYST WITH IFURITA IS OVER!
BUZZ
BUZZ
BUZZ
JIN-NAI?!
RUN, MAKOTO! HE'S MAD!
GREEP!
NOD
BY THE WAY, THERE'S SOMEONE HERE WHO'D LIKE TO SAY 'HI'!

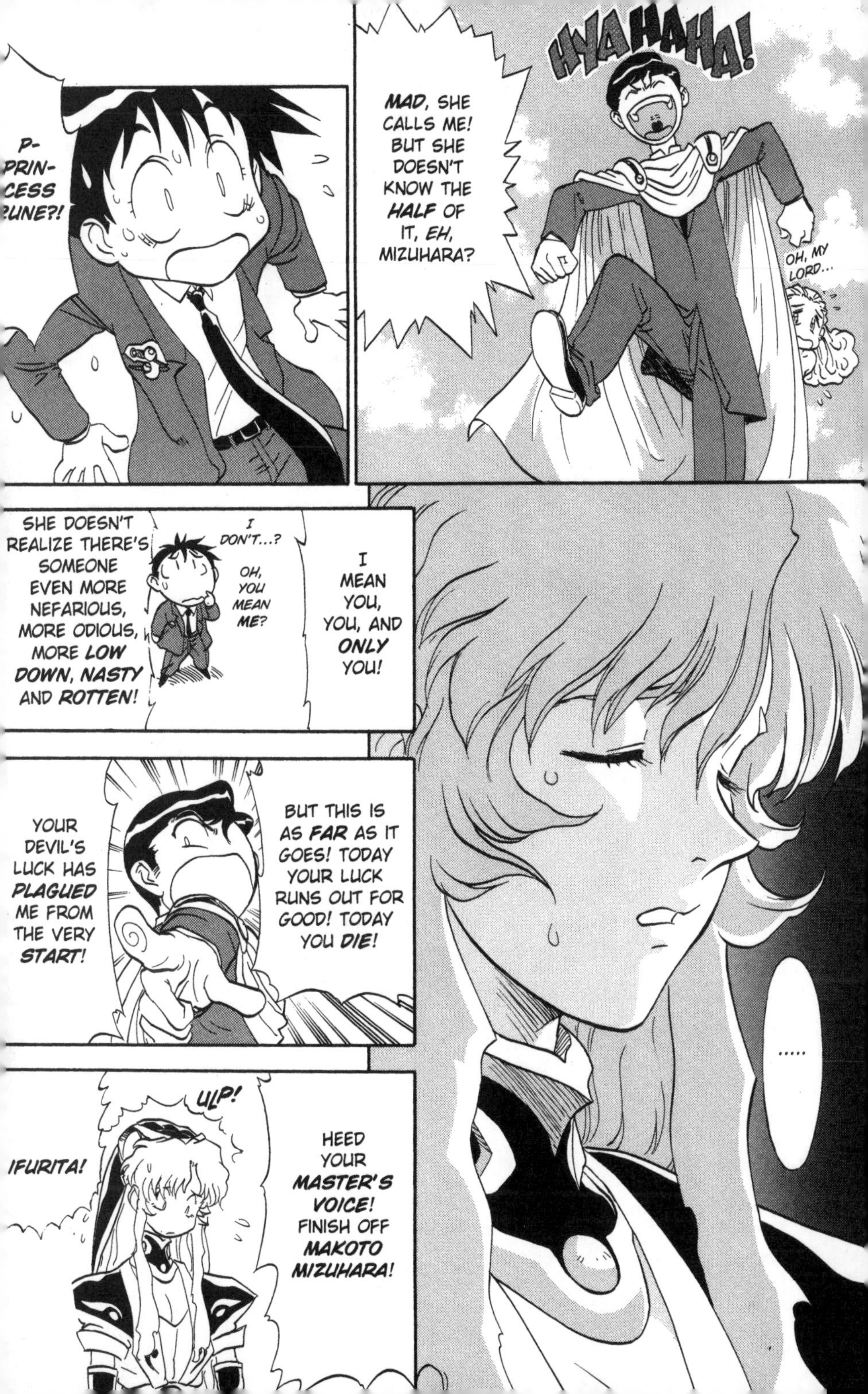
P-PRIN-CESS RUNE?!
HYAHAHA!
MAD, SHE CALLS ME! BUT SHE DOESN'T KNOW THE HALF OF IT, EH, MIZUHARA?
OH, MY LORD...
SHE DOESN'T REALIZE THERE'S SOMEONE EVEN MORE NEFARIOUS, MORE ODIOUS, MORE LOW DOWN, NASTY AND ROTTEN!
I DON'T...?
OH, YOU MEAN ME?
I MEAN YOU, YOU, AND ONLY YOU!
YOUR DEVIL'S LUCK HAS PLAGUED ME FROM THE VERY START!
BUT THIS IS AS FAR AS IT GOES! TODAY YOUR LUCK RUNS OUT FOR GOOD! TODAY YOU DIE!
.....
ULP!
IFURITA!
HEED YOUR MASTER'S VOICE! FINISH OFF MAKOTO MIZUHARA!

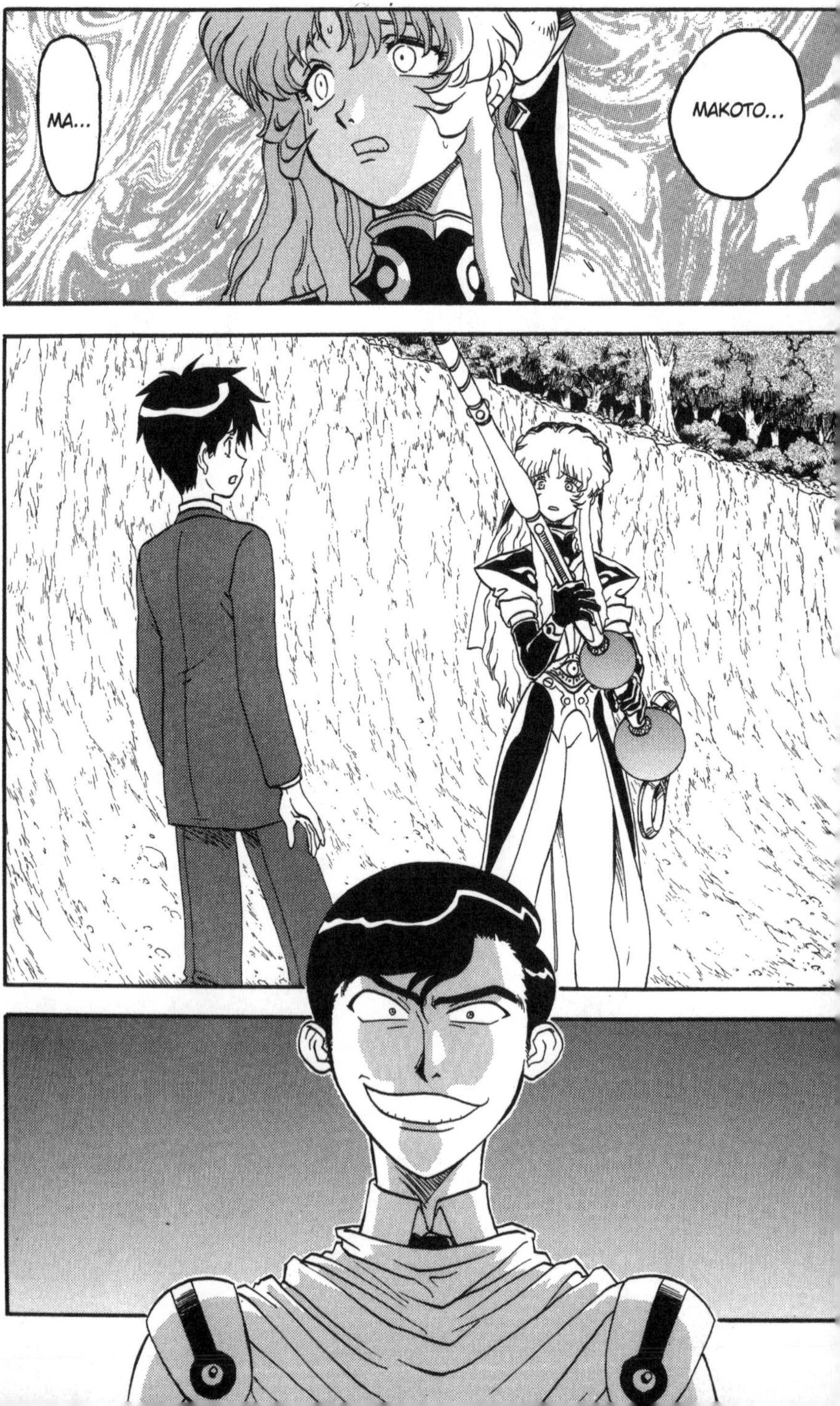
MAKOTO...
MA...

EL-HAZARD
THE MAGNIFICENT WORLD

EPISODE 13

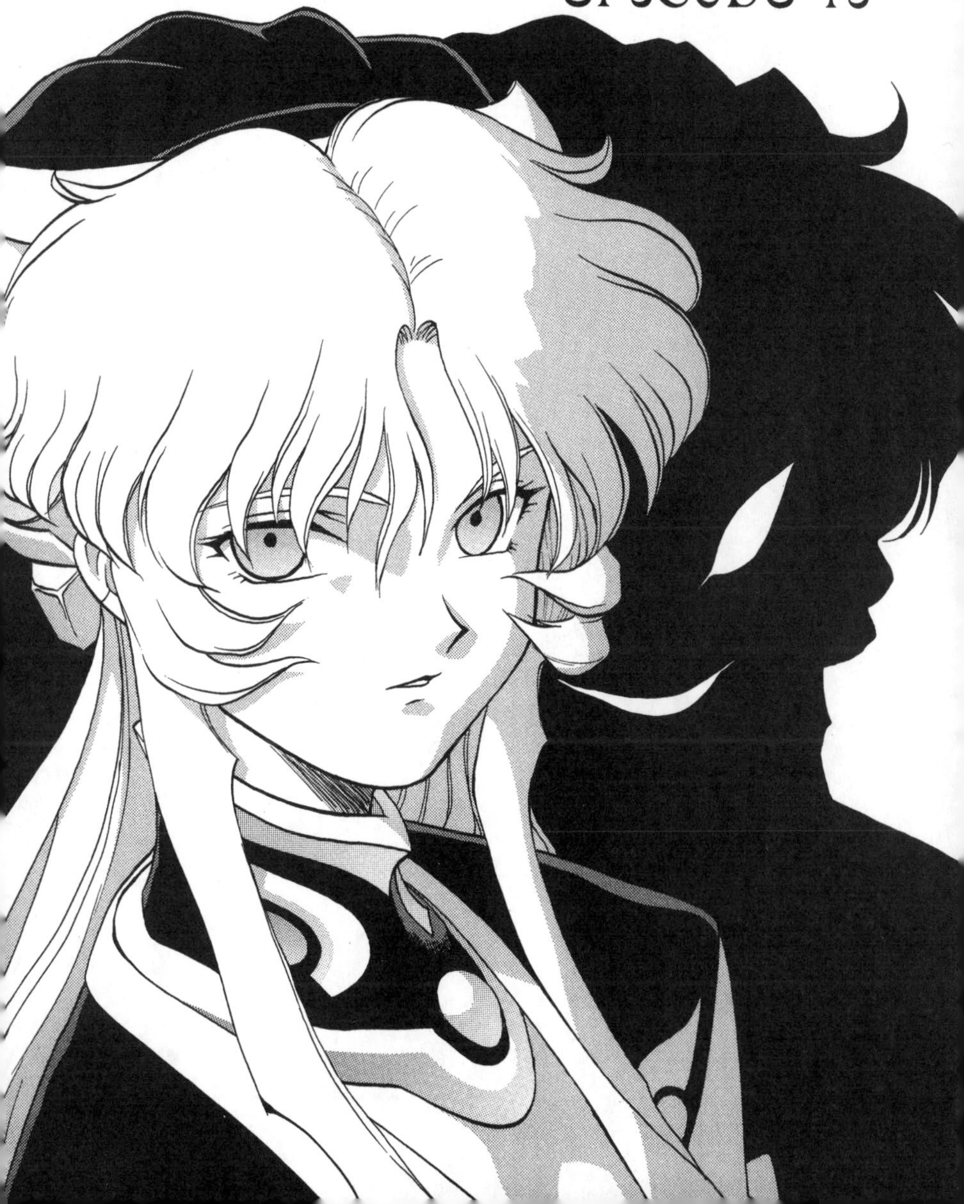

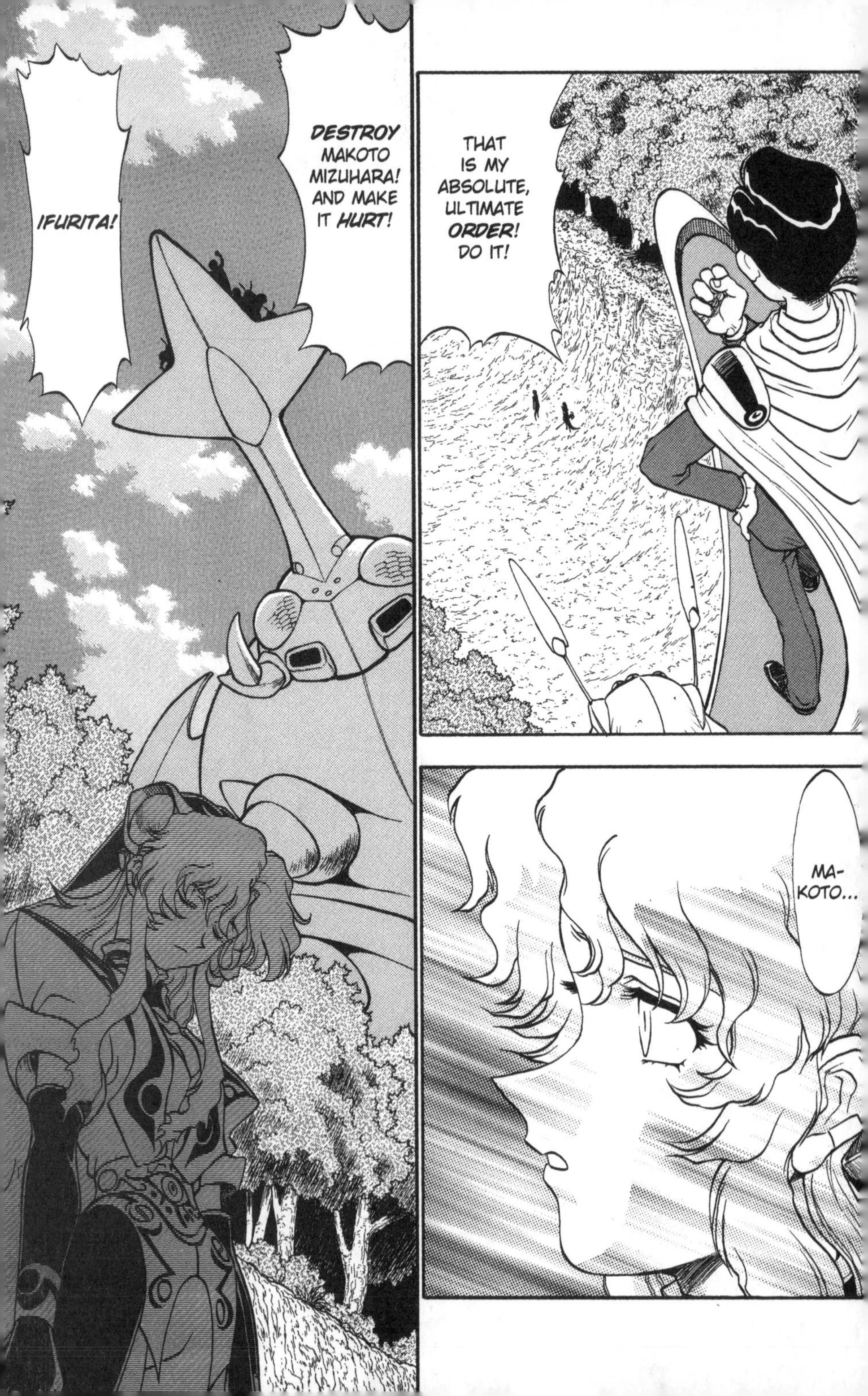
THAT IS MY ABSOLUTE, ULTIMATE ORDER! DO IT!
DESTROY MAKOTO MIZUHARA! AND MAKE IT HURT!
IFURITA!
MA-KOTO...

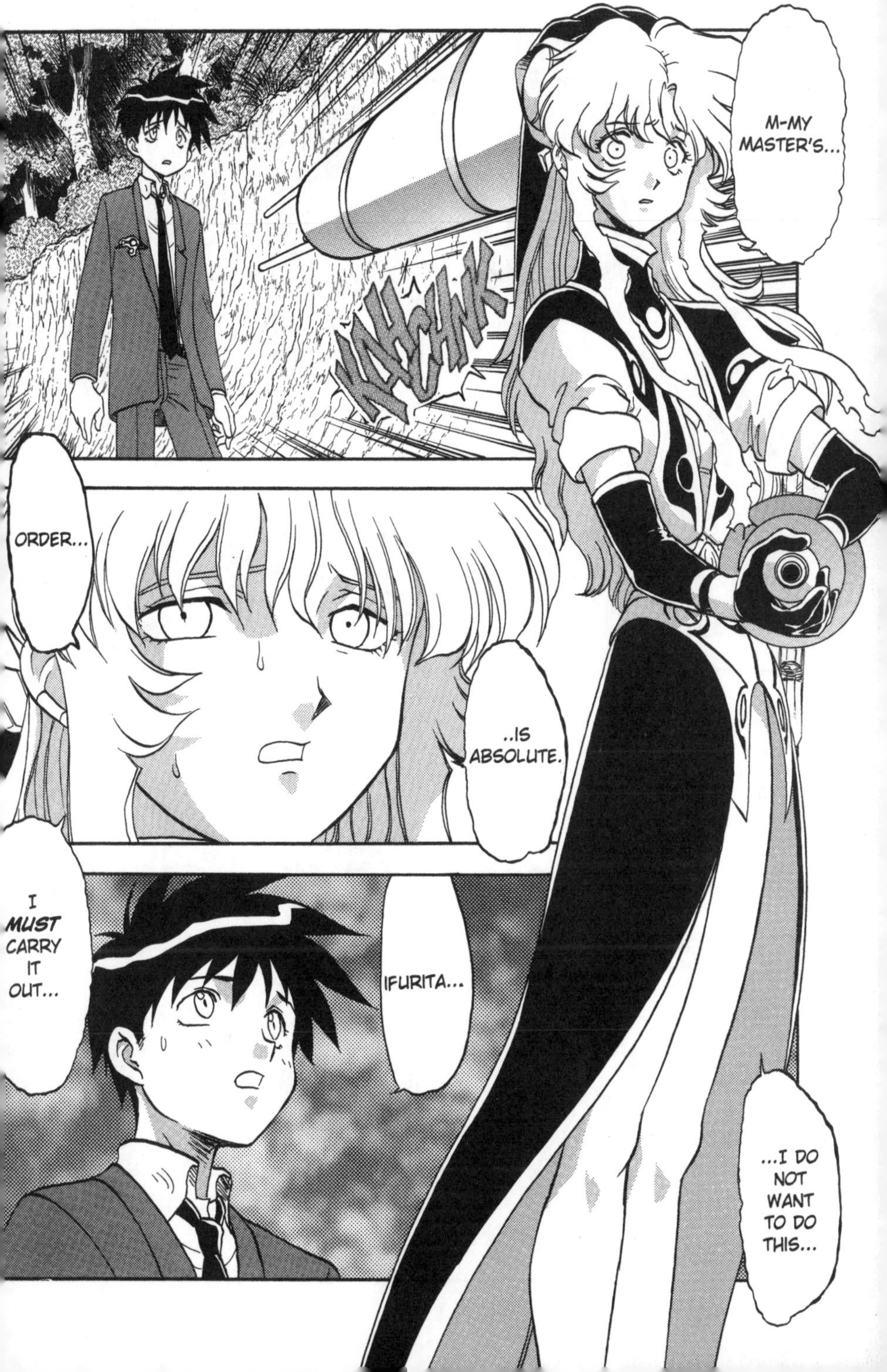
M-MY MASTER'S...
KACHINK
ORDER...
..IS ABSOLUTE.
I MUST CARRY IT OUT...
...I DO NOT WANT TO DO THIS...
IFURITA...

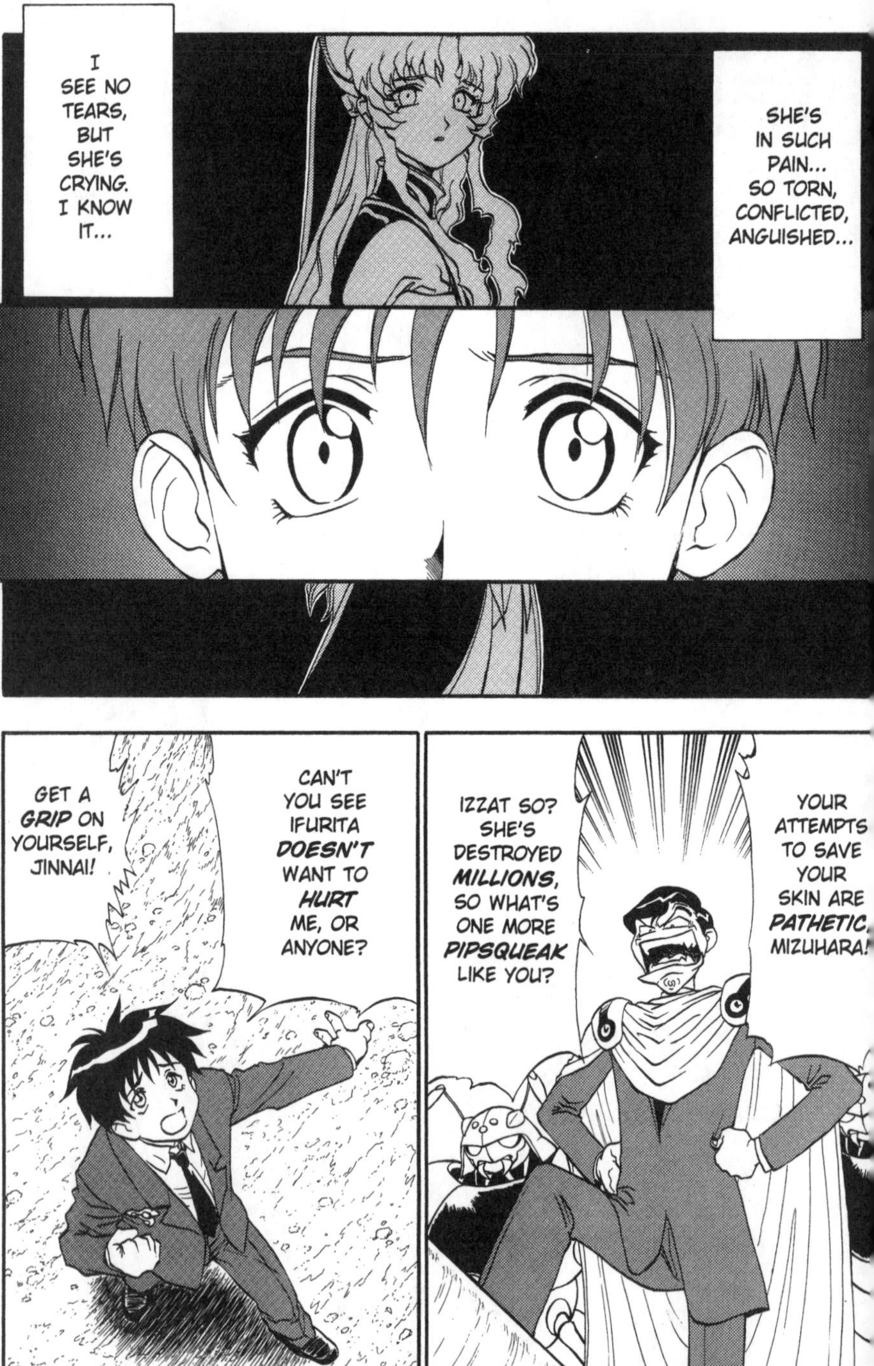
I SEE NO TEARS, BUT SHE'S CRYING. I KNOW IT...
SHE'S IN SUCH PAIN... SO TORN, CONFLICTED, ANGUISHED...
YOUR ATTEMPTS TO SAVE YOUR SKIN ARE PATHETIC, MIZUHARA!
IZZAT SO? SHE'S DESTROYED MILLIONS, SO WHAT'S ONE MORE PIPSQUEAK LIKE YOU?
GET A GRIP ON YOURSELF, JINNAI!
CAN'T YOU SEE IFURITA DOESN'T WANT TO HURT ME, OR ANYONE?

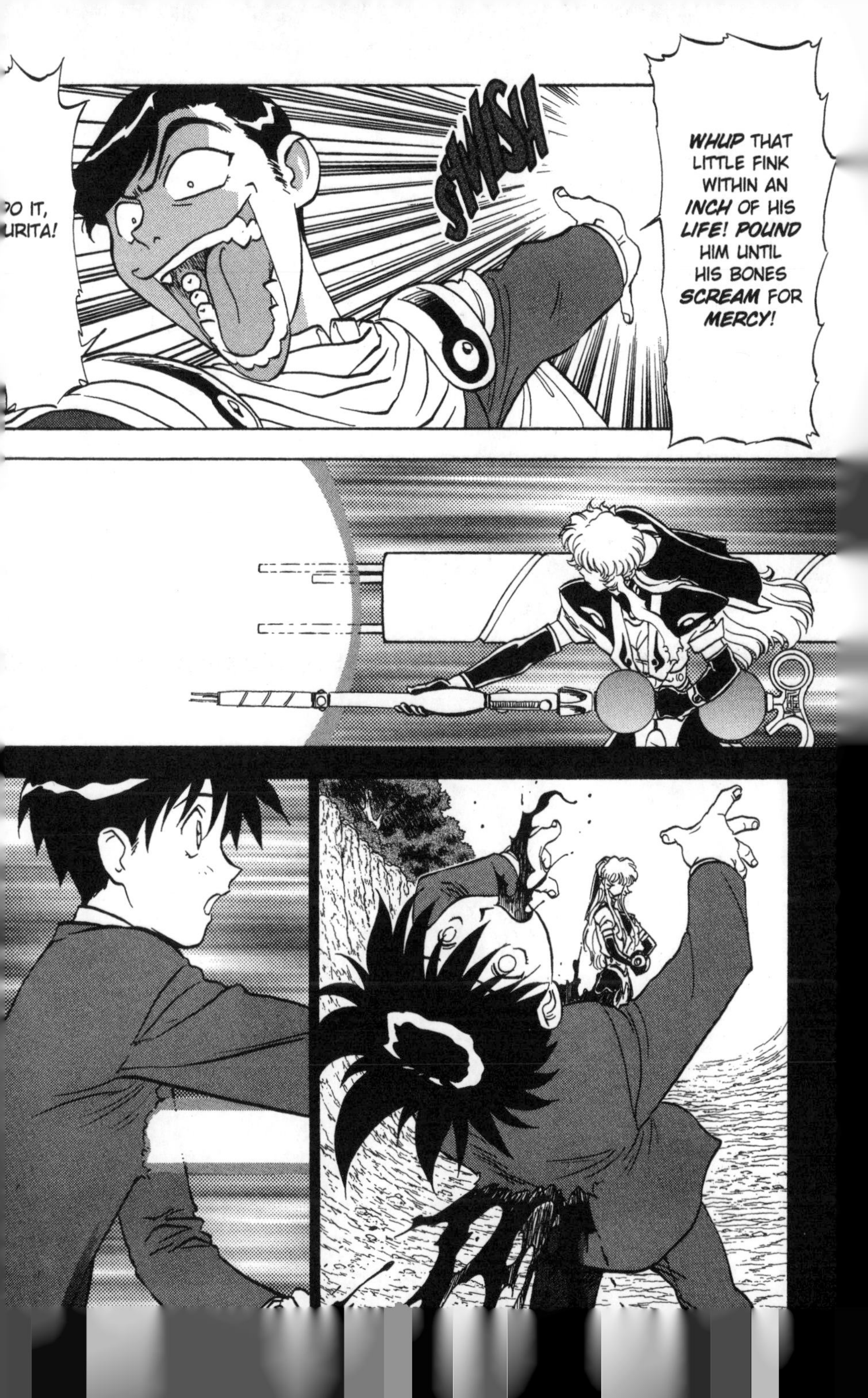
WHUP THAT LITTLE FINK WITHIN AN INCH OF HIS LIFE! POUND HIM UNTIL HIS BONES SCREAM FOR MERCY!
SWISH
DO IT, URITA!

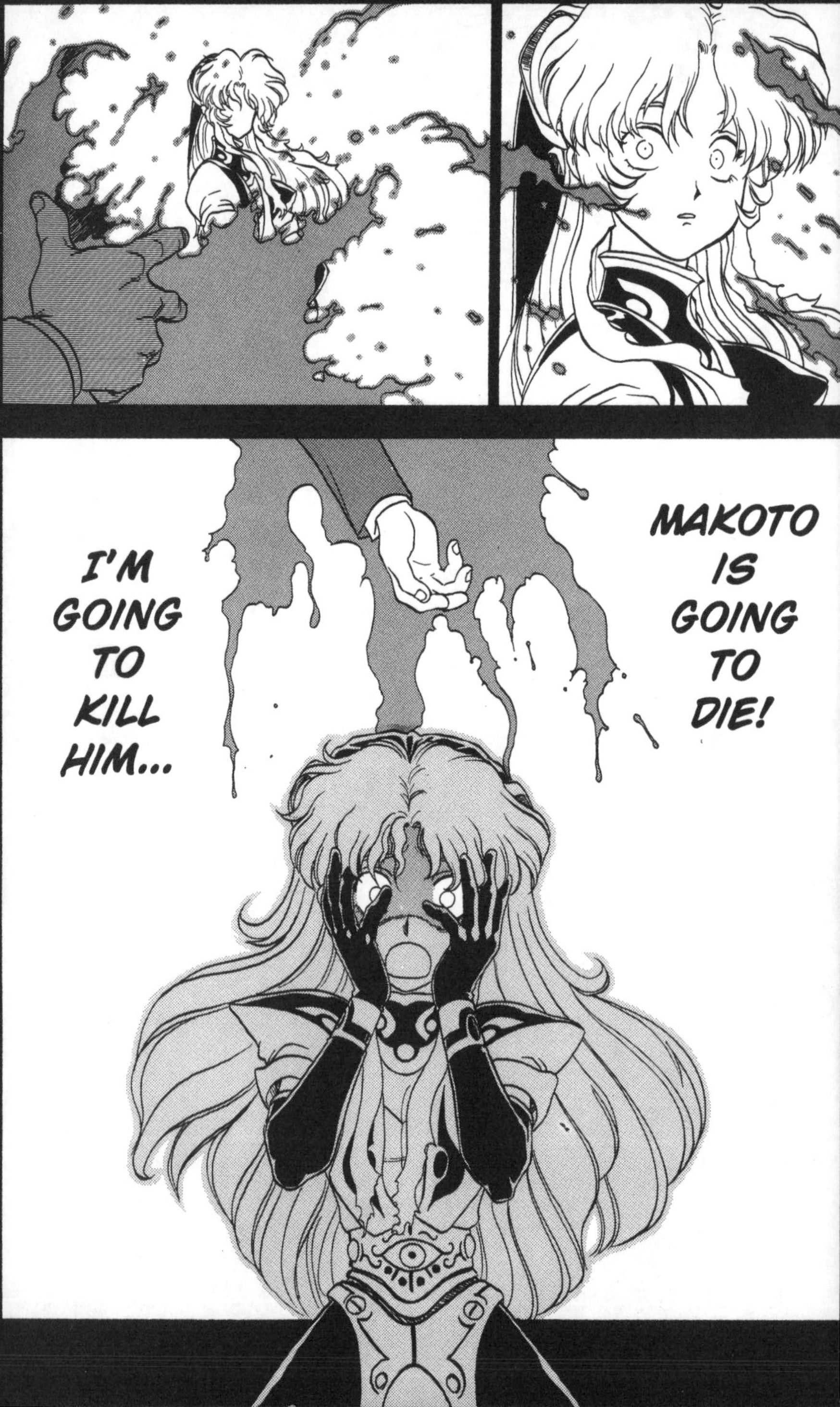
MAKOTO IS GOING TO DIE!
I'M GOING TO KILL HIM...

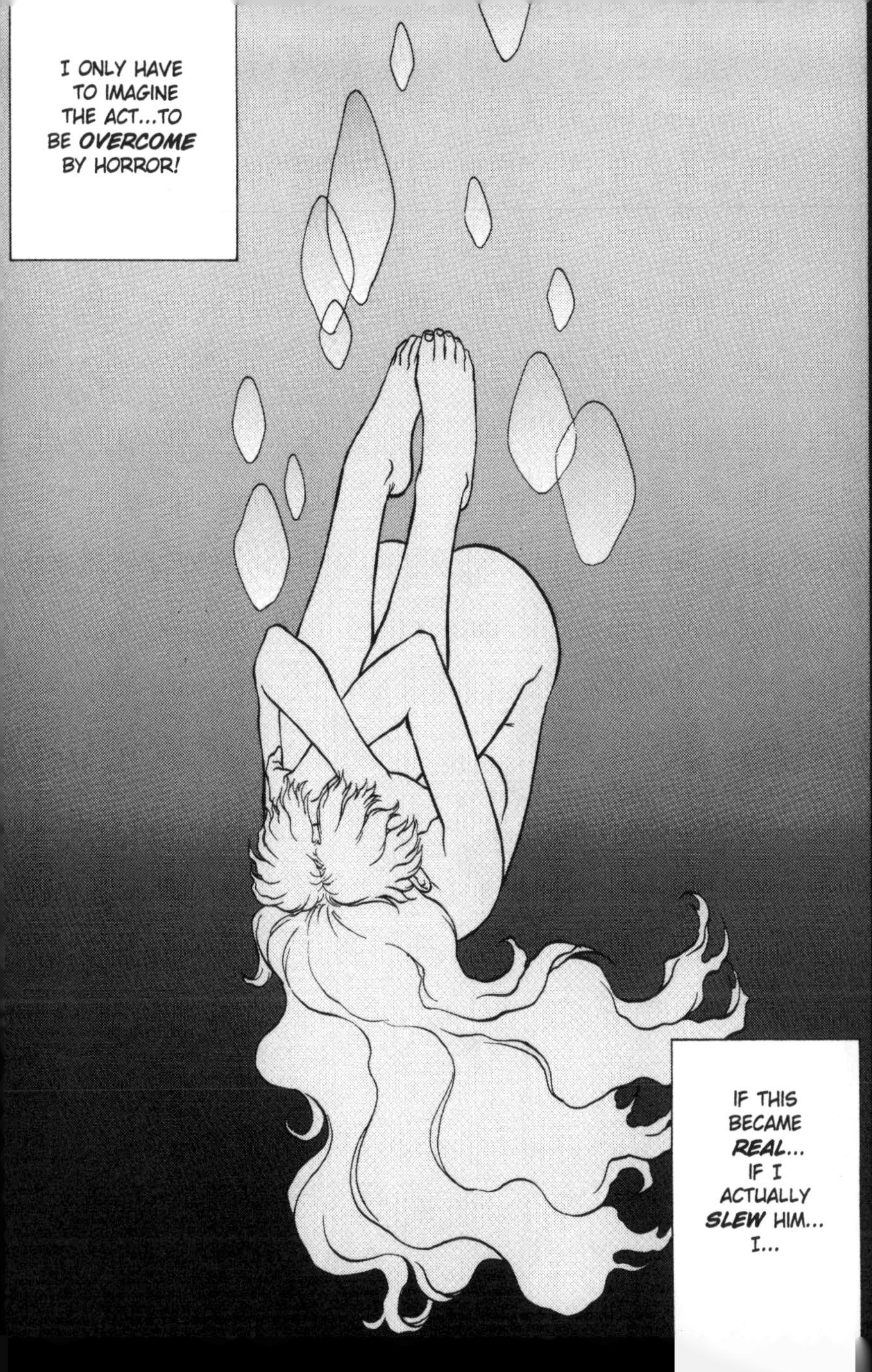
I ONLY HAVE TO IMAGINE THE ACT...TO BE OVERCOME BY HORROR!
IF THIS BECAME REAL... IF I ACTUALLY SLEW HIM... I...

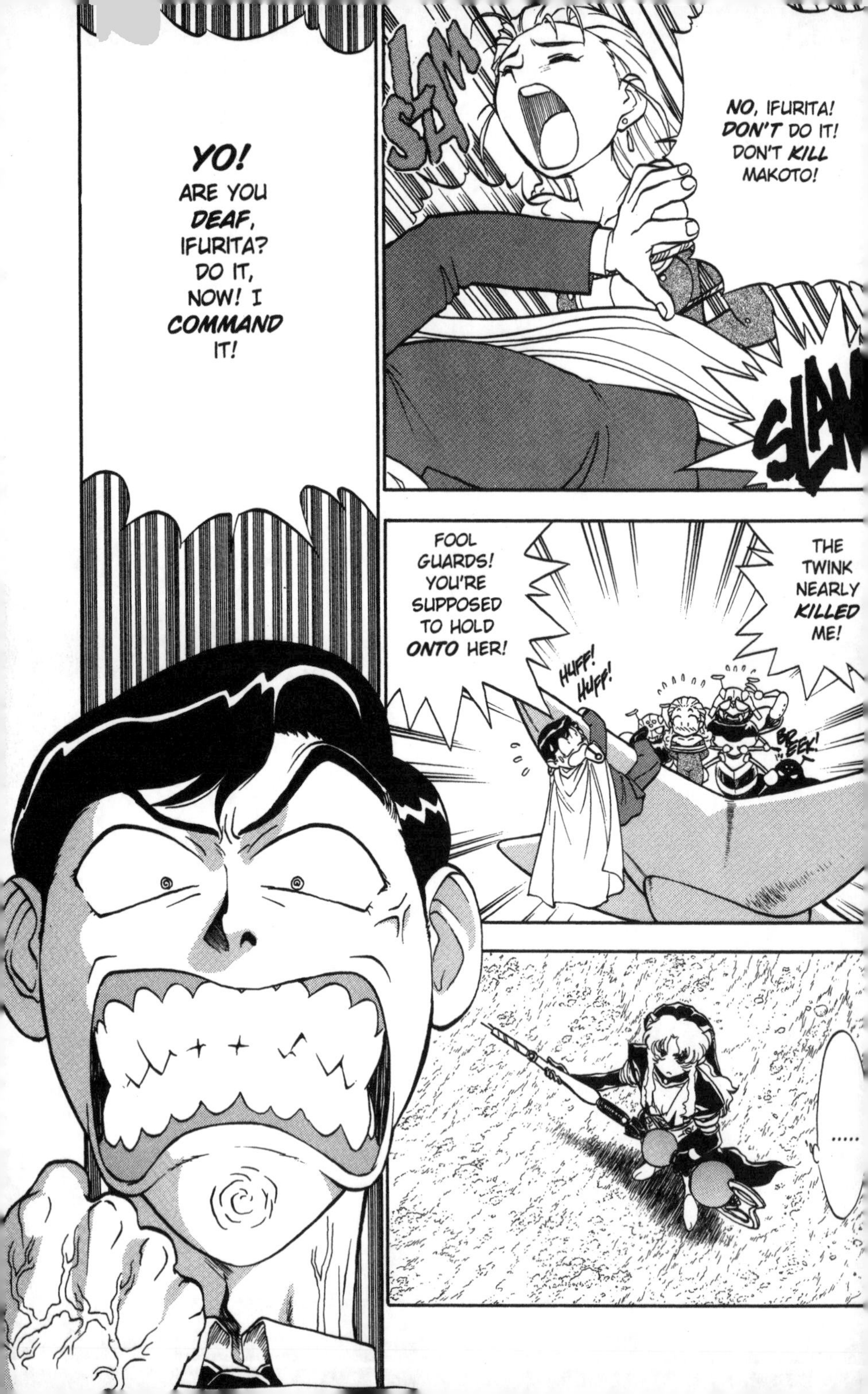

SLAM
NO, IFURITA! DON'T DO IT! DON'T KILL MAKOTO!
SLAM
YO! ARE YOU DEAF, IFURITA? DO IT, NOW! I COMMAND IT!
THE TWINK NEARLY KILLED ME!
FOOL GUARDS! YOU'RE SUPPOSED TO HOLD ONTO HER!
HUFF! HUFF!
BREEK!
.....

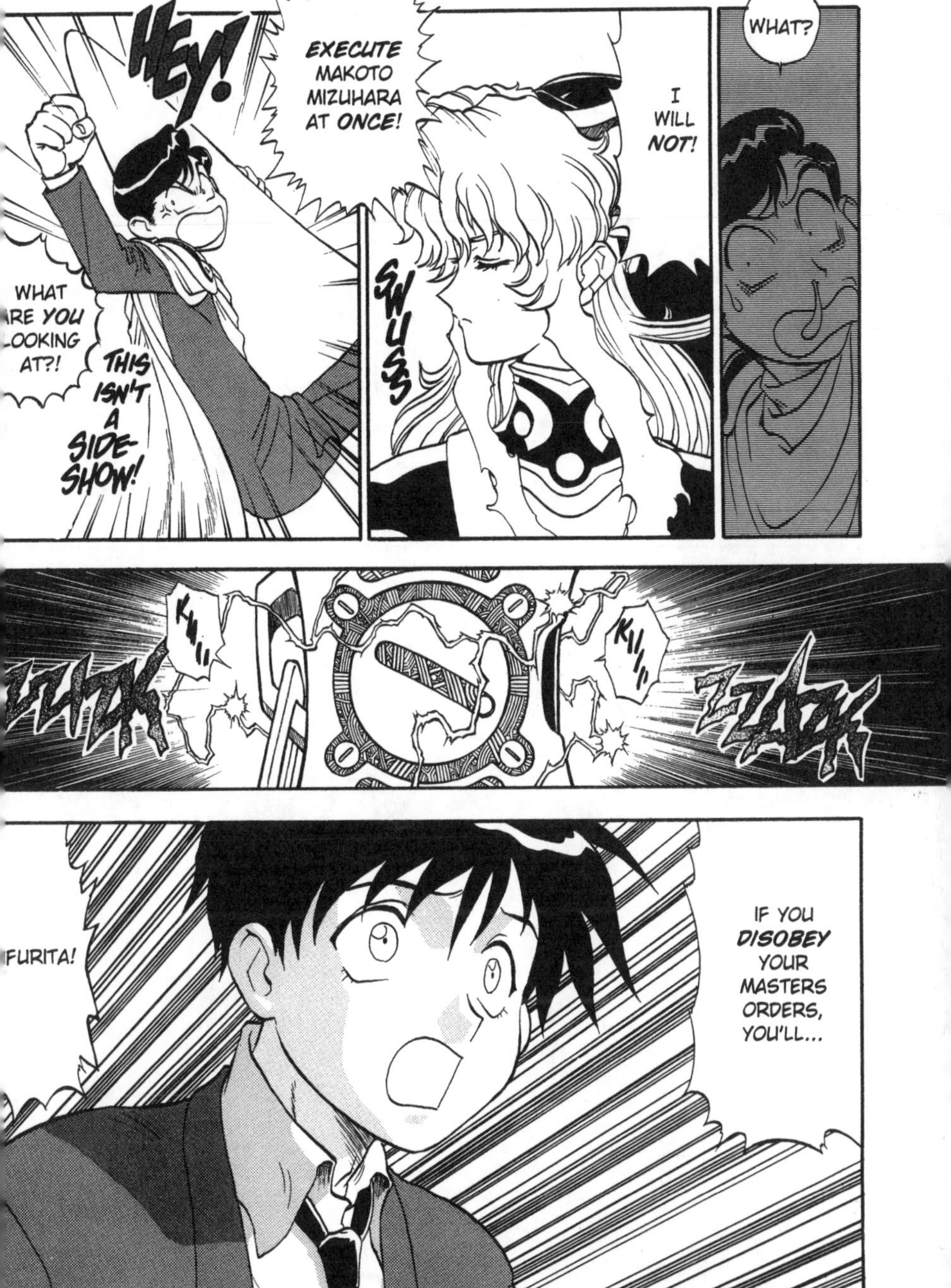
WHAT?
I WILL NOT!
EXECUTE MAKOTO MIZUHARA AT ONCE!
SWUSSS
HEY!
WHAT RE YOU OOKING AT?!
THIS ISN'T A SIDE-SHOW!
IF YOU DISOBEY YOUR MASTERS ORDERS, YOU'LL...
FURITA!

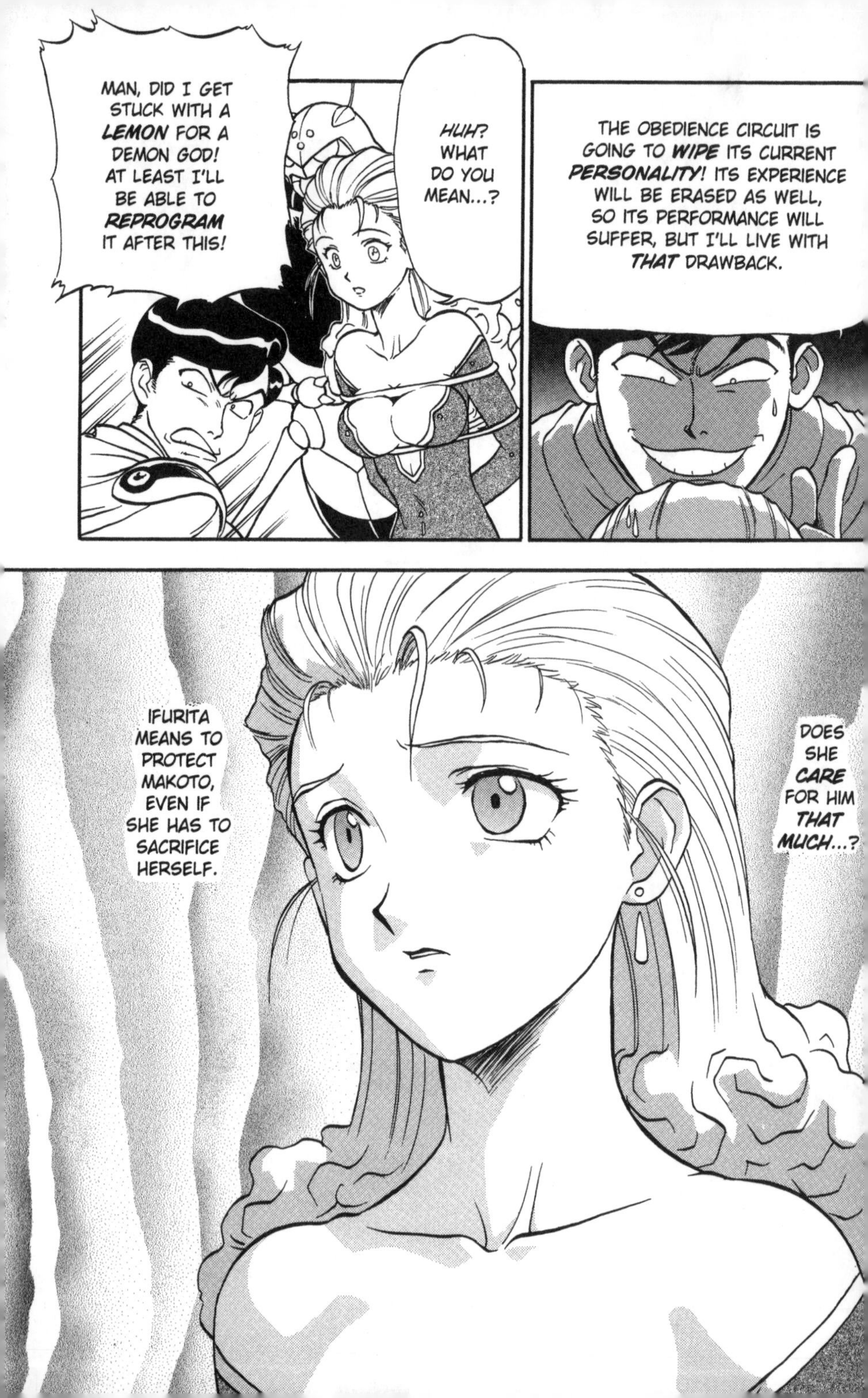
MAN, DID I GET STUCK WITH A LEMON FOR A DEMON GOD! AT LEAST I'LL BE ABLE TO REPROGRAM IT AFTER THIS!
HUH? WHAT DO YOU MEAN...?
THE OBEDIENCE CIRCUIT IS GOING TO WIPE ITS CURRENT PERSONALITY! ITS EXPERIENCE WILL BE ERASED AS WELL, SO ITS PERFORMANCE WILL SUFFER, BUT I'LL LIVE WITH THAT DRAWBACK.
IFURITA MEANS TO PROTECT MAKOTO, EVEN IF SHE HAS TO SACRIFICE HERSELF.
DOES SHE CARE FOR HIM THAT MUCH...?

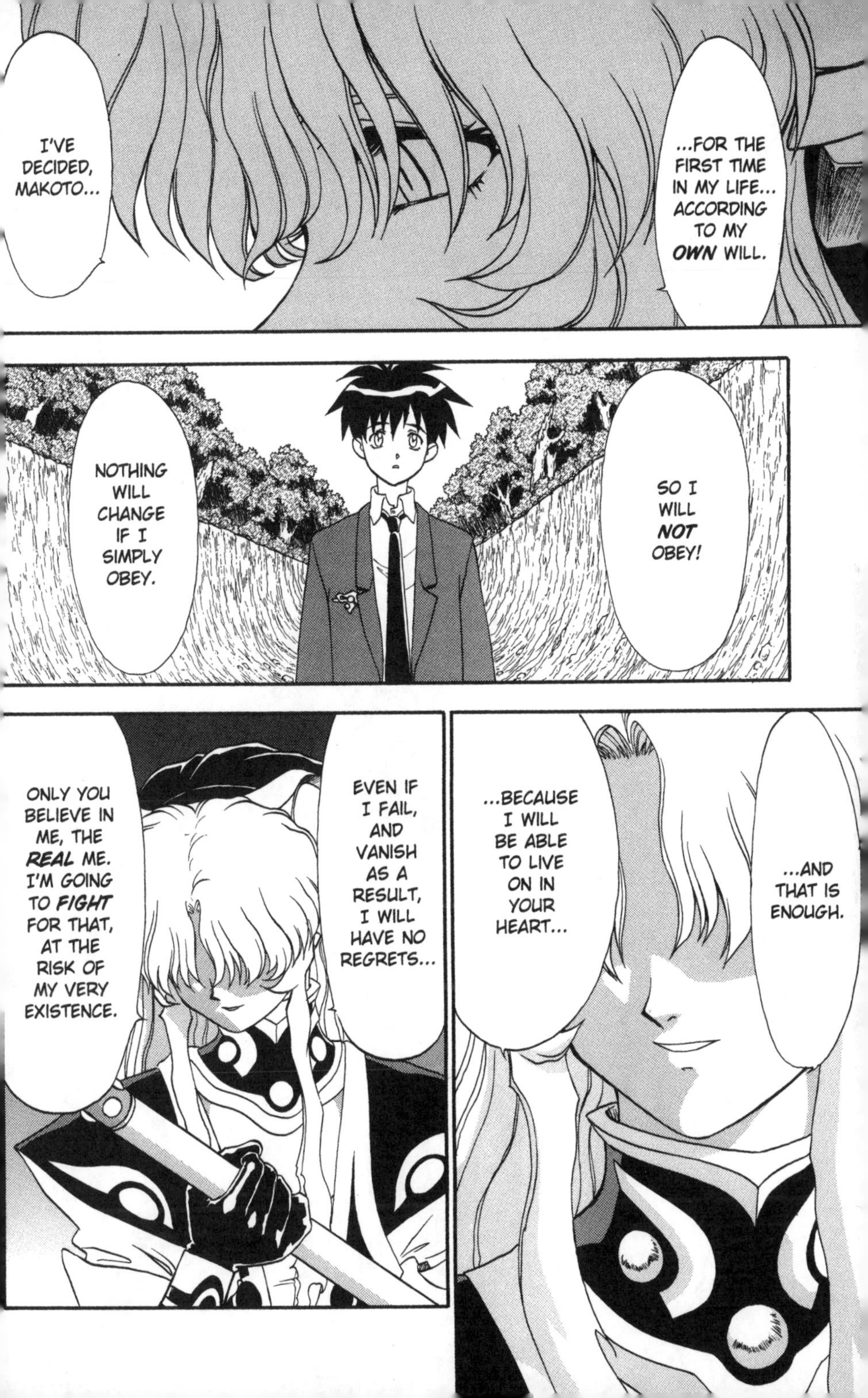
I'VE DECIDED, MAKOTO...
...FOR THE FIRST TIME IN MY LIFE... ACCORDING TO MY **OWN** WILL.
NOTHING WILL CHANGE IF I SIMPLY OBEY.
SO I WILL **NOT** OBEY!
ONLY YOU BELIEVE IN ME, THE **REAL** ME. I'M GOING TO **FIGHT** FOR THAT, AT THE RISK OF MY VERY EXISTENCE.
EVEN IF I FAIL, AND VANISH AS A RESULT, I WILL HAVE NO REGRETS...
...BECAUSE I WILL BE ABLE TO LIVE ON IN YOUR HEART...
...AND THAT IS ENOUGH.

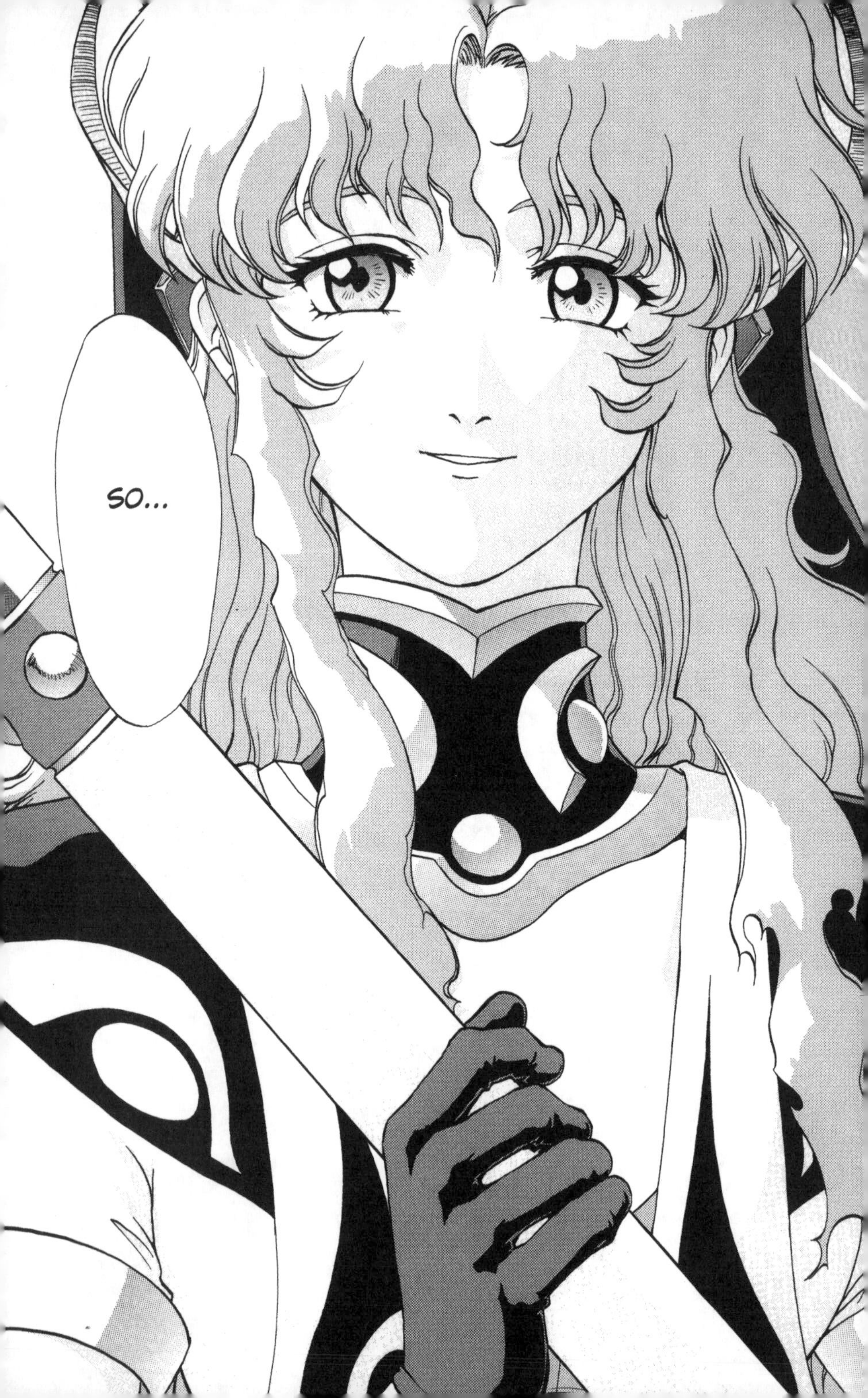
SO...

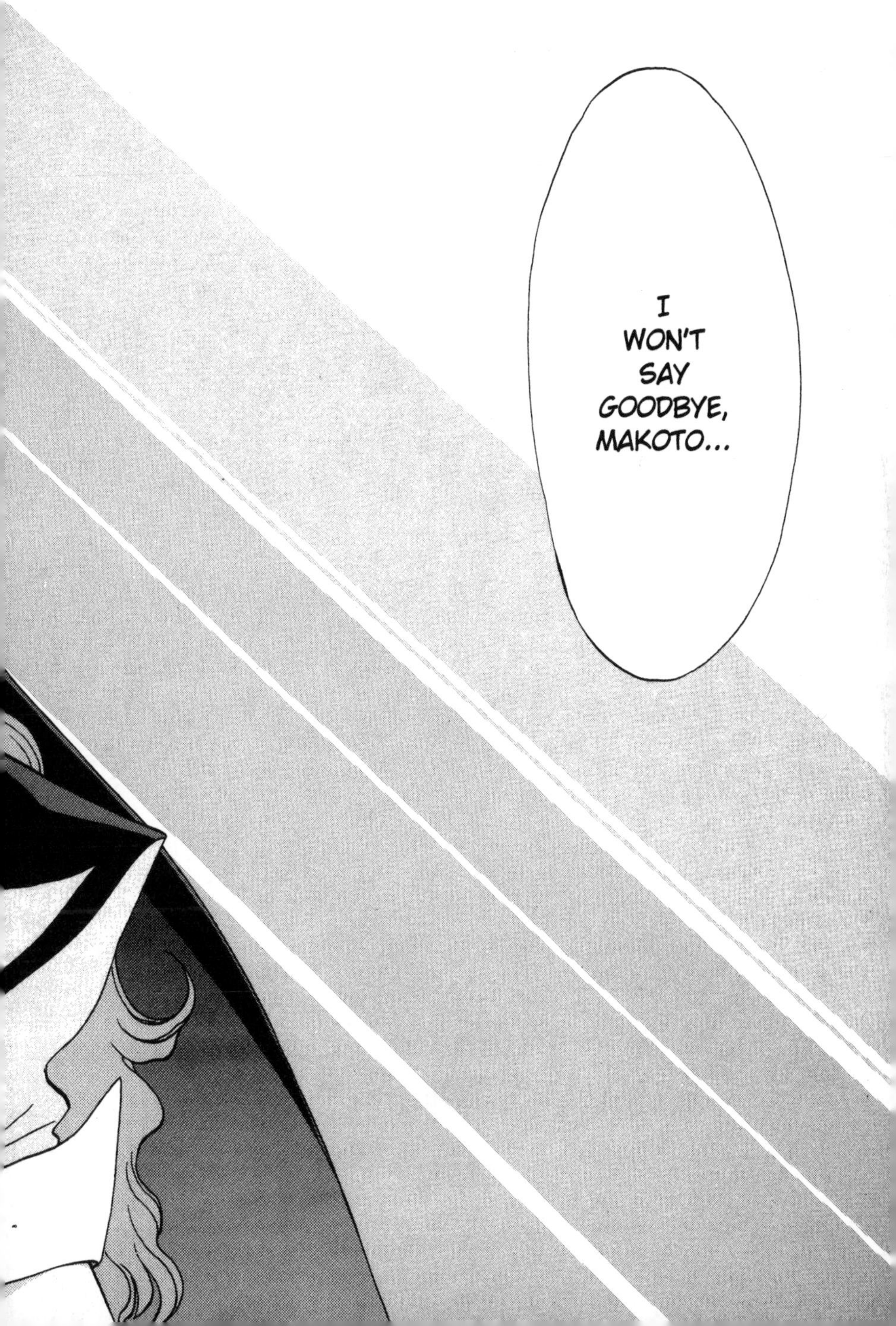
I WON'T SAY GOODBYE, MAKOTO...

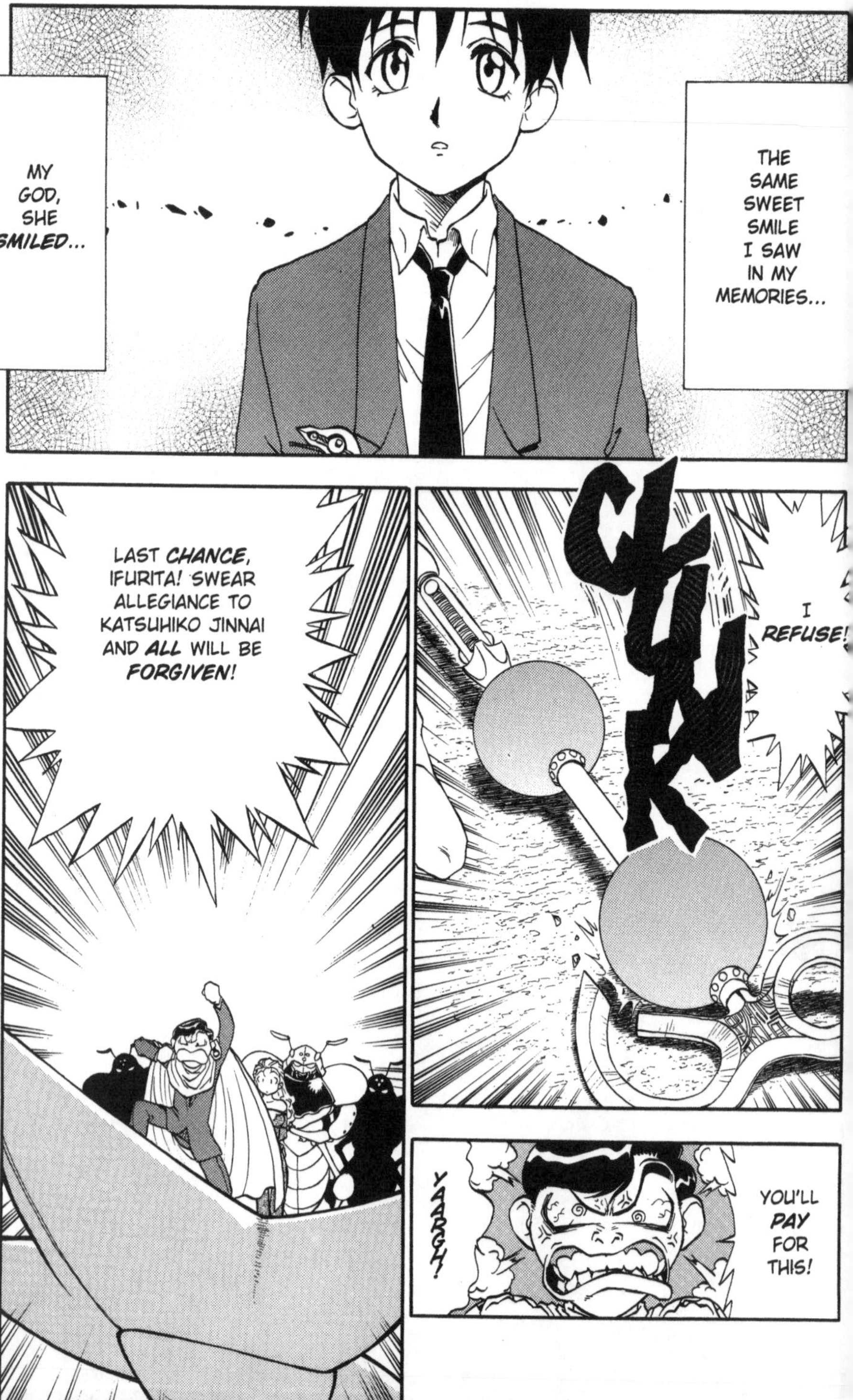
MY GOD, SHE SMILED...
THE SAME SWEET SMILE I SAW IN MY MEMORIES...
I REFUSE!
CLIKK
LAST CHANCE, IFURITA! SWEAR ALLEGIANCE TO KATSUHIKO JINNAI AND ALL WILL BE FORGIVEN!
YOU'LL PAY FOR THIS!
YAARGH!

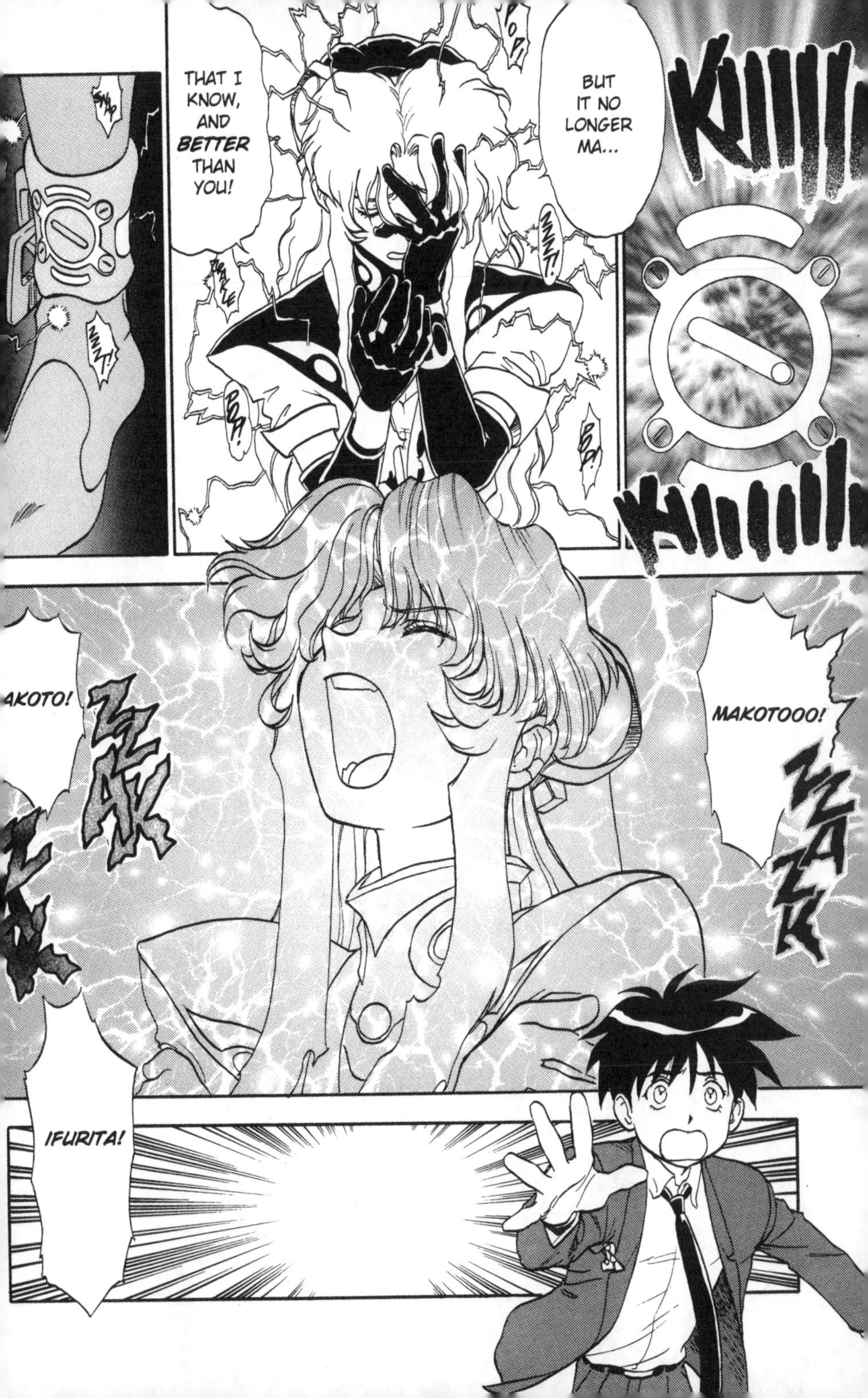
BUT IT NO LONGER MA...
THAT I KNOW, AND BETTER THAN YOU!
MAKOTOOO!
AKOTO!
IFURITA!

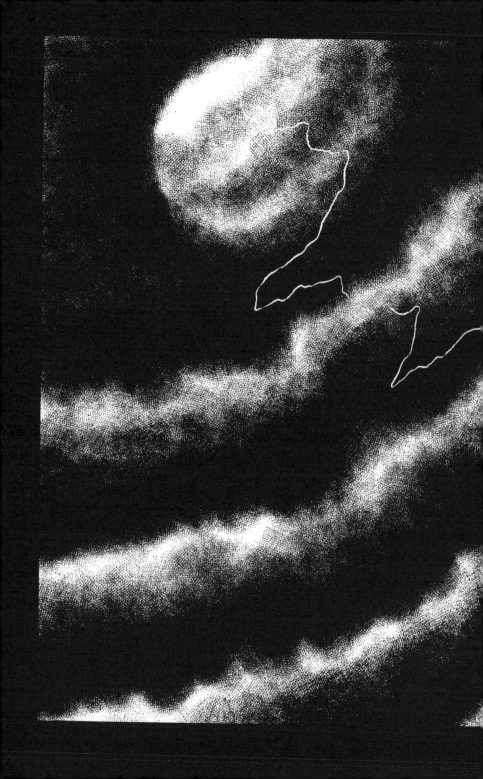

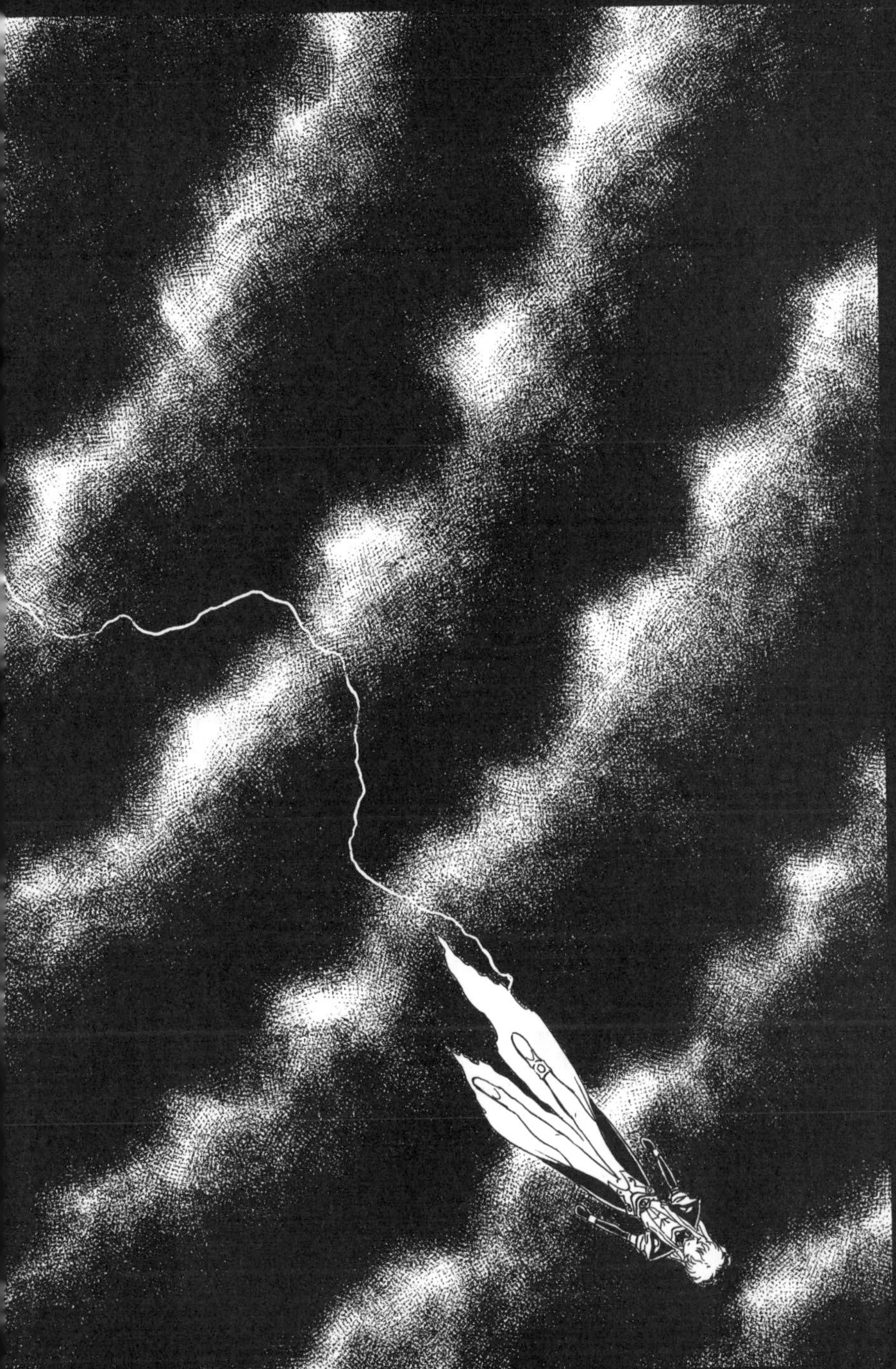

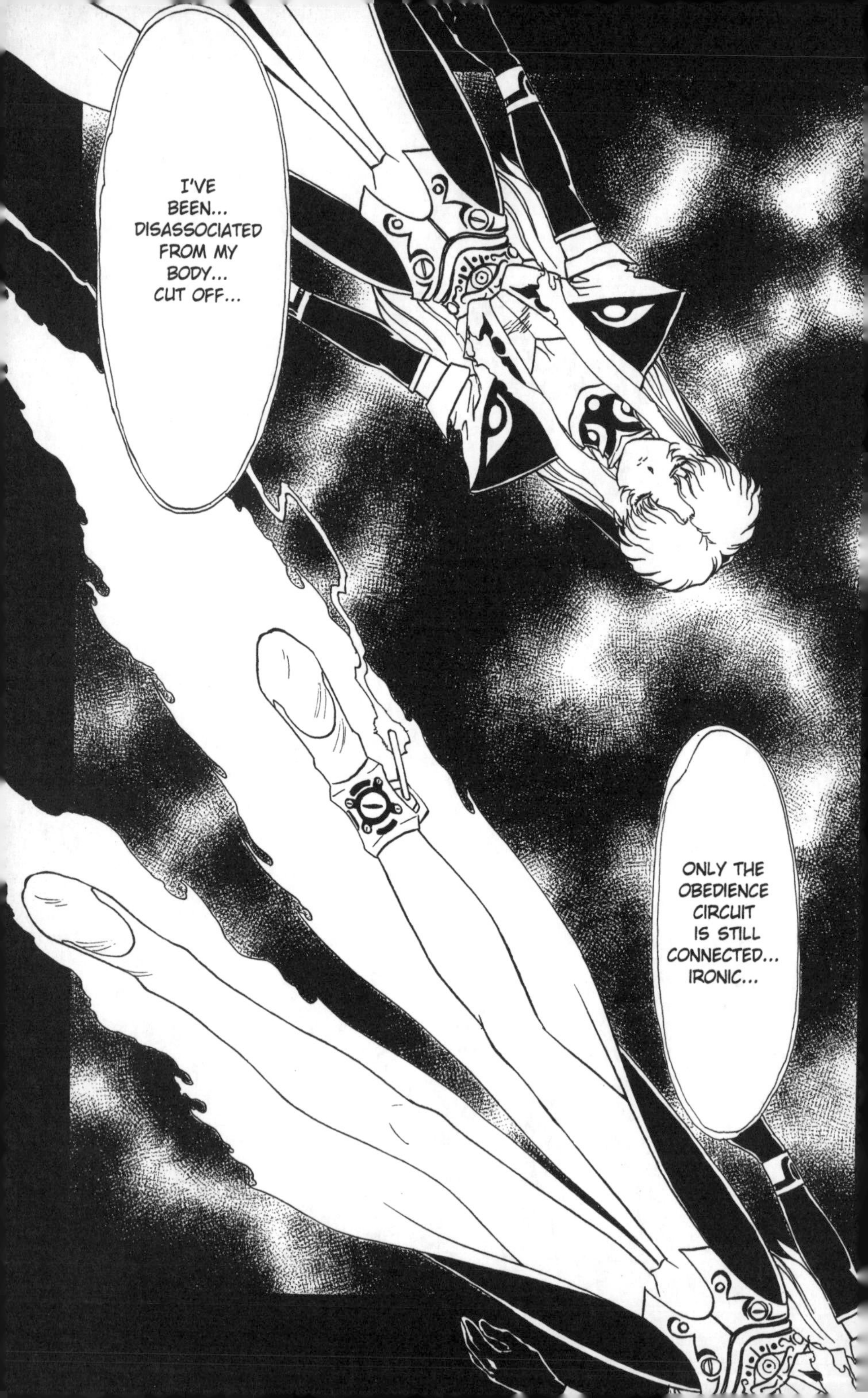
I'VE BEEN... DISASSOCIATED FROM MY BODY... CUT OFF...
ONLY THE OBEDIENCE CIRCUIT IS STILL CONNECTED... IRONIC...

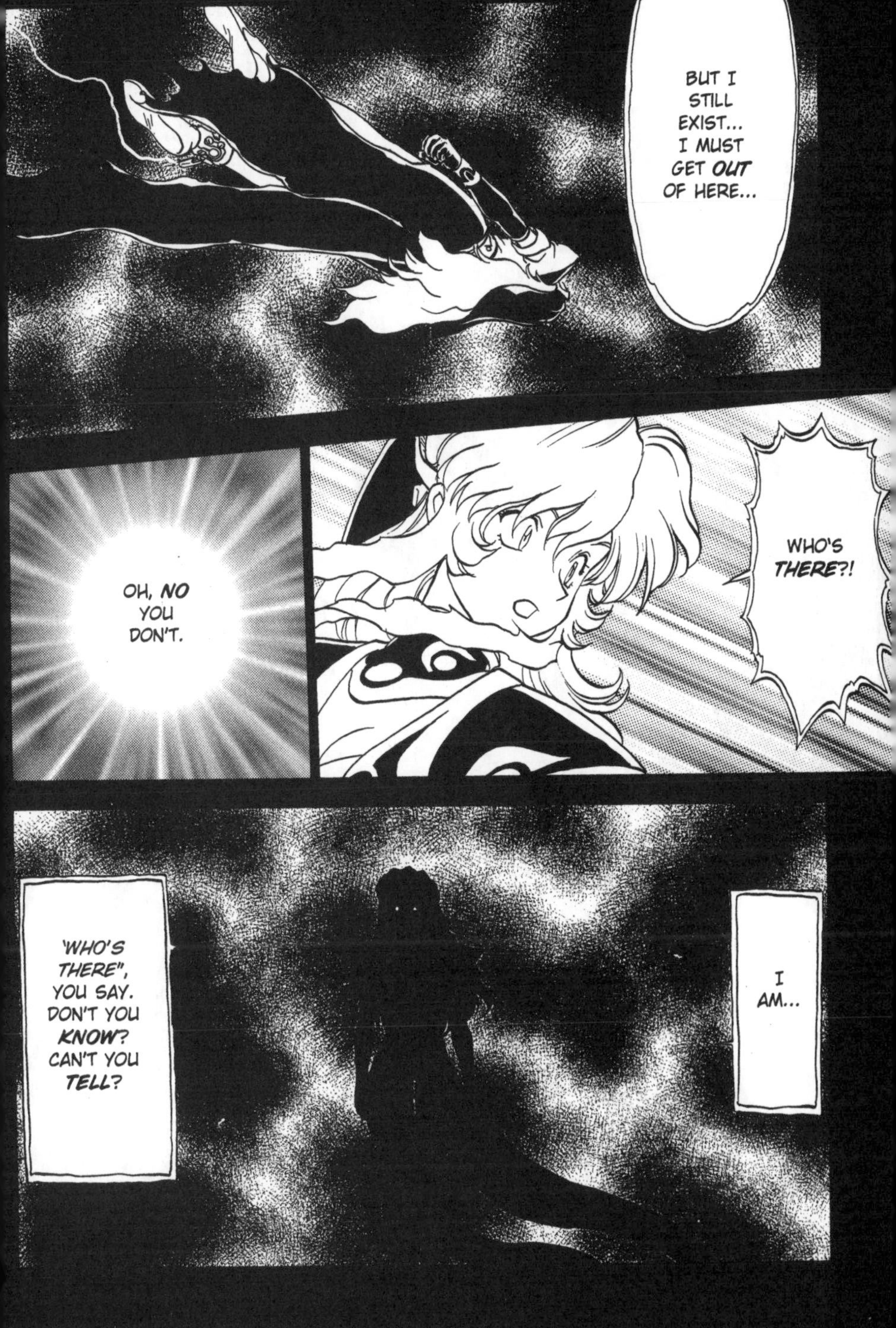
BUT I STILL EXIST... I MUST GET OUT OF HERE...
WHO'S THERE?!
OH, NO YOU DON'T.
I AM...
'WHO'S THERE", YOU SAY. DON'T YOU KNOW? CAN'T YOU TELL?

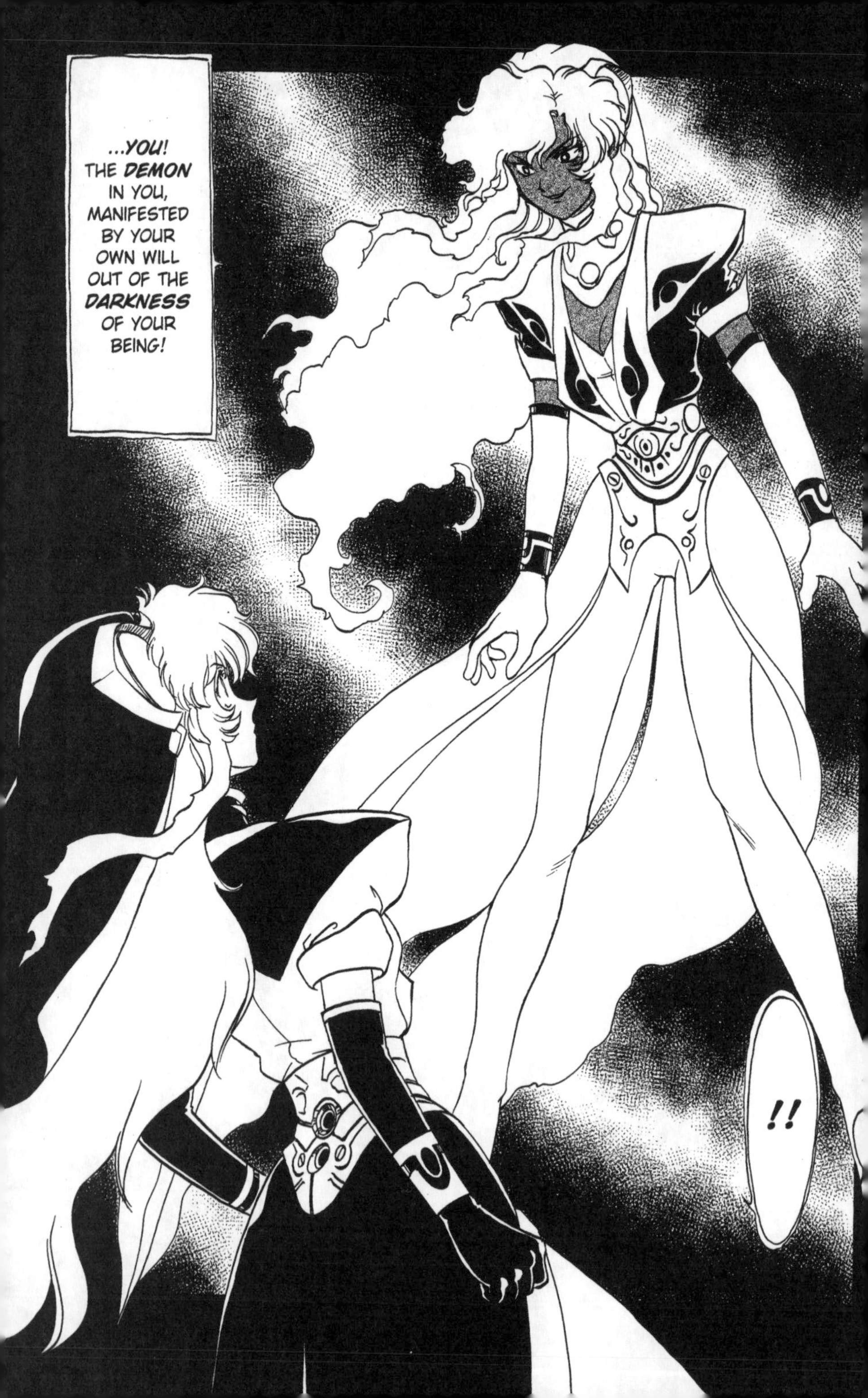
...YOU! THE DEMON IN YOU, MANIFESTED BY YOUR OWN WILL OUT OF THE DARKNESS OF YOUR BEING!
!!

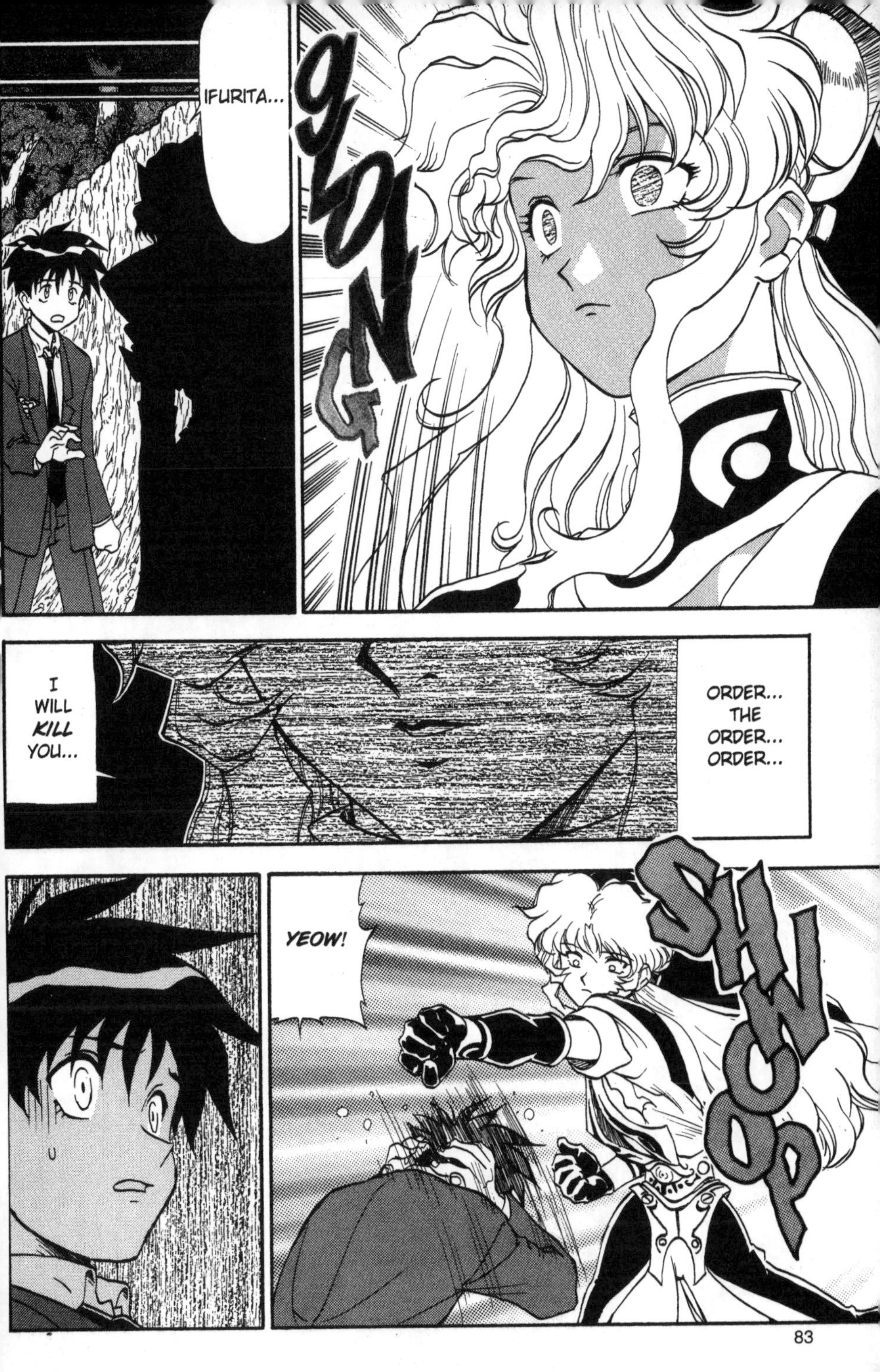
IFURITA...
GLOWG
ORDER... THE ORDER... ORDER...
I WILL KILL YOU...
SHOOOP
YEOW!

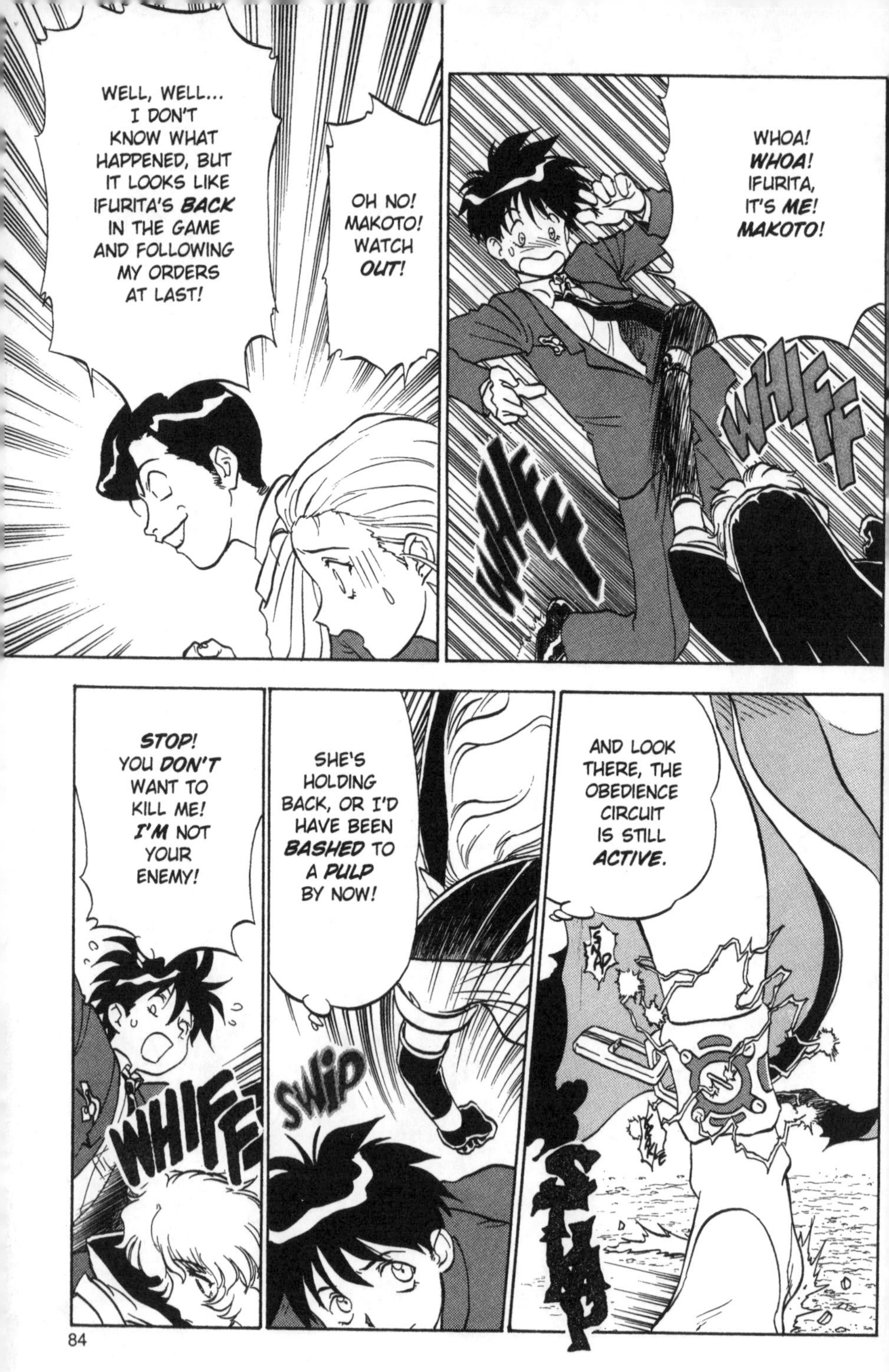
WELL, WELL... I DON'T KNOW WHAT HAPPENED, BUT IT LOOKS LIKE IFURITA'S BACK IN THE GAME AND FOLLOWING MY ORDERS AT LAST!
OH NO! MAKOTO! WATCH OUT!
WHOA! WHOA! IFURITA, IT'S ME! MAKOTO!
WHIFF
WHIFF
STOP! YOU DON'T WANT TO KILL ME! I'M NOT YOUR ENEMY!
WHIFF
SHE'S HOLDING BACK, OR I'D HAVE BEEN BASHED TO A PULP BY NOW!
SWIP
AND LOOK THERE, THE OBEDIENCE CIRCUIT IS STILL ACTIVE.

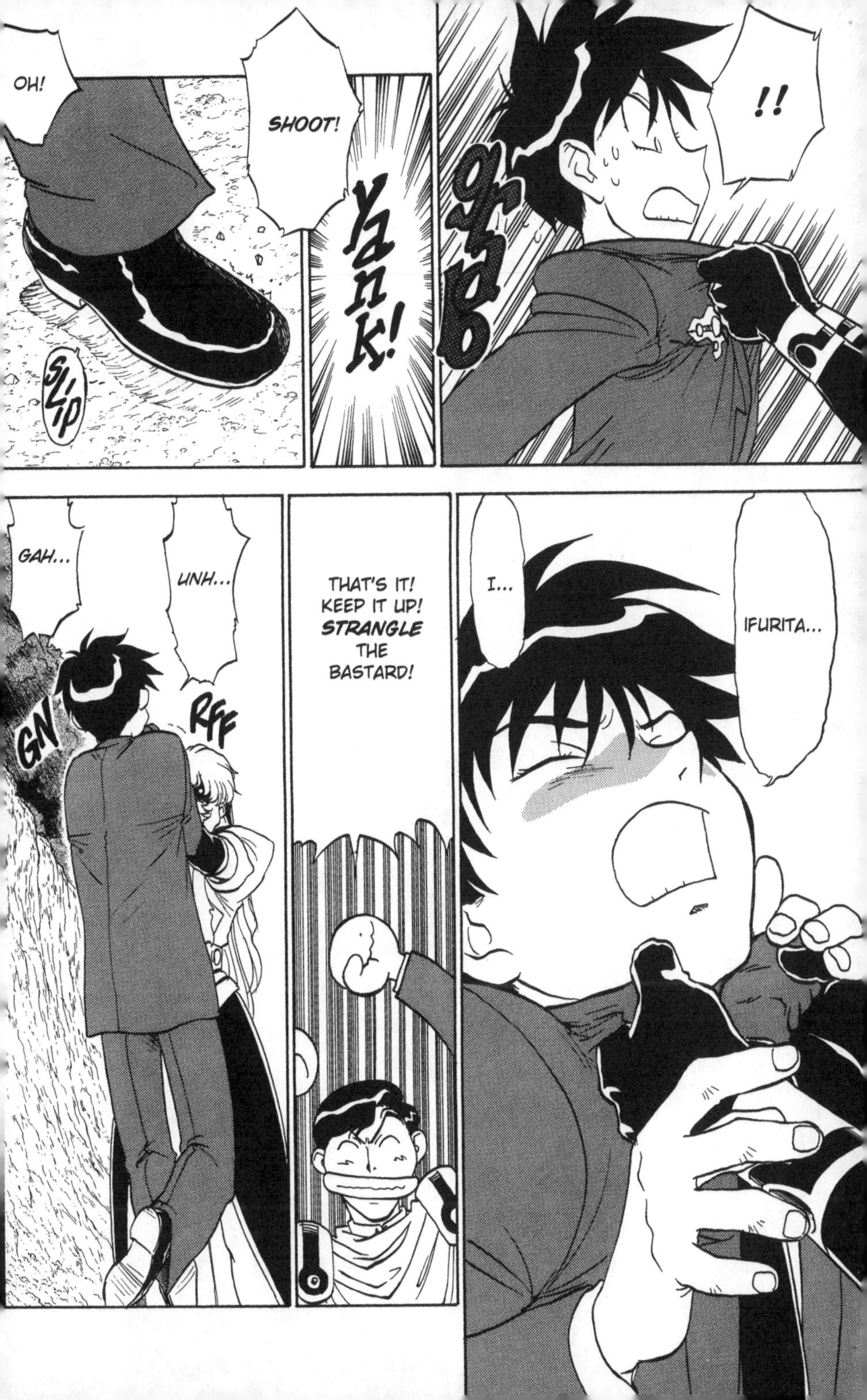

OH!
SHOOT!
SLIP
YANK!
GRAB
!!
GAH...
UNH...
GN
RFF
THAT'S IT! KEEP IT UP! STRANGLE THE BASTARD!
I...
IFURITA...

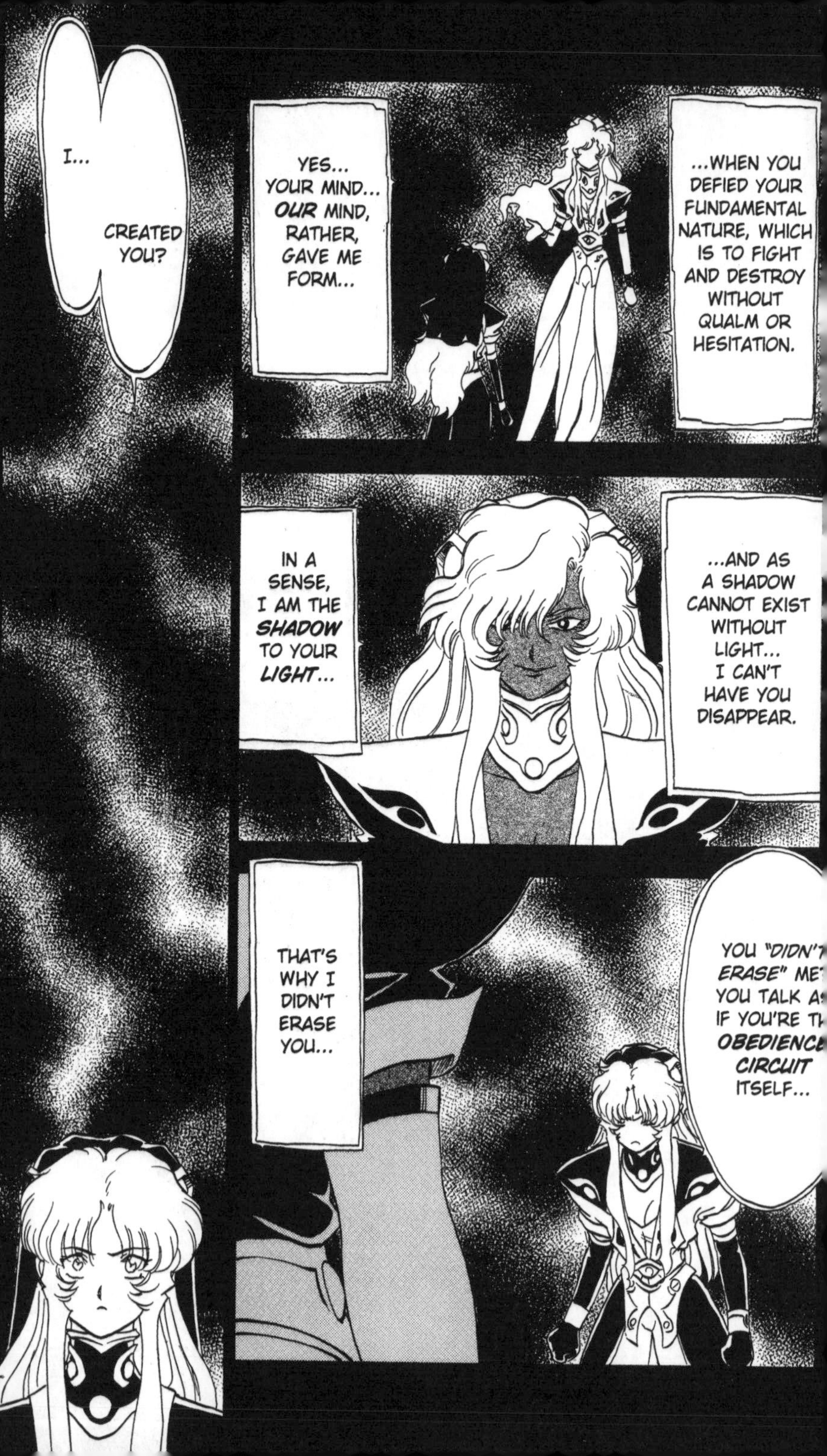
I...
CREATED YOU?
YES... YOUR MIND... OUR MIND, RATHER, GAVE ME FORM...
...WHEN YOU DEFIED YOUR FUNDAMENTAL NATURE, WHICH IS TO FIGHT AND DESTROY WITHOUT QUALM OR HESITATION.
IN A SENSE, I AM THE SHADOW TO YOUR LIGHT...
...AND AS A SHADOW CANNOT EXIST WITHOUT LIGHT... I CAN'T HAVE YOU DISAPPEAR.
THAT'S WHY I DIDN'T ERASE YOU...
YOU "DIDN' ERASE" ME YOU TALK A IF YOU'RE T OBEDIENC CIRCUIT ITSELF...

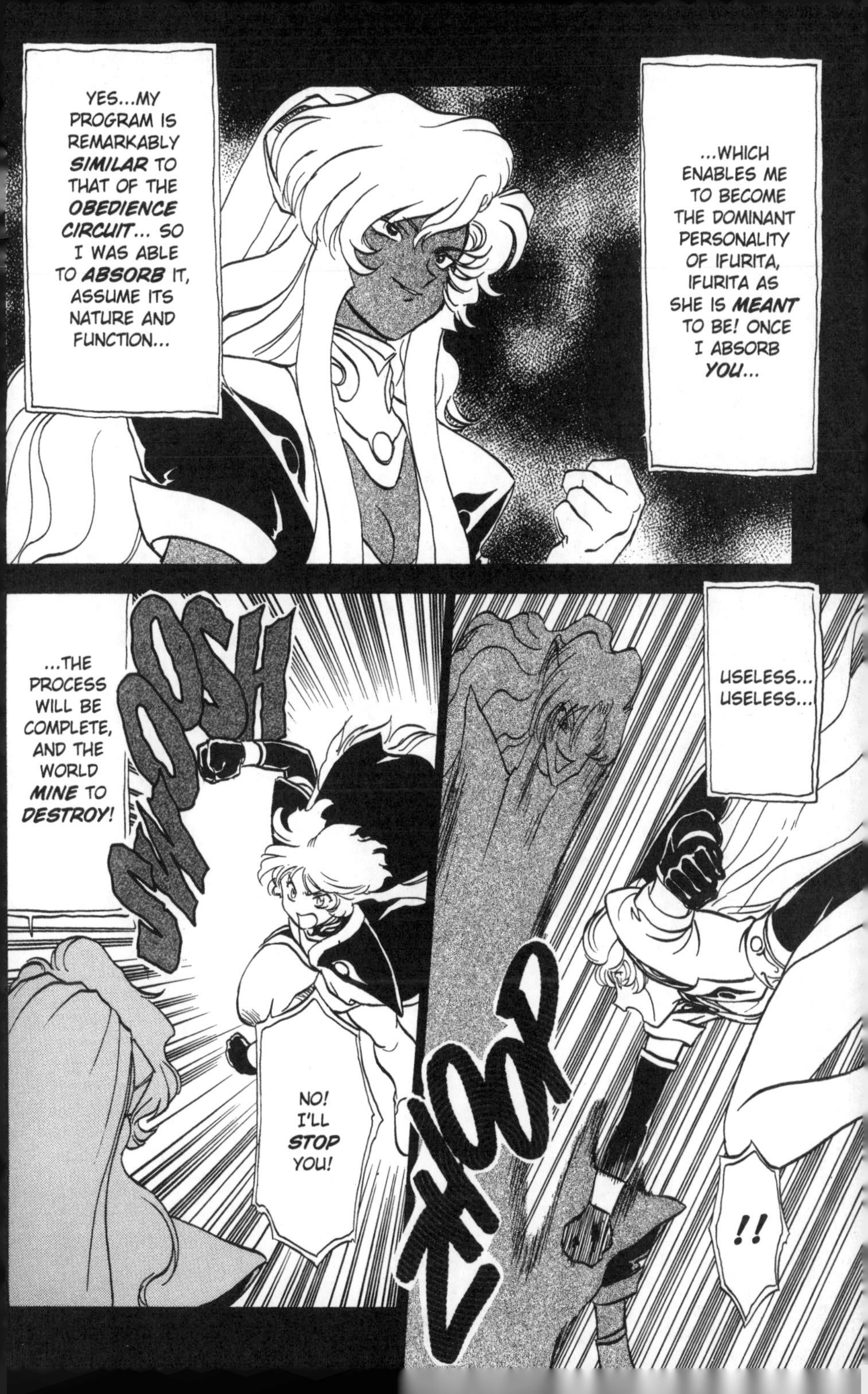

YES...MY PROGRAM IS REMARKABLY SIMILAR TO THAT OF THE OBEDIENCE CIRCUIT... SO I WAS ABLE TO ABSORB IT, ASSUME ITS NATURE AND FUNCTION...
...WHICH ENABLES ME TO BECOME THE DOMINANT PERSONALITY OF IFURITA, IFURITA AS SHE IS MEANT TO BE! ONCE I ABSORB YOU...
...THE PROCESS WILL BE COMPLETE, AND THE WORLD MINE TO DESTROY!
SWOOSH
USELESS... USELESS...
NO! I'LL STOP YOU!
ZHOOP
!!

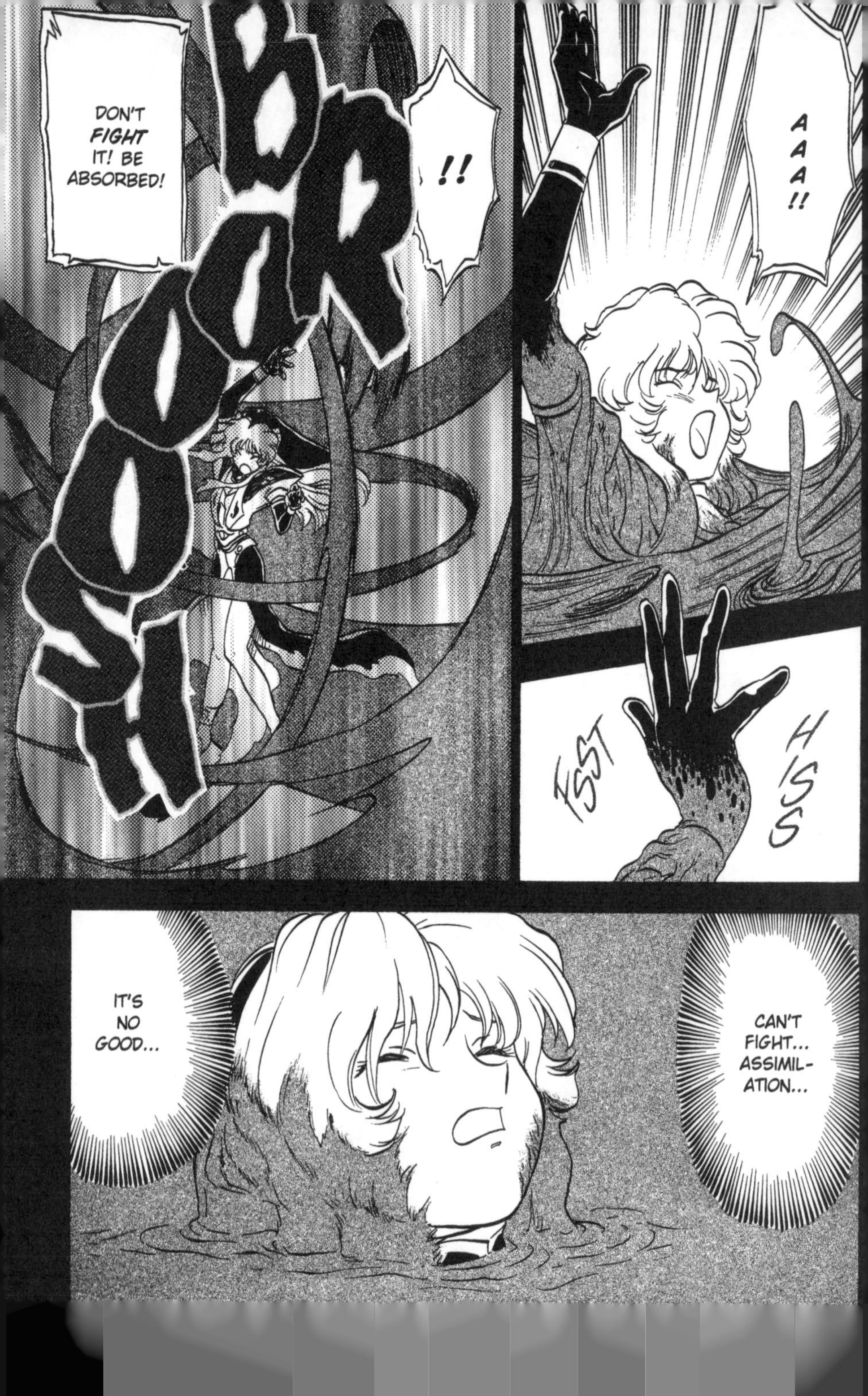
DON'T *FIGHT* IT! BE ABSORBED!
BROOOSH
!!
AAAA!!
FSST
HISS
IT'S NO GOOD...
CAN'T FIGHT... ASSIMIL-ATION...

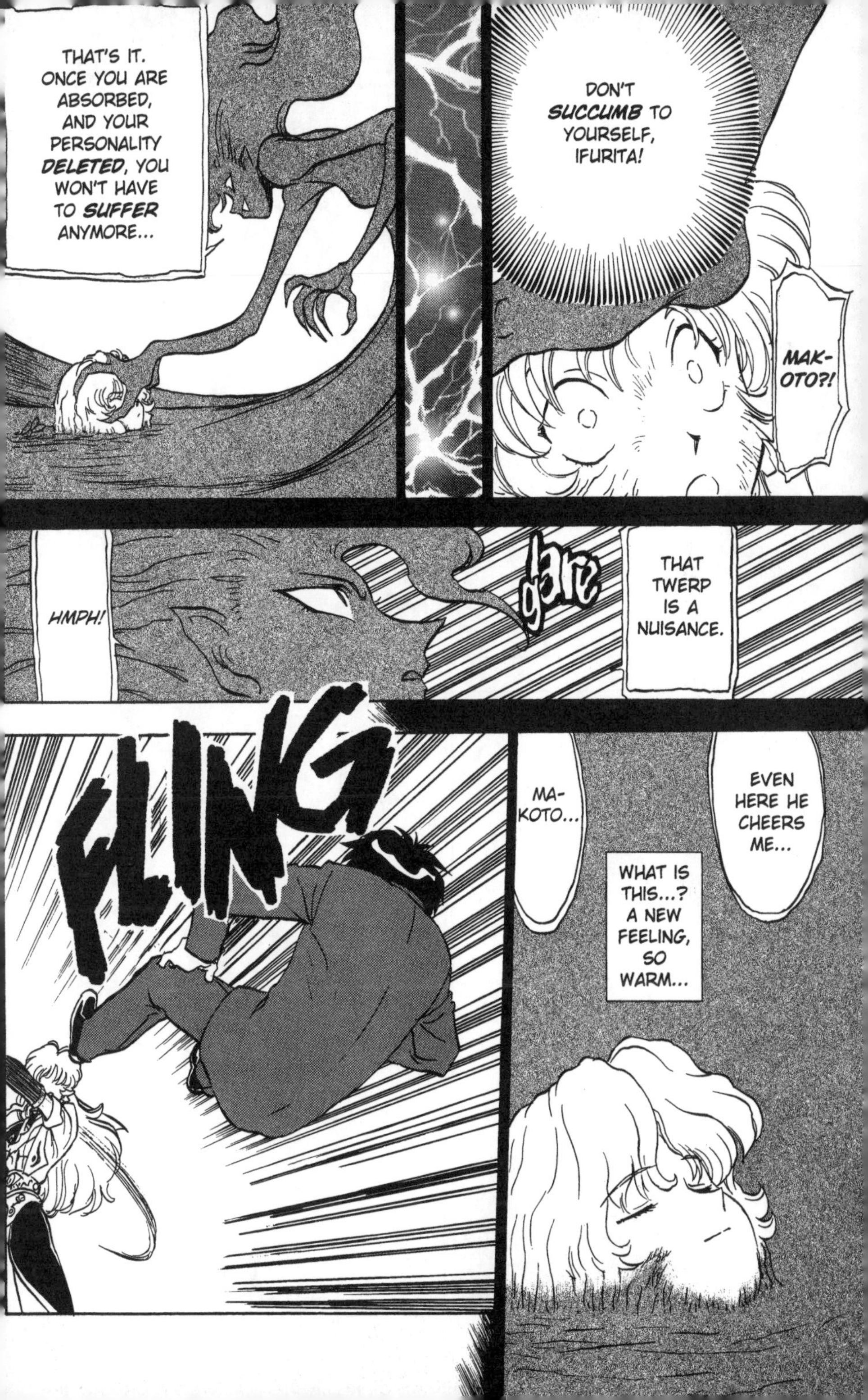
THAT'S IT. ONCE YOU ARE ABSORBED, AND YOUR PERSONALITY DELETED, YOU WON'T HAVE TO SUFFER ANYMORE...
DON'T SUCCUMB TO YOURSELF, IFURITA!
MAK-OTO?!
HMPH!
glare
THAT TWERP IS A NUISANCE.
FLING
MA-KOTO...
EVEN HERE HE CHEERS ME...
WHAT IS THIS...? A NEW FEELING, SO WARM...

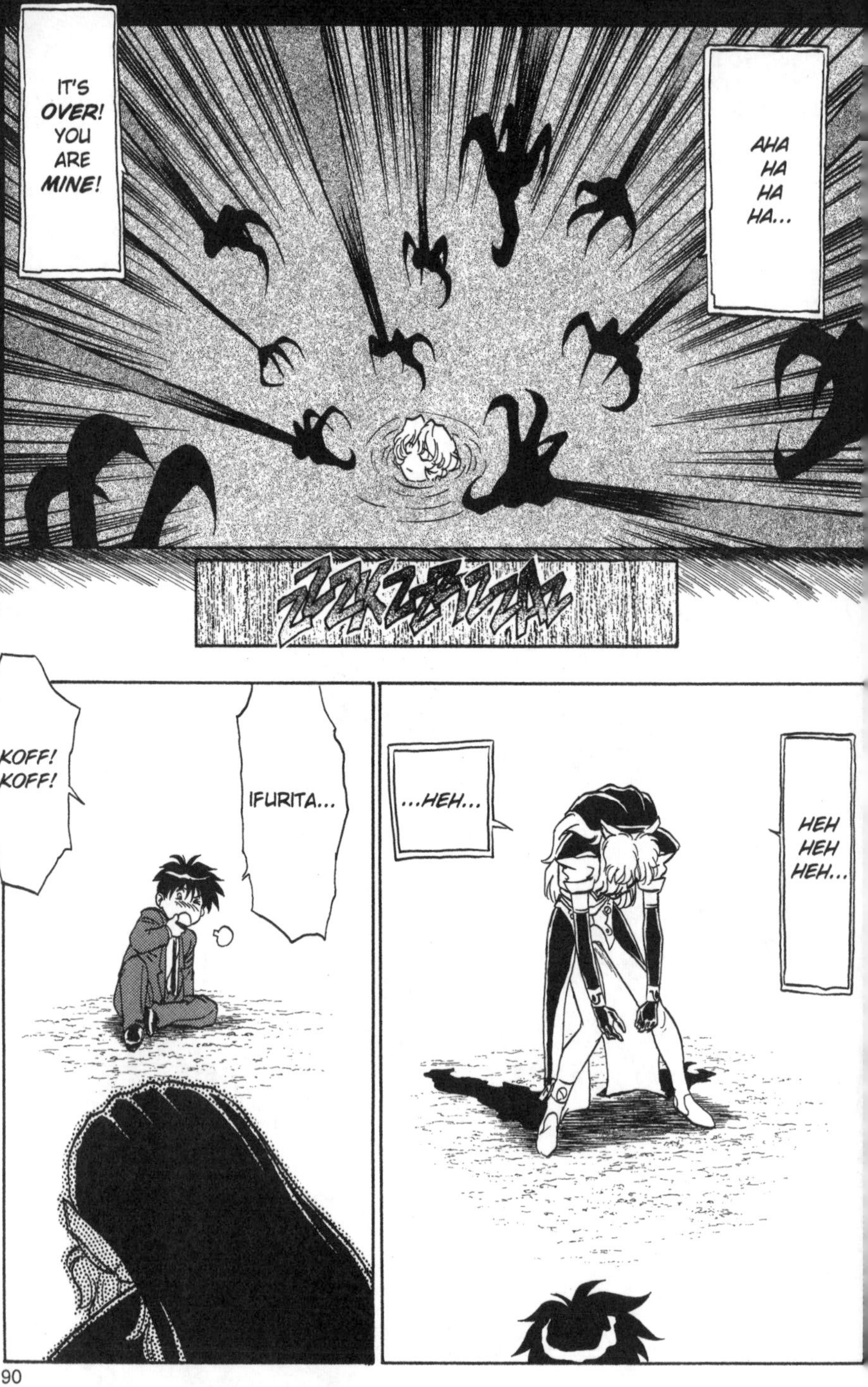
IT'S OVER! YOU ARE MINE!
AHA HA HA HA...
KOFF! KOFF!
IFURITA...
...HEH...
HEH HEH HEH...

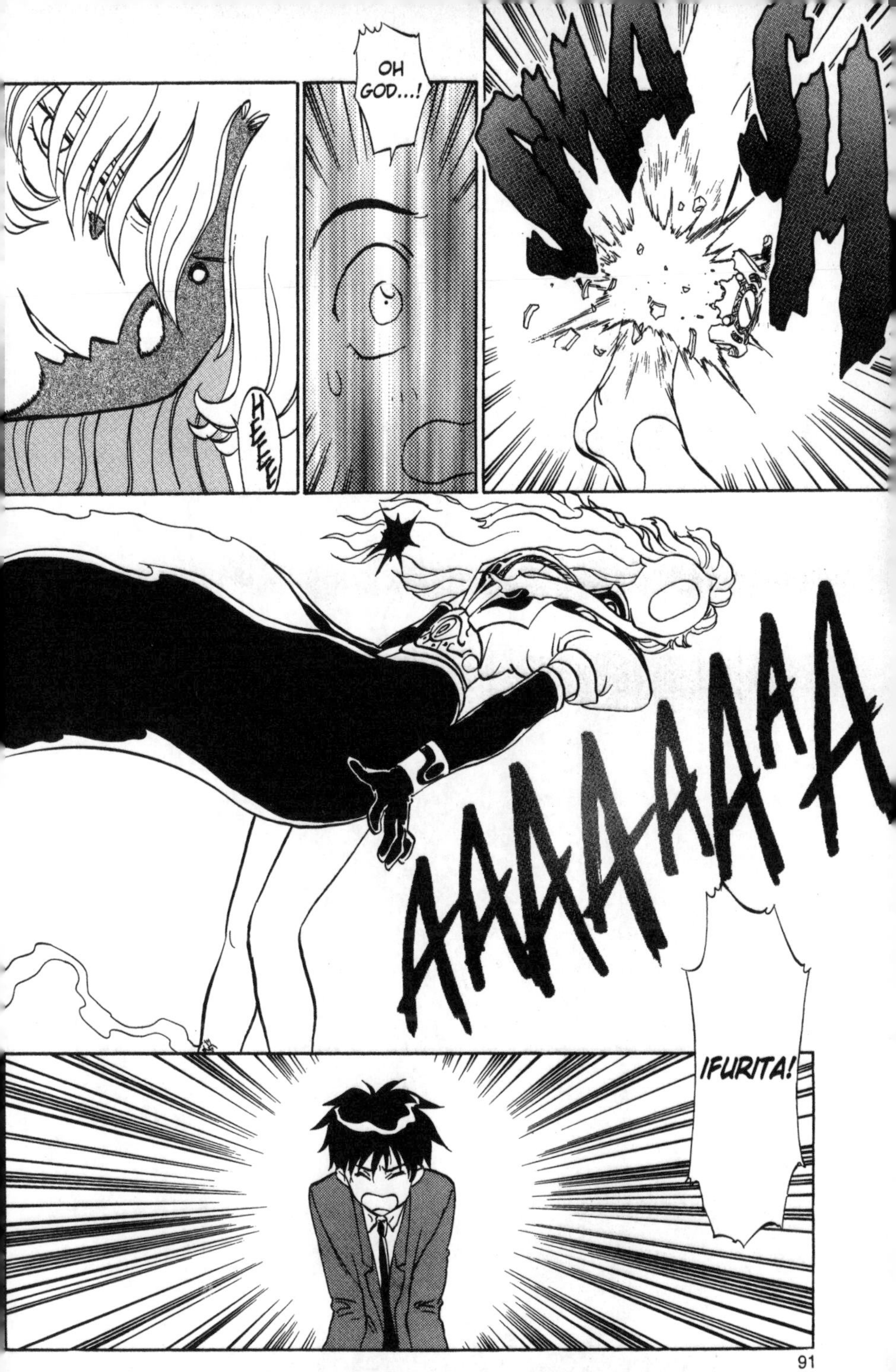
OH GOD...!
HEEEE
SMASH
AAAAAAA
IFURITA!

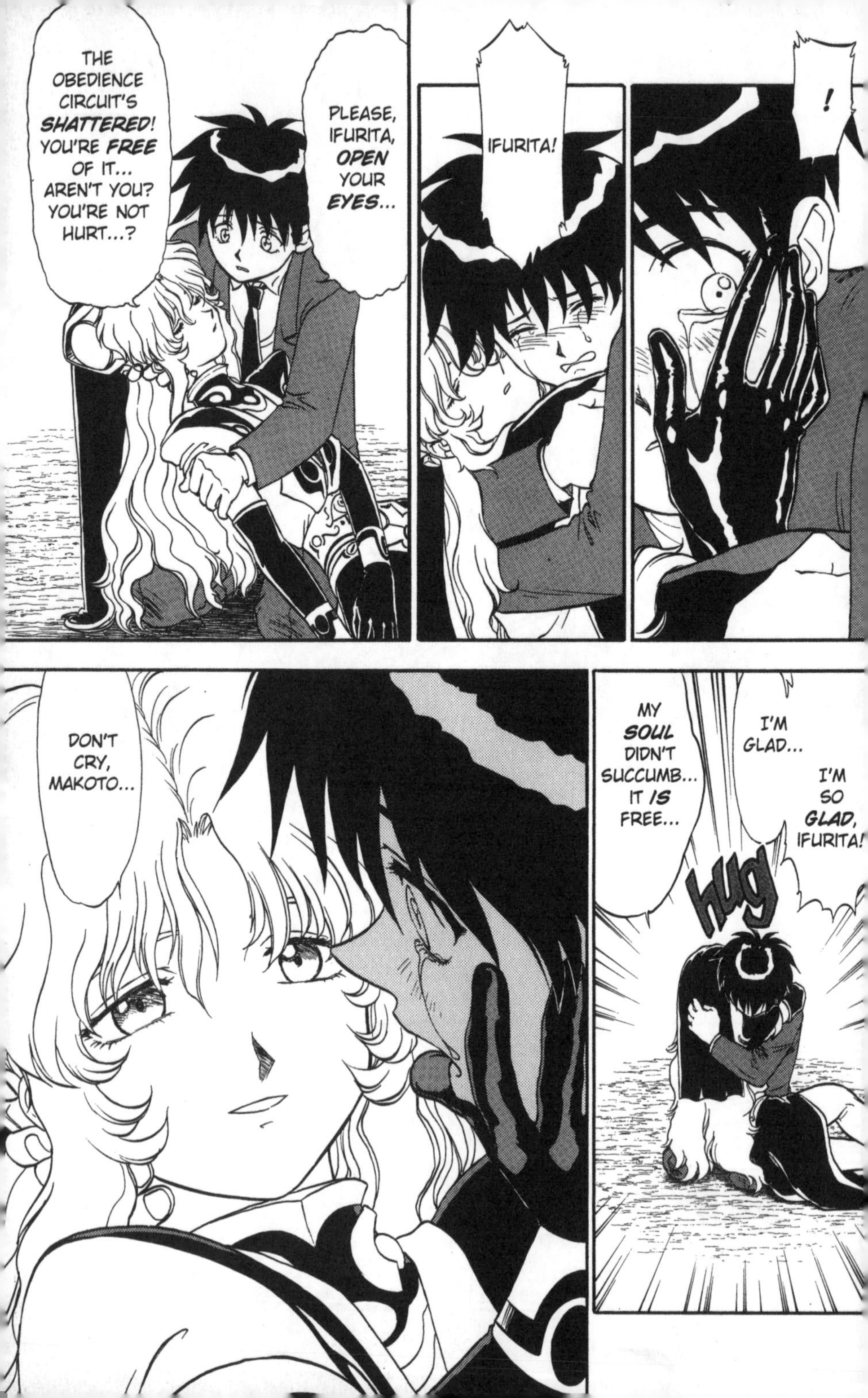

THE OBEDIENCE CIRCUIT'S SHATTERED! YOU'RE FREE OF IT... AREN'T YOU? YOU'RE NOT HURT...?
PLEASE, IFURITA, OPEN YOUR EYES...
IFURITA!
!
DON'T CRY, MAKOTO...
MY SOUL DIDN'T SUCCUMB... IT IS FREE...
I'M GLAD...
I'M SO GLAD, IFURITA!
hug

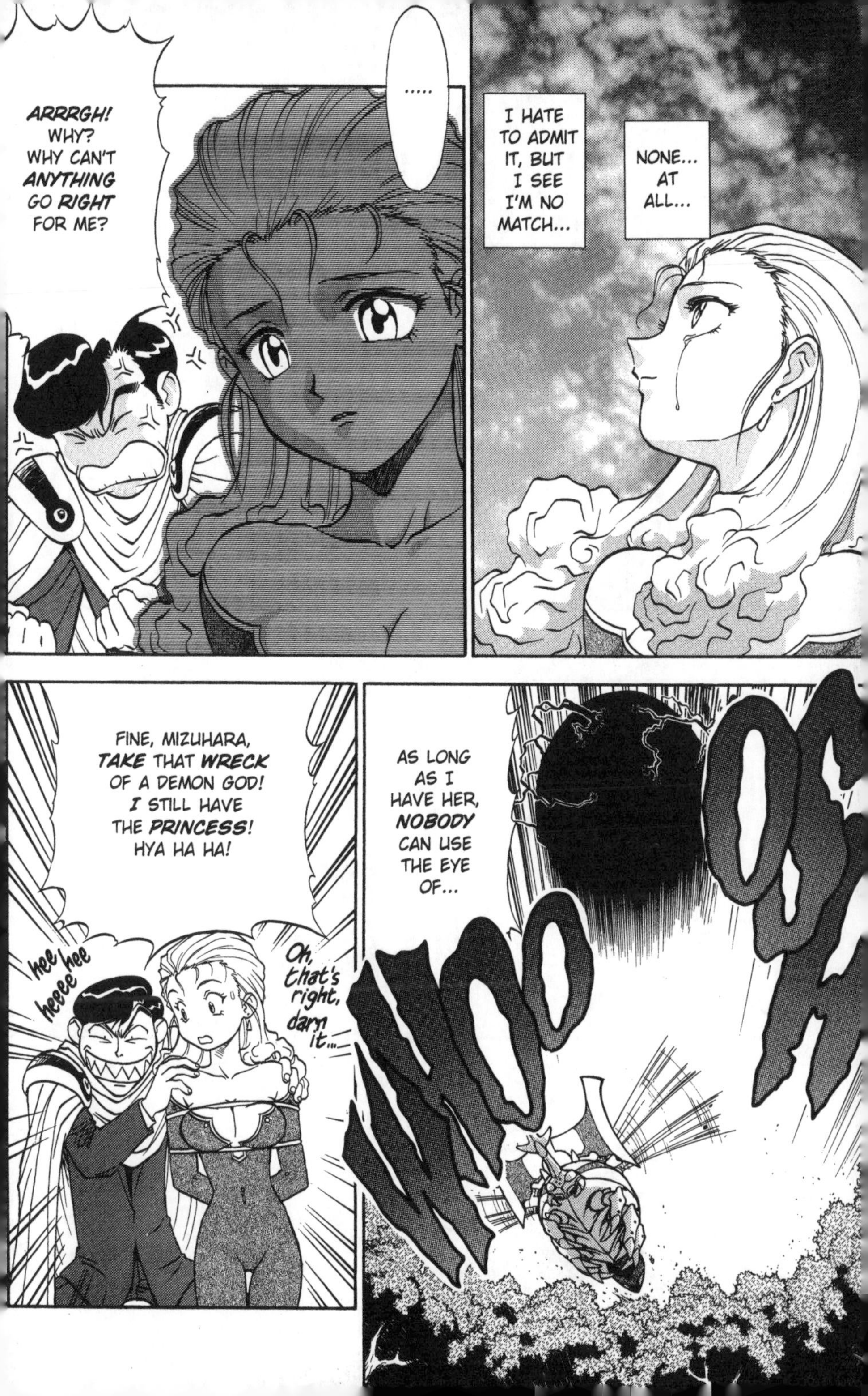
ARRRGH! WHY? WHY CAN'T ANYTHING GO RIGHT FOR ME?
.....
I HATE TO ADMIT IT, BUT I SEE I'M NO MATCH...
NONE... AT ALL...
FINE, MIZUHARA, TAKE THAT WRECK OF A DEMON GOD! I STILL HAVE THE PRINCESS! HYA HA HA!
hee hee heeee
Oh, that's right, darn it...
AS LONG AS I HAVE HER, NOBODY CAN USE THE EYE OF...

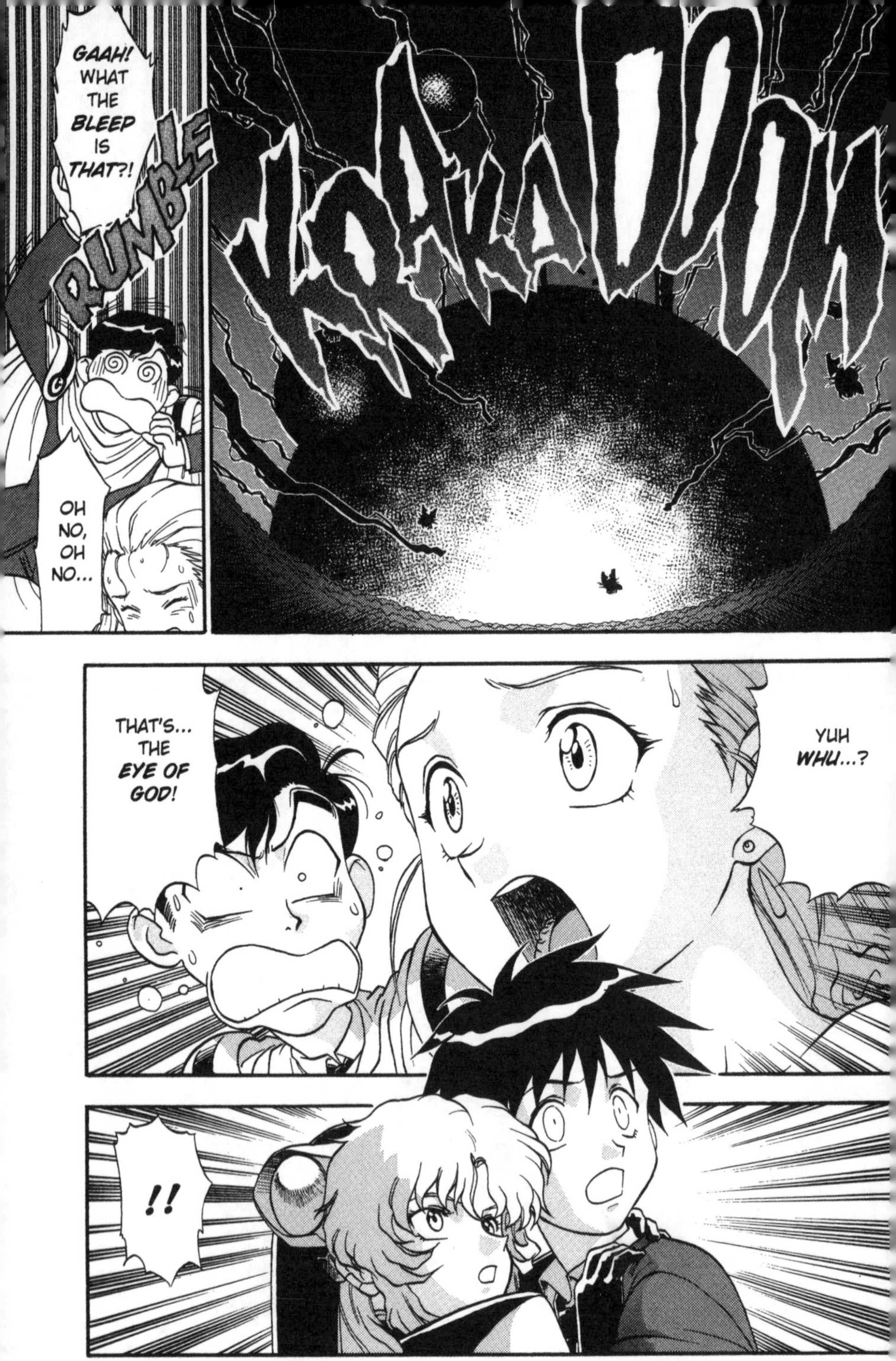
KRAKADOOM
GAAH! WHAT THE BLEEP IS THAT?!
RUMBLE
OH NO, OH NO...
YUH WHU...?
THAT'S... THE EYE OF GOD!
!!

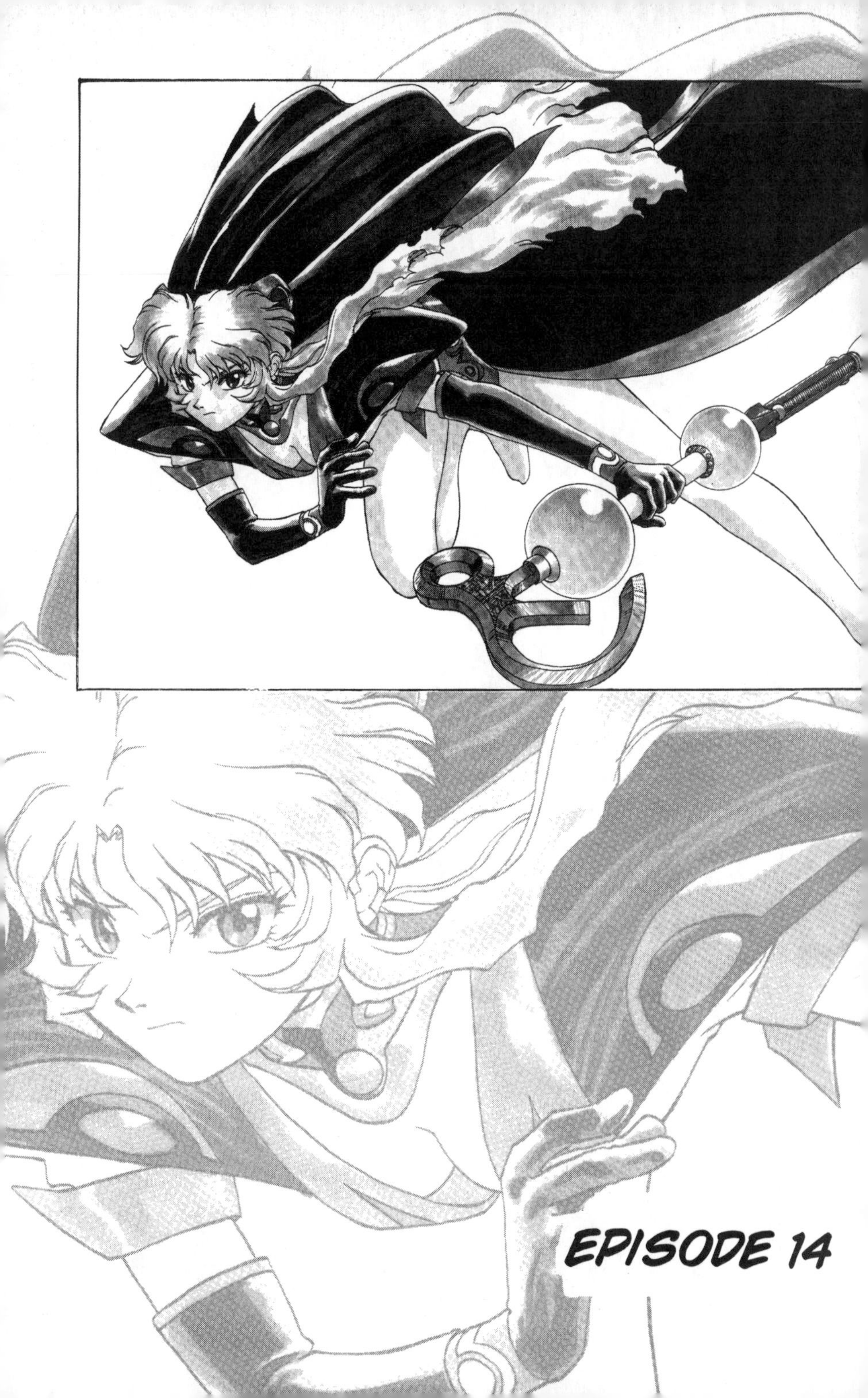
EPISODE 14

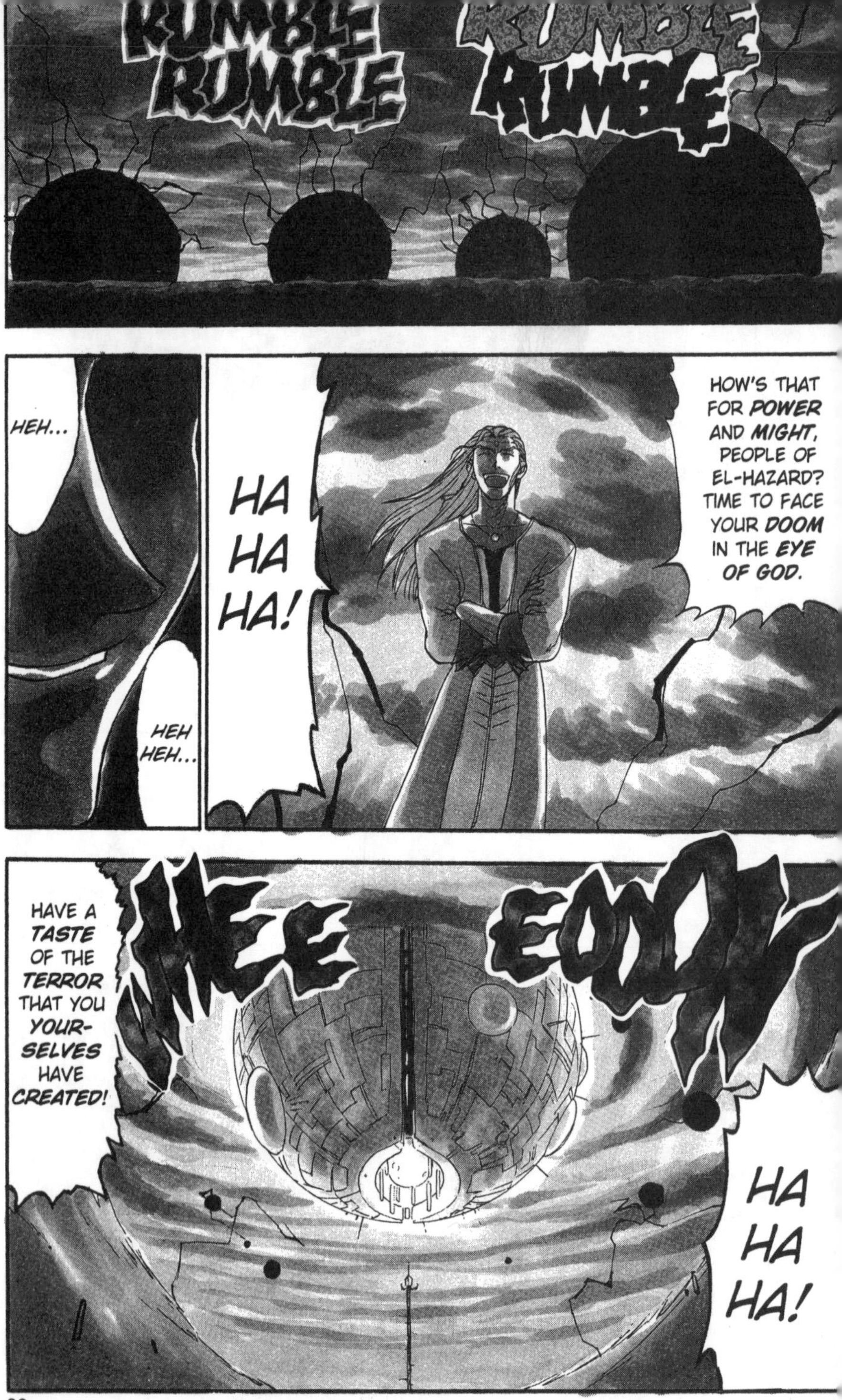
RUMBLE RUMBLE
RUMBLE RUMBLE
HEH...
HA HA HA!
HOW'S THAT FOR POWER AND MIGHT, PEOPLE OF EL-HAZARD? TIME TO FACE YOUR DOOM IN THE EYE OF GOD.
HEH HEH...
HAVE A TASTE OF THE TERROR THAT YOU YOURSELVES HAVE CREATED!
HA HA HA!

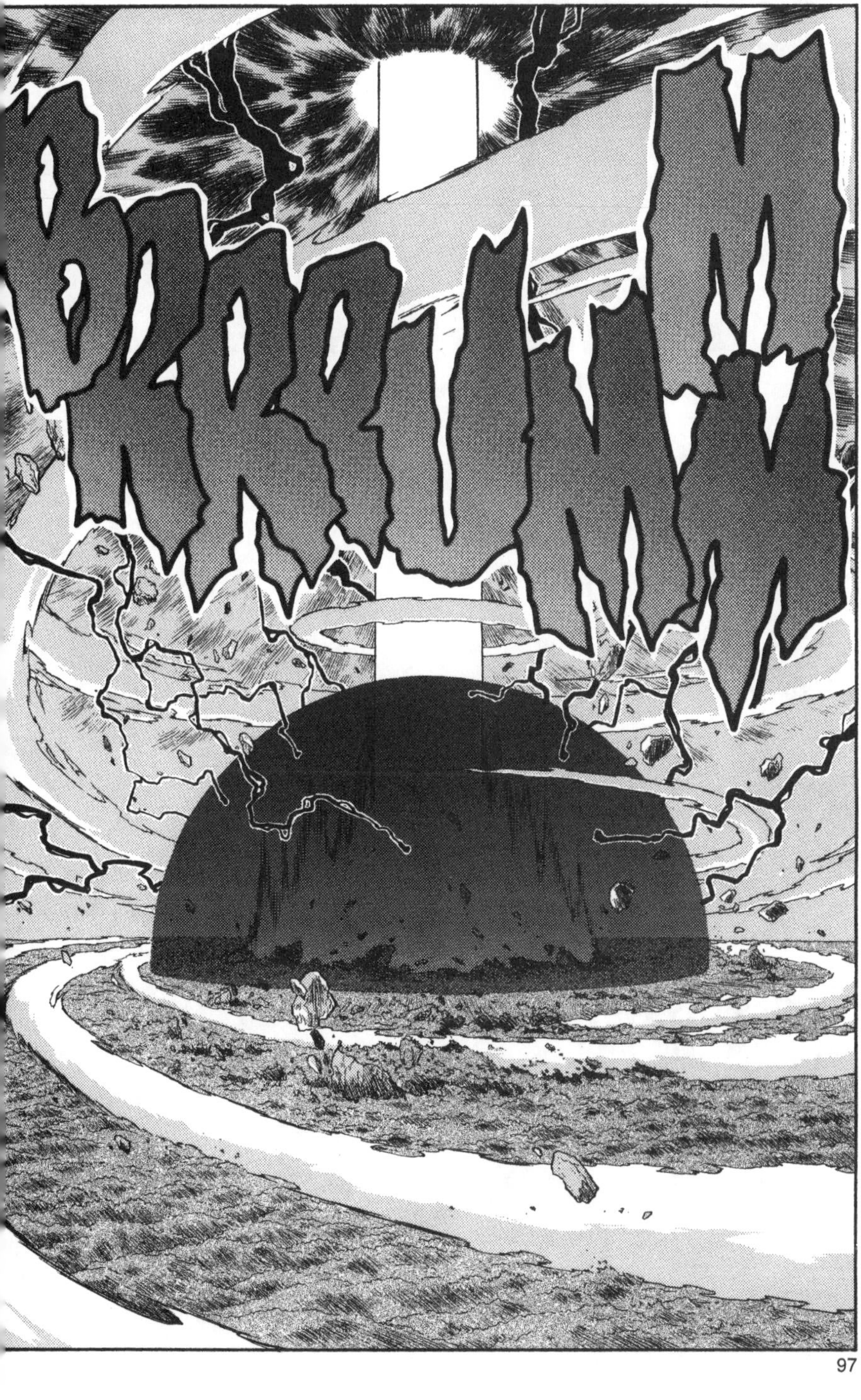
BRRRUMMM

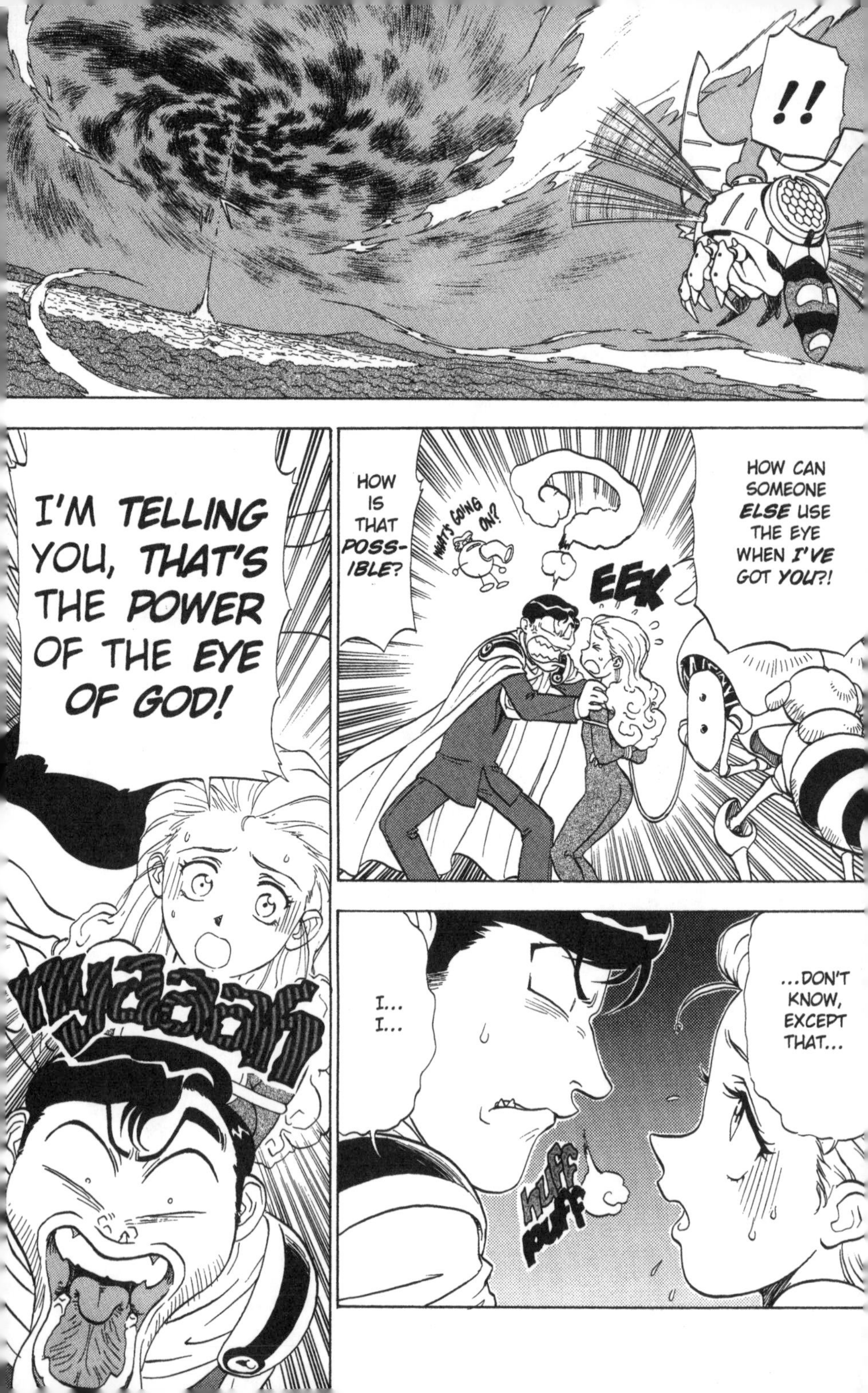

!!
I'M TELLING YOU, THAT'S THE POWER OF THE EYE OF GOD!
HOW IS THAT POSSIBLE?
WHAT'S GOING ON?
EEK
HOW CAN SOMEONE ELSE USE THE EYE WHEN I'VE GOT YOU?!
I... I...
...DON'T KNOW, EXCEPT THAT...
HUFF PUFF

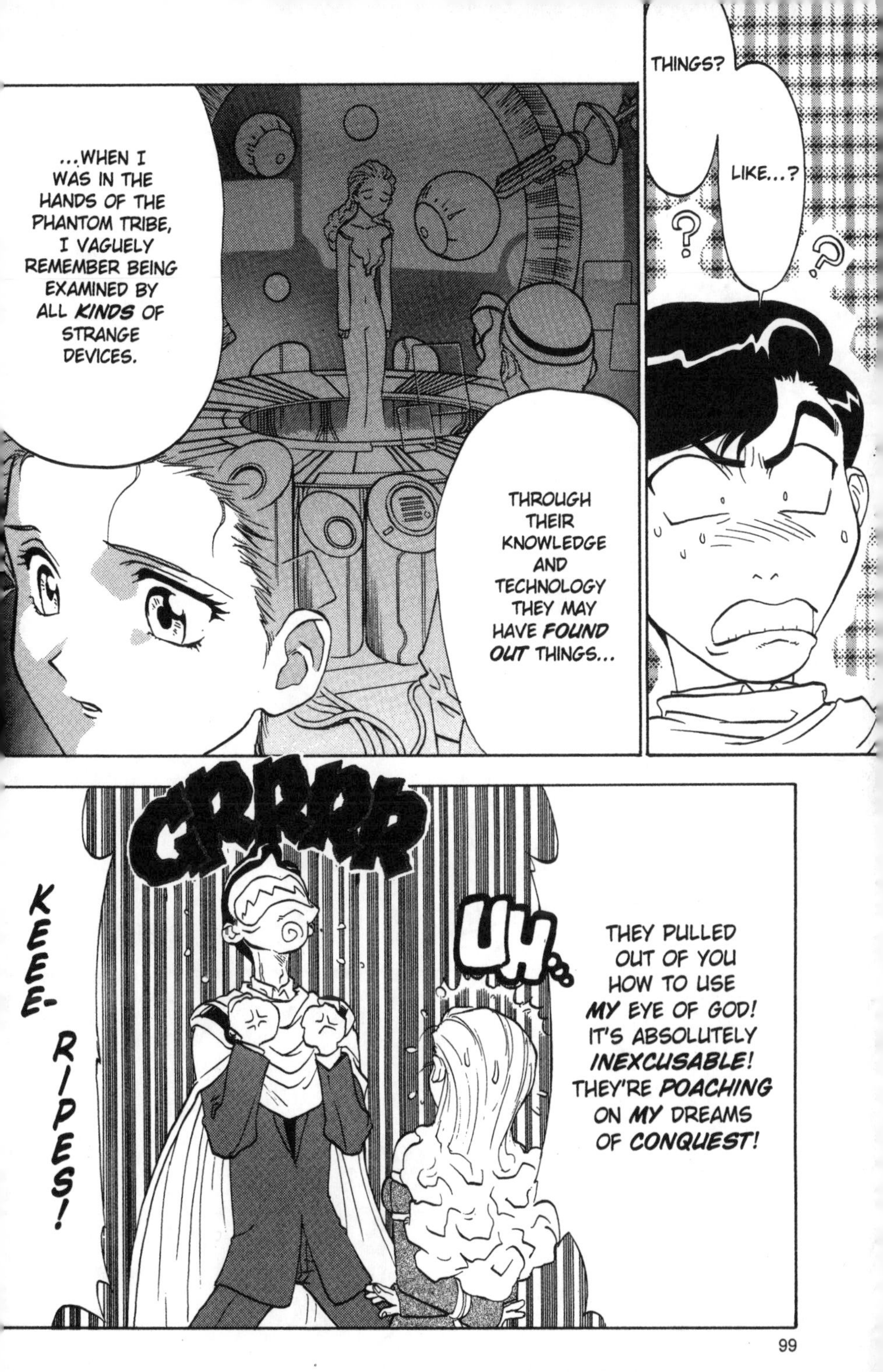

...WHEN I WAS IN THE HANDS OF THE PHANTOM TRIBE, I VAGUELY REMEMBER BEING EXAMINED BY ALL KINDS OF STRANGE DEVICES.
THROUGH THEIR KNOWLEDGE AND TECHNOLOGY THEY MAY HAVE FOUND OUT THINGS...
THINGS?
LIKE...?
?
?
GRRRR
KEEE-RIPES!
UH...
THEY PULLED OUT OF YOU HOW TO USE MY EYE OF GOD! IT'S ABSOLUTELY INEXCUSABLE! THEY'RE POACHING ON MY DREAMS OF CONQUEST!

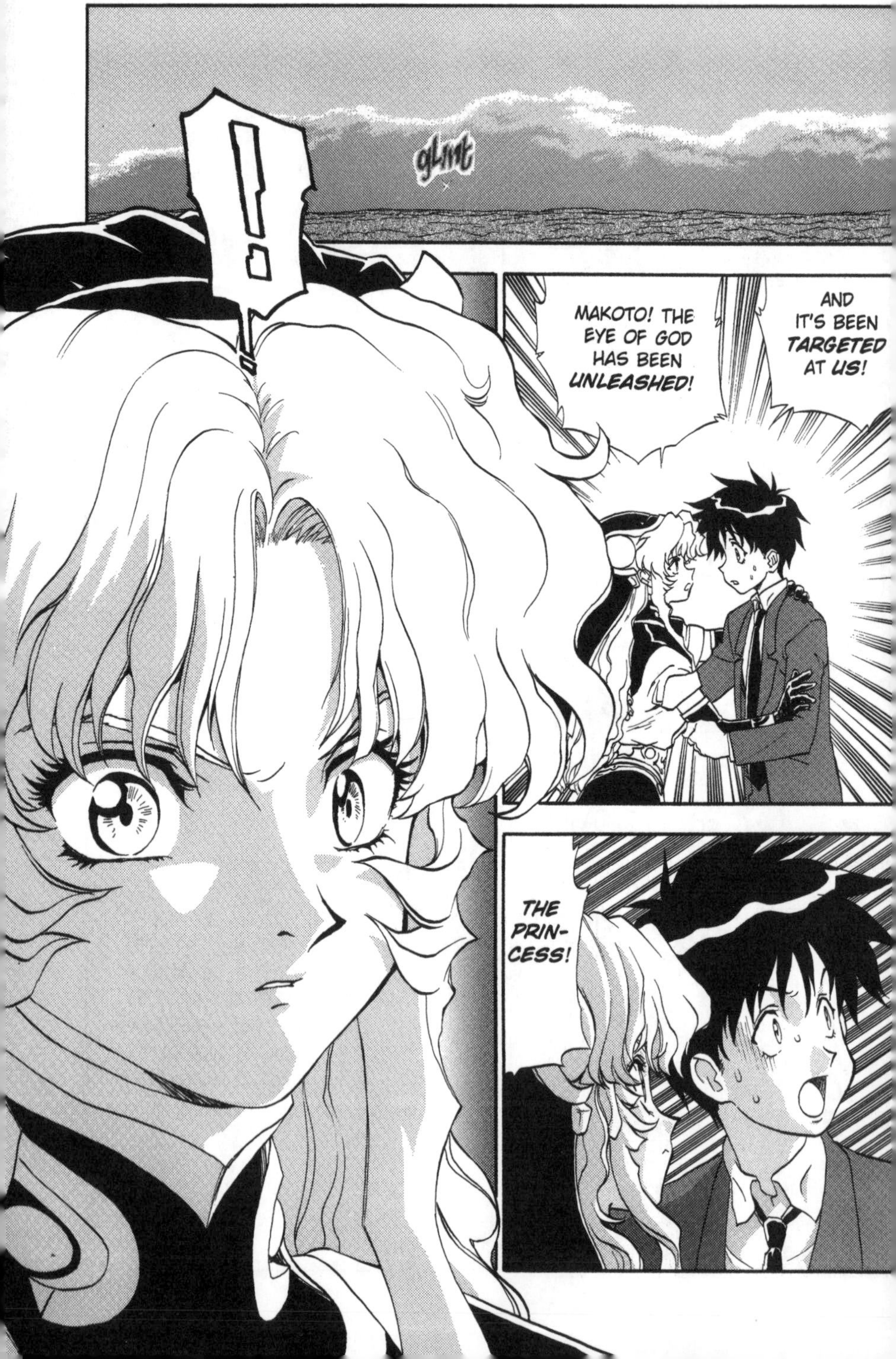
glint
!
MAKOTO! THE EYE OF GOD HAS BEEN UNLEASHED!
AND IT'S BEEN TARGETED AT US!
THE PRINCESS!

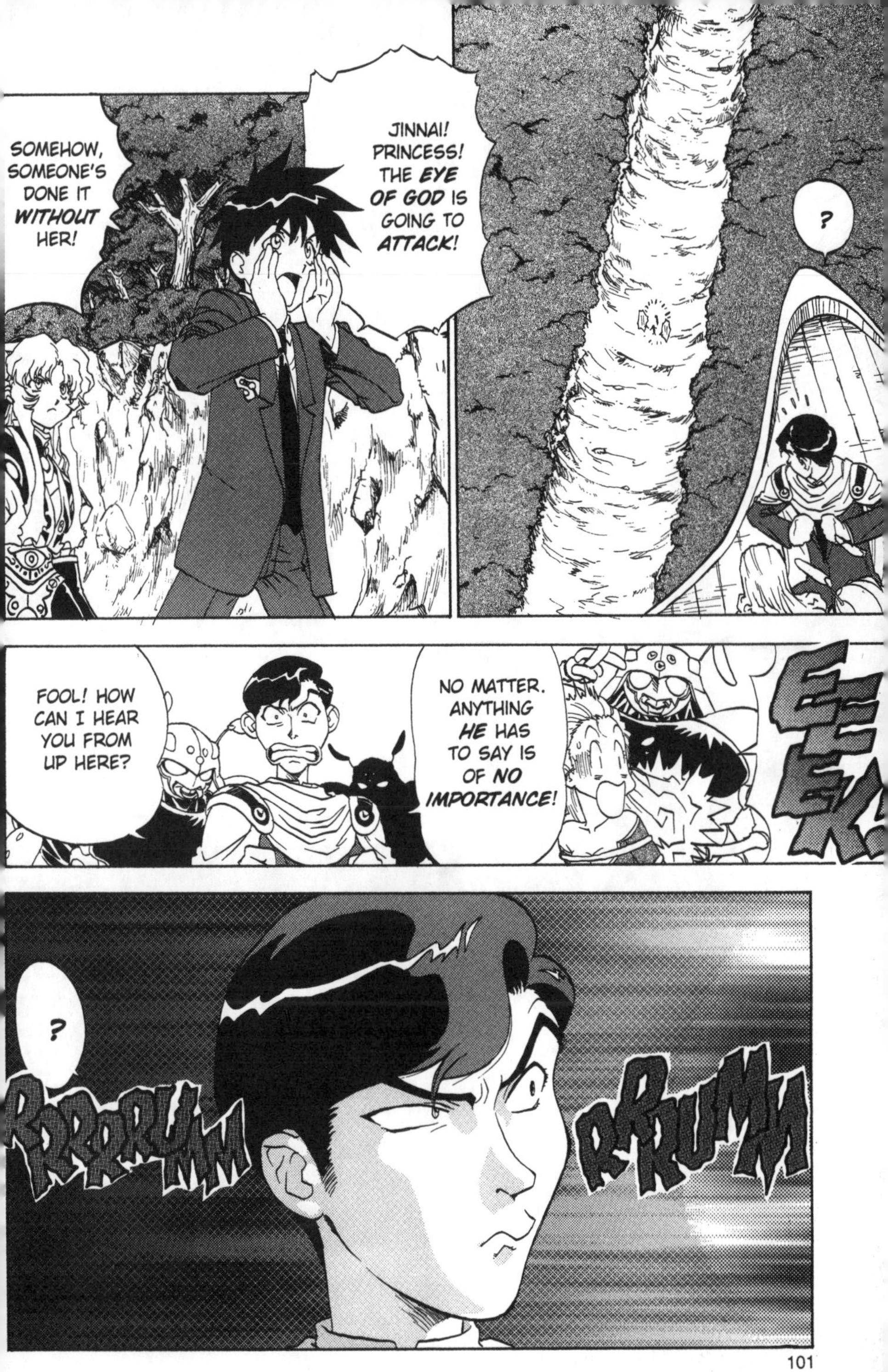
SOMEHOW, SOMEONE'S DONE IT WITHOUT HER!
JINNAI! PRINCESS! THE EYE OF GOD IS GOING TO ATTACK!
?
FOOL! HOW CAN I HEAR YOU FROM UP HERE?
NO MATTER. ANYTHING HE HAS TO SAY IS OF NO IMPORTANCE!
EEEEK!!
?
RRRRUMM
RRUMM

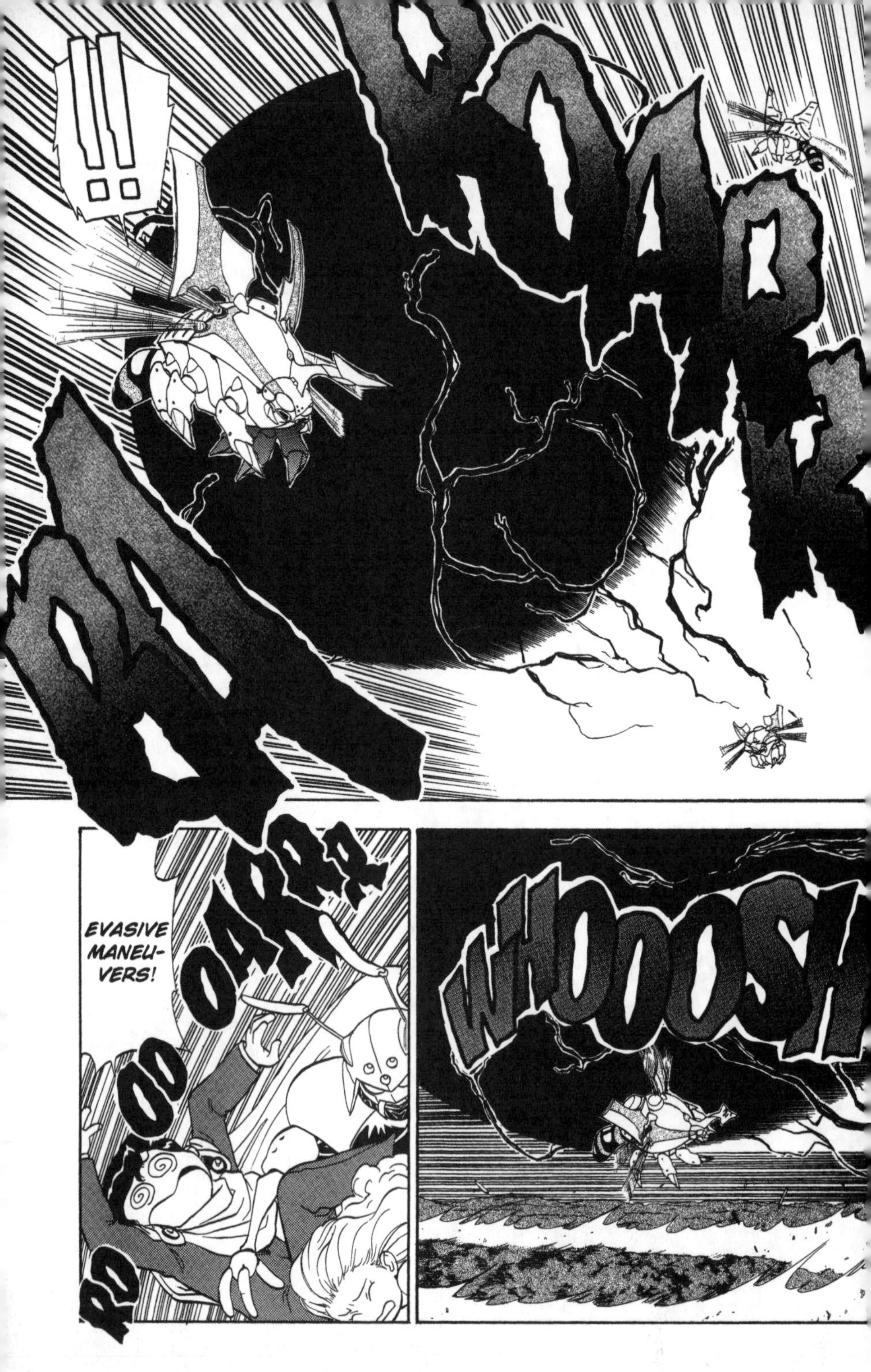
!!
EVASIVE MANEU-VERS!
WHOOOSH

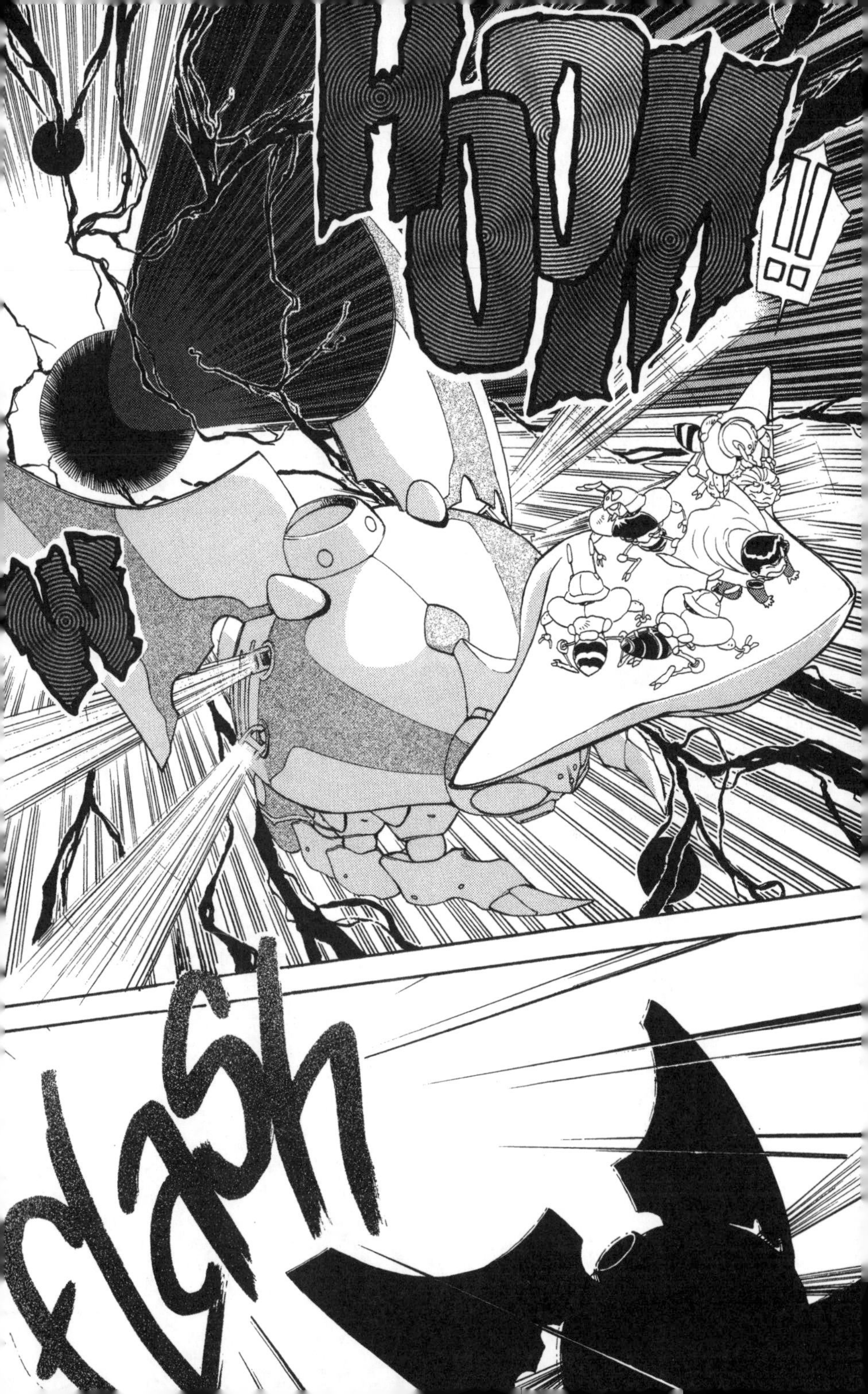
HOOM!!
flash

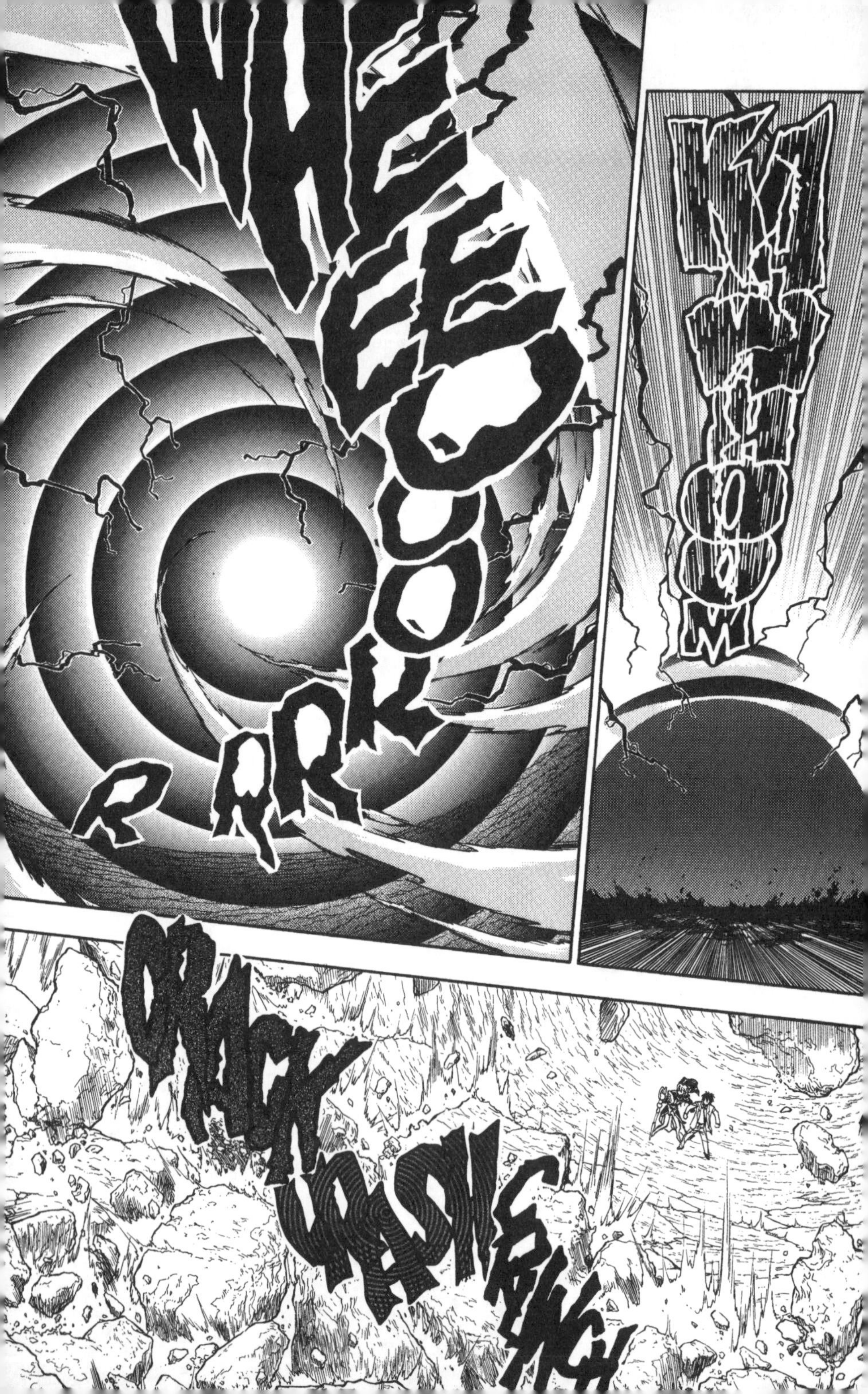
WHOOOM
CRACK

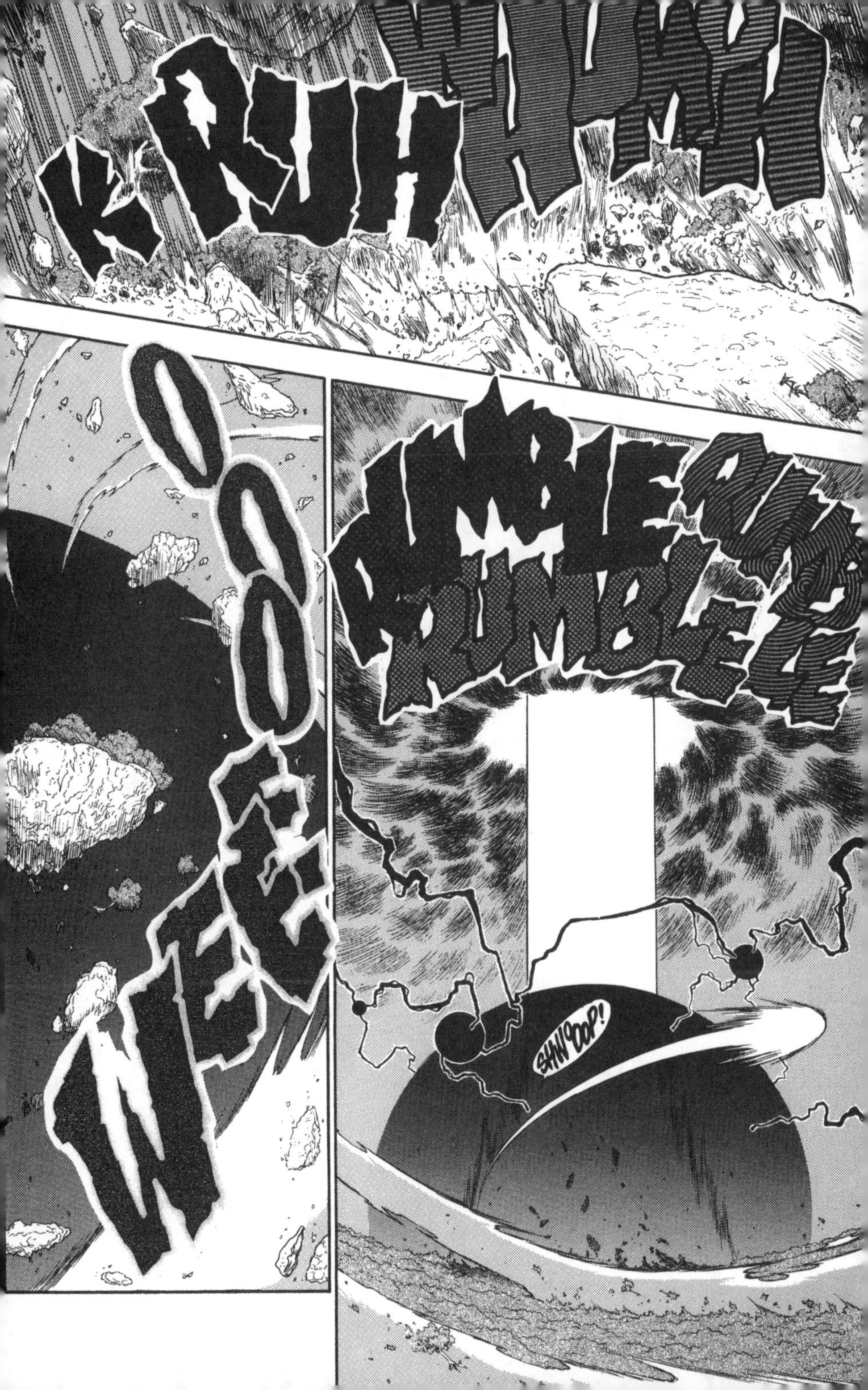
KRUH
RUMBLE
RUMBLE
SHWOOOP!

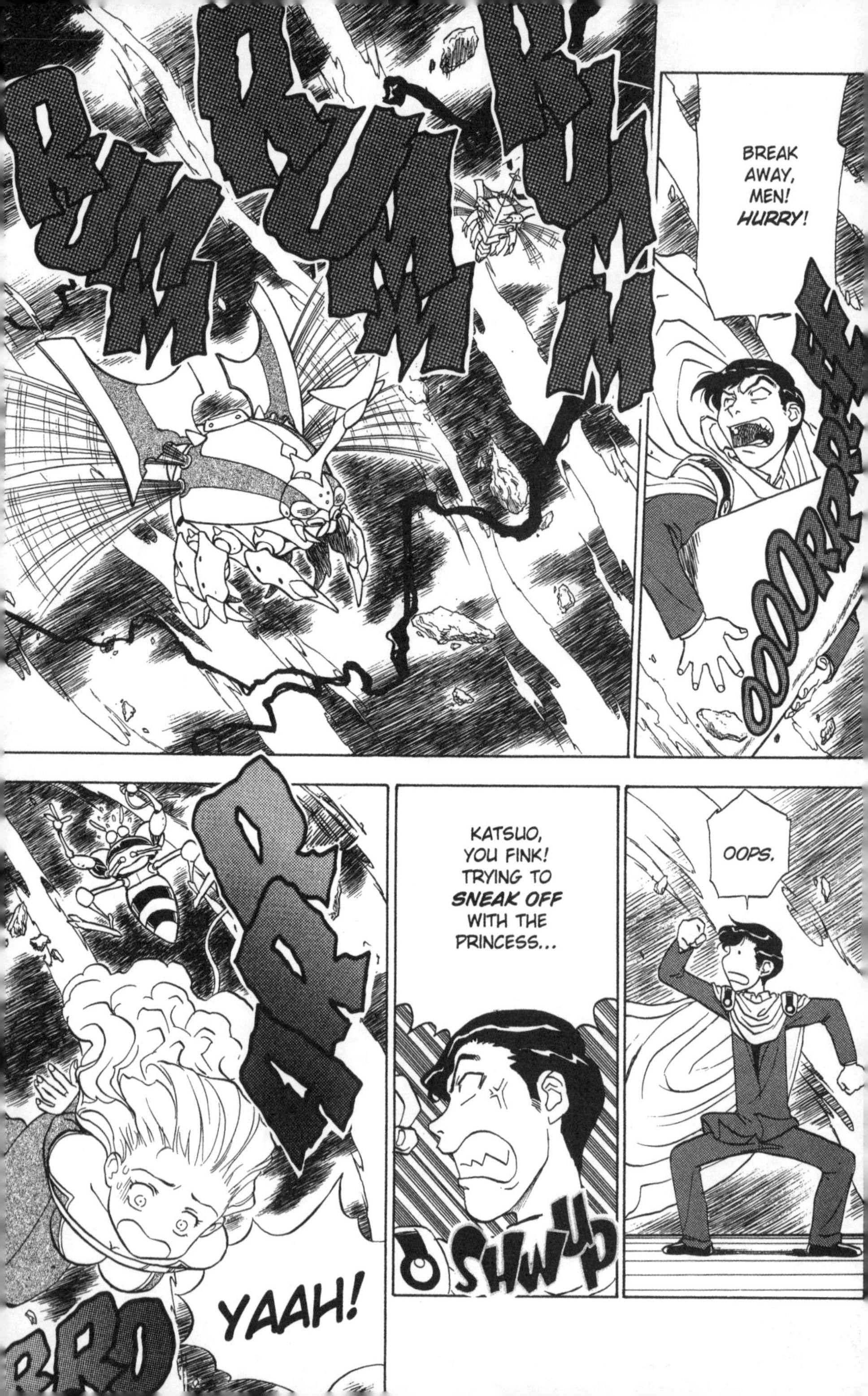
BREAK AWAY, MEN! *HURRY*!
YAAH!
KATSUO, YOU FINK! TRYING TO **SNEAK OFF** WITH THE PRINCESS...
SHWUP
OOPS.

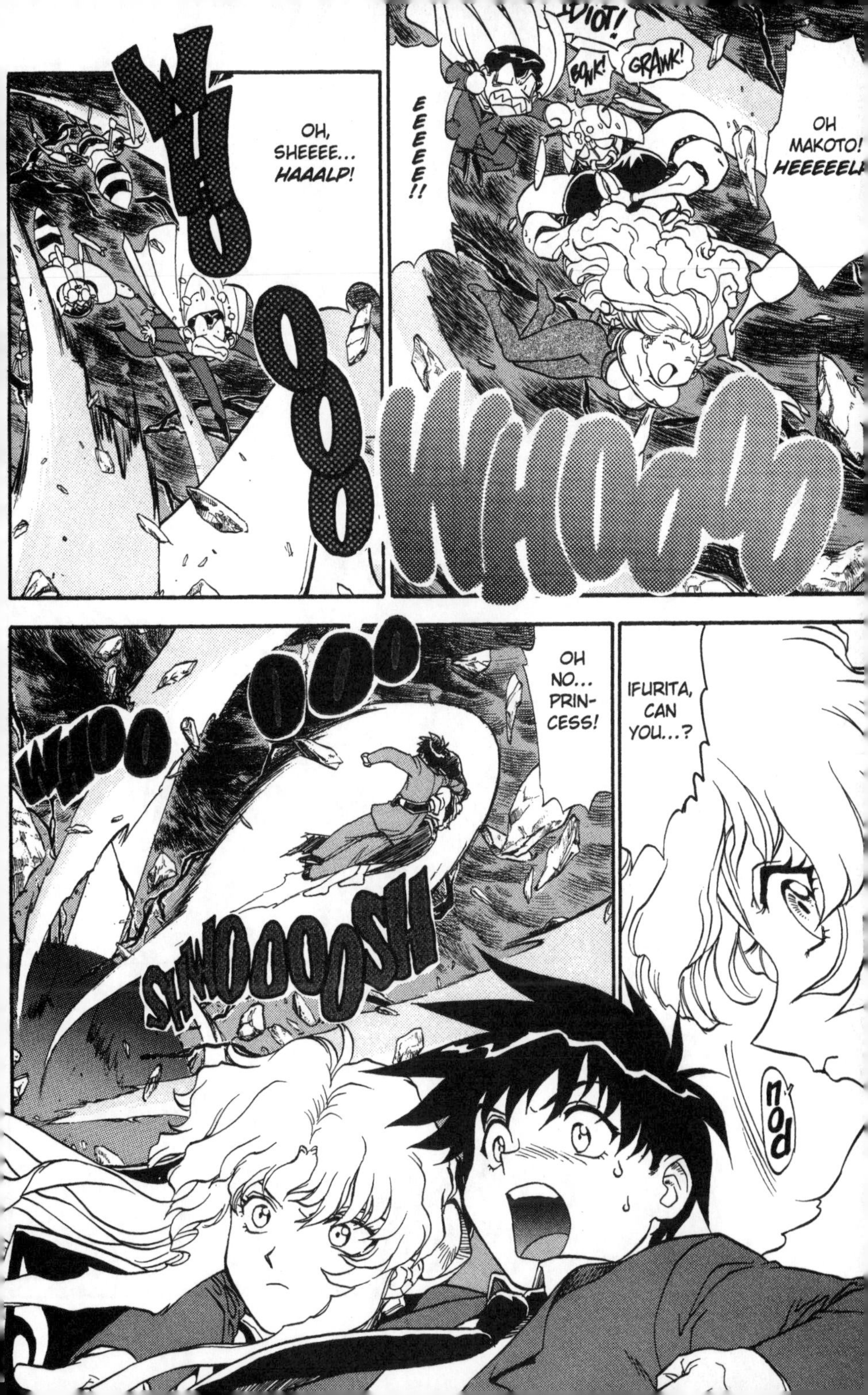
IDIOT!
BONK!
GRAWK!
EEEEEE!!
OH MAKOTO! HEEEEEL
OH, SHEEEE... HAAALP!
IFURITA, CAN YOU...?
nod
OH NO... PRINCESS!
SHWOOOOOSH

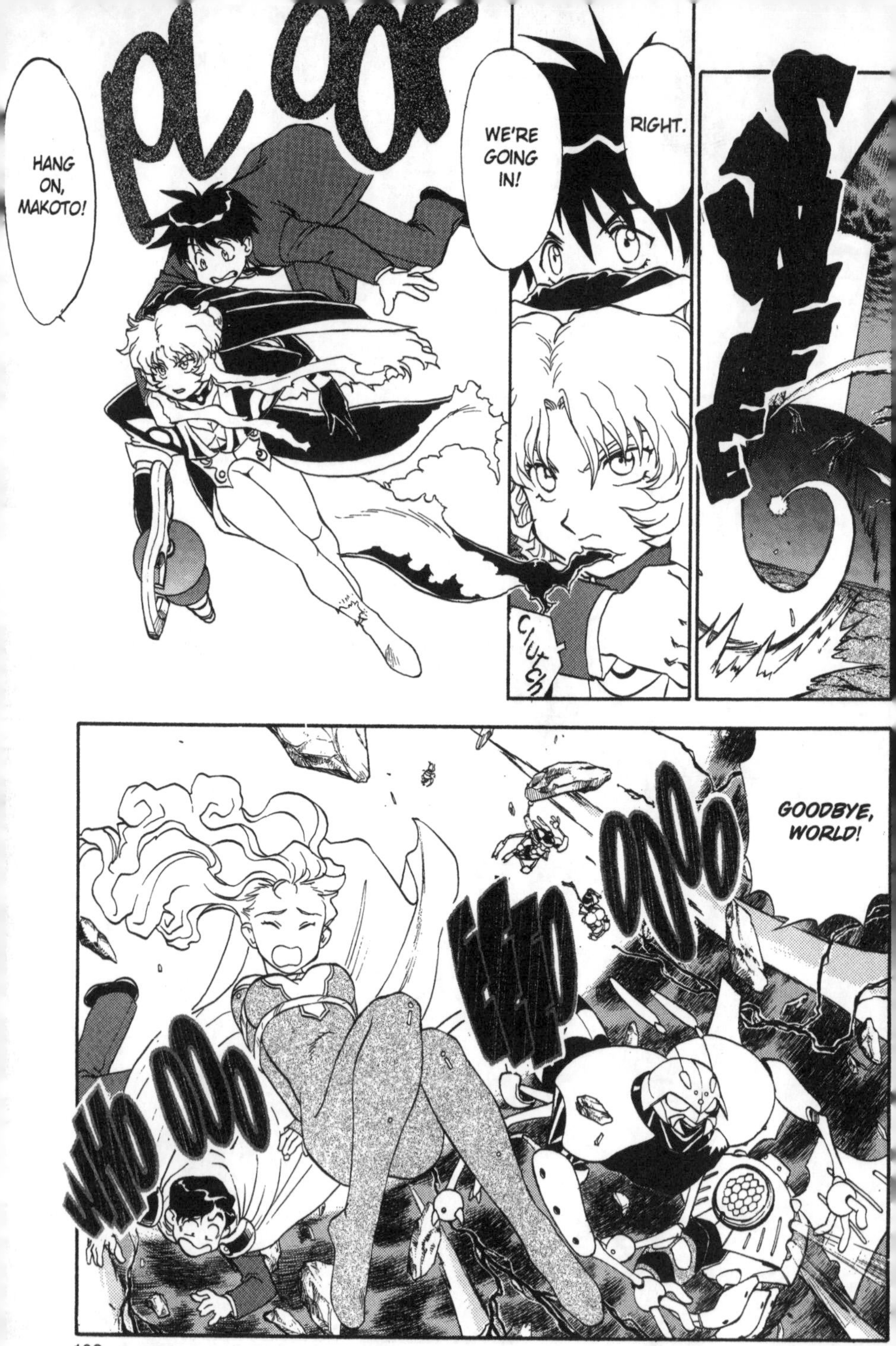
HANG ON, MAKOTO!
WE'RE GOING IN!
RIGHT.
CLUTCH
GOODBYE, WORLD!

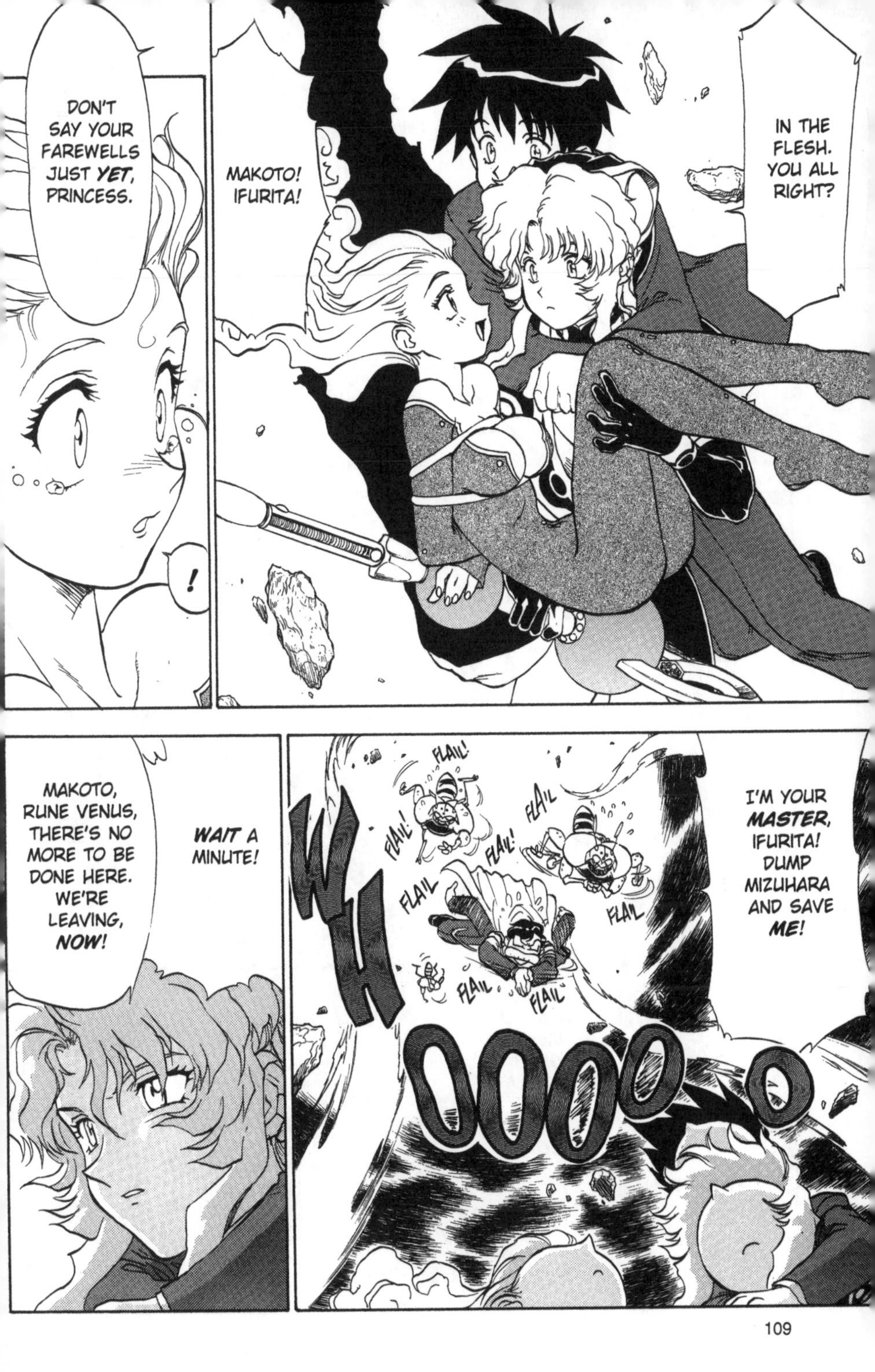
DON'T SAY YOUR FAREWELLS JUST *YET*, PRINCESS.
!
MAKOTO! IFURITA!
IN THE FLESH. YOU ALL RIGHT?
MAKOTO, RUNE VENUS, THERE'S NO MORE TO BE DONE HERE. WE'RE LEAVING, *NOW*!
WAIT A MINUTE!
I'M YOUR *MASTER*, IFURITA! DUMP MIZUHARA AND SAVE *ME*!
FLAIL! FLAIL! FLAIL! FLAIL! FLAIL FLAIL FLAIL FLAIL FLAIL
WHOOOOO-O

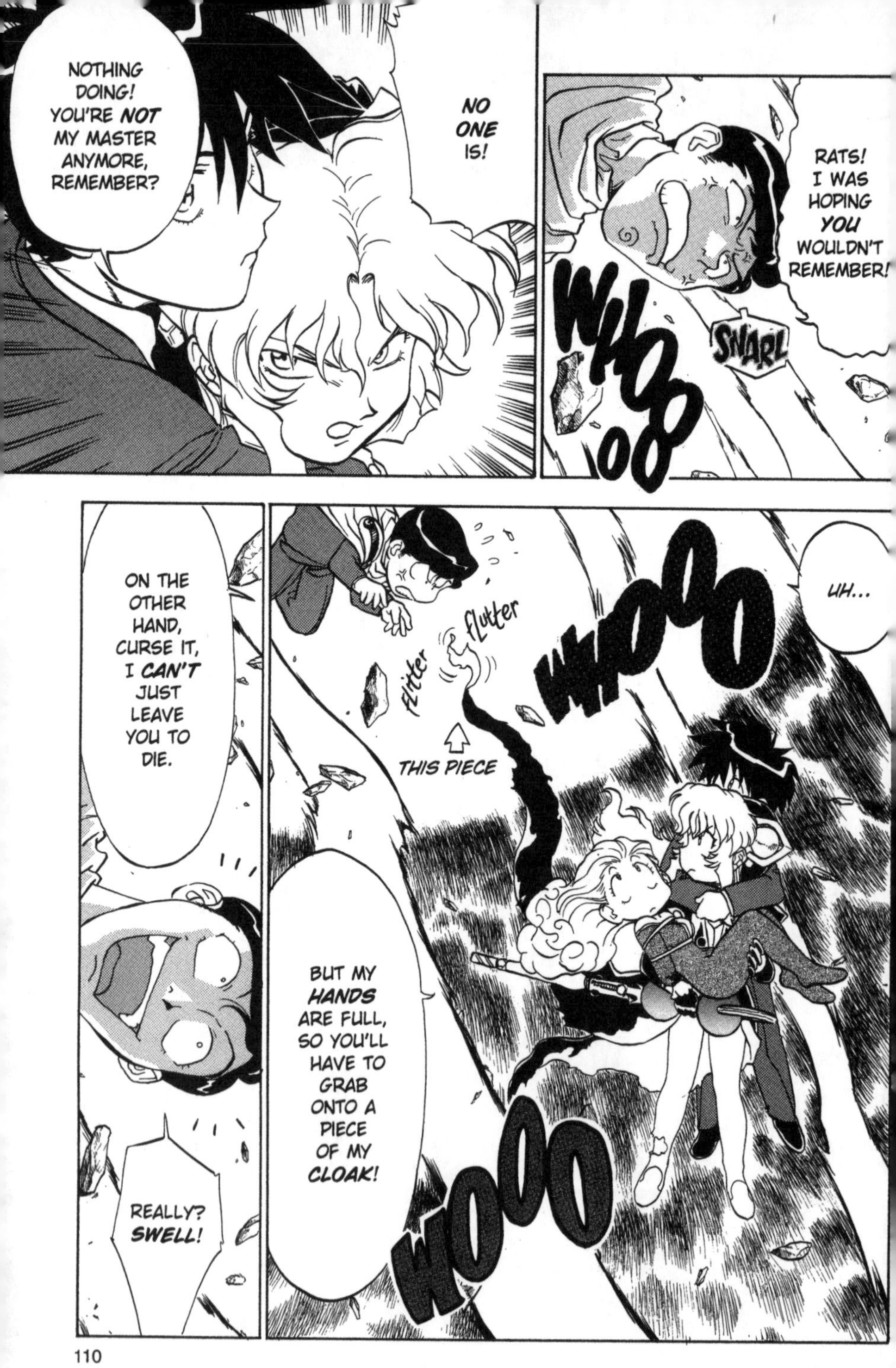
NOTHING DOING! YOU'RE NOT MY MASTER ANYMORE, REMEMBER?
NO ONE IS!
RATS! I WAS HOPING YOU WOULDN'T REMEMBER!
SNARL
WHOOOO
UH...
WHOOOO
ON THE OTHER HAND, CURSE IT, I CAN'T JUST LEAVE YOU TO DIE.
flitter flutter
THIS PIECE
BUT MY HANDS ARE FULL, SO YOU'LL HAVE TO GRAB ONTO A PIECE OF MY CLOAK!
REALLY? SWELL!
WHOOOO

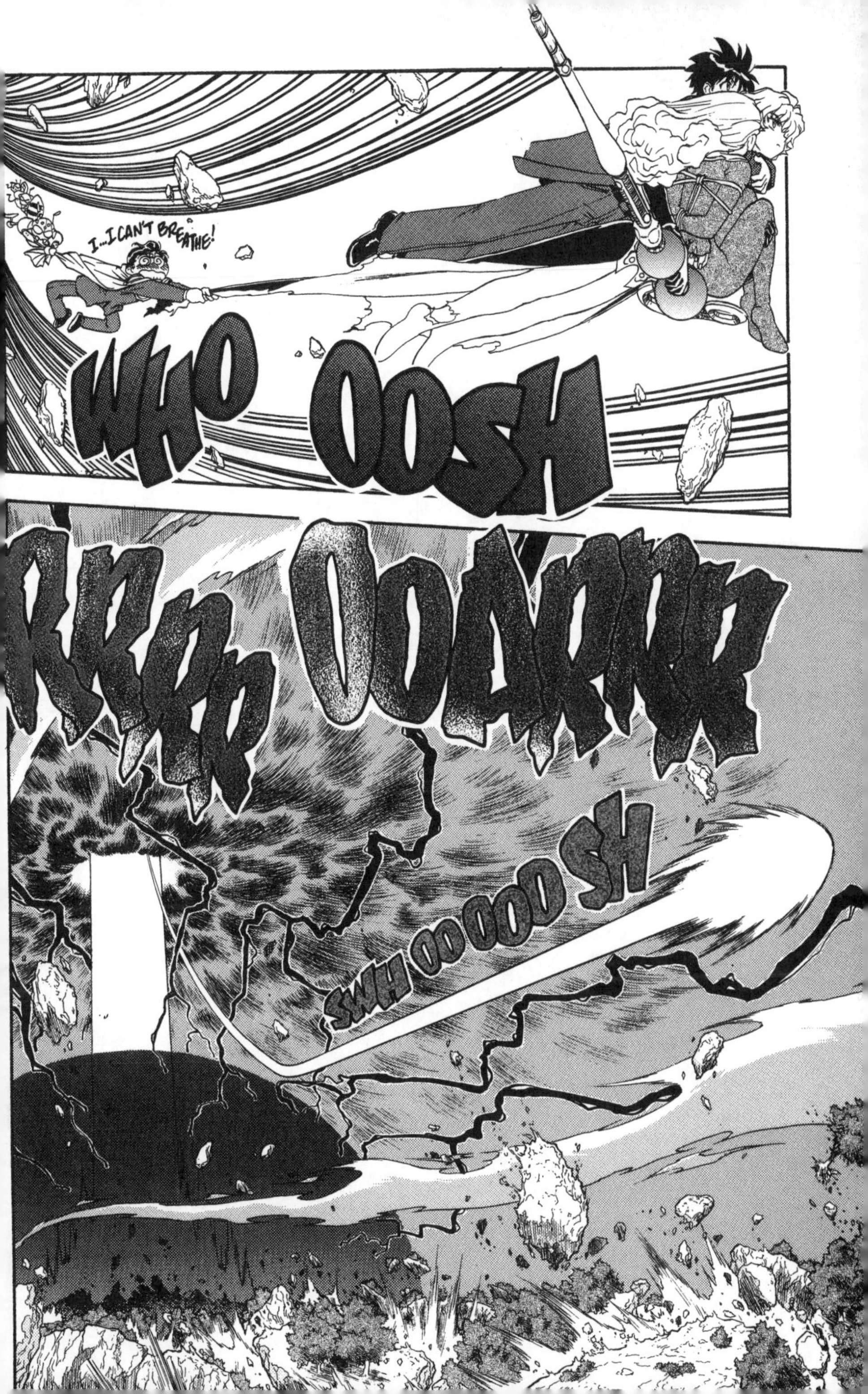
I...I CAN'T BREATHE!
WHOOOSH
RRRR OOAAARR
SWHOOOOOOSH

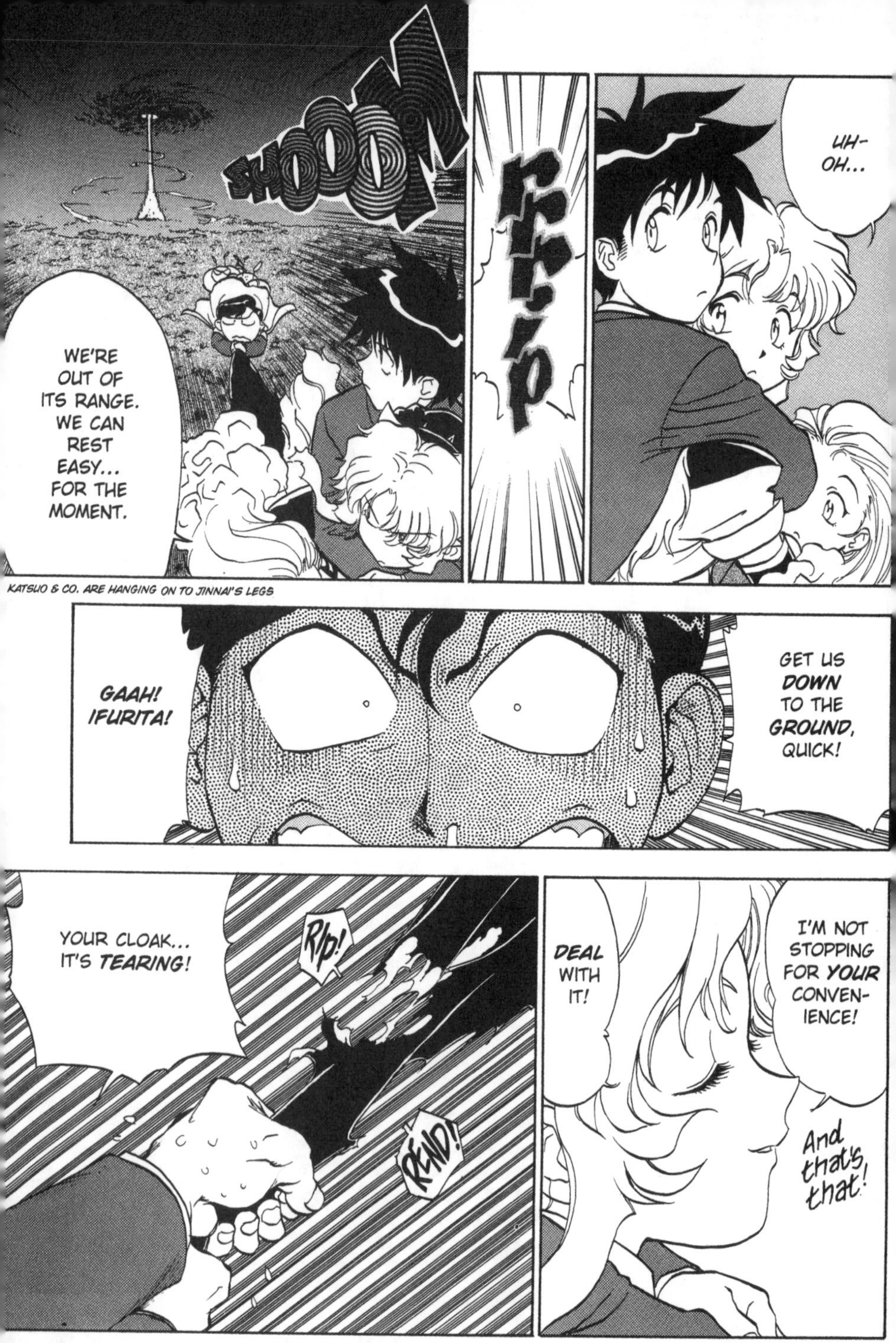
UH- OH...
SHOOOOM
WE'RE OUT OF ITS RANGE. WE CAN REST EASY... FOR THE MOMENT.
KATSUO & CO. ARE HANGING ON TO JINNAI'S LEGS
GET US DOWN TO THE GROUND, QUICK!
GAAH! IFURITA!
I'M NOT STOPPING FOR YOUR CONVENIENCE!
DEAL WITH IT!
And that's that!
YOUR CLOAK... IT'S TEARING!
RIP!
REND!

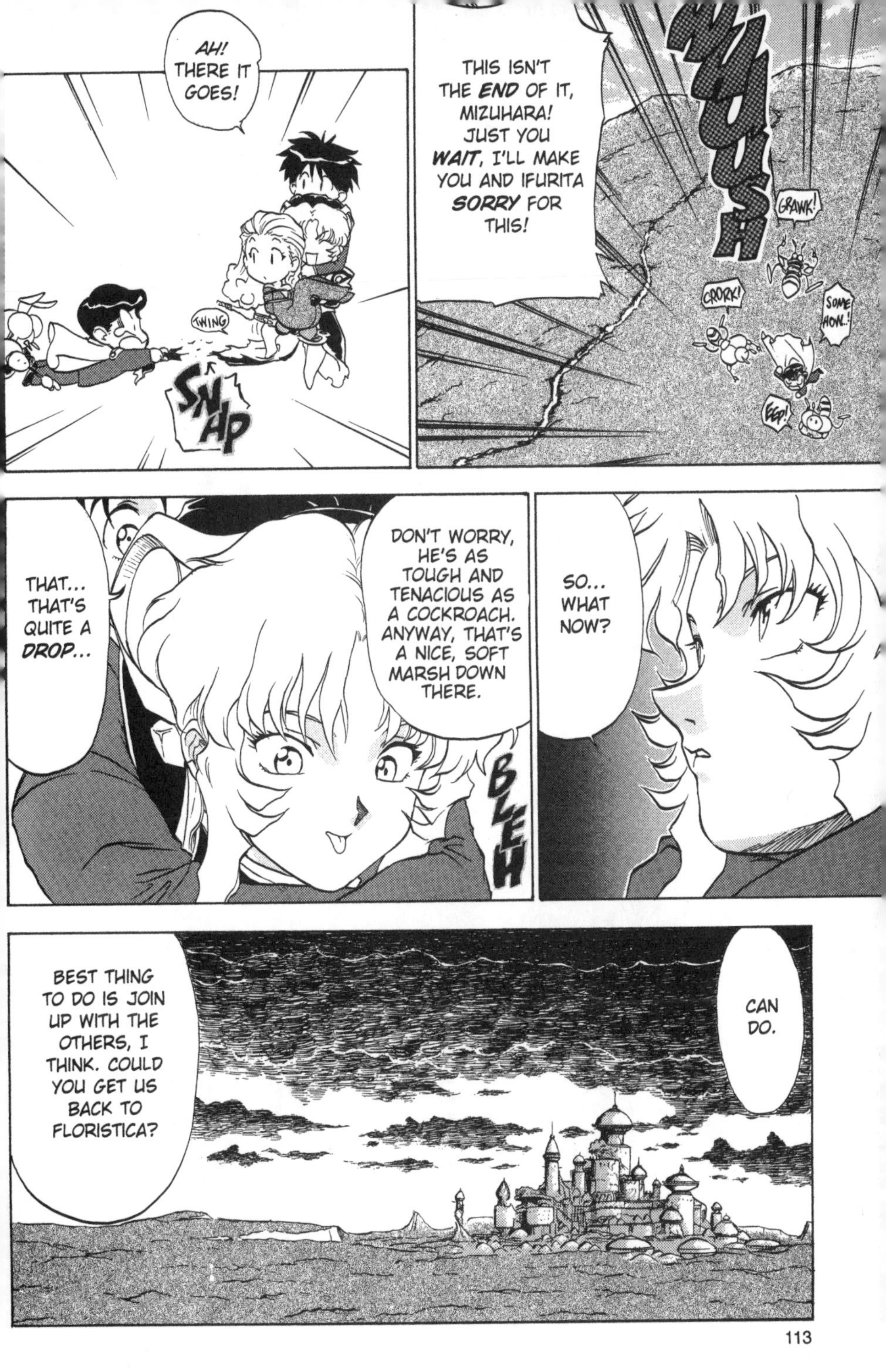
AH! THERE IT GOES!
TWING
SNAP
THIS ISN'T THE END OF IT, MIZUHARA! JUST YOU WAIT, I'LL MAKE YOU AND IFURITA SORRY FOR THIS!
WHOOSH
GRAWK!
CRORK!
SOME HOW..!
EEP!
THAT... THAT'S QUITE A DROP...
DON'T WORRY, HE'S AS TOUGH AND TENACIOUS AS A COCKROACH. ANYWAY, THAT'S A NICE, SOFT MARSH DOWN THERE.
BLEH
SO... WHAT NOW?
BEST THING TO DO IS JOIN UP WITH THE OTHERS, I THINK. COULD YOU GET US BACK TO FLORISTICA?
CAN DO.

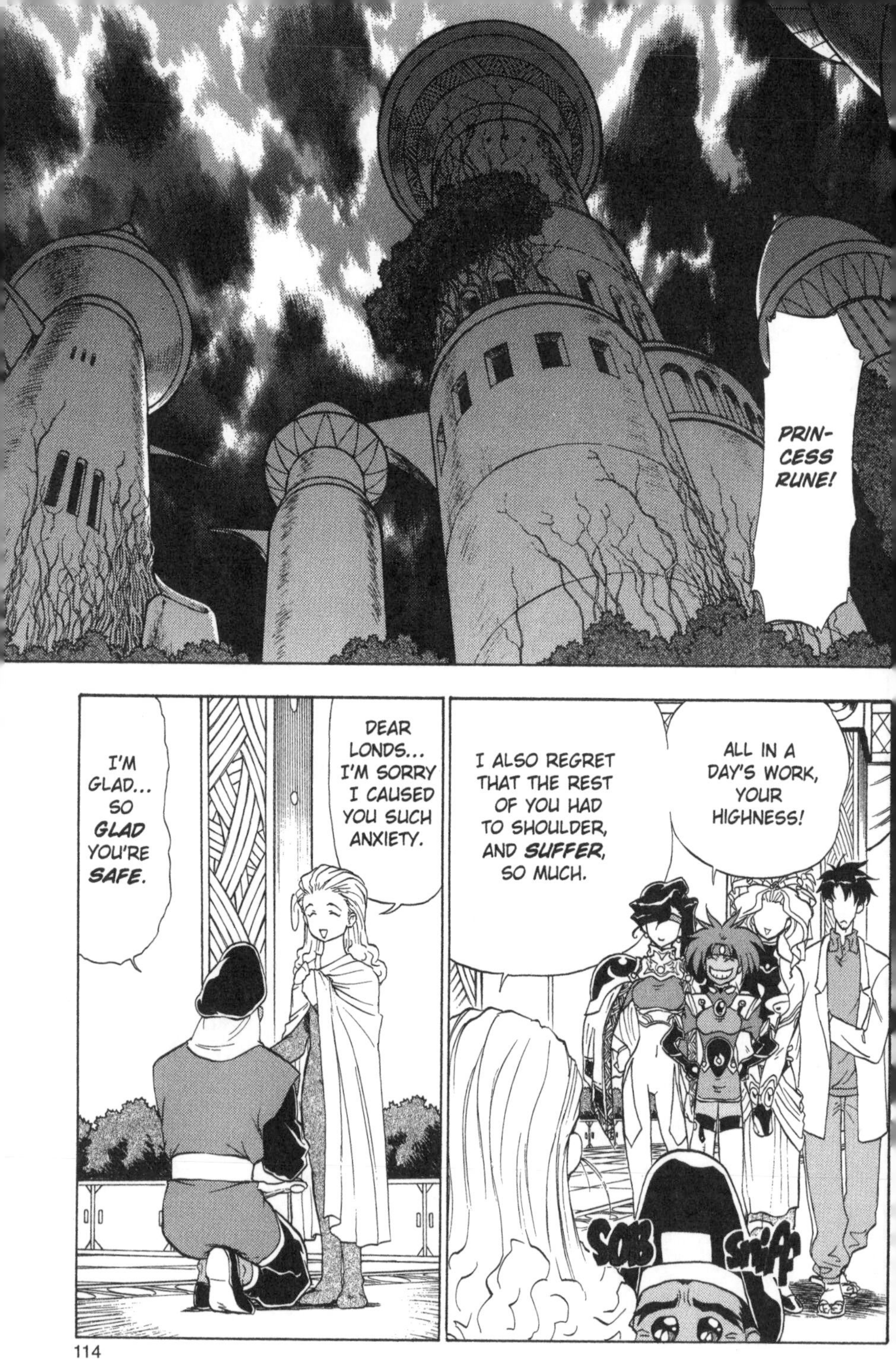
PRINCESS RUNE!
I'M GLAD... SO GLAD YOU'RE SAFE.
DEAR LONDS... I'M SORRY I CAUSED YOU SUCH ANXIETY.
I ALSO REGRET THAT THE REST OF YOU HAD TO SHOULDER, AND SUFFER, SO MUCH.
ALL IN A DAY'S WORK, YOUR HIGHNESS!
SOB
SNIFF

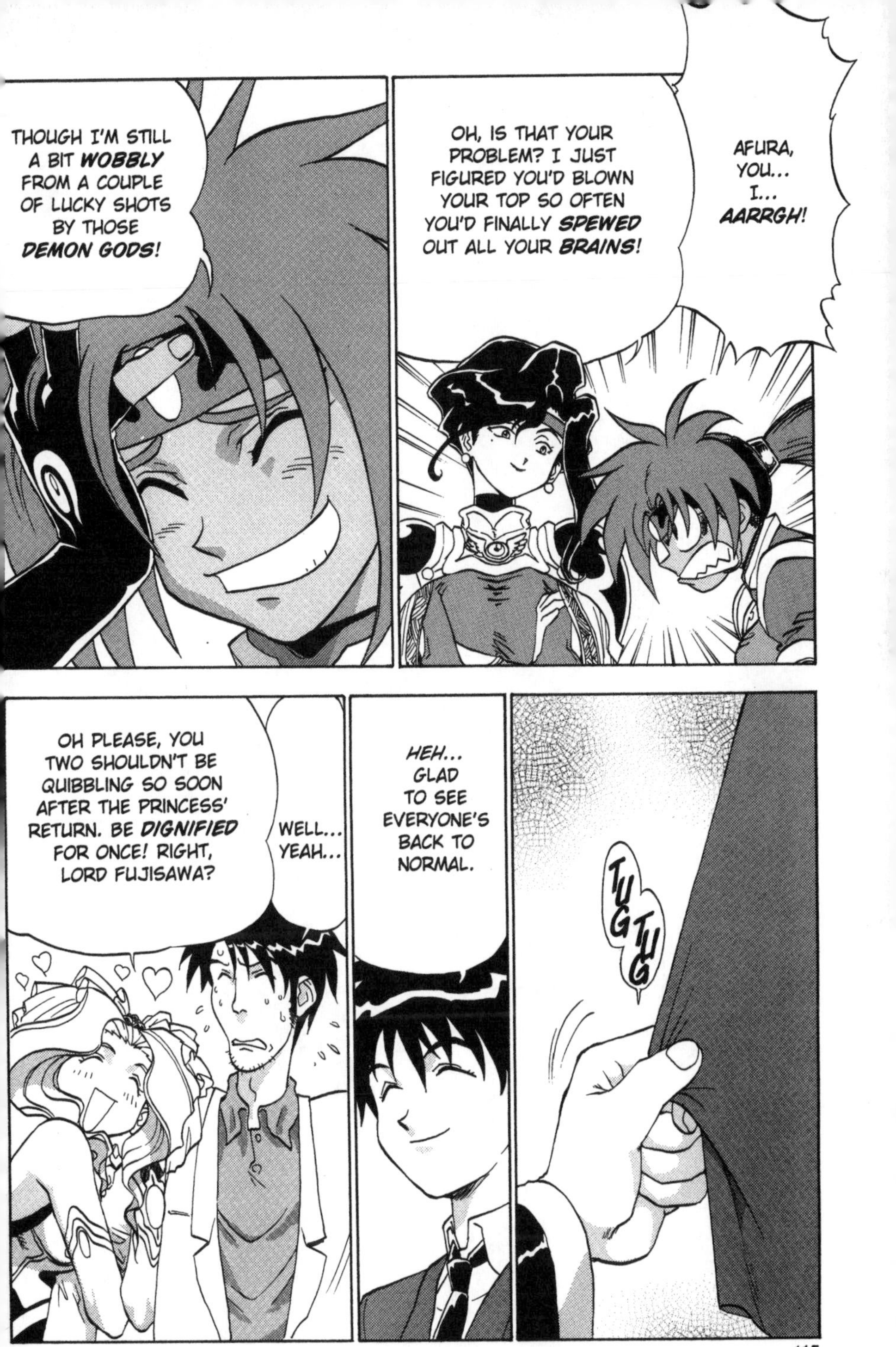
THOUGH I'M STILL A BIT WOBBLY FROM A COUPLE OF LUCKY SHOTS BY THOSE DEMON GODS!
OH, IS THAT YOUR PROBLEM? I JUST FIGURED YOU'D BLOWN YOUR TOP SO OFTEN YOU'D FINALLY SPEWED OUT ALL YOUR BRAINS!
AFURA, YOU... I... AARRGH!
OH PLEASE, YOU TWO SHOULDN'T BE QUIBBLING SO SOON AFTER THE PRINCESS' RETURN. BE DIGNIFIED FOR ONCE! RIGHT, LORD FUJISAWA?
WELL... YEAH...
HEH... GLAD TO SEE EVERYONE'S BACK TO NORMAL.
TUG TUG

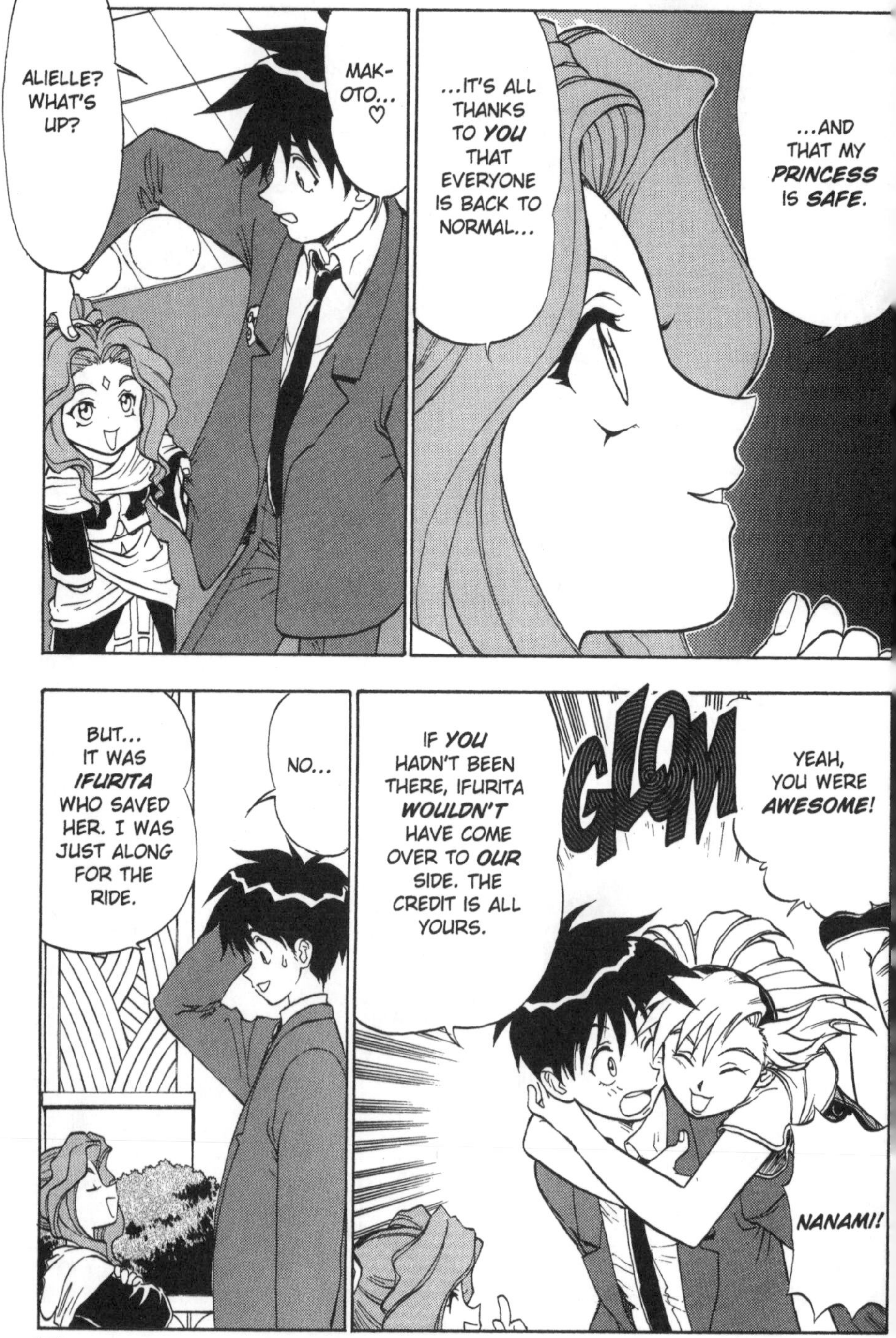
MAK-OTO... ♡
ALIELLE? WHAT'S UP?
...IT'S ALL THANKS TO YOU THAT EVERYONE IS BACK TO NORMAL...
...AND THAT MY PRINCESS IS SAFE.
NO...
BUT... IT WAS IFURITA WHO SAVED HER. I WAS JUST ALONG FOR THE RIDE.
IF YOU HADN'T BEEN THERE, IFURITA WOULDN'T HAVE COME OVER TO OUR SIDE. THE CREDIT IS ALL YOURS.
GLOM
YEAH, YOU WERE AWESOME!
NANAMI!

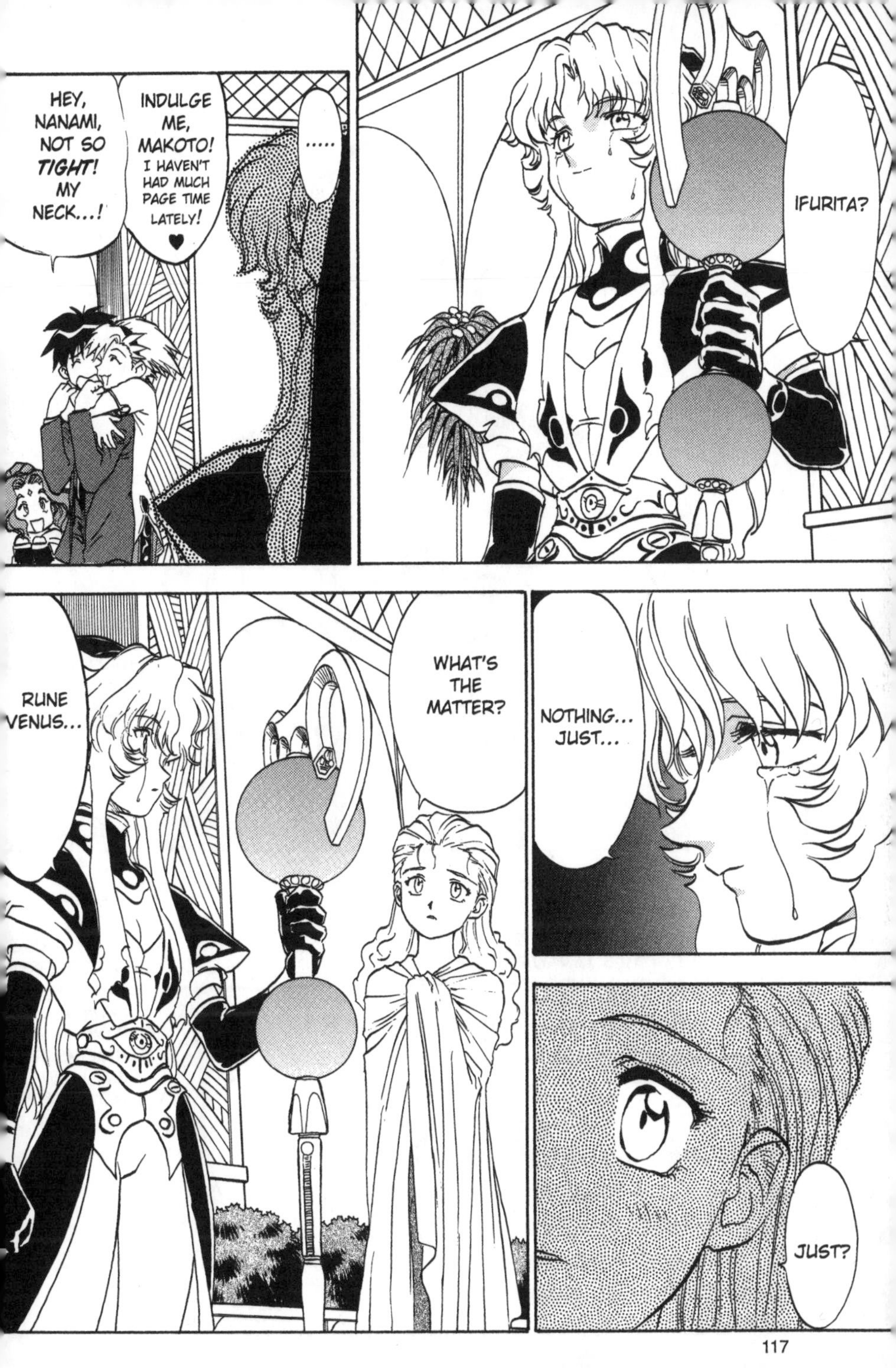
IFURITA?
.....
INDULGE ME, MAKOTO! I HAVEN'T HAD MUCH PAGE TIME LATELY! ♥
HEY, NANAMI, NOT SO TIGHT! MY NECK...!
NOTHING... JUST...
WHAT'S THE MATTER?
RUNE VENUS...
JUST?

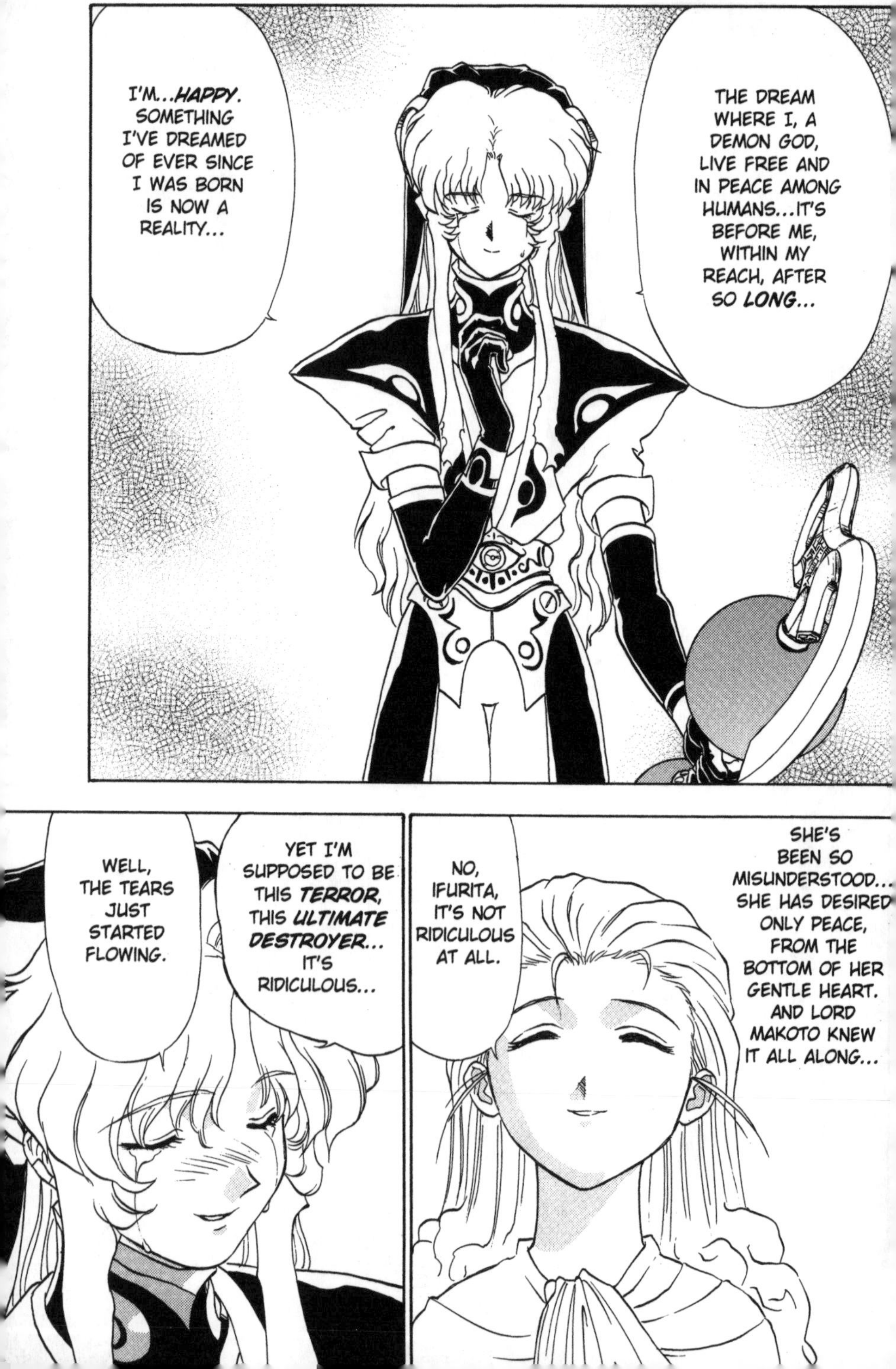
I'M...*HAPPY*. SOMETHING I'VE DREAMED OF EVER SINCE I WAS BORN IS NOW A REALITY...
THE DREAM WHERE I, A DEMON GOD, LIVE FREE AND IN PEACE AMONG HUMANS...IT'S BEFORE ME, WITHIN MY REACH, AFTER SO *LONG*...
WELL, THE TEARS JUST STARTED FLOWING.
YET I'M SUPPOSED TO BE THIS *TERROR*, THIS *ULTIMATE DESTROYER*... IT'S RIDICULOUS...
NO, IFURITA, IT'S NOT RIDICULOUS AT ALL.
SHE'S BEEN SO MISUNDERSTOOD... SHE HAS DESIRED ONLY PEACE, FROM THE BOTTOM OF HER GENTLE HEART. AND LORD MAKOTO KNEW IT ALL ALONG...

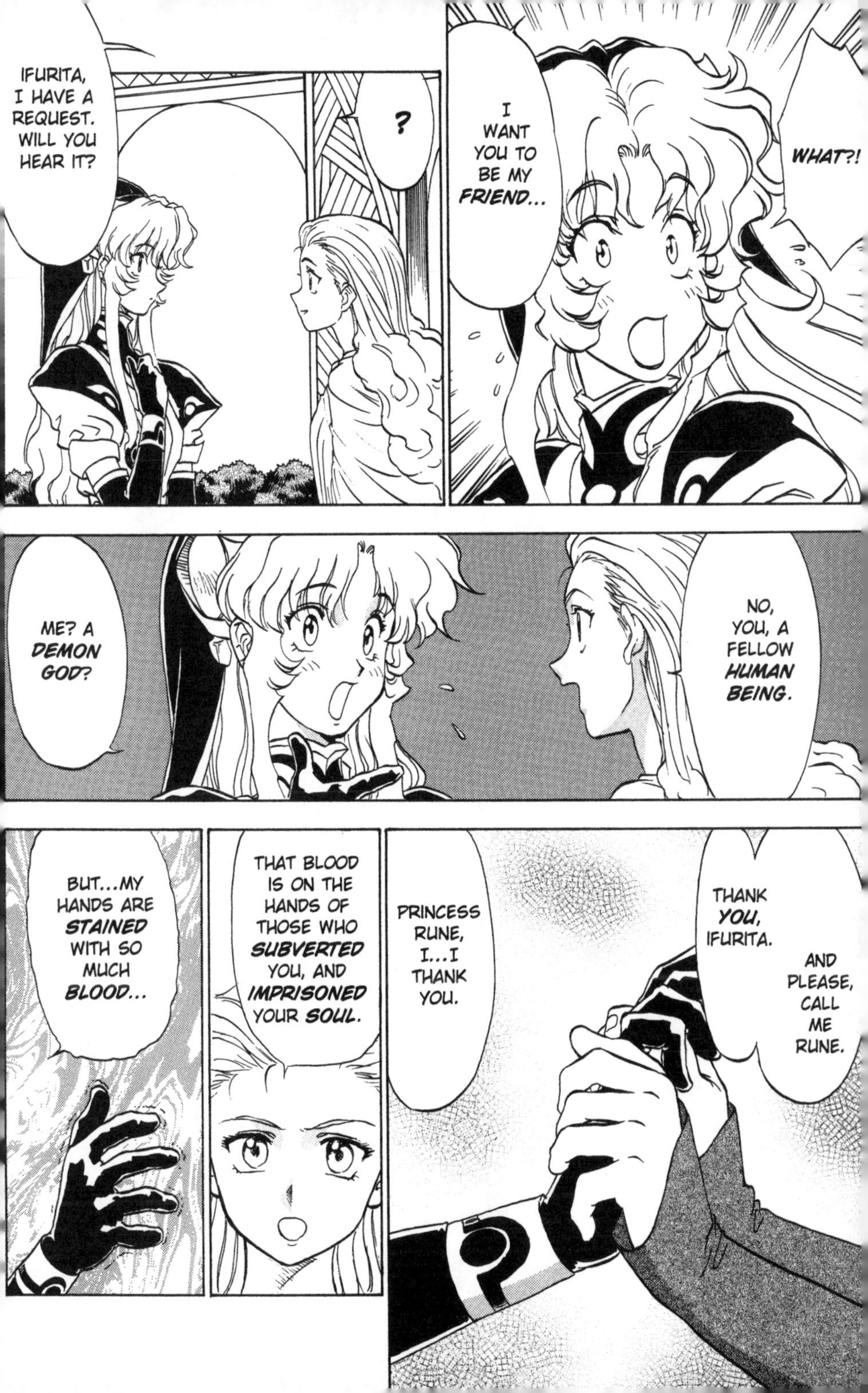
IFURITA, I HAVE A REQUEST. WILL YOU HEAR IT?
?
I WANT YOU TO BE MY FRIEND...
WHAT?!
ME? A DEMON GOD?
NO, YOU, A FELLOW HUMAN BEING.
BUT...MY HANDS ARE STAINED WITH SO MUCH BLOOD...
THAT BLOOD IS ON THE HANDS OF THOSE WHO SUBVERTED YOU, AND IMPRISONED YOUR SOUL.
PRINCESS RUNE, I...I THANK YOU.
THANK YOU, IFURITA.
AND PLEASE, CALL ME RUNE.

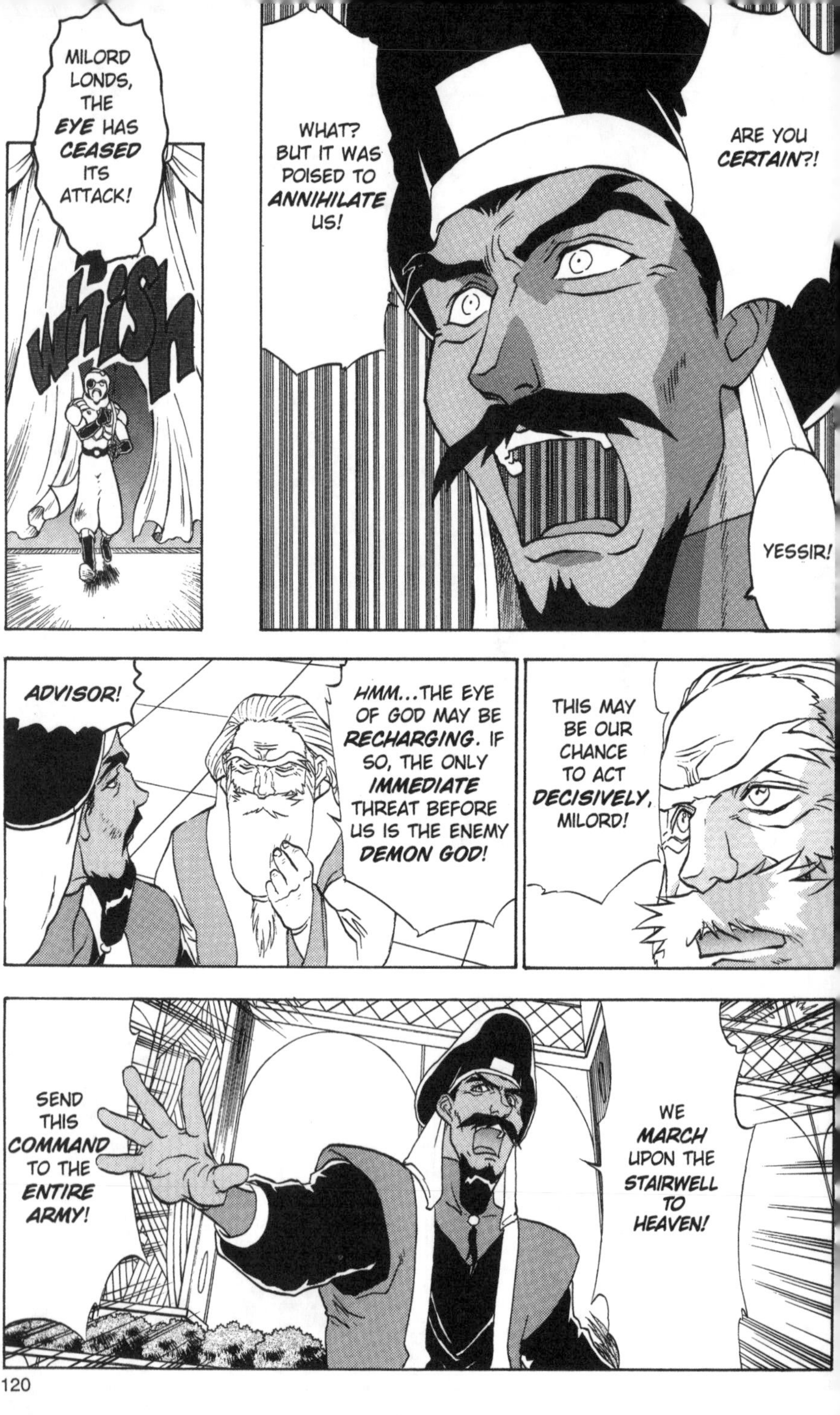
MILORD LONDS, THE EYE HAS CEASED ITS ATTACK!
WHISH
ARE YOU CERTAIN?!
WHAT? BUT IT WAS POISED TO ANNIHILATE US!
YESSIR!
ADVISOR!
HMM...THE EYE OF GOD MAY BE RECHARGING. IF SO, THE ONLY IMMEDIATE THREAT BEFORE US IS THE ENEMY DEMON GOD!
THIS MAY BE OUR CHANCE TO ACT DECISIVELY, MILORD!
SEND THIS COMMAND TO THE ENTIRE ARMY!
WE MARCH UPON THE STAIRWELL TO HEAVEN!

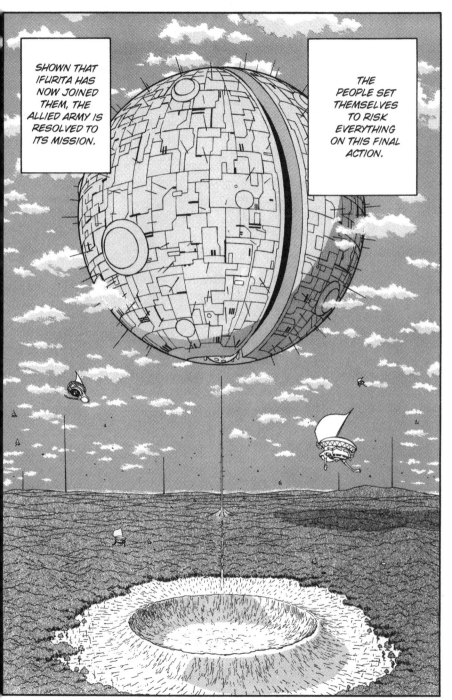

SHOWN THAT IFURITA HAS NOW JOINED THEM, THE ALLIED ARMY IS RESOLVED TO ITS MISSION.

THE PEOPLE SET THEMSELVES TO RISK EVERYTHING ON THIS FINAL ACTION.

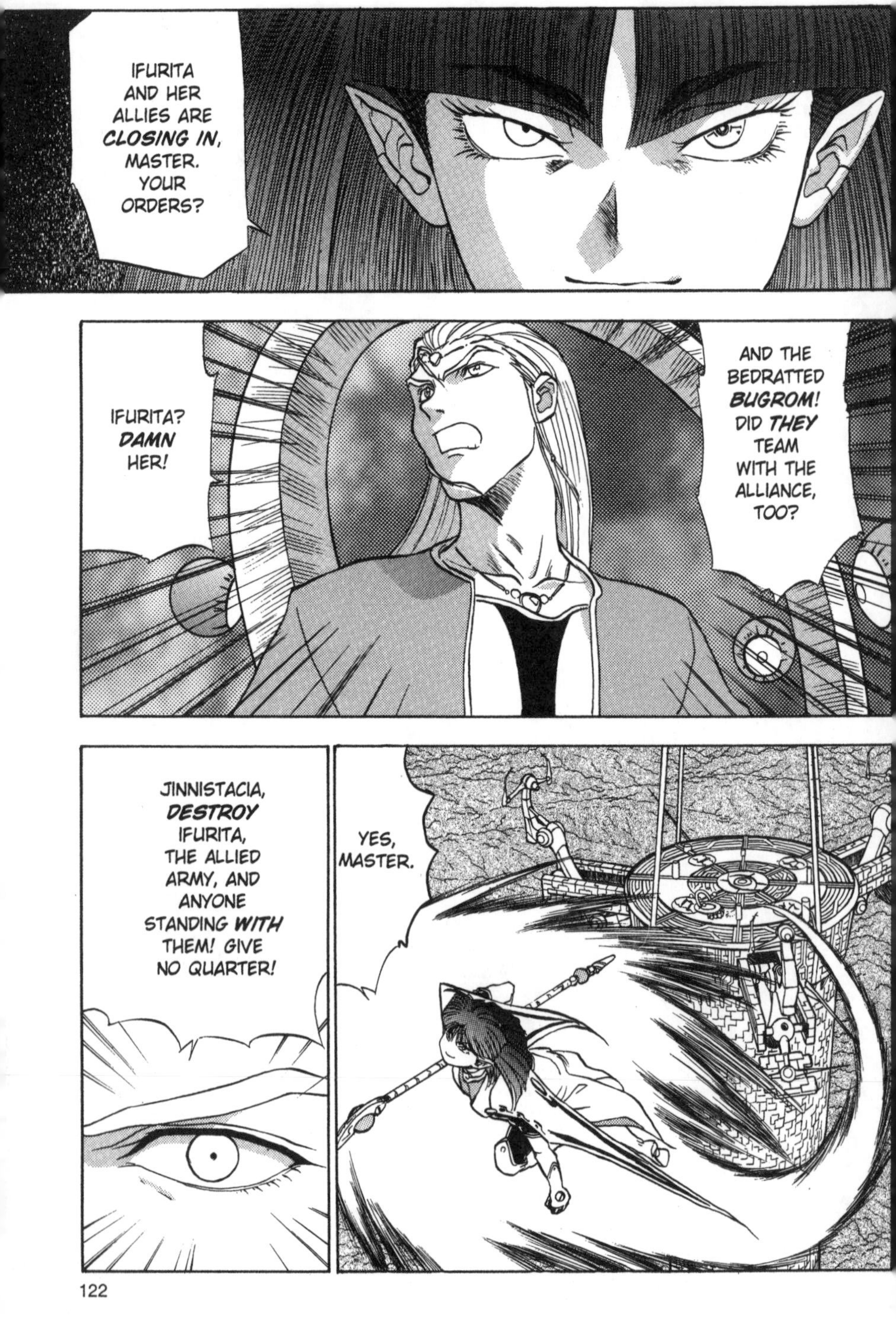
IFURITA AND HER ALLIES ARE **CLOSING IN**, MASTER. YOUR ORDERS?
AND THE BEDRATTED **BUGROM**! DID **THEY** TEAM WITH THE ALLIANCE, TOO?
IFURITA? **DAMN** HER!
JINNISTACIA, **DESTROY** IFURITA, THE ALLIED ARMY, AND ANYONE STANDING **WITH** THEM! GIVE NO QUARTER!
YES, MASTER.

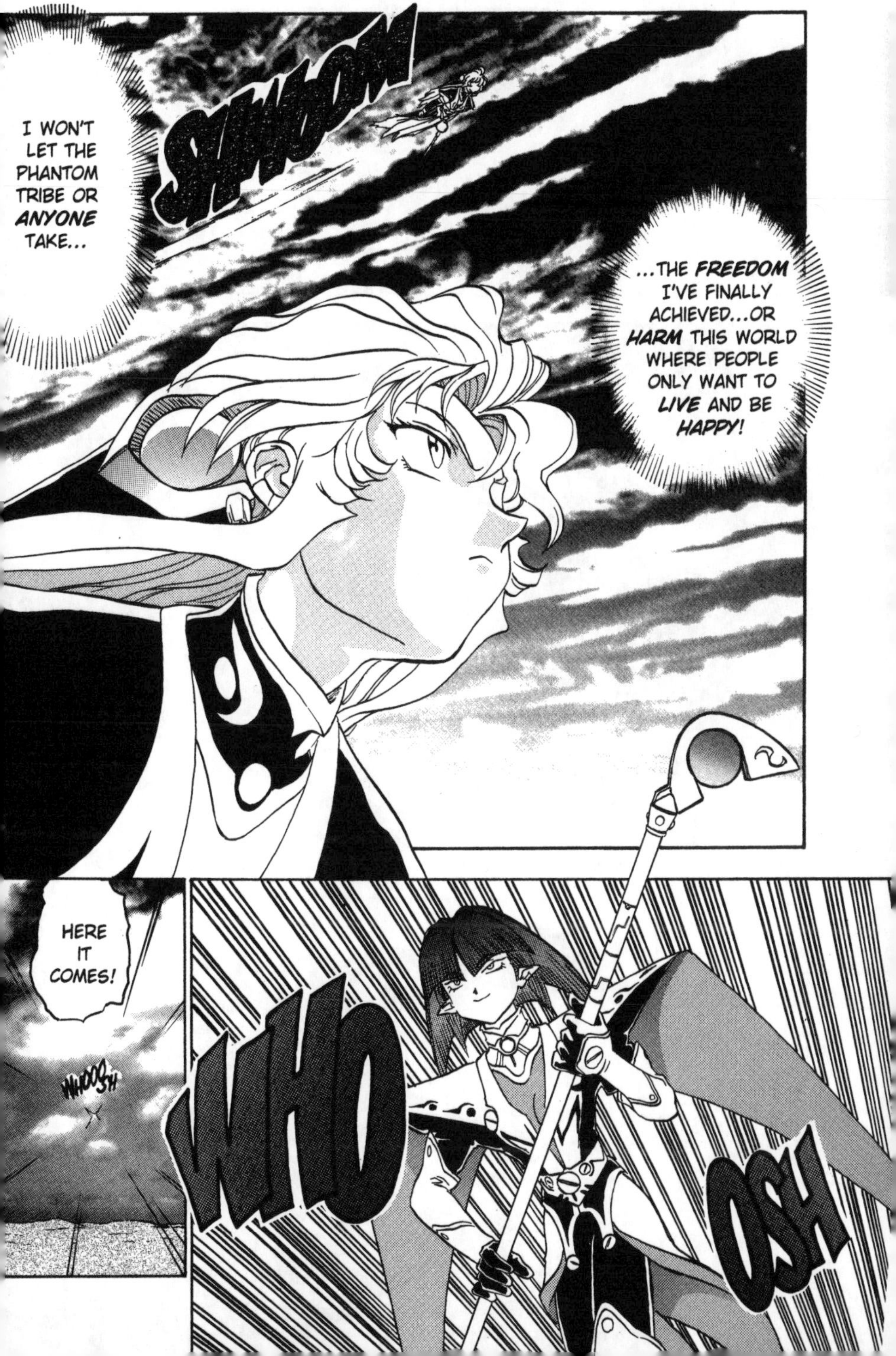
SHWOOM
I WON'T LET THE PHANTOM TRIBE OR ANYONE TAKE...
...THE FREEDOM I'VE FINALLY ACHIEVED...OR HARM THIS WORLD WHERE PEOPLE ONLY WANT TO LIVE AND BE HAPPY!
HERE IT COMES!
WHOOSH
WHOOSH

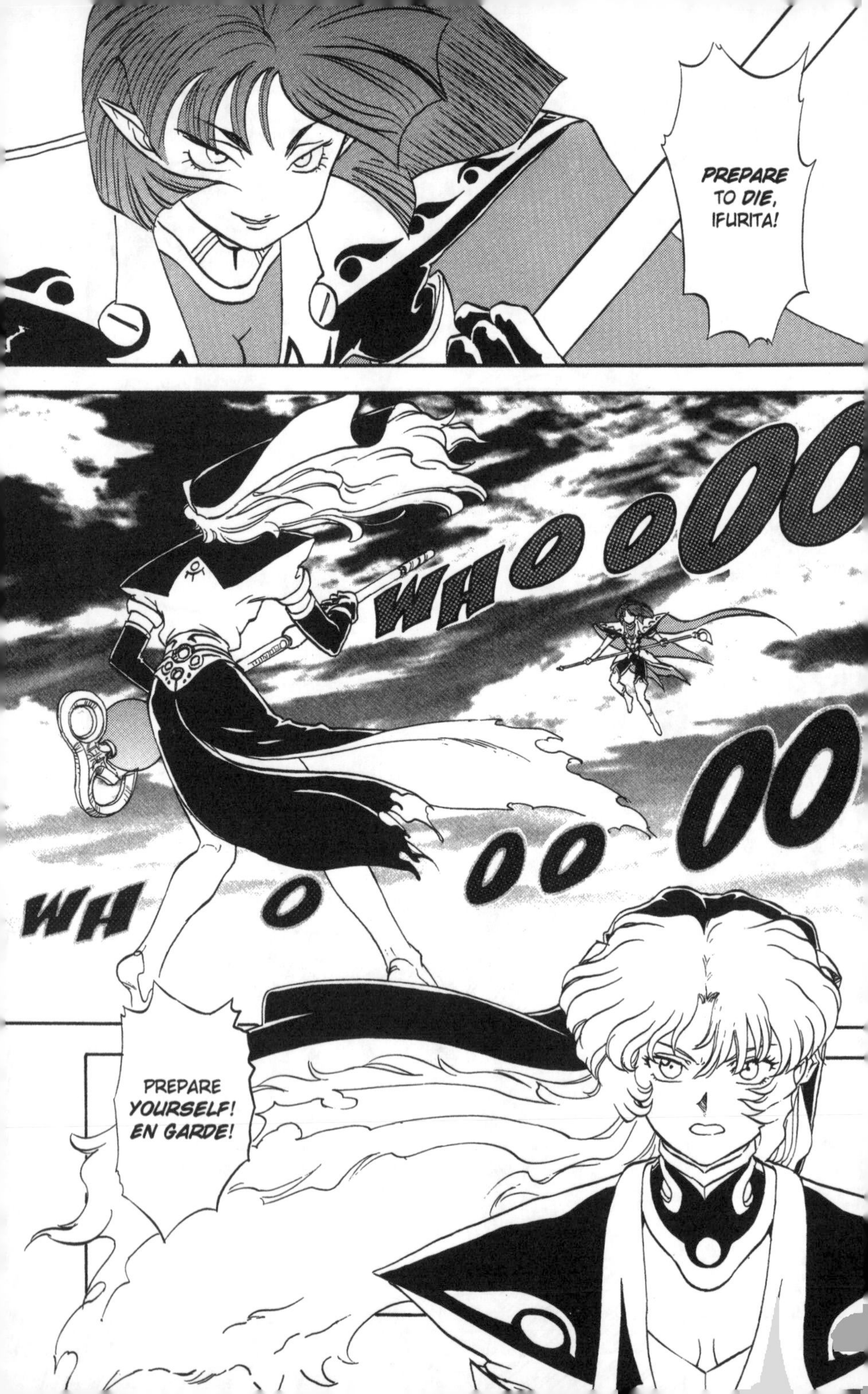

PREPARE TO DIE, IFURITA!
WHOOOOOO
WHOOOOOO
PREPARE YOURSELF! EN GARDE!

EPISODE 15

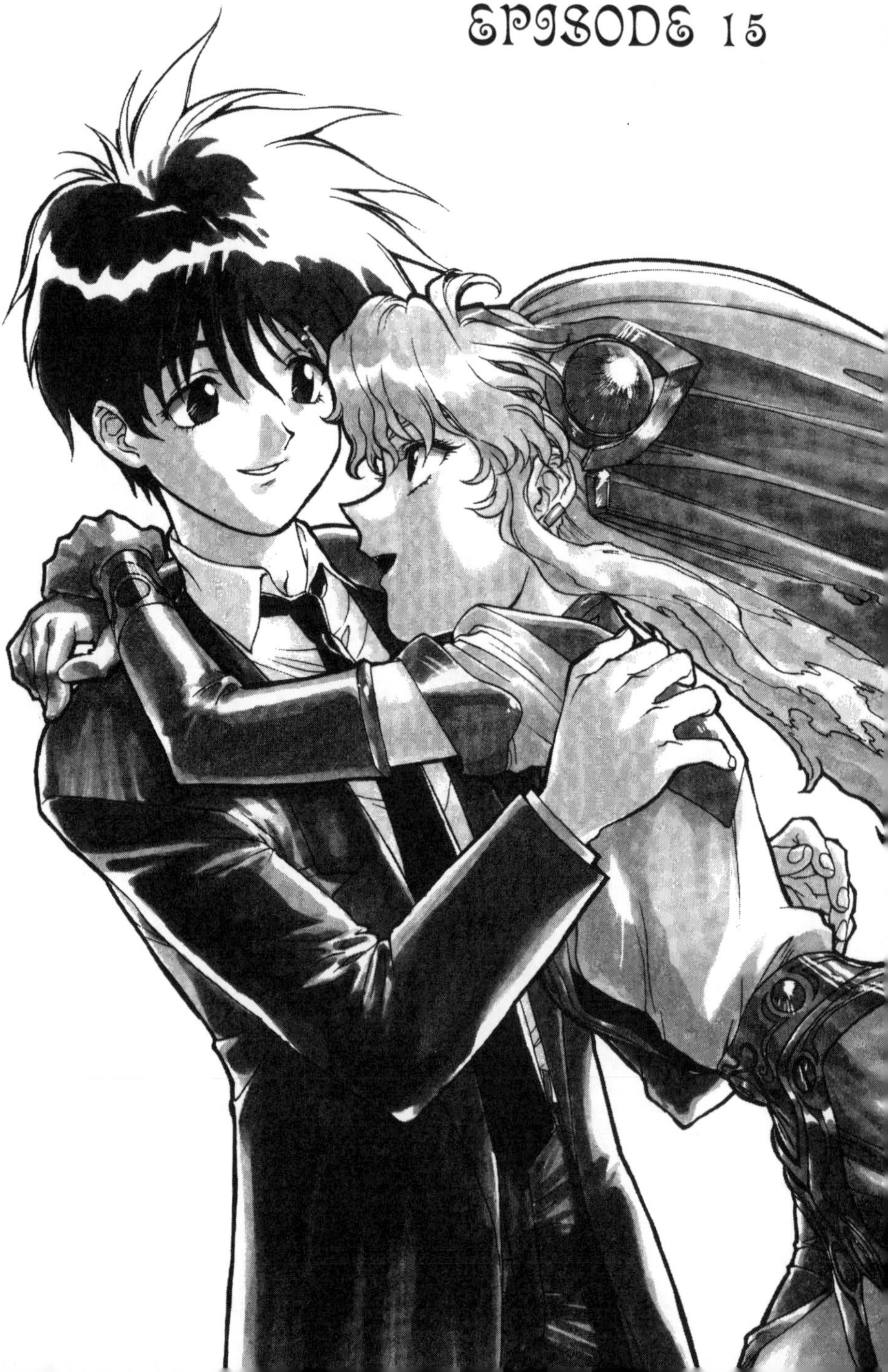

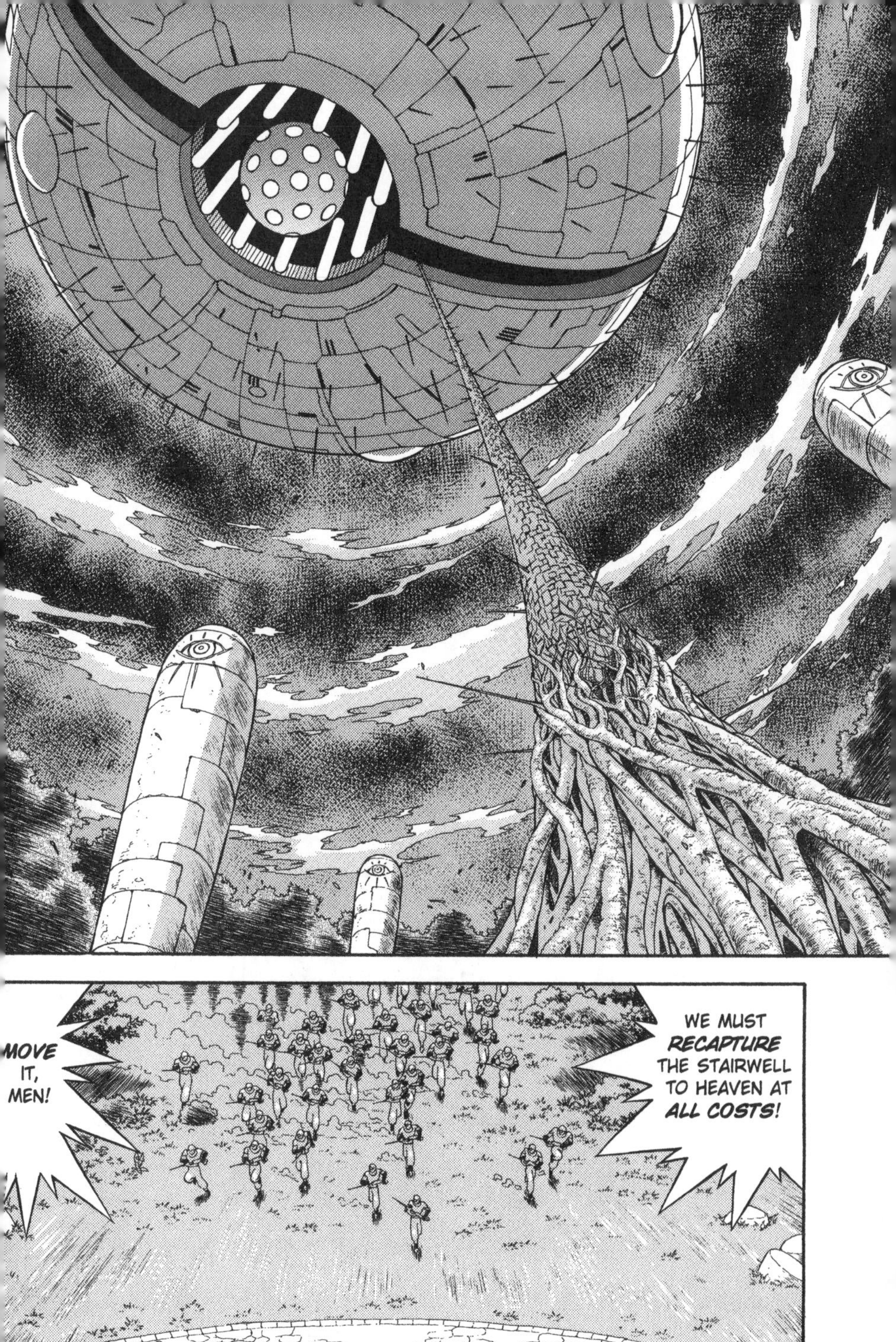
WE MUST RECAPTURE THE STAIRWELL TO HEAVEN AT ALL COSTS!
MOVE IT, MEN!

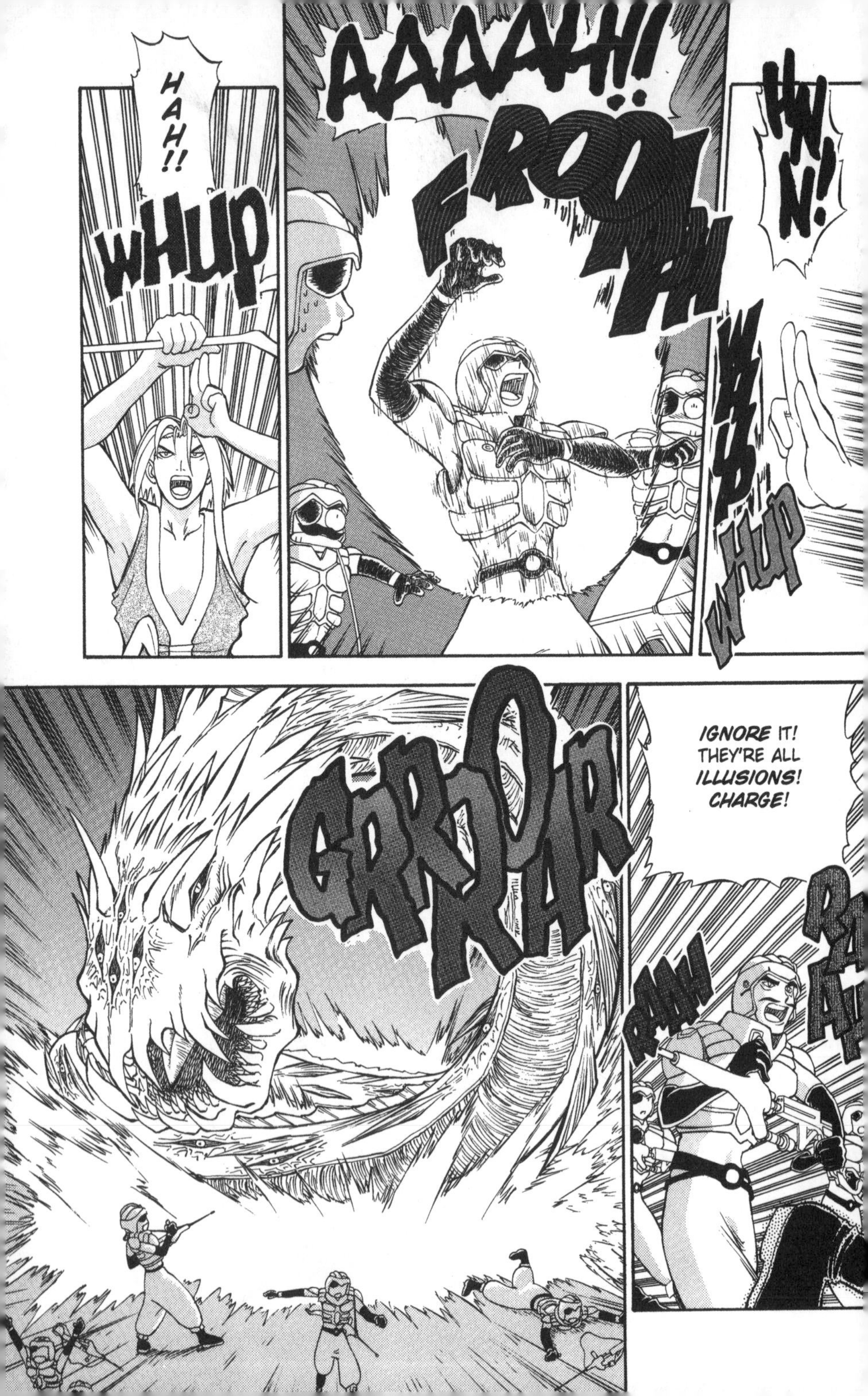
HAH!!
wHUP
AAAAH!!
FROOM
HNNN!
WHUP
GRRROAR
IGNORE IT! THEY'RE ALL ILLUSIONS! CHARGE!
RAAH

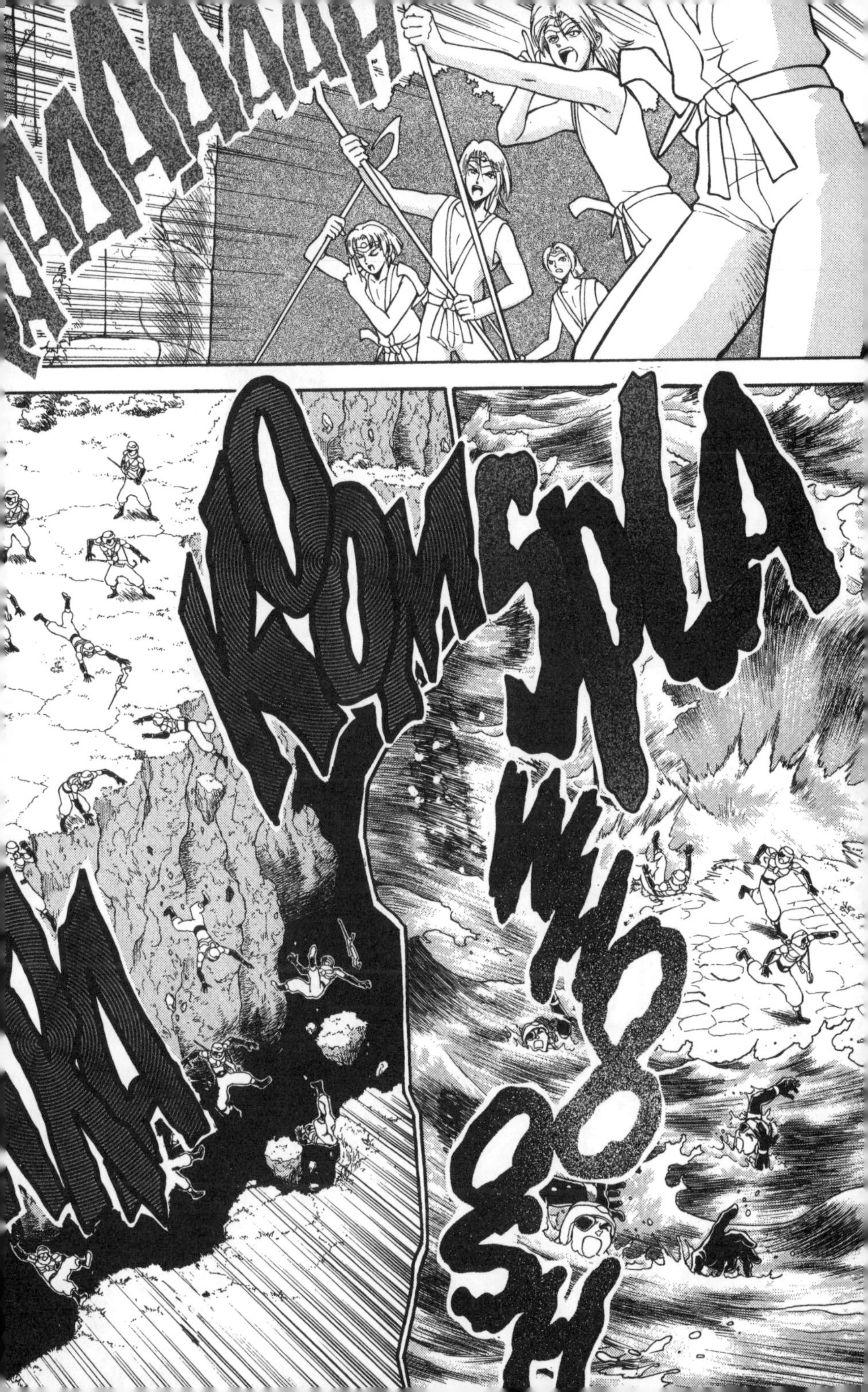

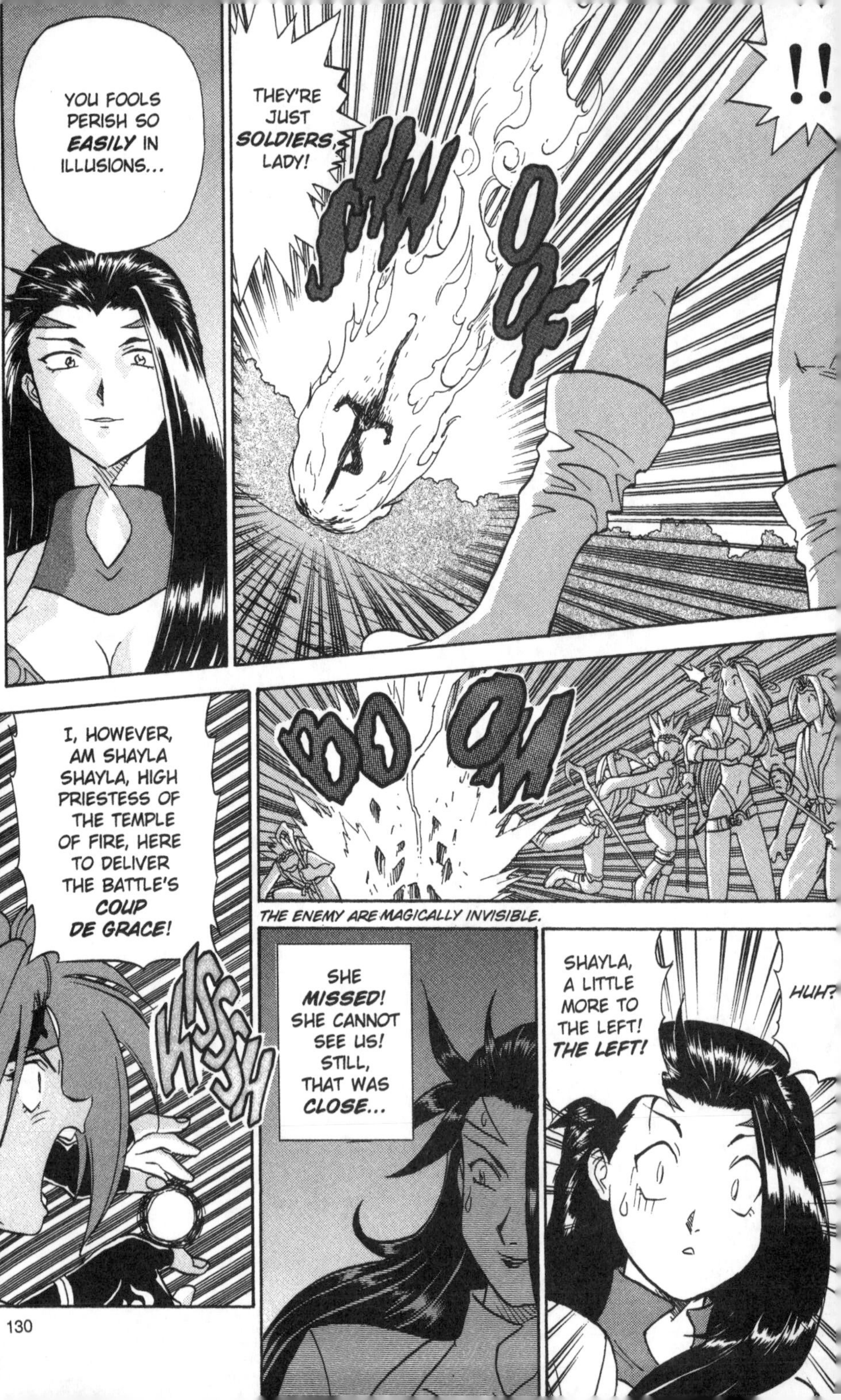
YOU FOOLS PERISH SO EASILY IN ILLUSIONS...
THEY'RE JUST SOLDIERS, LADY!
SHHWOOF
!!
I, HOWEVER, AM SHAYLA SHAYLA, HIGH PRIESTESS OF THE TEMPLE OF FIRE, HERE TO DELIVER THE BATTLE'S COUP DE GRACE!
BOOM
THE ENEMY ARE MAGICALLY INVISIBLE.
WSSSH
SHE MISSED! SHE CANNOT SEE US! STILL, THAT WAS CLOSE...
SHAYLA, A LITTLE MORE TO THE LEFT! THE LEFT!
HUH?

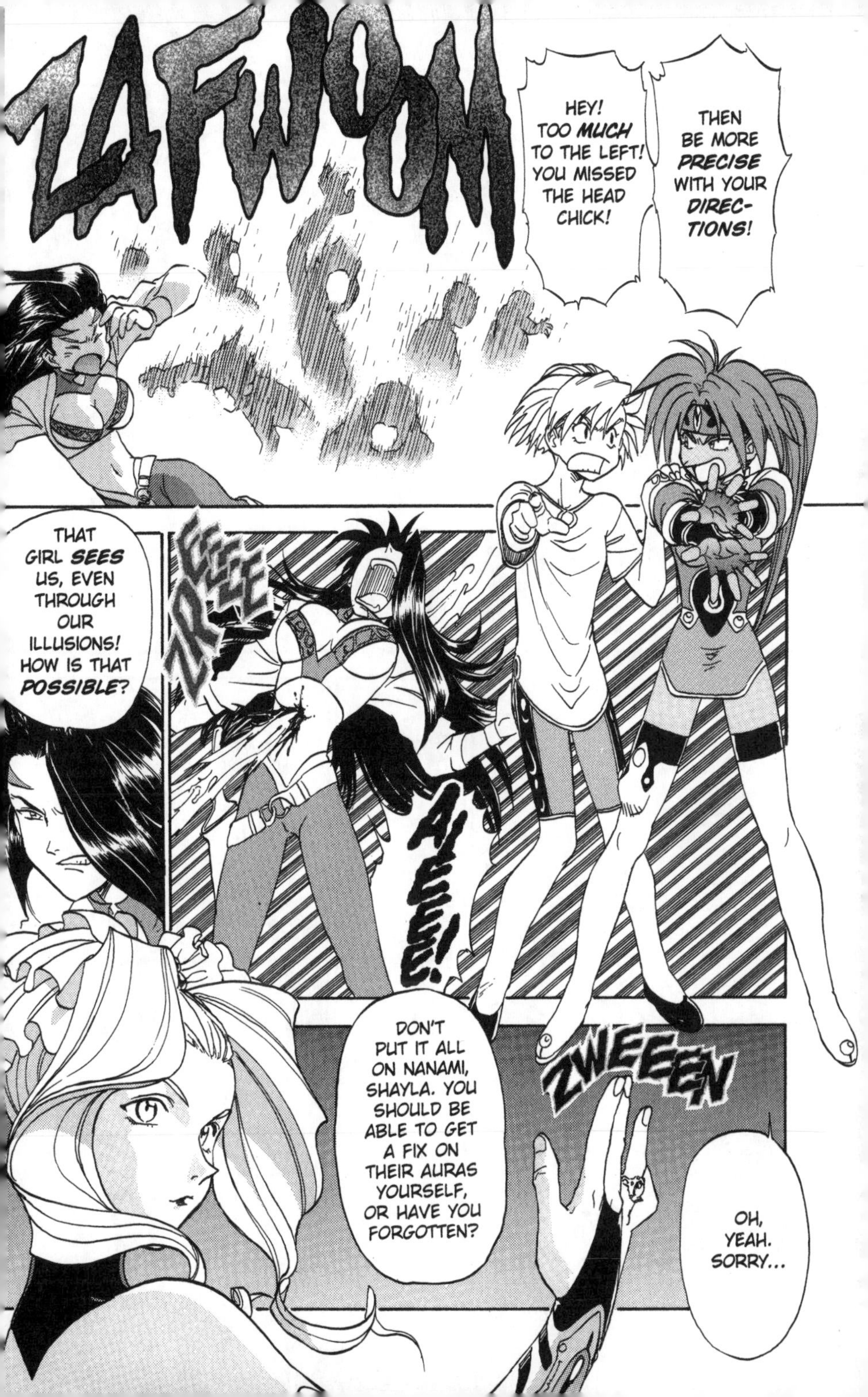
ZAFWOOM
HEY! TOO *MUCH* TO THE LEFT! YOU MISSED THE HEAD CHICK!
THEN BE MORE *PRECISE* WITH YOUR *DIRECTIONS!*
THAT GIRL *SEES* US, EVEN THROUGH OUR ILLUSIONS! HOW IS THAT *POSSIBLE?*
AIEEEE!
DON'T PUT IT ALL ON NANAMI, SHAYLA. YOU SHOULD BE ABLE TO GET A FIX ON THEIR AURAS YOURSELF, OR HAVE YOU FORGOTTEN?
ZWEEEN
OH, YEAH. SORRY...

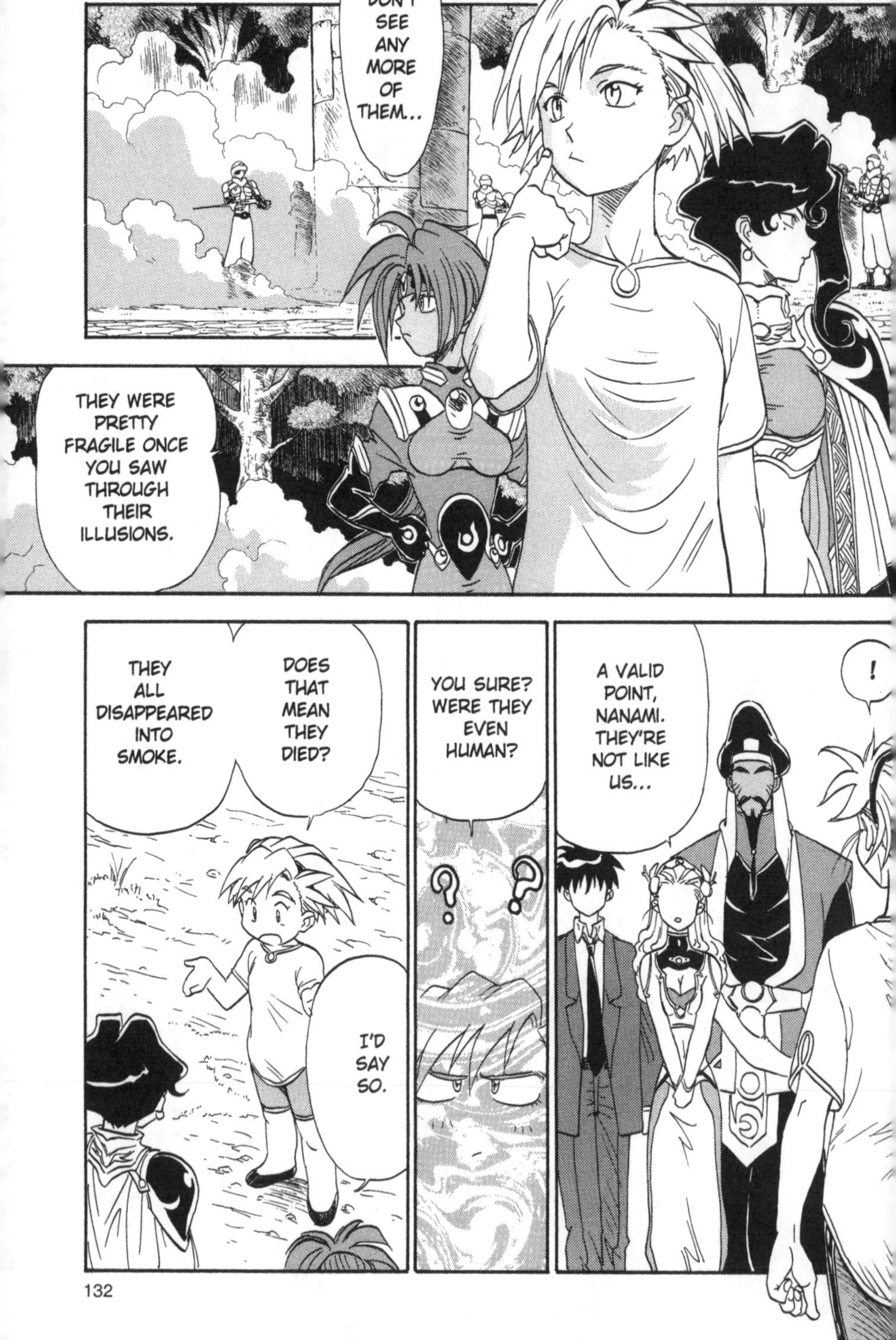
I DON'T SEE ANY MORE OF THEM...
THEY WERE PRETTY FRAGILE ONCE YOU SAW THROUGH THEIR ILLUSIONS.
THEY ALL DISAPPEARED INTO SMOKE.
DOES THAT MEAN THEY DIED?
I'D SAY SO.
YOU SURE? WERE THEY EVEN HUMAN?
A VALID POINT, NANAMI. THEY'RE NOT LIKE US...
!

...AND THAT MAY HAVE KEPT US FROM BEING ABLE TO **UNDERSTAND** EACH OTHER. IT'S A SAD THING...

SUCH TALK'S FOR COUNCIL ROOMS! RIGHT NOW IT'S DOWN TO WHO WINS AND WHO LOSES, WHO **LIVES** AND WHO **DIES**!

WHICH ARE **WE** GOING TO BE, HIGHNESS?

OH, WELL, THE WIN-NERS...

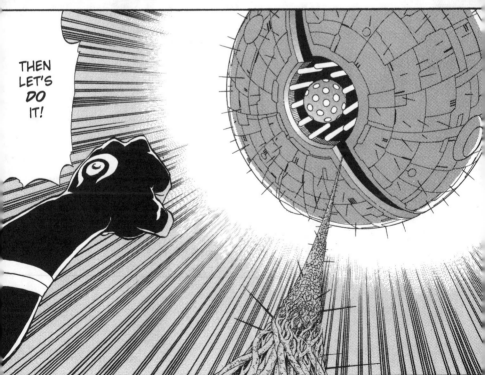

THEN LET'S **DO** IT!

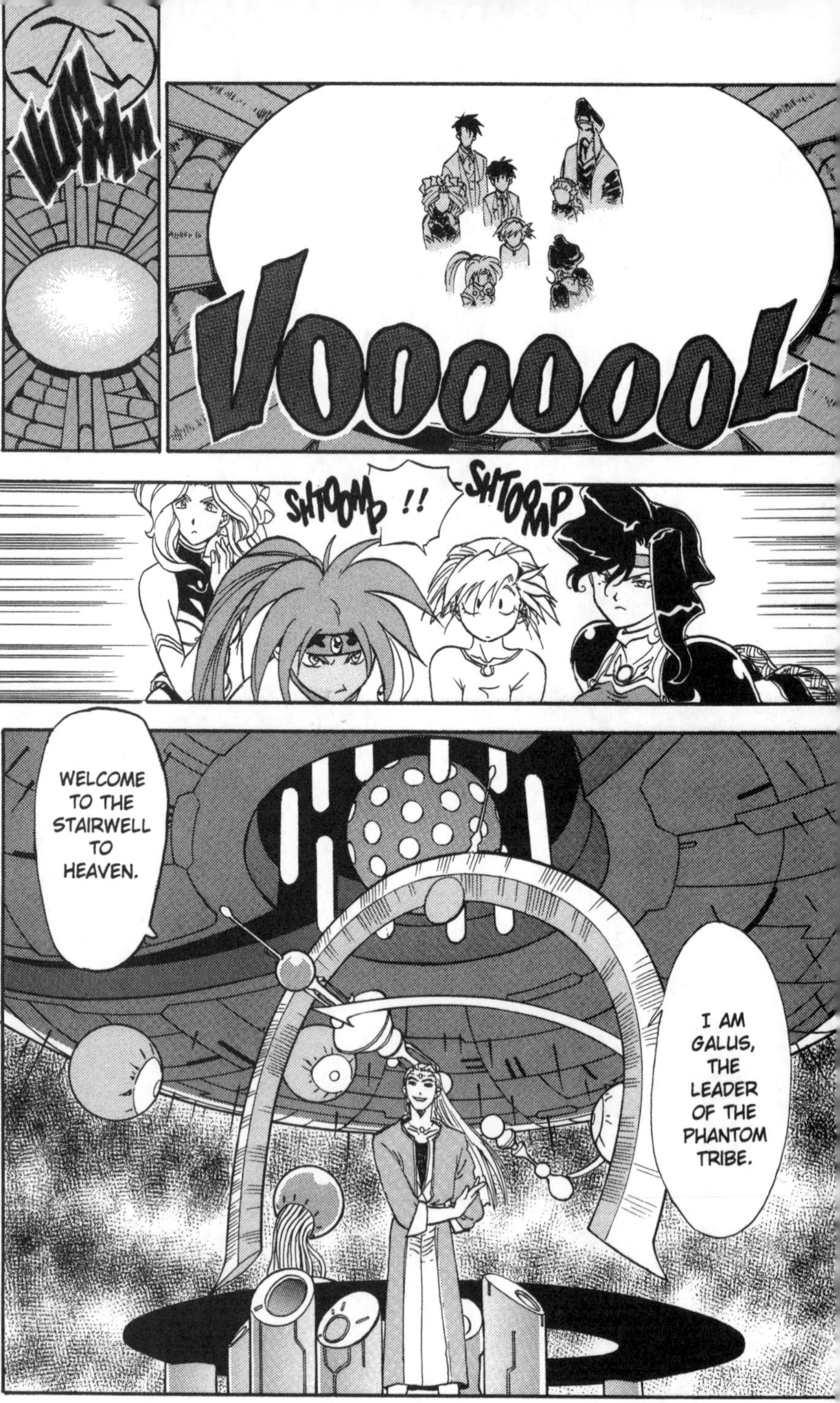
VUMMMM
VOOOOOOL
SHTOOMP
!!
SHTOOMP
WELCOME TO THE STAIRWELL TO HEAVEN.
I AM GALUS, THE LEADER OF THE PHANTOM TRIBE.

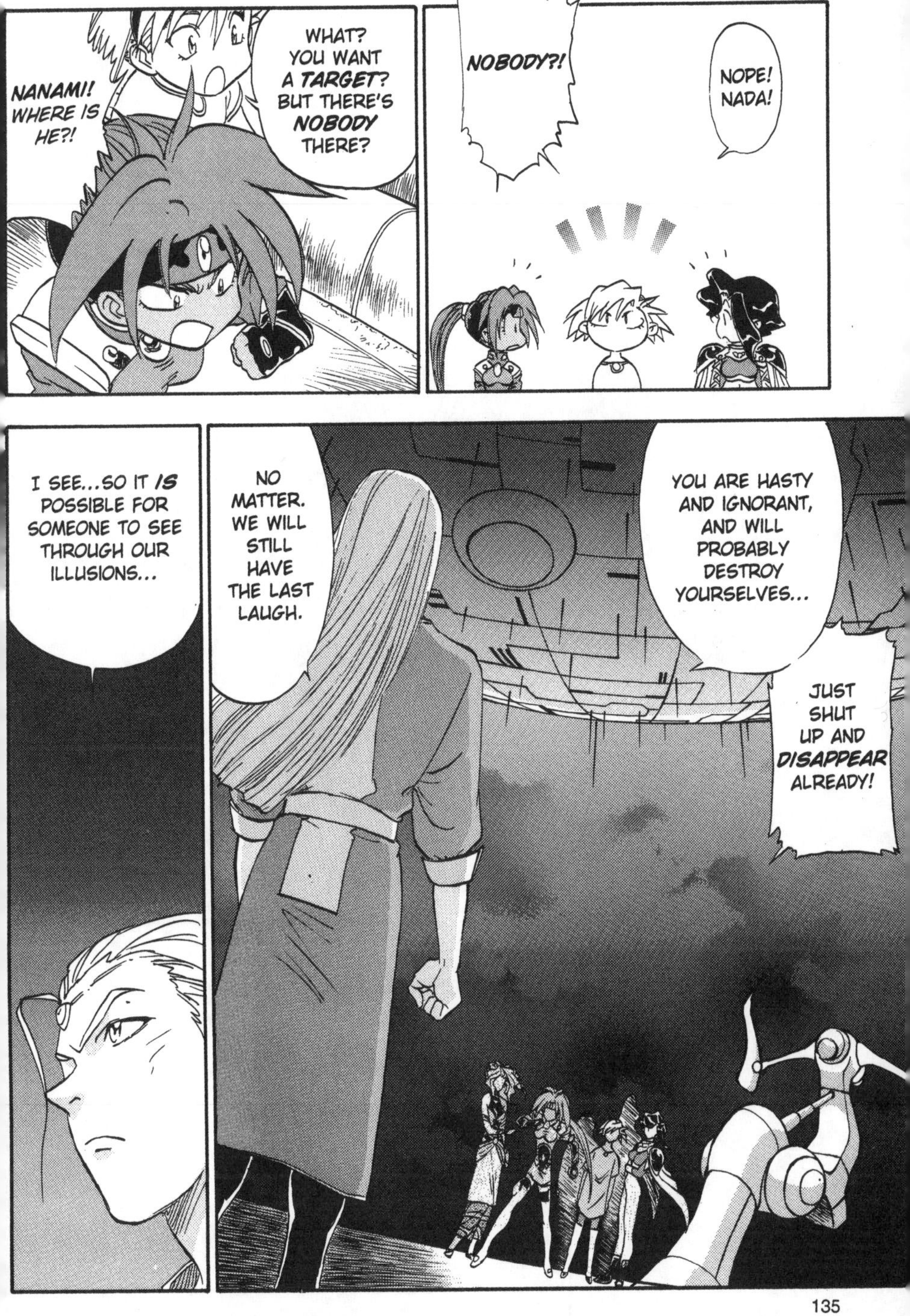
NANAMI! WHERE IS HE?!
WHAT? YOU WANT A *TARGET*? BUT THERE'S *NOBODY* THERE?
NOBODY?!
NOPE! NADA!
I SEE...SO IT *IS* POSSIBLE FOR SOMEONE TO SEE THROUGH OUR ILLUSIONS...
NO MATTER. WE WILL STILL HAVE THE LAST LAUGH.
YOU ARE HASTY AND IGNORANT, AND WILL PROBABLY DESTROY YOURSELVES...
JUST SHUT UP AND *DISAPPEAR* ALREADY!

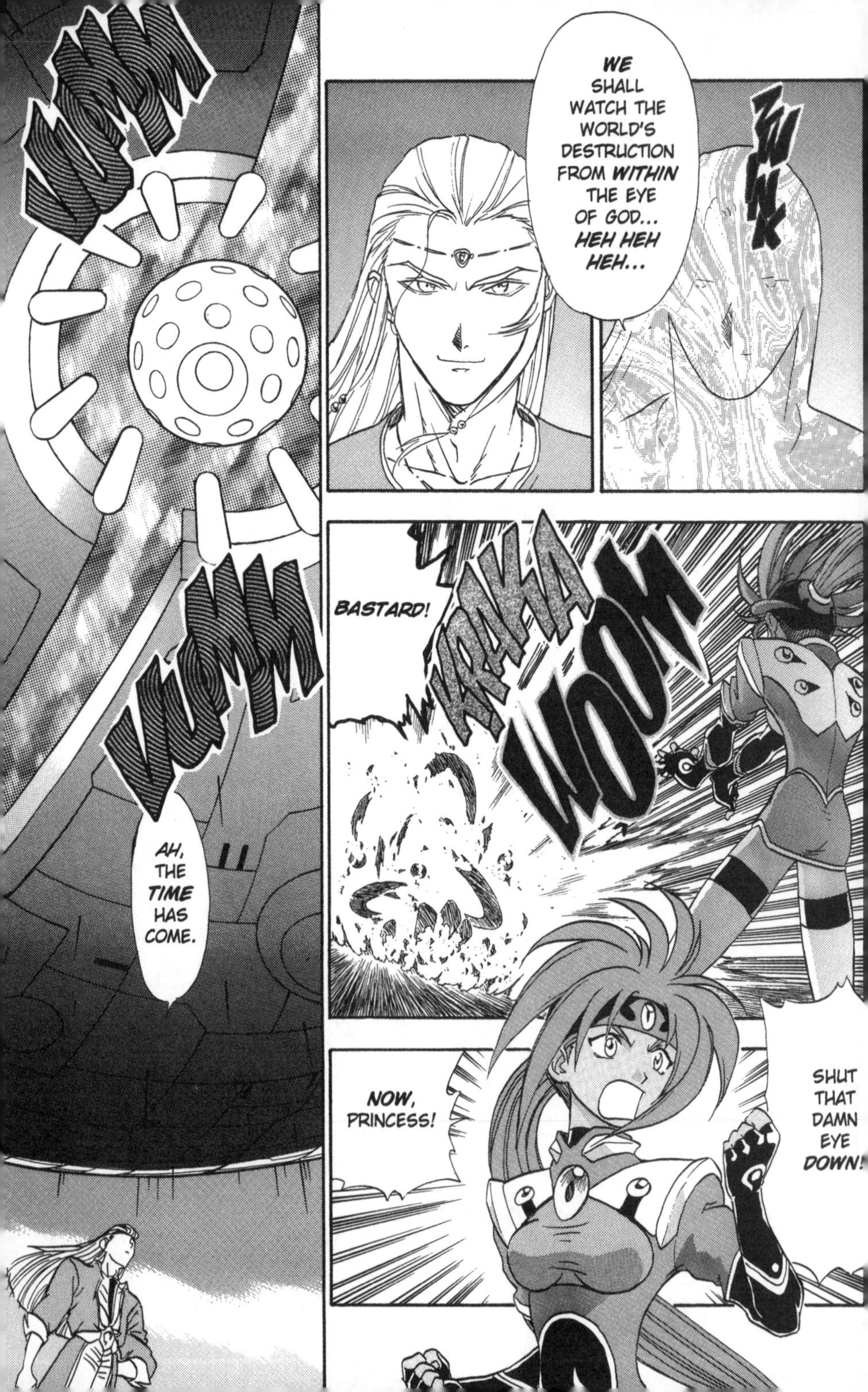

WUMMM
WUMMM
AH, THE TIME HAS COME.
WE SHALL WATCH THE WORLD'S DESTRUCTION FROM WITHIN THE EYE OF GOD... HEH HEH HEH...
ZWINK
BASTARD!
KRAKA WOOM
NOW, PRINCESS!
SHUT THAT DAMN EYE DOWN!

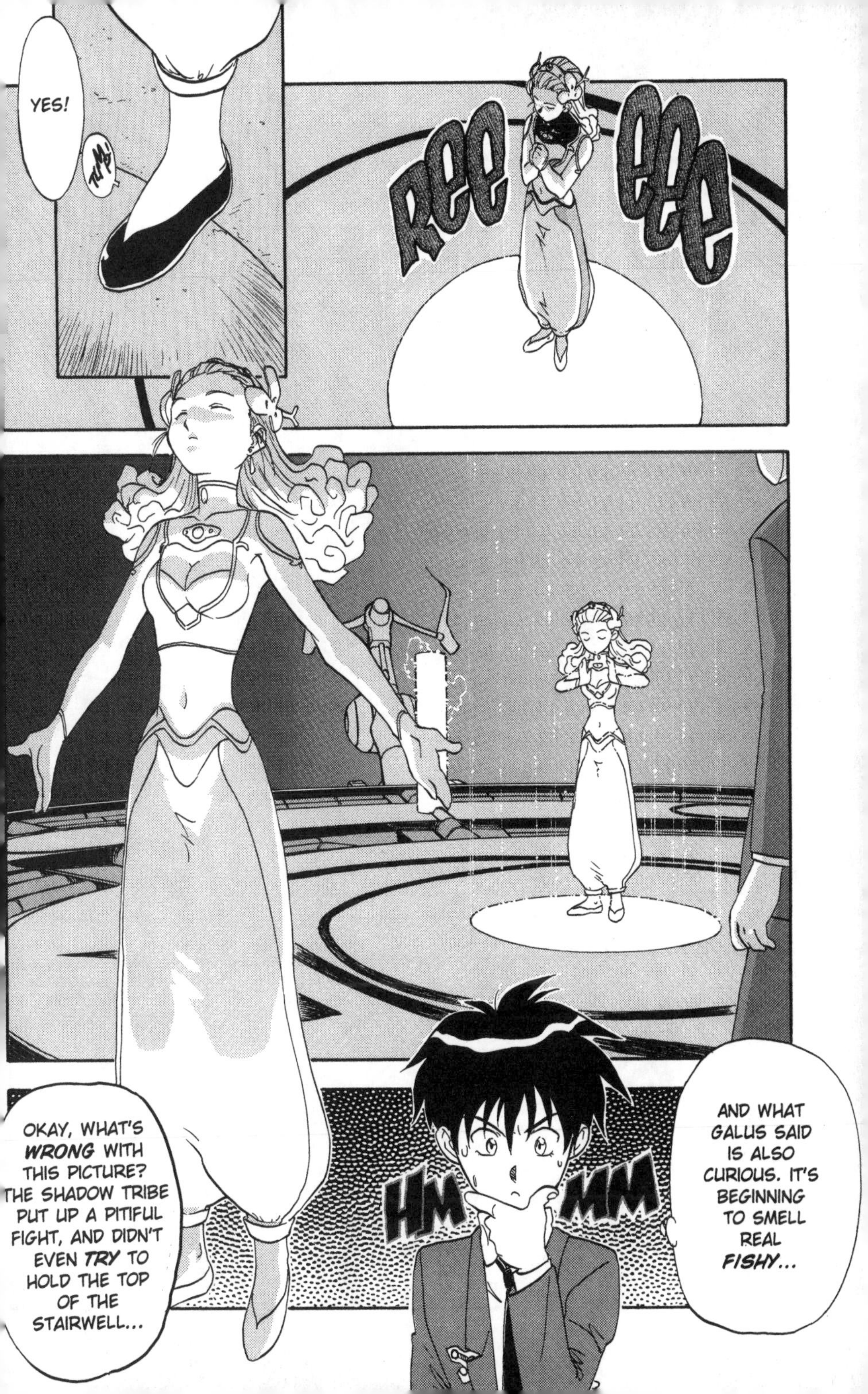
YES!
TUMP!
REE EEE
OKAY, WHAT'S *WRONG* WITH THIS PICTURE? THE SHADOW TRIBE PUT UP A PITIFUL FIGHT, AND DIDN'T EVEN *TRY* TO HOLD THE TOP OF THE STAIRWELL...
HM MM
AND WHAT GALUS SAID IS ALSO CURIOUS. IT'S BEGINNING TO SMELL REAL *FISHY*...

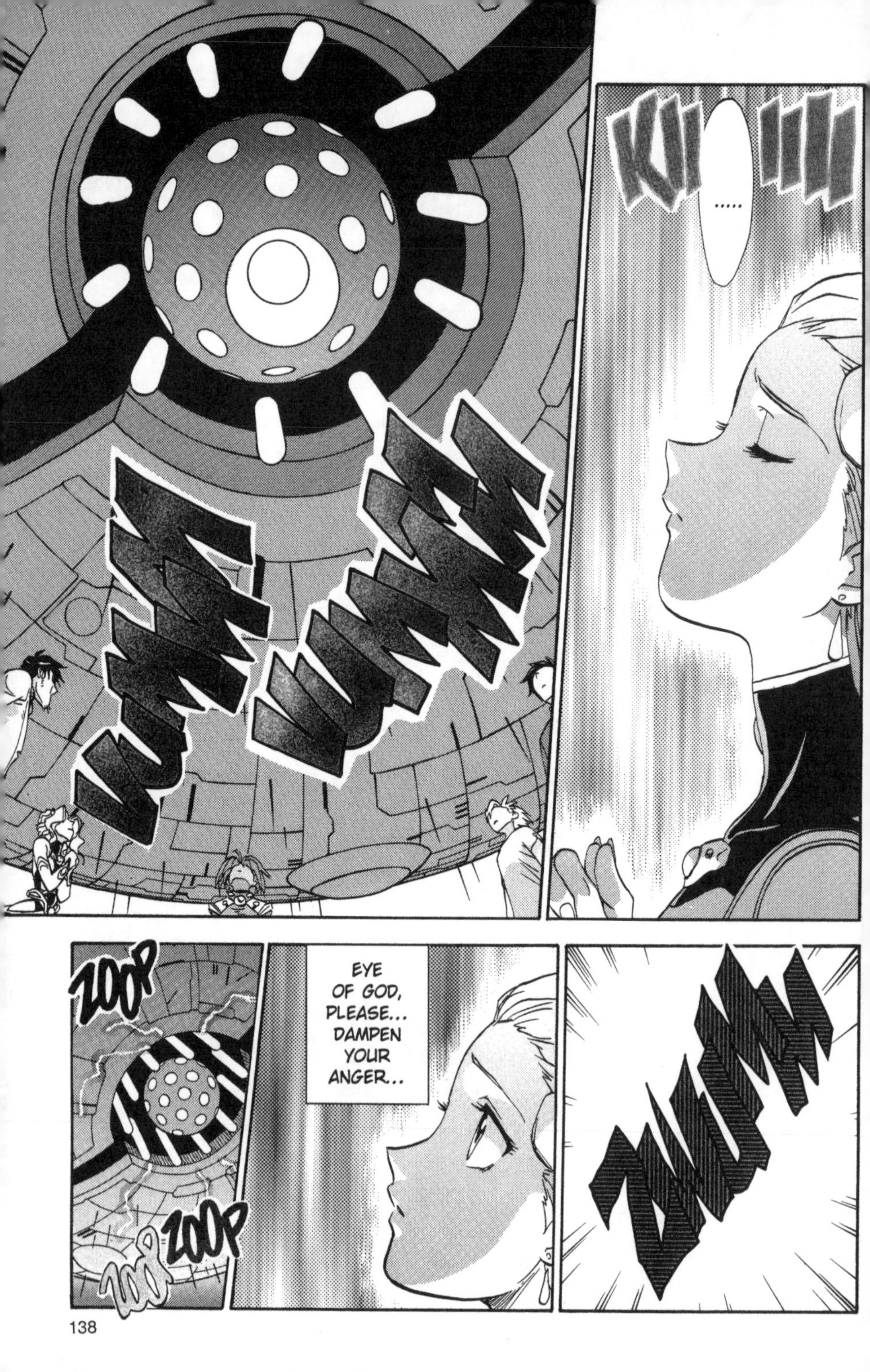
......
EYE OF GOD, PLEASE... DAMPEN YOUR ANGER...
ZOOP
ZOOP

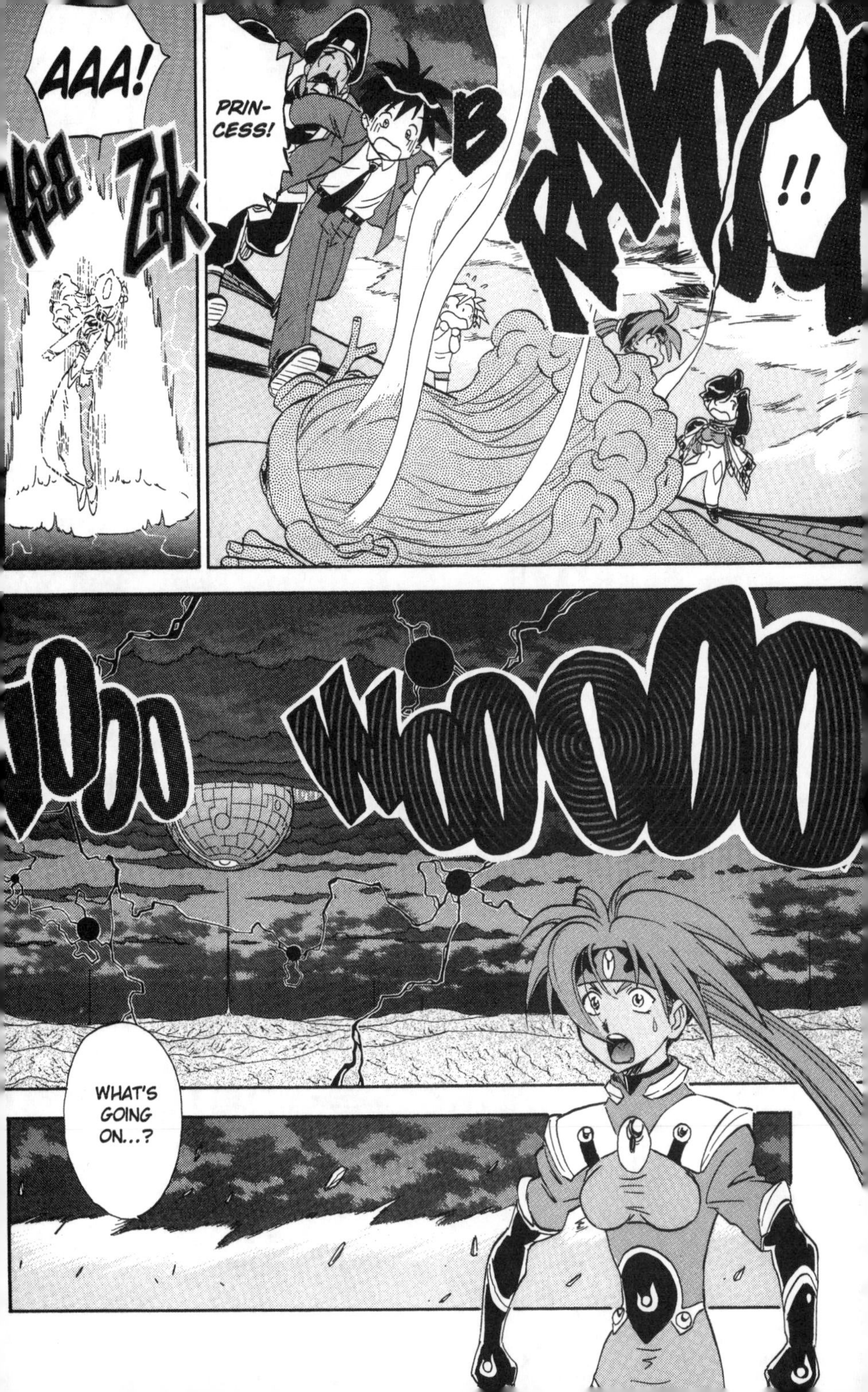
AAA!
ZAK
PRIN-CESS!
!!
WHAT'S GOING ON...?

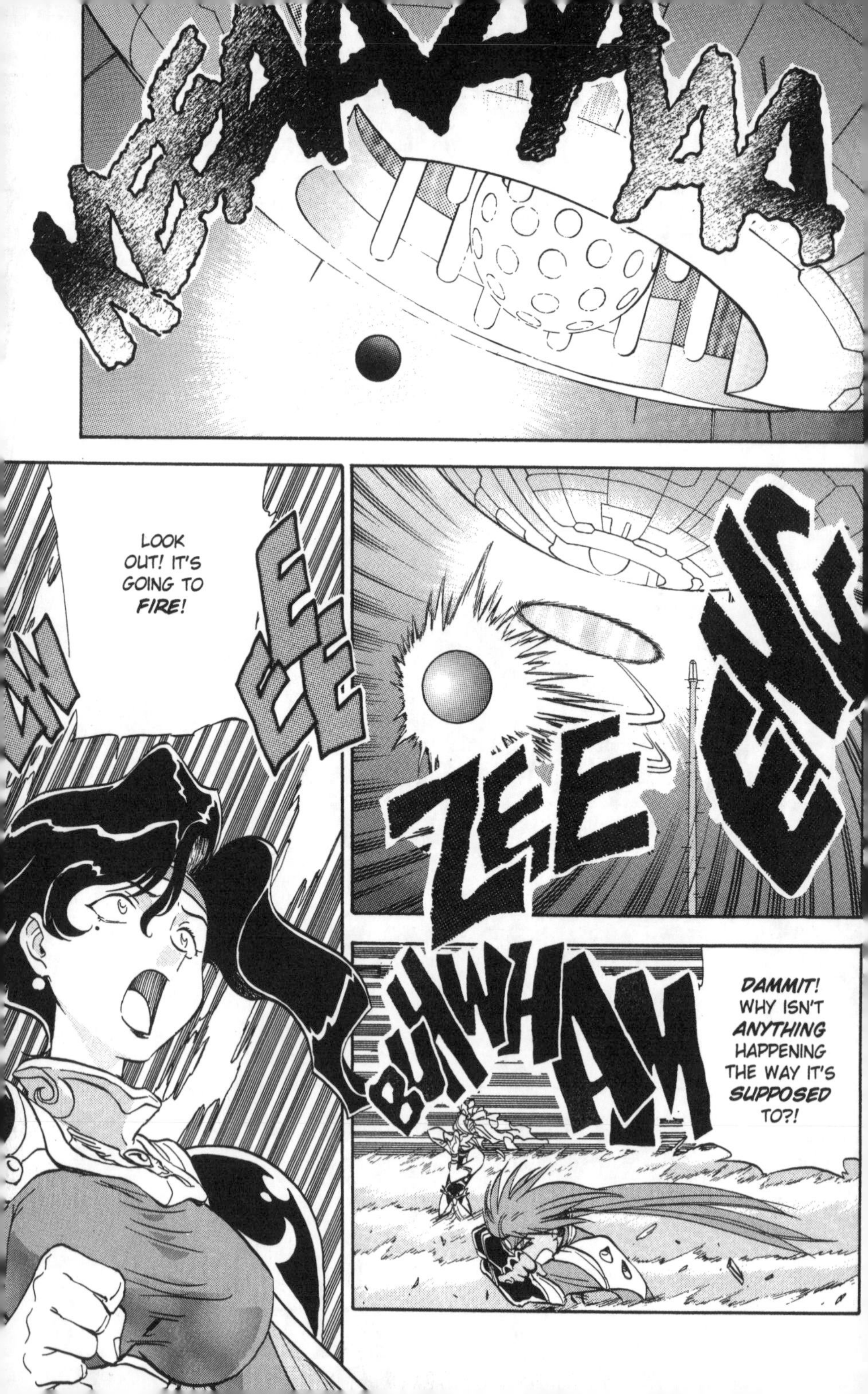
LOOK OUT! IT'S GOING TO *FIRE!*
ZEE
DAMMIT! WHY ISN'T *ANYTHING* HAPPENING THE WAY IT'S *SUPPOSED* TO?!

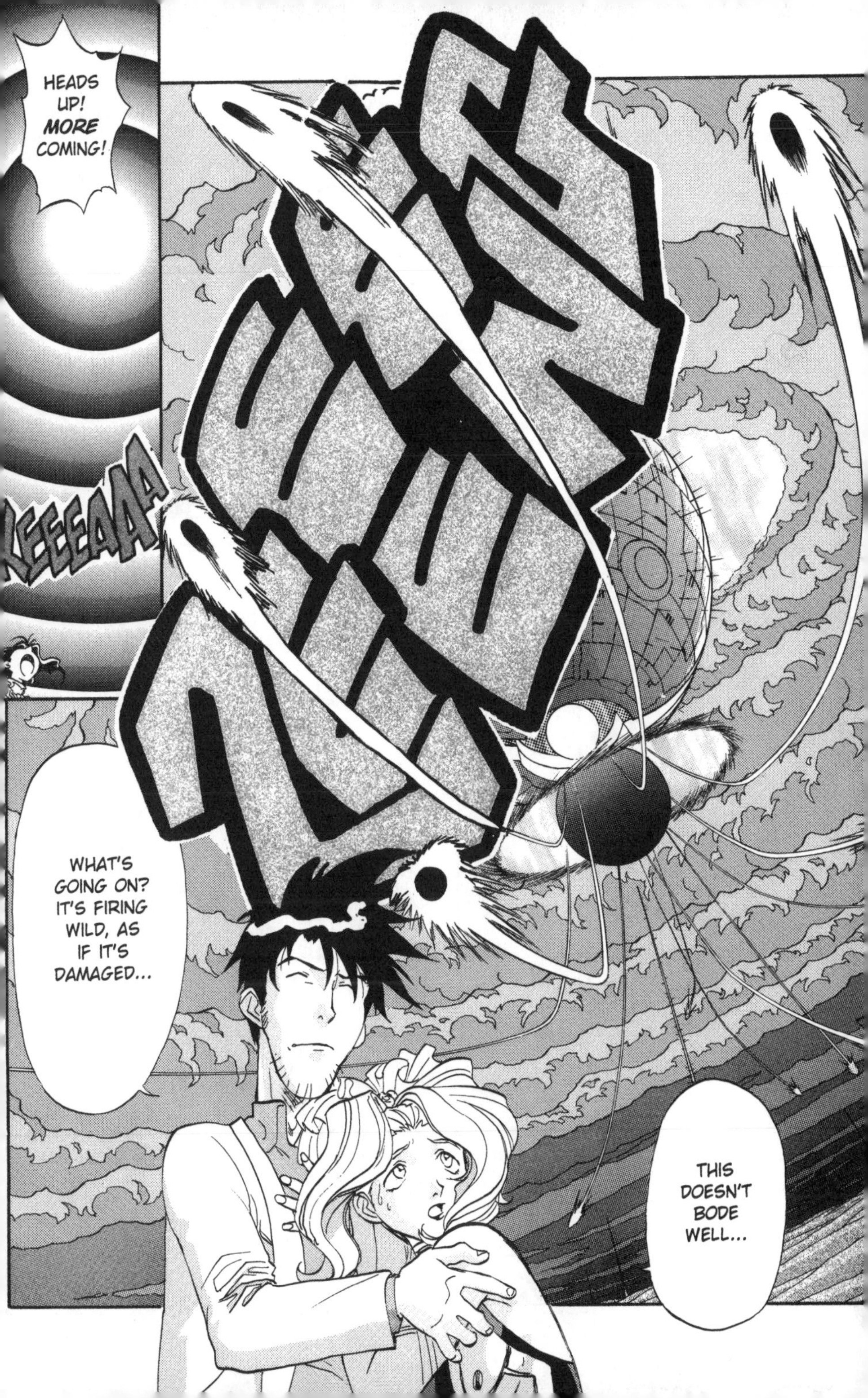
HEADS UP! MORE COMING!
KEEEAAA
WHAT'S GOING ON? IT'S FIRING WILD, AS IF IT'S DAMAGED...
THIS DOESN'T BODE WELL...

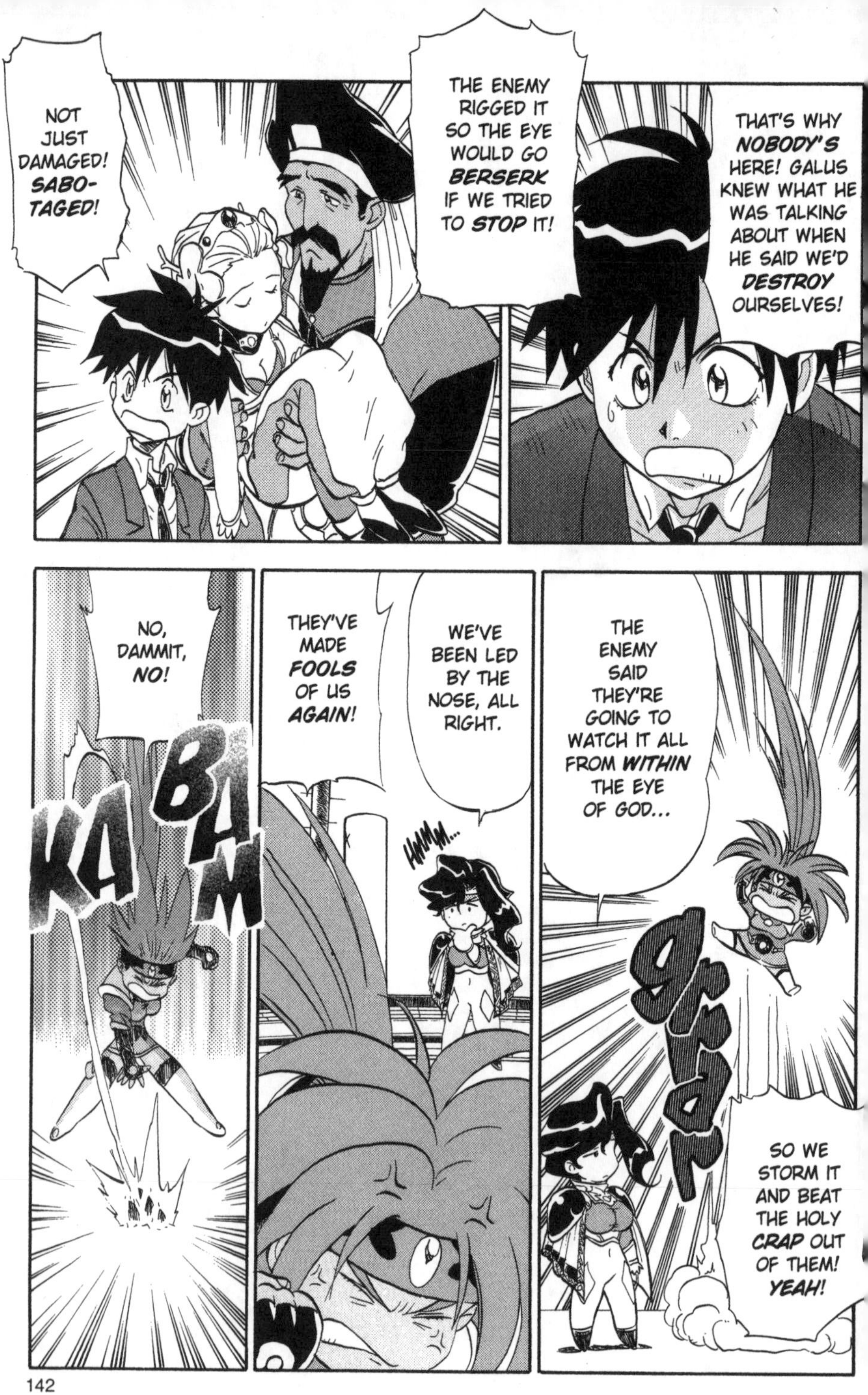
NOT JUST DAMAGED! SABO-TAGED!
THE ENEMY RIGGED IT SO THE EYE WOULD GO BERSERK IF WE TRIED TO STOP IT!
THAT'S WHY NOBODY'S HERE! GALUS KNEW WHAT HE WAS TALKING ABOUT WHEN HE SAID WE'D DESTROY OURSELVES!
THE ENEMY SAID THEY'RE GOING TO WATCH IT ALL FROM WITHIN THE EYE OF GOD...
GRRR
SO WE STORM IT AND BEAT THE HOLY CRAP OUT OF THEM! YEAH!
WE'VE BEEN LED BY THE NOSE, ALL RIGHT.
HMMM...
THEY'VE MADE FOOLS OF US AGAIN!
NO, DAMMIT, NO!
KABAM

NANAMI! WE NEED YOUR *EYES* AGAIN!

SURE THING!

JUST PROMISE YOU'LL *INVEST* IN MY NEW SHOP.

WHAT? YOU WANT TO DRUM UP *FUNDING* AT A TIME LIKE *THIS*?

I MUST GO WITH YOU.

PRINCESS RUNE! WHAT ARE YOU *SAYING*?!

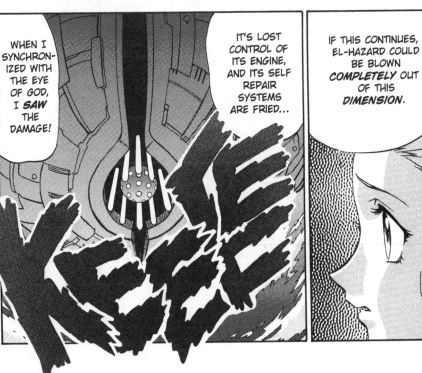

WHEN I SYNCHRONIZED WITH THE EYE OF GOD, I *SAW* THE DAMAGE!

IT'S LOST CONTROL OF ITS ENGINE, AND ITS SELF REPAIR SYSTEMS ARE FRIED...

IF THIS CONTINUES, EL-HAZARD COULD BE BLOWN *COMPLETELY* OUT OF THIS *DIMENSION*.

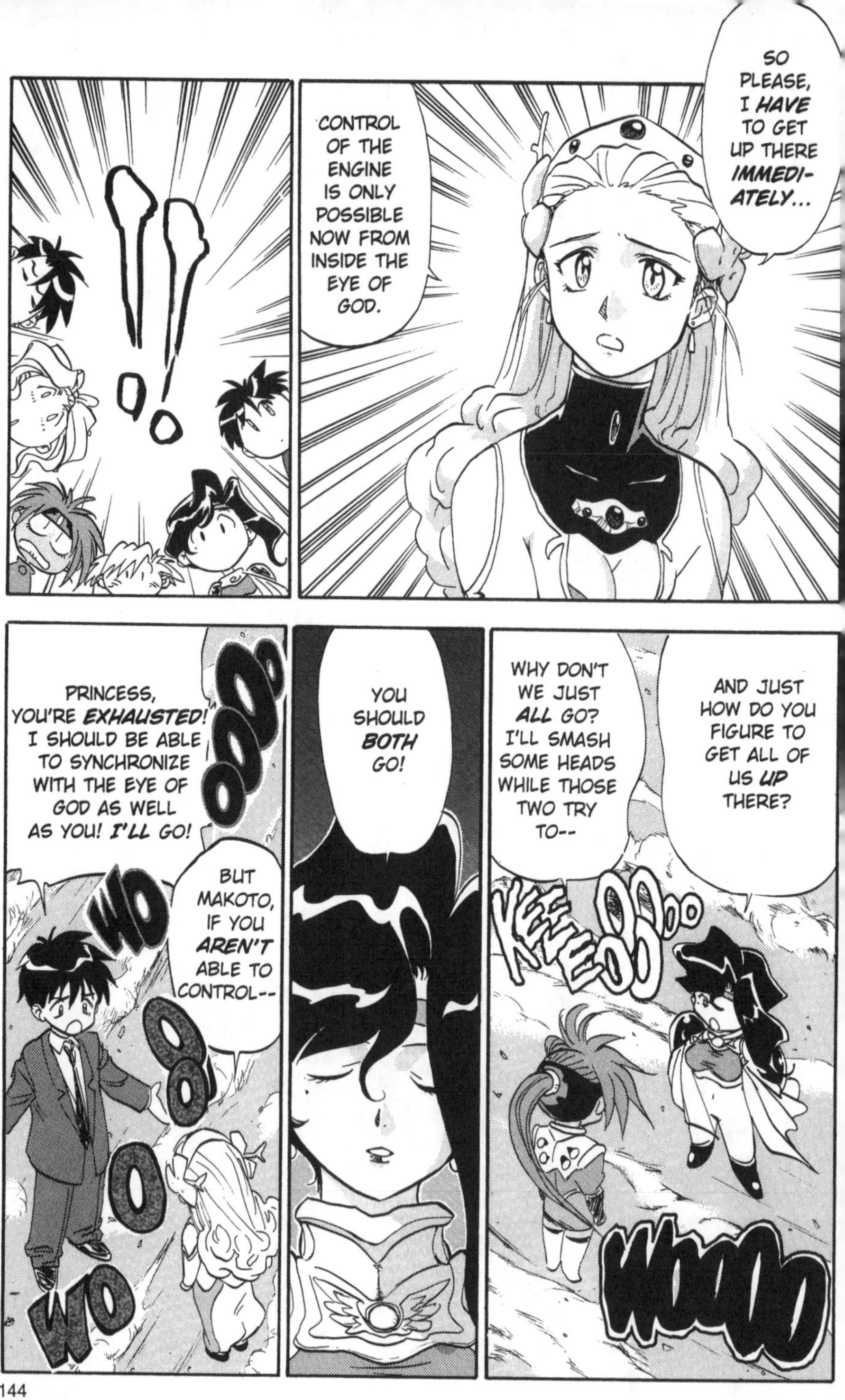
!!
CONTROL OF THE ENGINE IS ONLY POSSIBLE NOW FROM INSIDE THE EYE OF GOD.
SO PLEASE, I *HAVE* TO GET UP THERE *IMMEDIATELY...*
PRINCESS, YOU'RE *EXHAUSTED!* I SHOULD BE ABLE TO SYNCHRONIZE WITH THE EYE OF GOD AS WELL AS YOU! *I'LL* GO!
BUT MAKOTO, IF YOU *AREN'T* ABLE TO CONTROL--
YOU SHOULD *BOTH* GO!
WHY DON'T WE JUST *ALL* GO? I'LL SMASH SOME HEADS WHILE THOSE TWO TRY TO--
AND JUST HOW DO YOU FIGURE TO GET ALL OF US *UP* THERE?
WOOOO

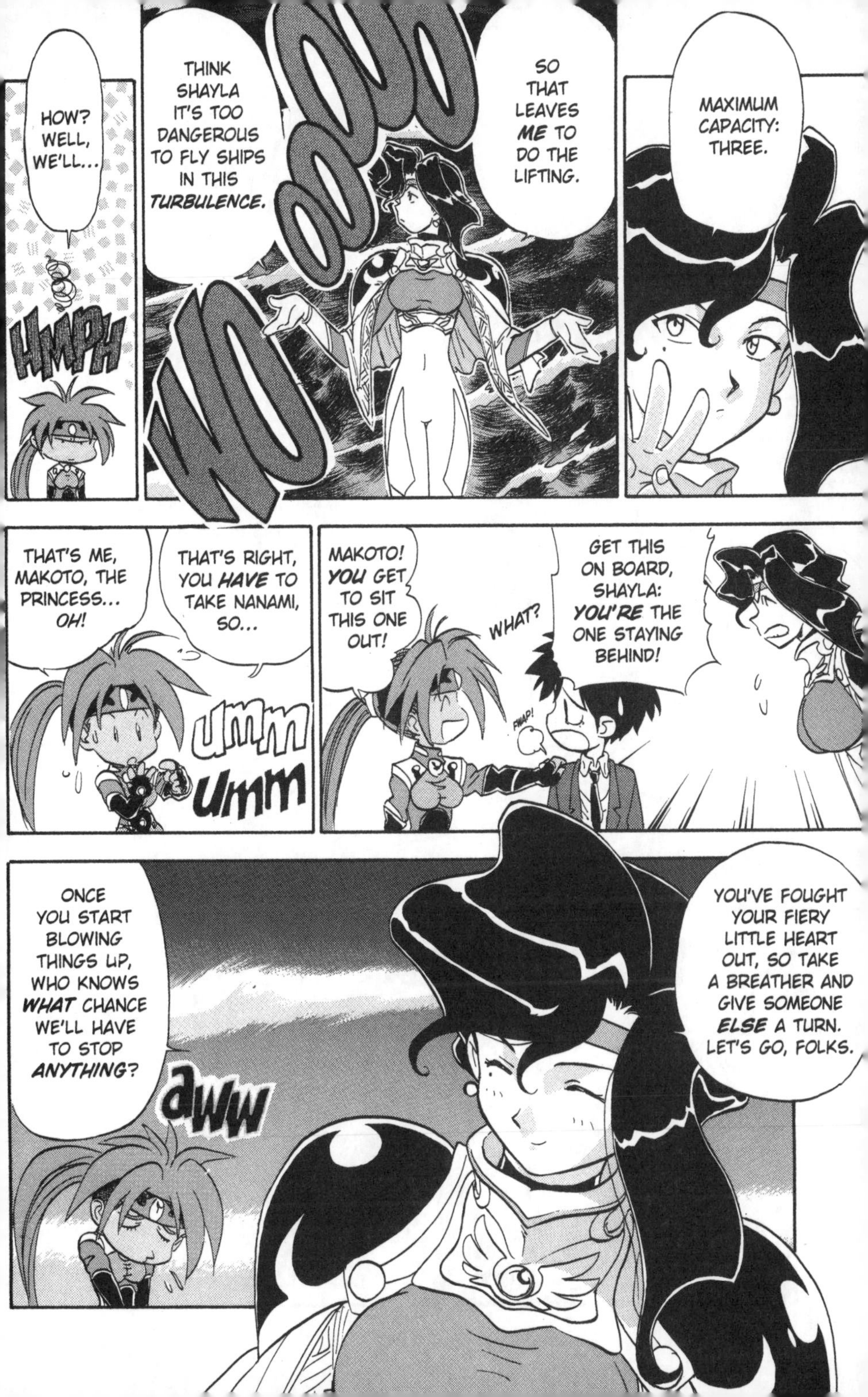

HOW? WELL, WE'LL...
HMPH
THINK SHAYLA IT'S TOO DANGEROUS TO FLY SHIPS IN THIS *TURBULENCE.*
SO THAT LEAVES *ME* TO DO THE LIFTING.
MAXIMUM CAPACITY: THREE.
THAT'S ME, MAKOTO, THE PRINCESS... *OH!*
THAT'S RIGHT, YOU *HAVE* TO TAKE NANAMI, SO...
UMM
UMM
MAKOTO! *YOU* GET TO SIT THIS ONE OUT!
WHAT?
FWAP!
GET THIS ON BOARD, SHAYLA: *YOU'RE* THE ONE STAYING BEHIND!
ONCE YOU START BLOWING THINGS UP, WHO KNOWS *WHAT* CHANCE WE'LL HAVE TO STOP *ANYTHING*?
AWW
YOU'VE FOUGHT YOUR FIERY LITTLE HEART OUT, SO TAKE A BREATHER AND GIVE SOMEONE *ELSE* A TURN. LET'S GO, FOLKS.

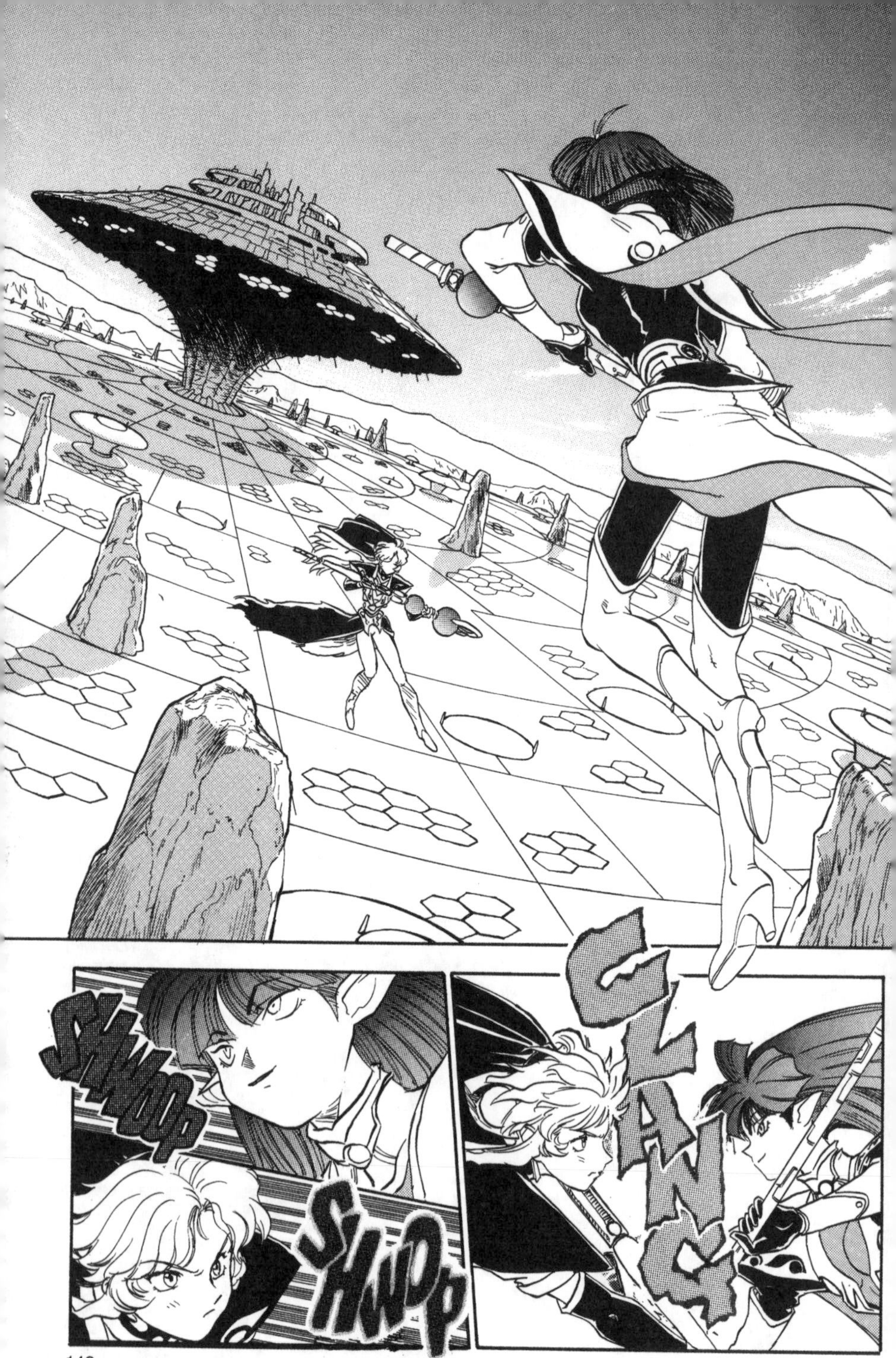
SHWOOP
SHWOOP
CLANG

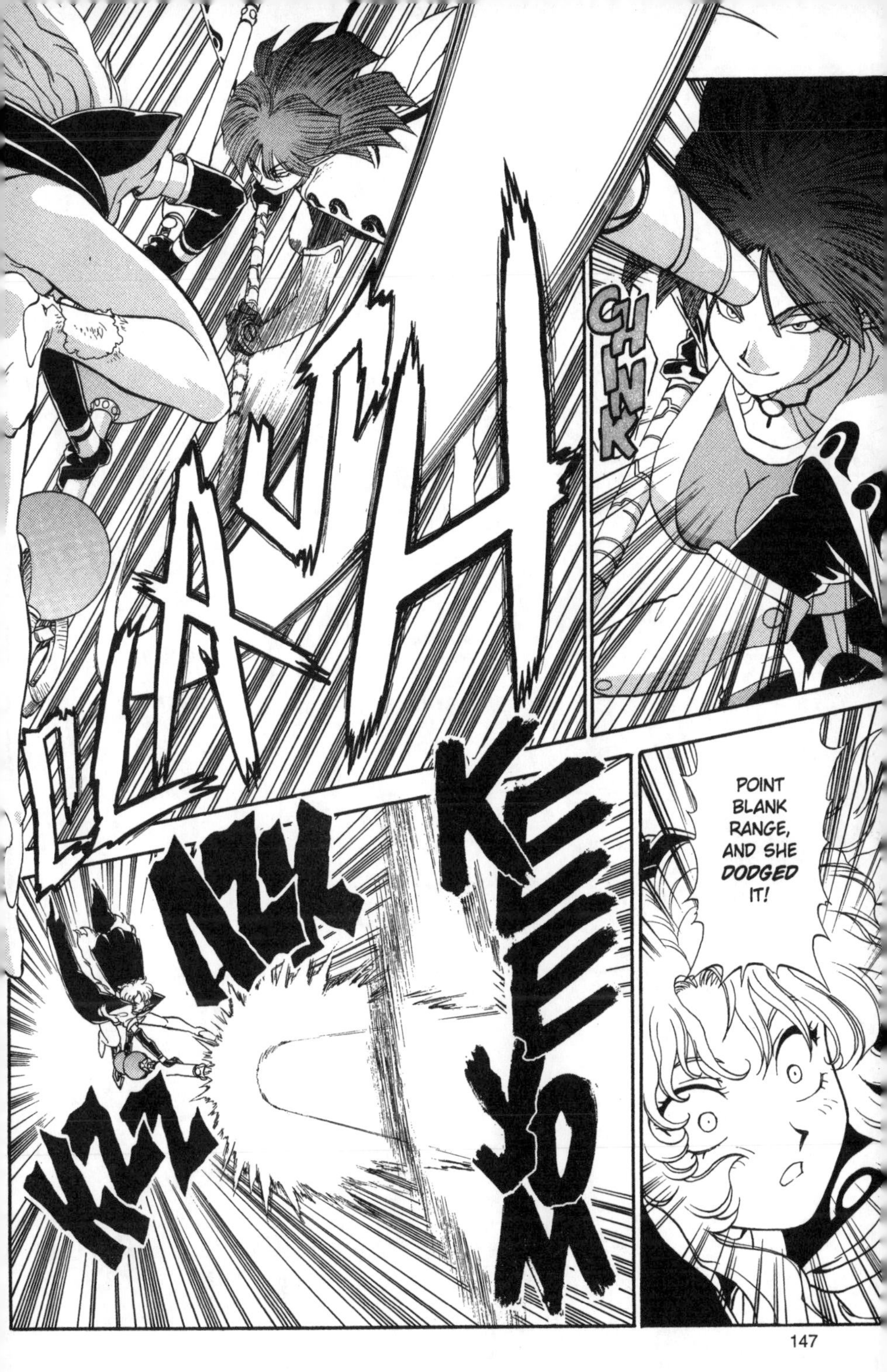
CHINK
POINT BLANK RANGE, AND SHE *DODGED* IT!

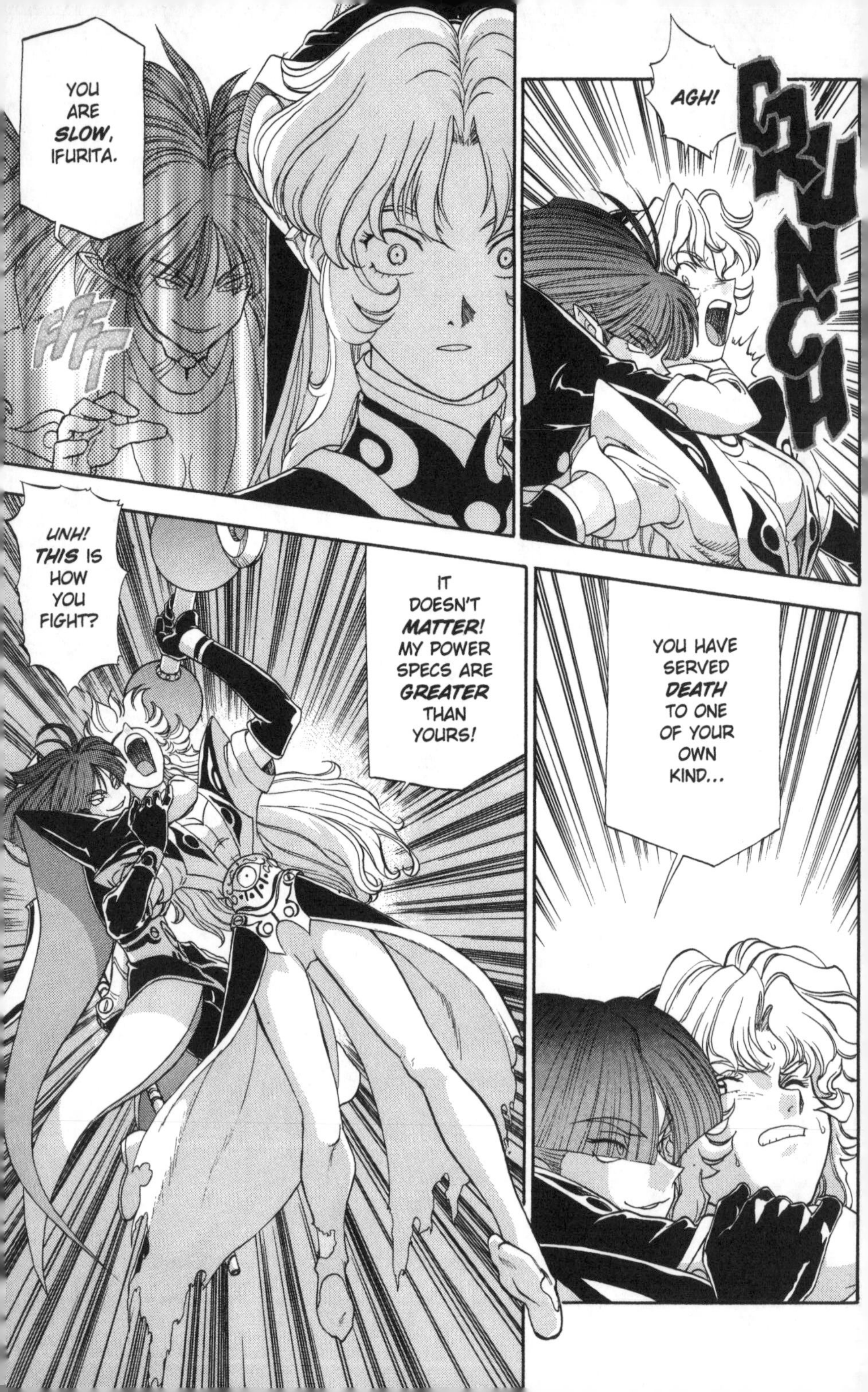
AGH!
CRUNCH
YOU ARE SLOW, IFURITA.
FFFT
YOU HAVE SERVED DEATH TO ONE OF YOUR OWN KIND...
IT DOESN'T MATTER! MY POWER SPECS ARE GREATER THAN YOURS!
UNH! THIS IS HOW YOU FIGHT?

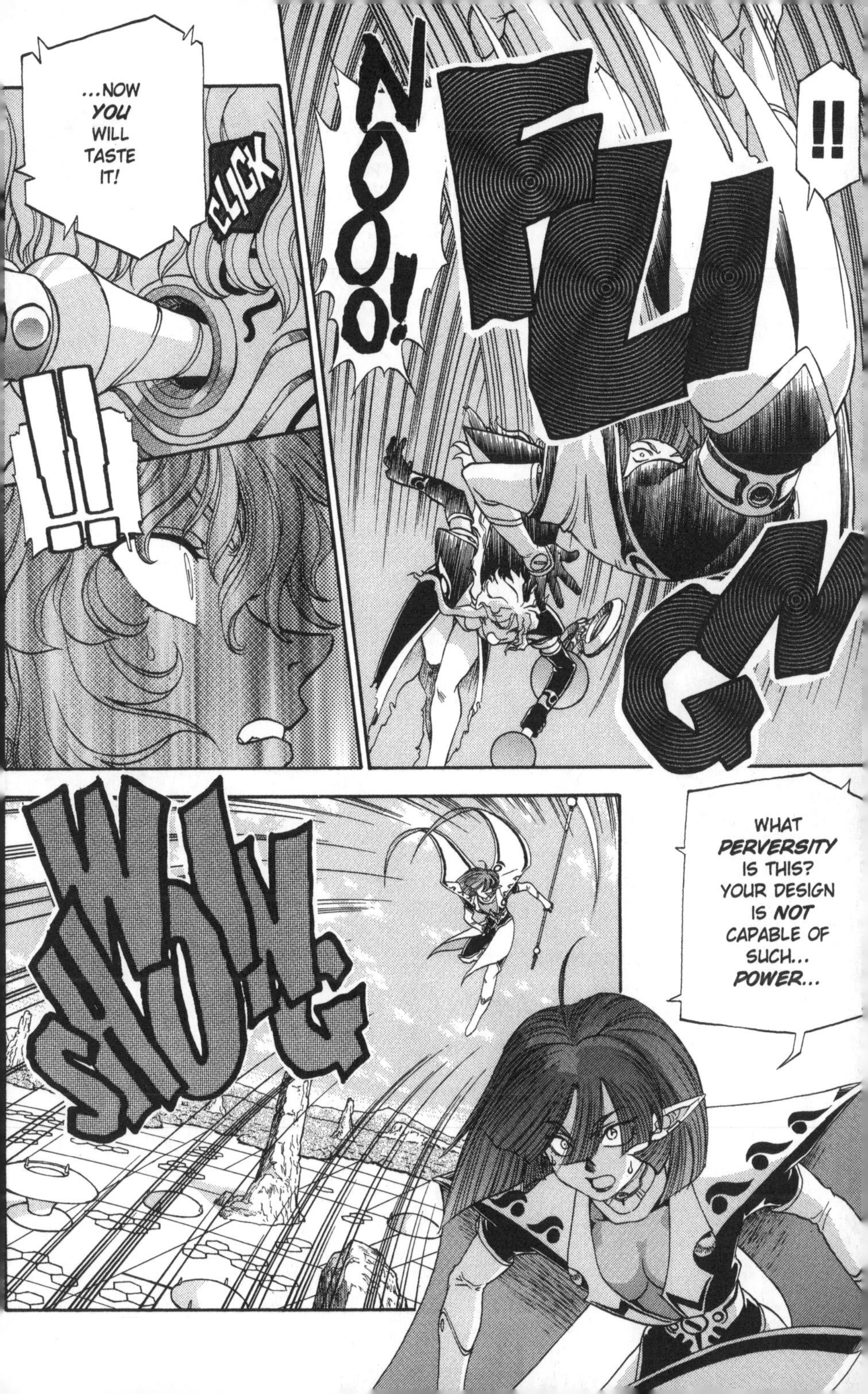
...NOW YOU WILL TASTE IT!
CLICK
!!
NOOOO!
!!
WHAT PERVERSITY IS THIS? YOUR DESIGN IS NOT CAPABLE OF SUCH... POWER...

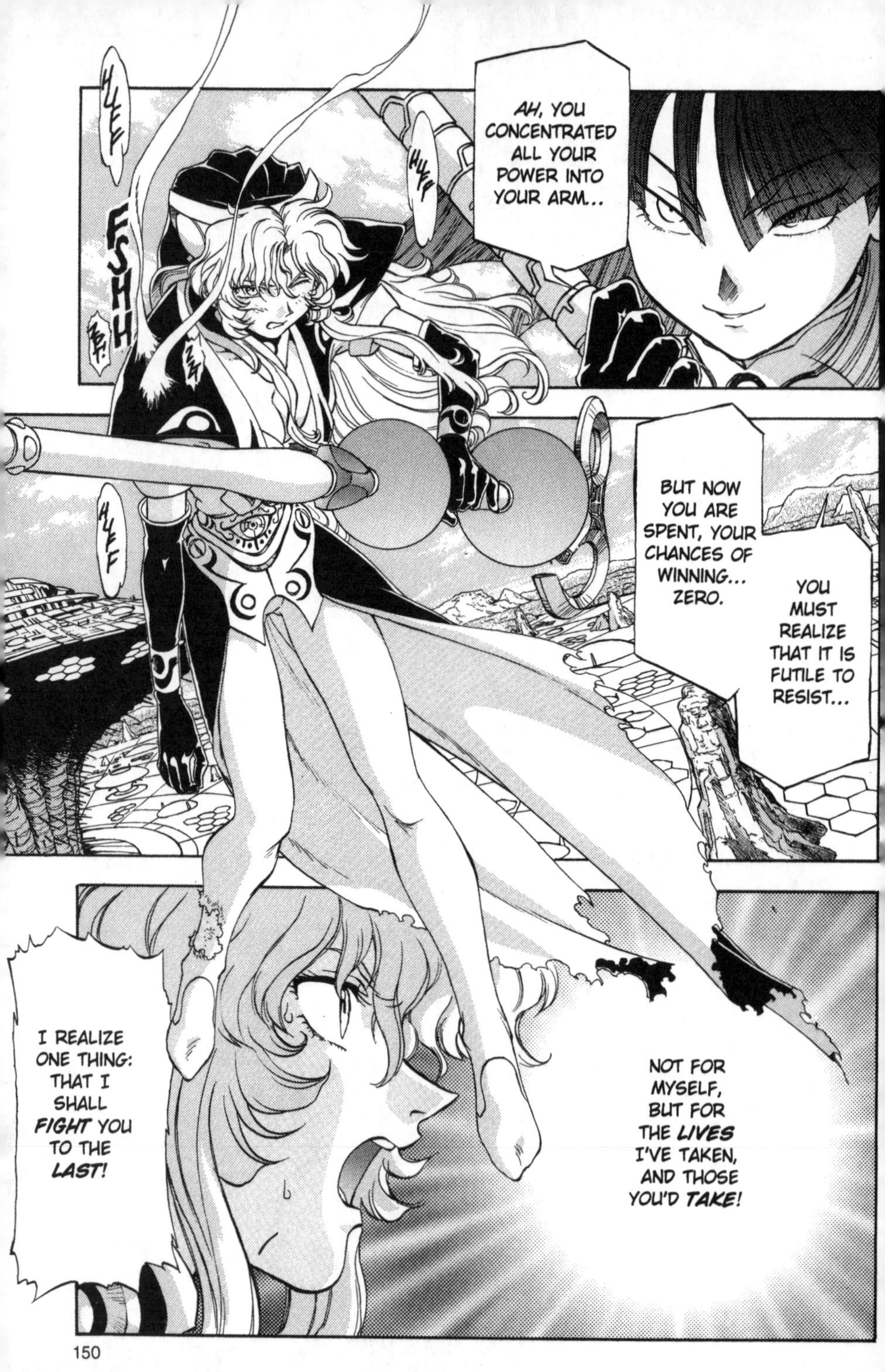
AH, YOU CONCENTRATED ALL YOUR POWER INTO YOUR ARM...
HUFF
HUFF
FSHH
BUT NOW YOU ARE SPENT, YOUR CHANCES OF WINNING... ZERO.
YOU MUST REALIZE THAT IT IS FUTILE TO RESIST...
HUFF
I REALIZE ONE THING: THAT I SHALL FIGHT YOU TO THE LAST!
NOT FOR MYSELF, BUT FOR THE LIVES I'VE TAKEN, AND THOSE YOU'D TAKE!

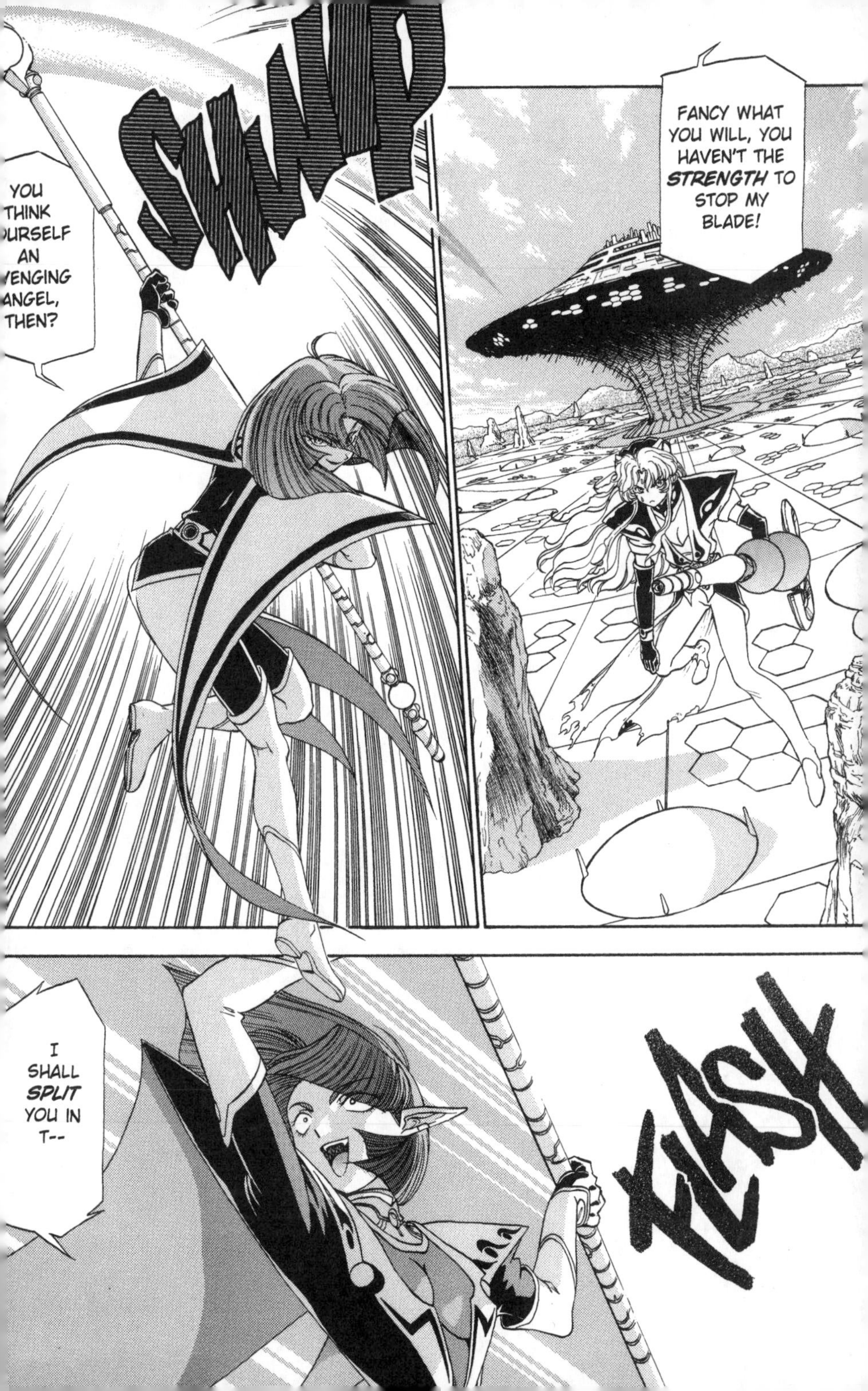

SHWIP
YOU THINK URSELF AN VENGING ANGEL, THEN?
FANCY WHAT YOU WILL, YOU HAVEN'T THE *STRENGTH* TO STOP MY BLADE!
I SHALL *SPLIT* YOU IN T--
KLASH

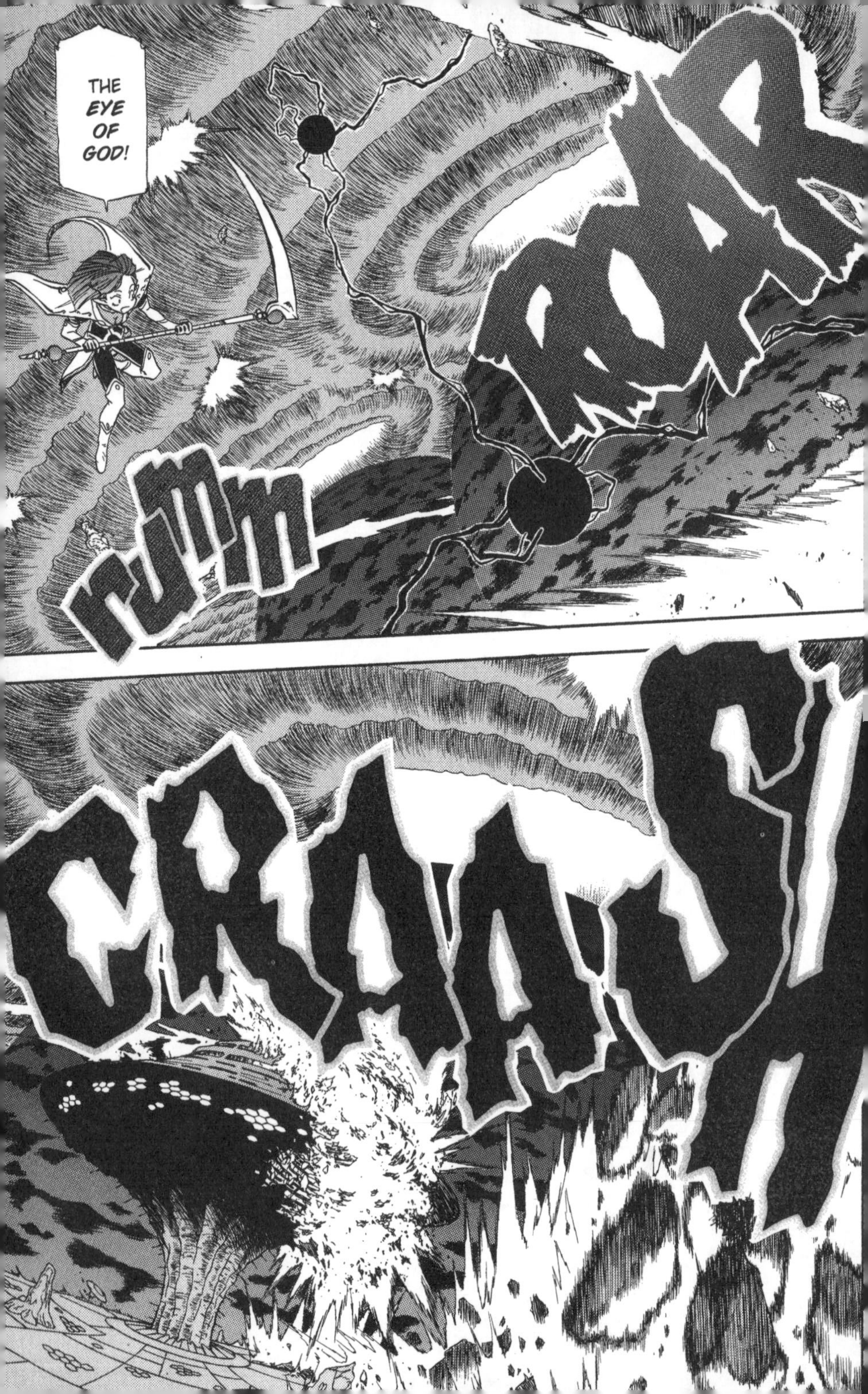
THE *EYE* OF GOD!
ROAR

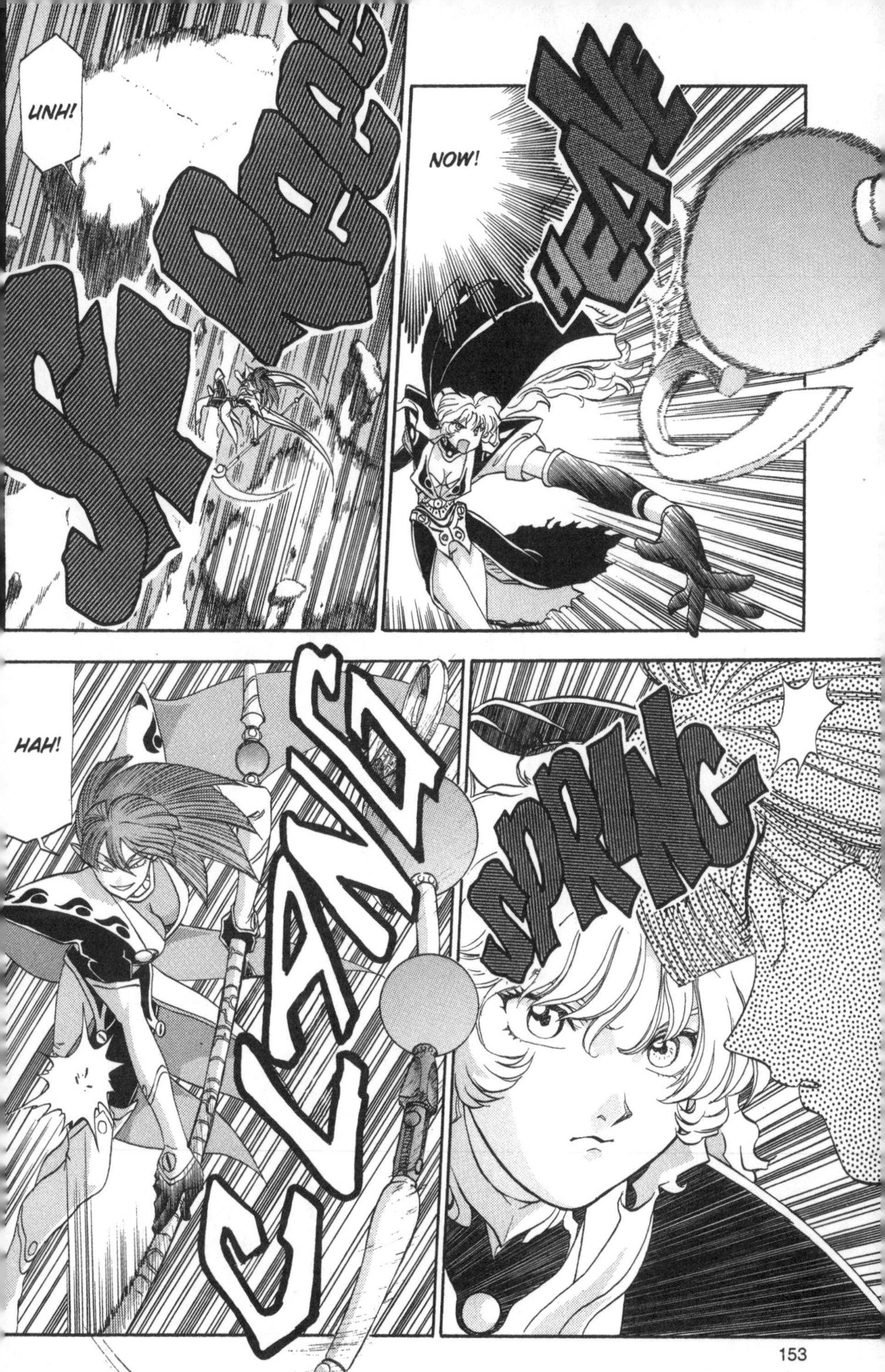
UNH!
NOW!
HAH!

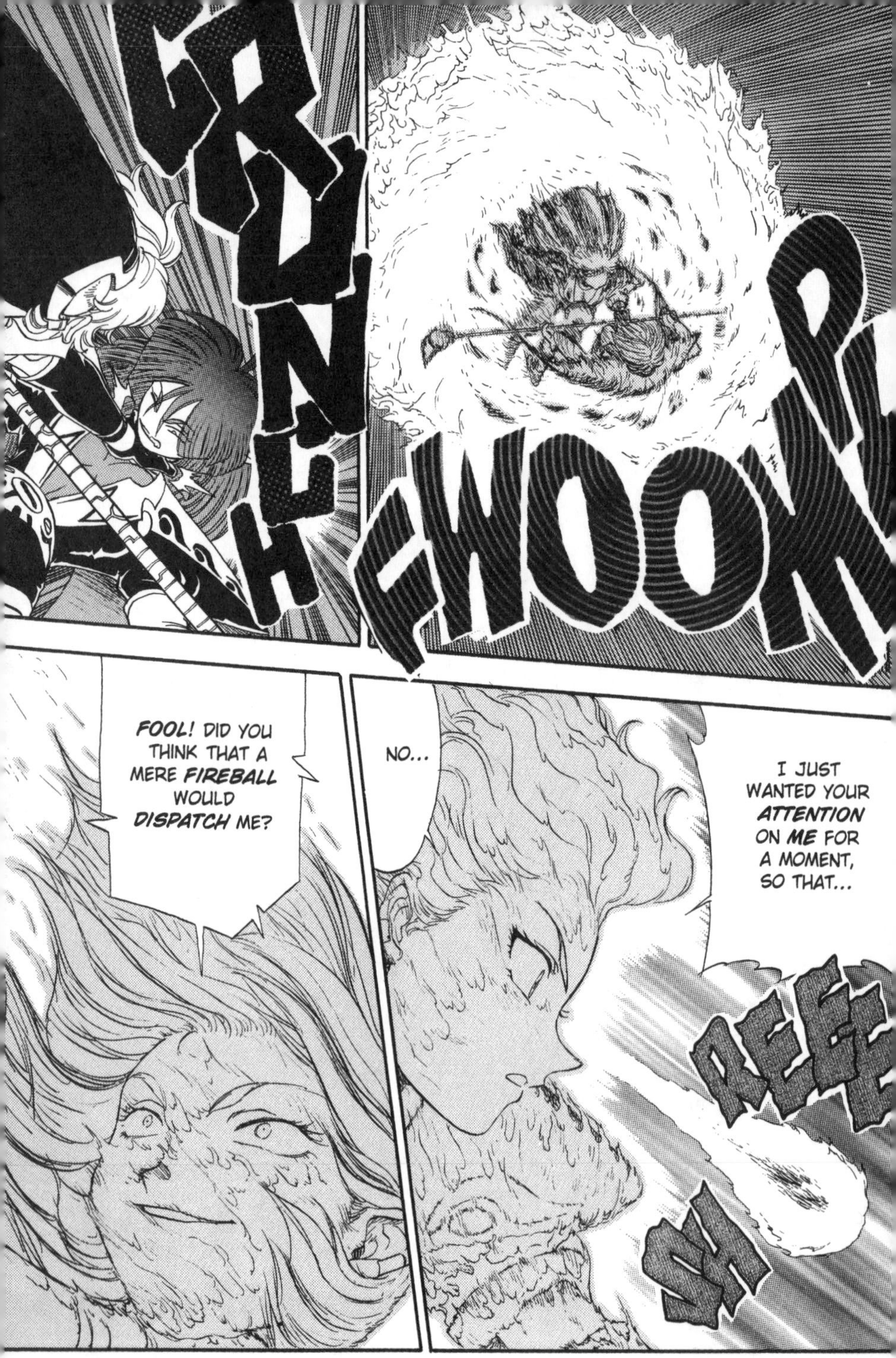
CRUNCH
FWOOM
FOOL! DID YOU THINK THAT A MERE FIREBALL WOULD DISPATCH ME?
NO...
I JUST WANTED YOUR ATTENTION ON ME FOR A MOMENT, SO THAT...
SHREEE

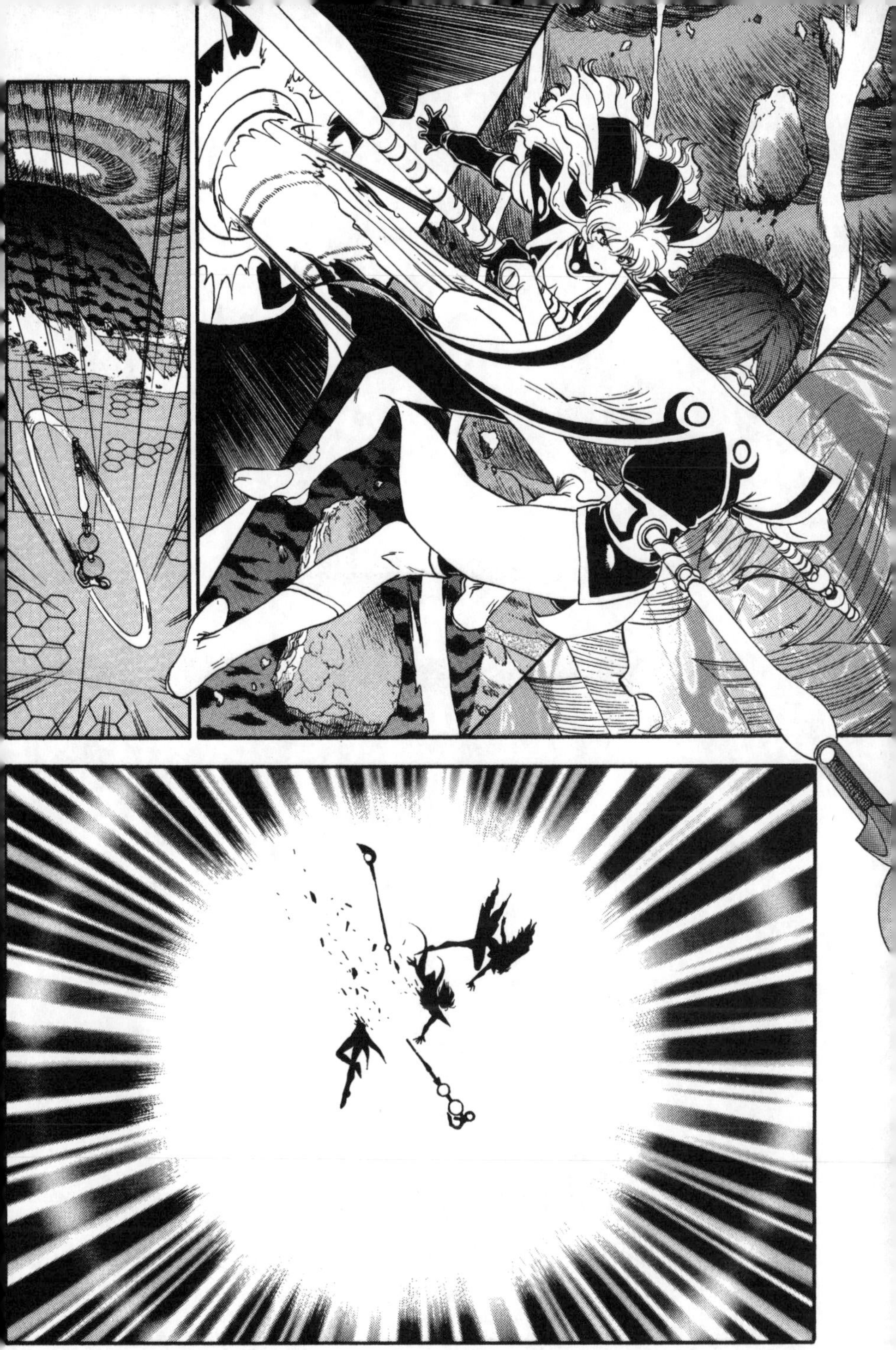

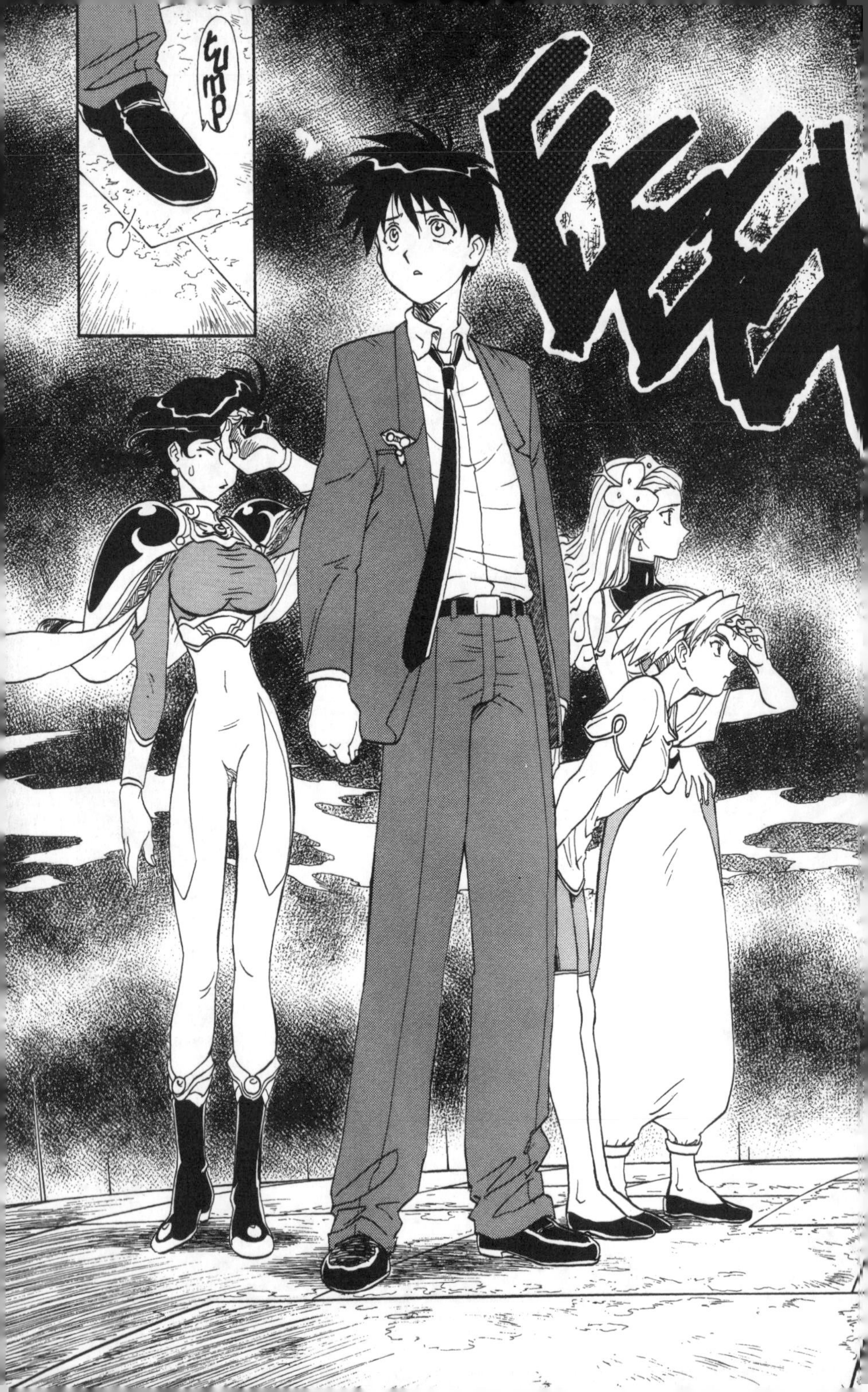
tump

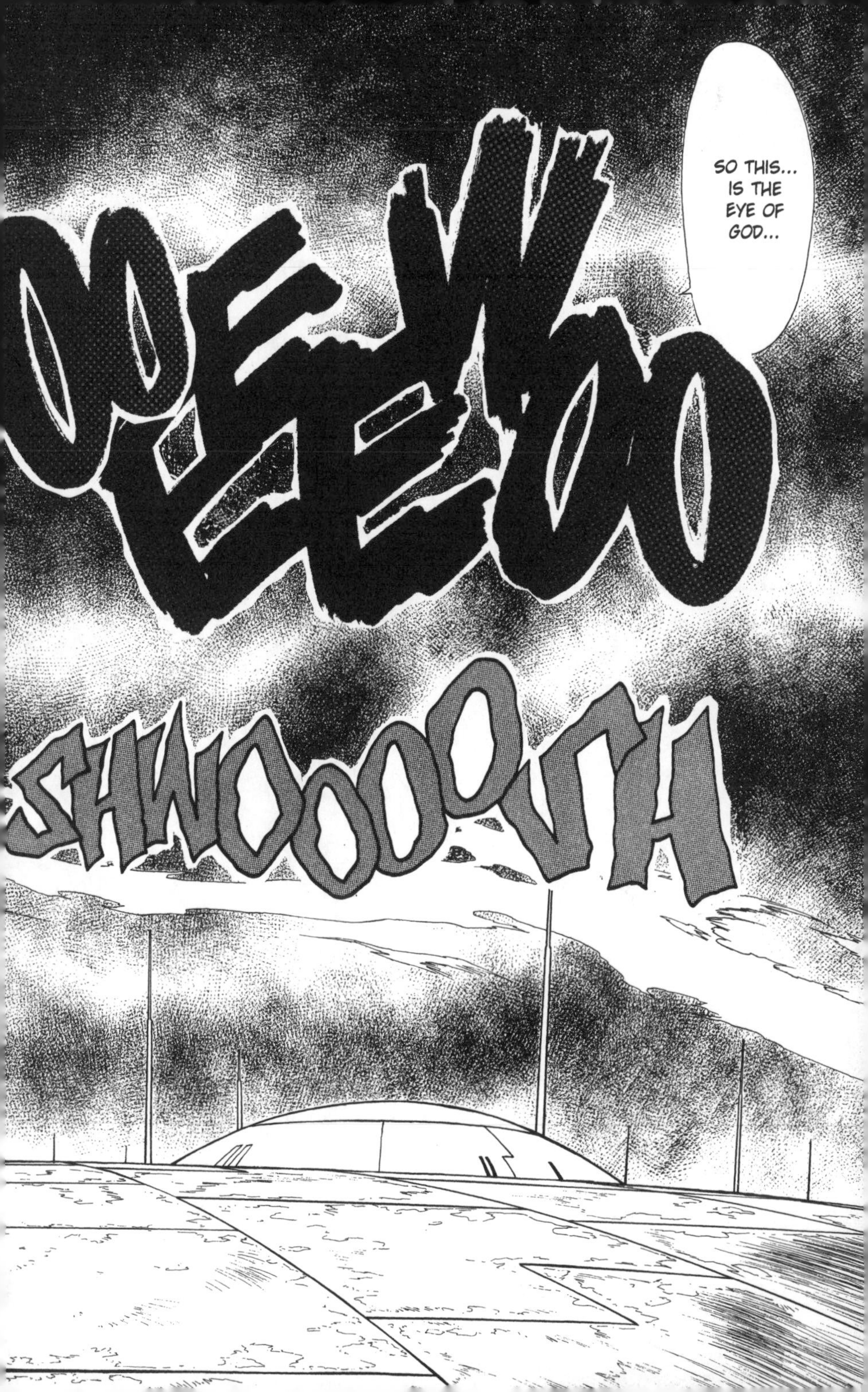
SO THIS... IS THE EYE OF GOD...

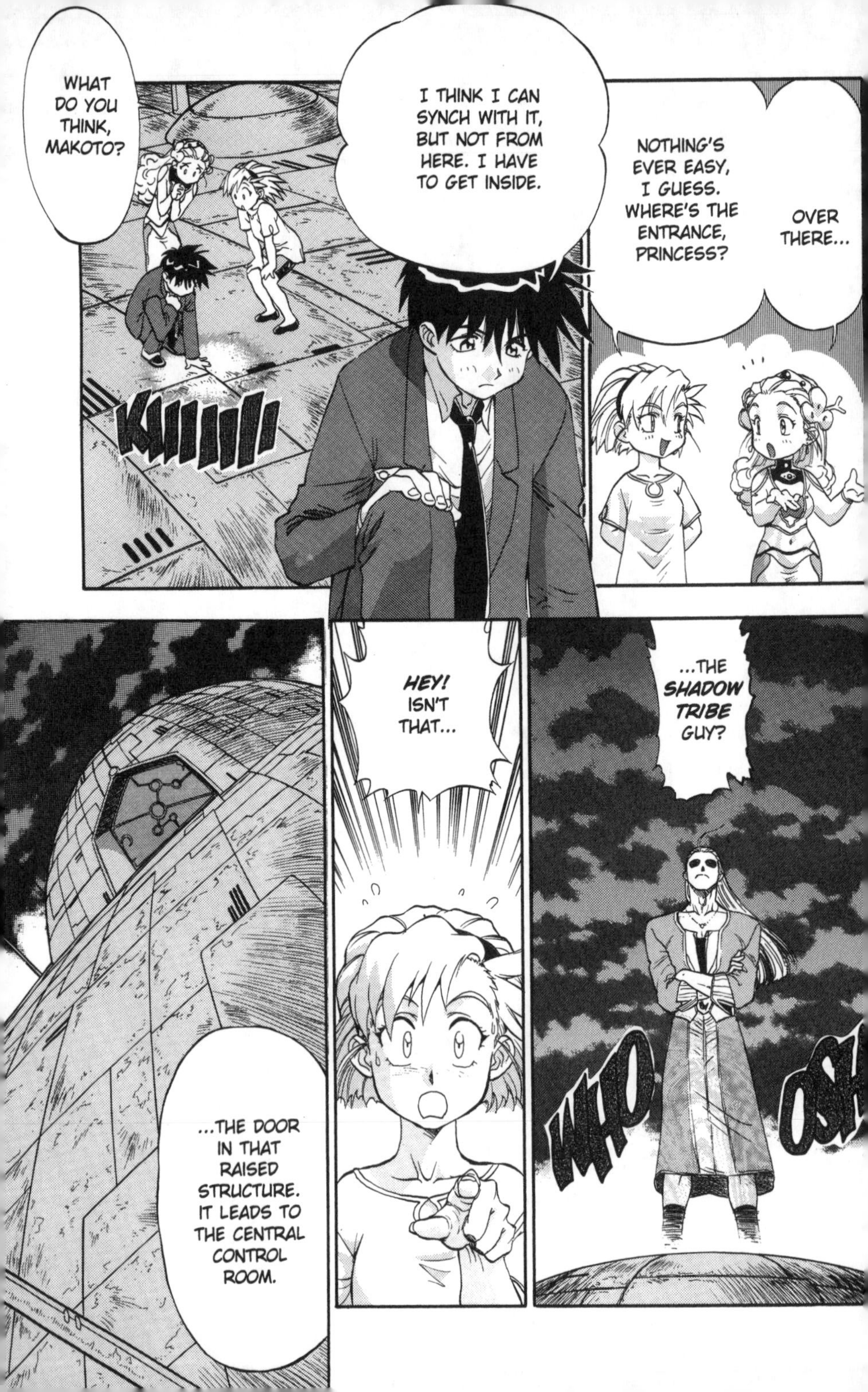
WHAT DO YOU THINK, MAKOTO?
I THINK I CAN SYNCH WITH IT, BUT NOT FROM HERE. I HAVE TO GET INSIDE.
NOTHING'S EVER EASY, I GUESS. WHERE'S THE ENTRANCE, PRINCESS?
OVER THERE...
...THE DOOR IN THAT RAISED STRUCTURE. IT LEADS TO THE CENTRAL CONTROL ROOM.
HEY! ISN'T THAT...
...THE *SHADOW TRIBE* GUY?

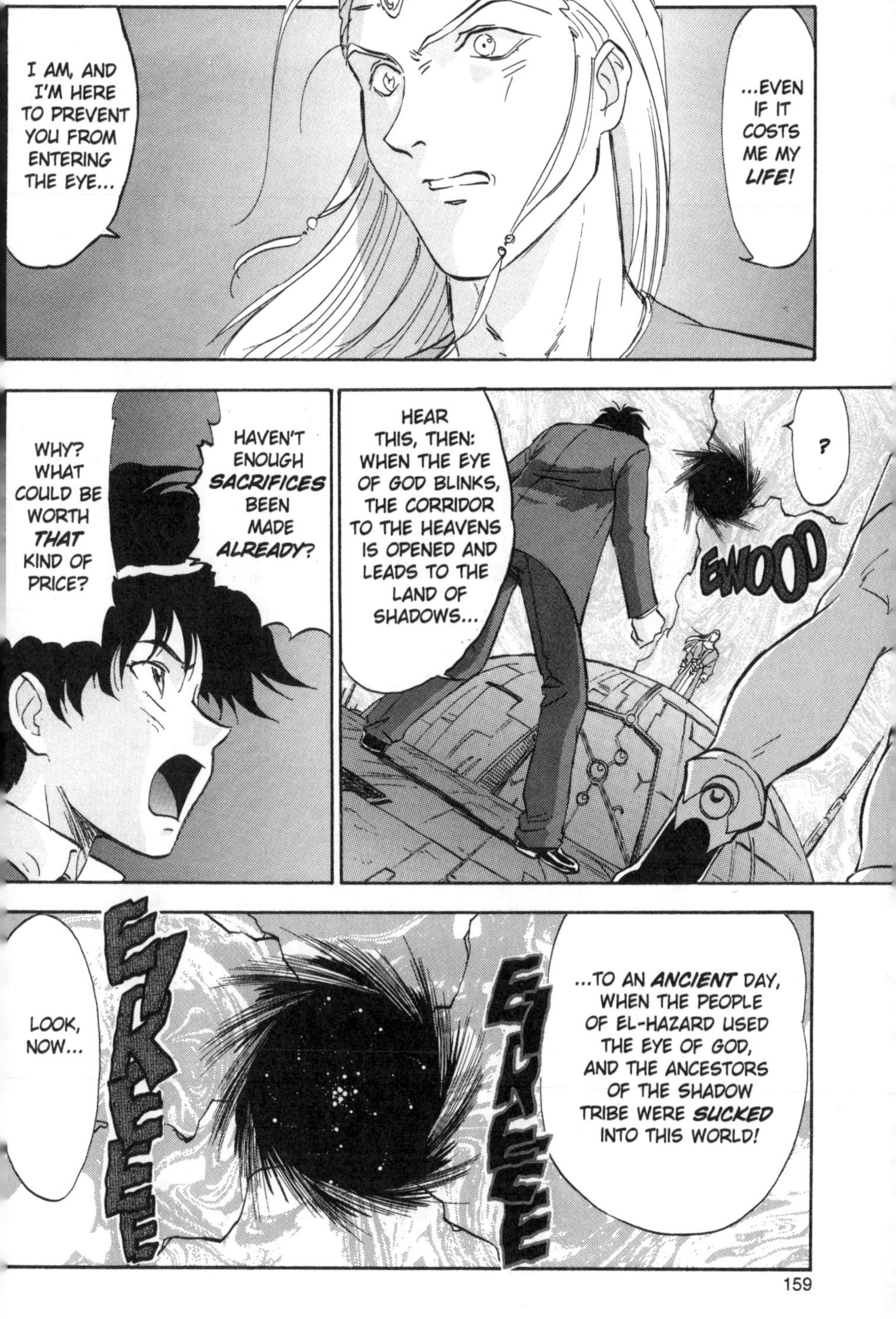
I AM, AND I'M HERE TO PREVENT YOU FROM ENTERING THE EYE...
...EVEN IF IT COSTS ME MY *LIFE*!
WHY? WHAT COULD BE WORTH *THAT* KIND OF PRICE?
HAVEN'T ENOUGH *SACRIFICES* BEEN MADE *ALREADY*?
HEAR THIS, THEN: WHEN THE EYE OF GOD BLINKS, THE CORRIDOR TO THE HEAVENS IS OPENED AND LEADS TO THE LAND OF SHADOWS...
?
EWOOO
LOOK, NOW...
...TO AN *ANCIENT* DAY, WHEN THE PEOPLE OF EL-HAZARD USED THE EYE OF GOD, AND THE ANCESTORS OF THE SHADOW TRIBE WERE *SUCKED* INTO THIS WORLD!

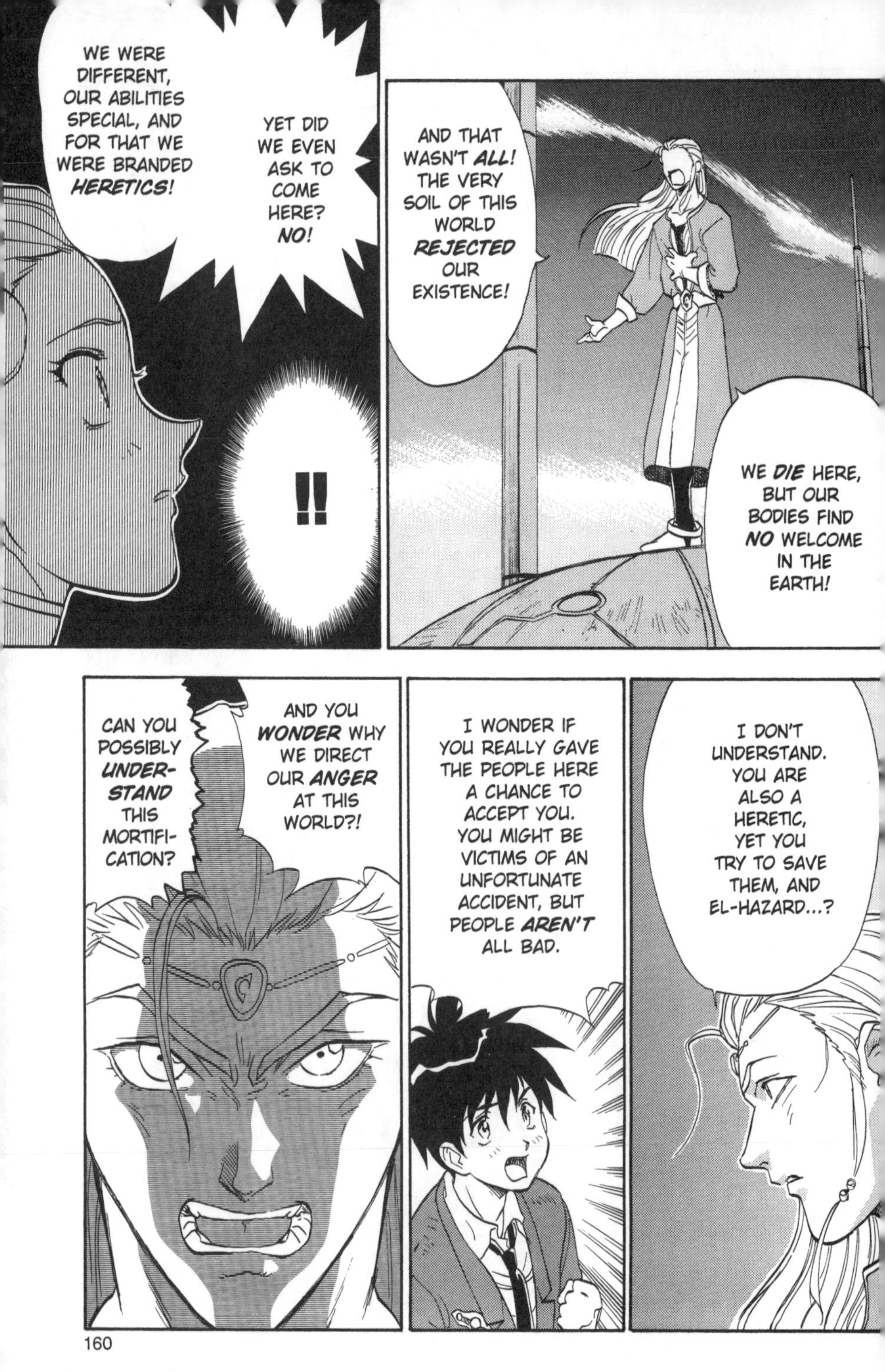

WE WERE DIFFERENT, OUR ABILITIES SPECIAL, AND FOR THAT WE WERE BRANDED *HERETICS*!
YET DID WE EVEN ASK TO COME HERE? *NO*!
!!
AND THAT WASN'T *ALL*! THE VERY SOIL OF THIS WORLD *REJECTED* OUR EXISTENCE!
WE *DIE* HERE, BUT OUR BODIES FIND *NO* WELCOME IN THE EARTH!
CAN YOU POSSIBLY *UNDER-STAND* THIS MORTIFI-CATION?
AND YOU *WONDER* WHY WE DIRECT OUR *ANGER* AT THIS WORLD?!
I WONDER IF YOU REALLY GAVE THE PEOPLE HERE A CHANCE TO ACCEPT YOU. YOU MIGHT BE VICTIMS OF AN UNFORTUNATE ACCIDENT, BUT PEOPLE *AREN'T* ALL BAD.
I DON'T UNDERSTAND. YOU ARE ALSO A HERETIC, YET YOU TRY TO SAVE THEM, AND EL-HAZARD...?

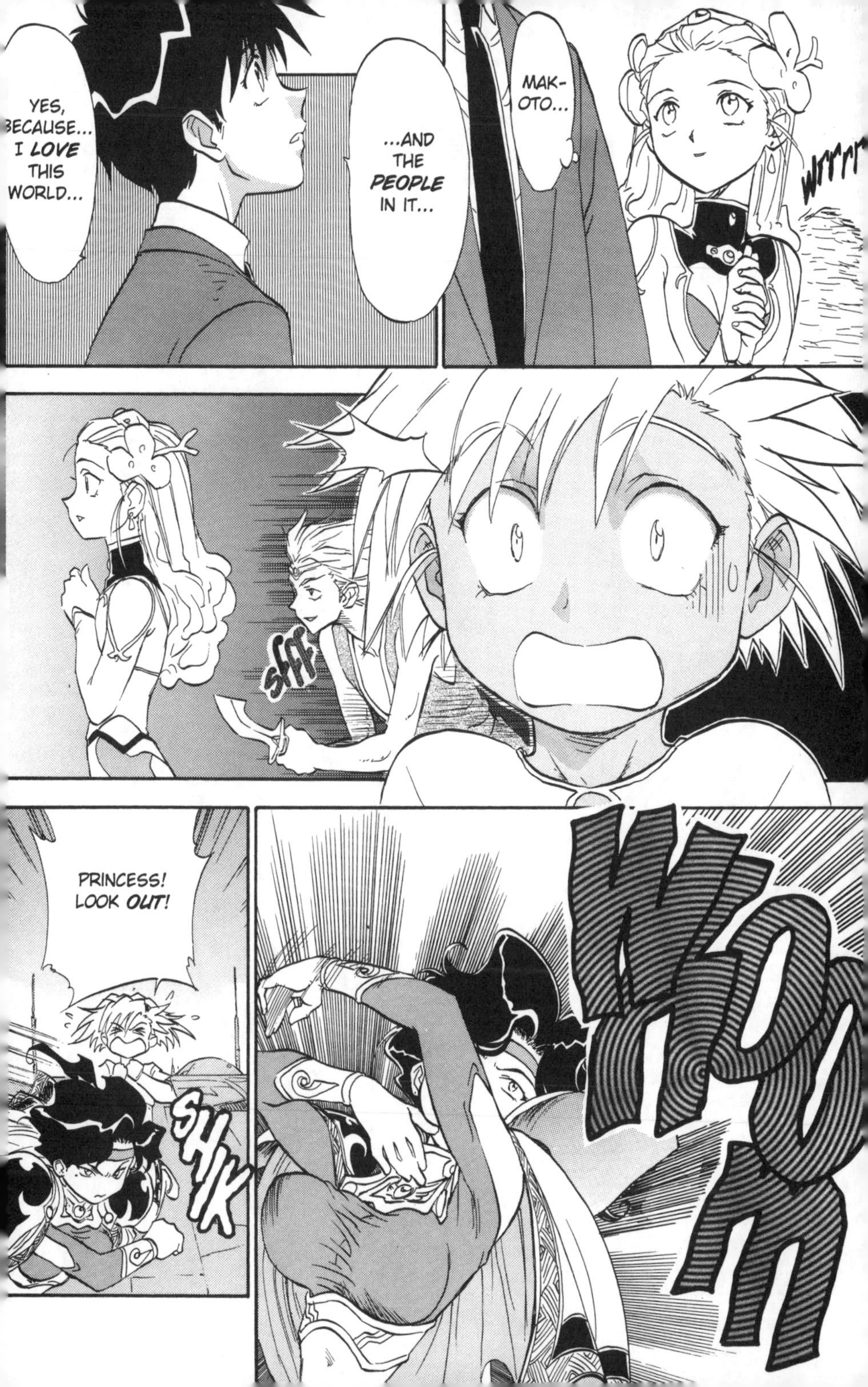
MAK-
OTO...
...AND
THE
PEOPLE
IN IT...
YES,
BECAUSE...
I LOVE
THIS
WORLD...
Wrrrr
SFFF
PRINCESS!
LOOK OUT!
SHIK
WHOOM

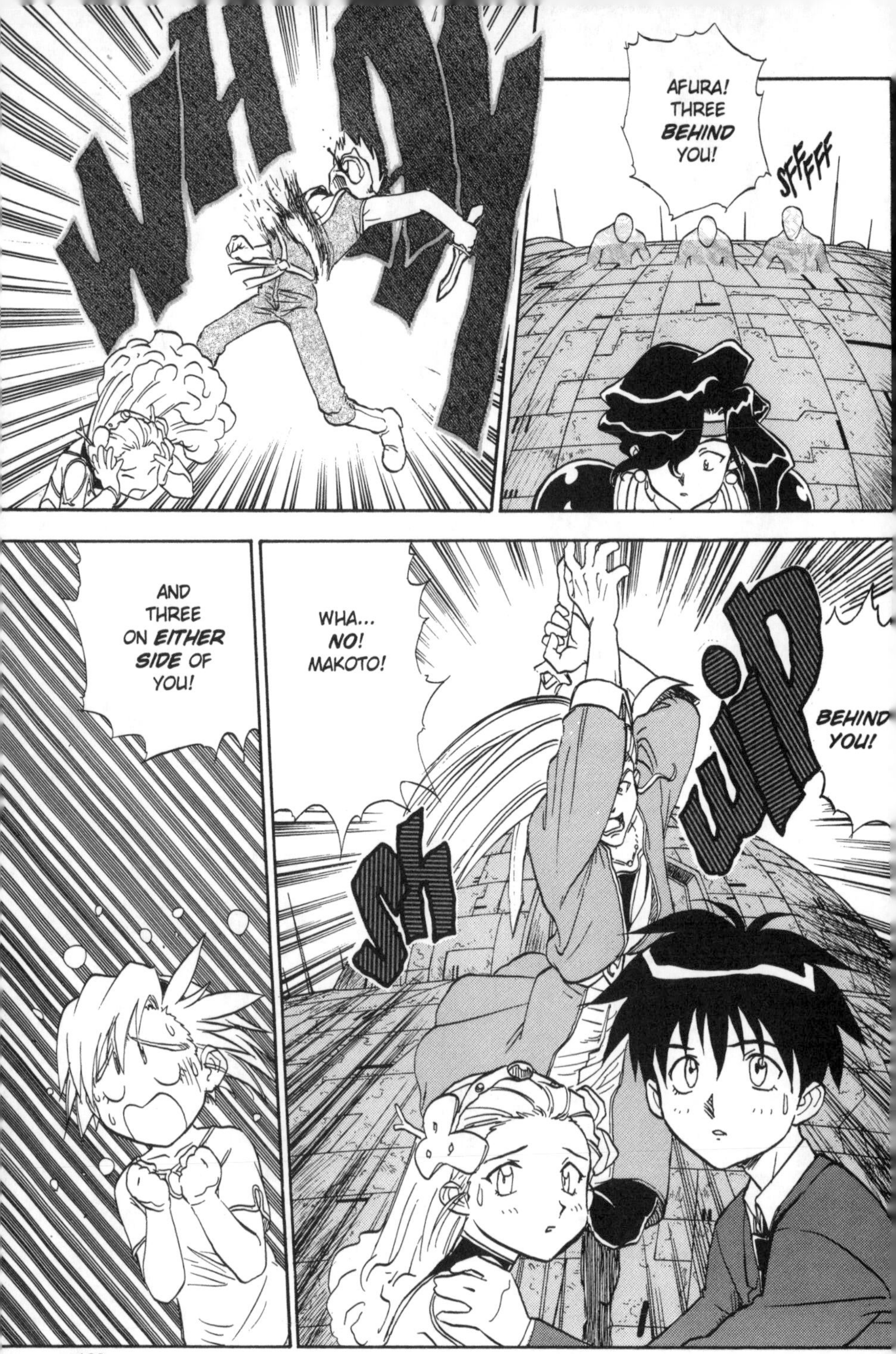
AFURA! THREE BEHIND YOU!
SFFFFFF
WHAM
BEHIND YOU!
WHA... NO! MAKOTO!
AND THREE ON EITHER SIDE OF YOU!

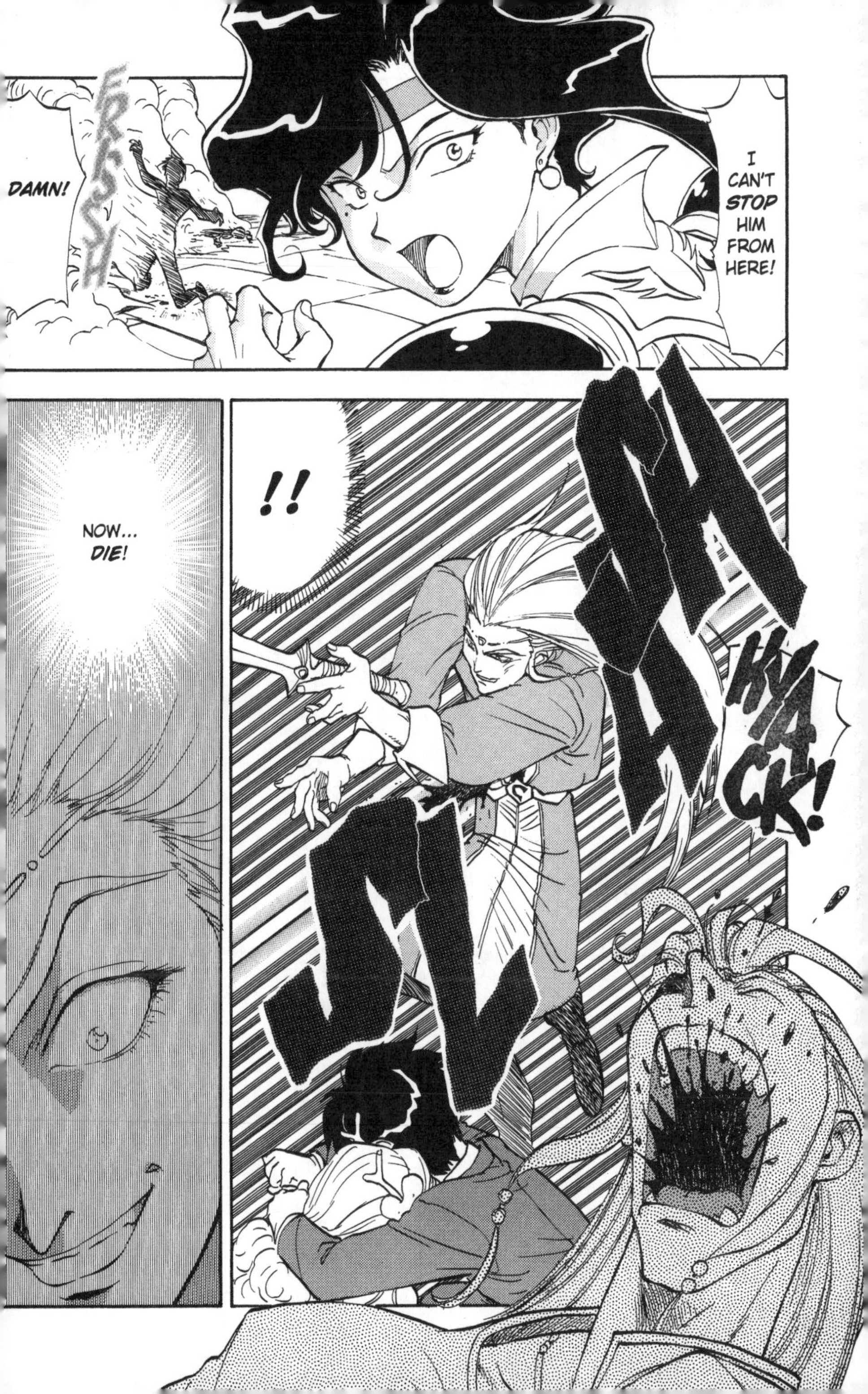
I CAN'T STOP HIM FROM HERE!
FRSSH
DAMN!
!!
SHA
SHA
KYAACK!
NOW... DIE!

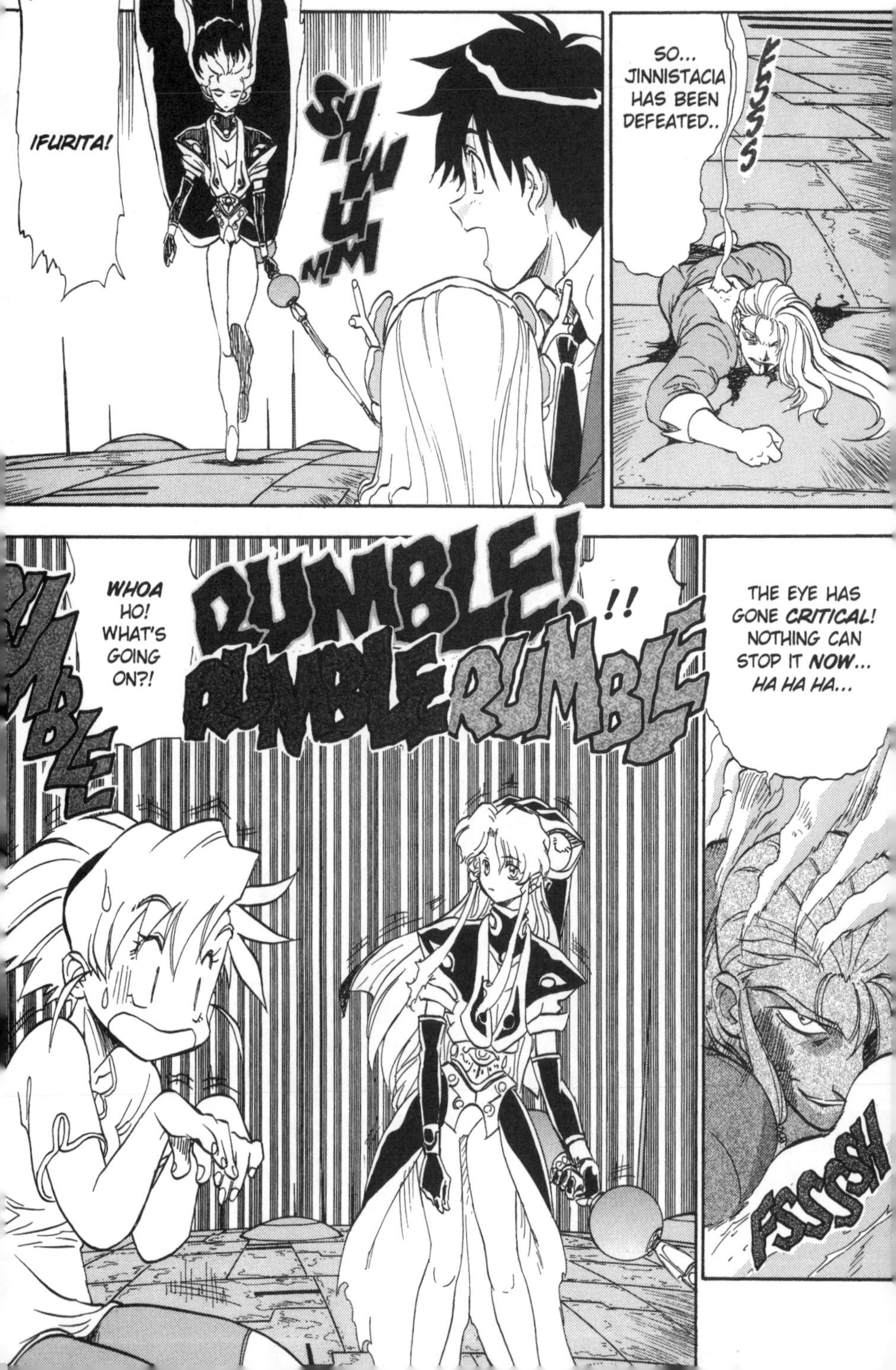
SO... JINNISTACIA HAS BEEN DEFEATED..
SHWUMM
IFURITA!
THE EYE HAS GONE CRITICAL! NOTHING CAN STOP IT NOW... HA HA HA...
FSSSH
!!
RUMBLE! RUMBLE RUMBLE
WHOA HO! WHAT'S GOING ON?!
RUMBLE

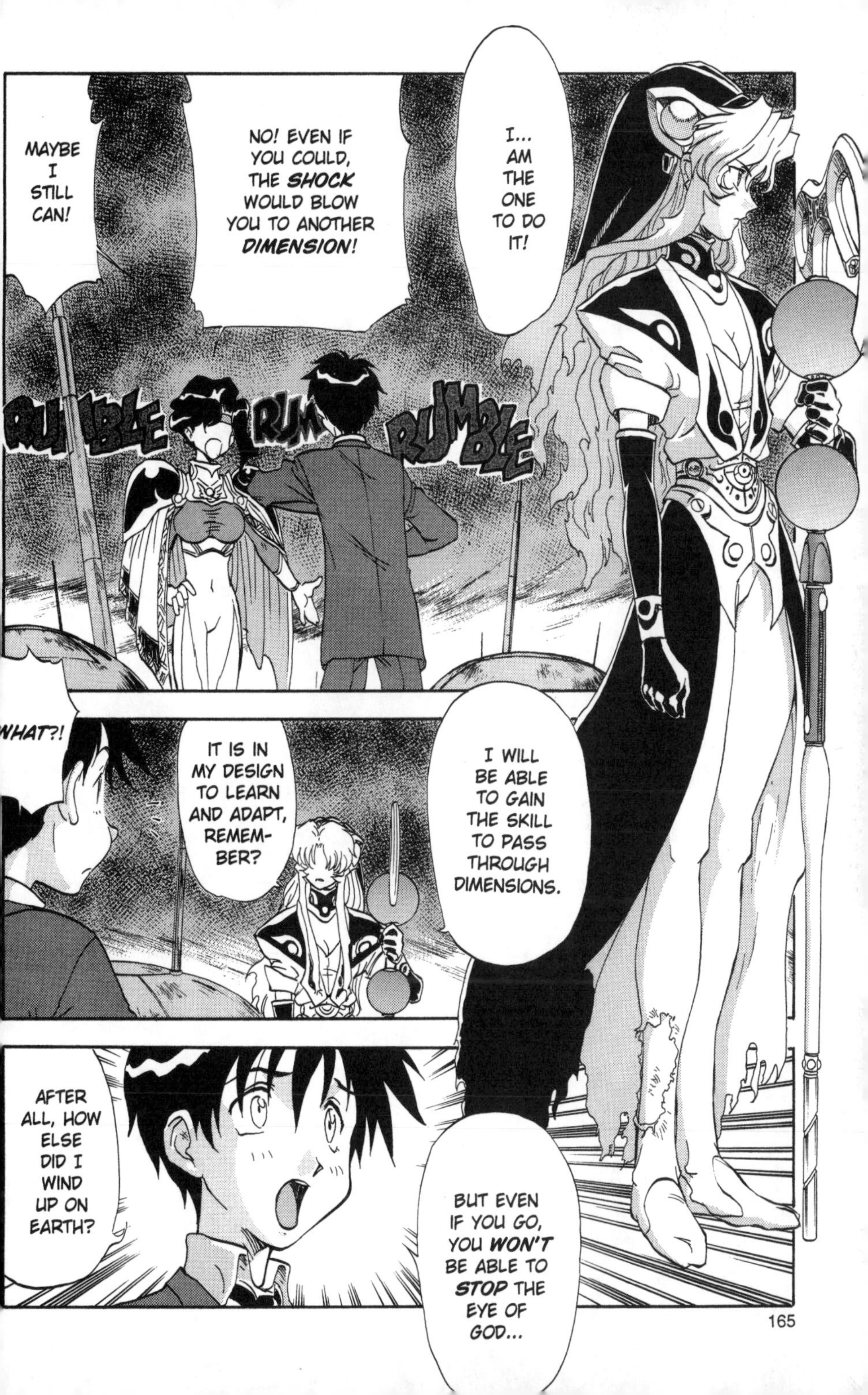
MAYBE I STILL CAN!
NO! EVEN IF YOU COULD, THE SHOCK WOULD BLOW YOU TO ANOTHER DIMENSION!
I... AM THE ONE TO DO IT!
RUMBLE RUMBLE RUMBLE
WHAT?!
IT IS IN MY DESIGN TO LEARN AND ADAPT, REMEMBER?
I WILL BE ABLE TO GAIN THE SKILL TO PASS THROUGH DIMENSIONS.
AFTER ALL, HOW ELSE DID I WIND UP ON EARTH?
BUT EVEN IF YOU GO, YOU WON'T BE ABLE TO STOP THE EYE OF GOD...

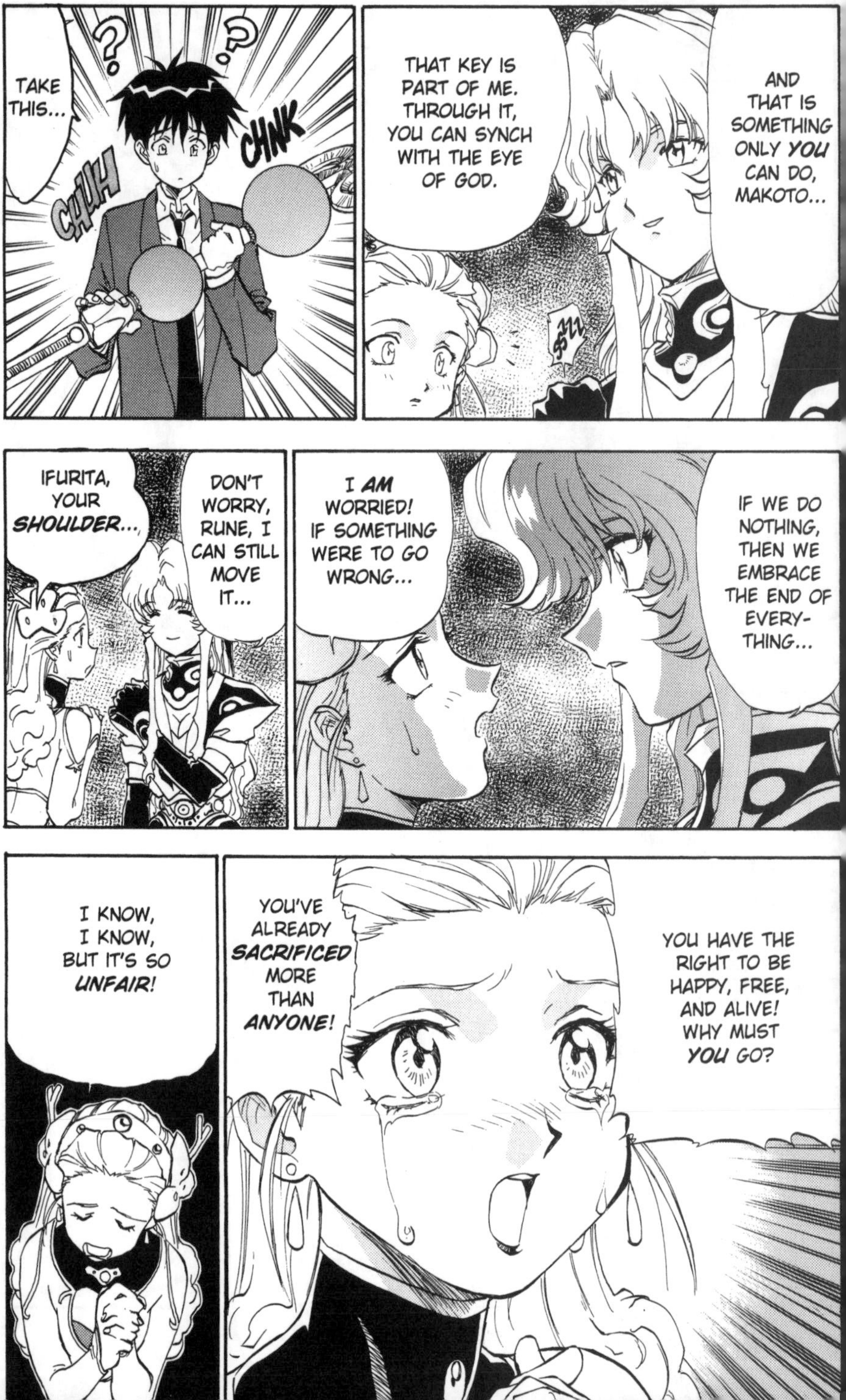

TAKE THIS...
CHUH
CHNK
THAT KEY IS PART OF ME. THROUGH IT, YOU CAN SYNCH WITH THE EYE OF GOD.
AND THAT IS SOMETHING ONLY *YOU* CAN DO, MAKOTO...
IFURITA, YOUR *SHOULDER*...
DON'T WORRY, RUNE, I CAN STILL MOVE IT...
I *AM* WORRIED! IF SOMETHING WERE TO GO WRONG...
IF WE DO NOTHING, THEN WE EMBRACE THE END OF EVERY-THING...
I KNOW, I KNOW, BUT IT'S SO *UNFAIR*!
YOU'VE ALREADY *SACRIFICED* MORE THAN *ANYONE*!
YOU HAVE THE RIGHT TO BE HAPPY, FREE, AND ALIVE! WHY MUST *YOU* GO?

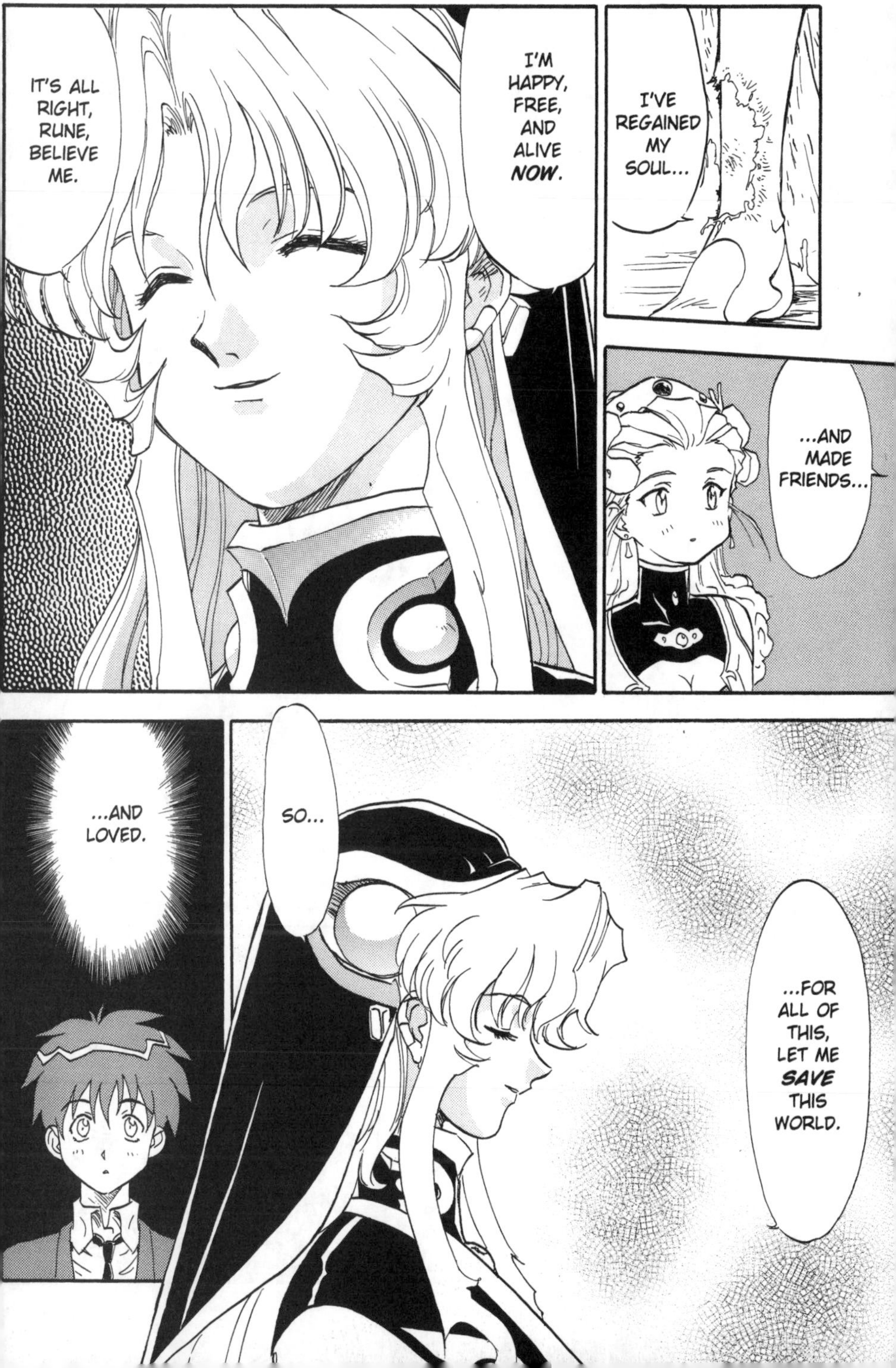
IT'S ALL RIGHT, RUNE, BELIEVE ME.
I'M HAPPY, FREE, AND ALIVE *NOW*.
I'VE REGAINED MY SOUL...
...AND MADE FRIENDS...
...AND LOVED.
SO...
...FOR ALL OF THIS, LET ME *SAVE* THIS WORLD.

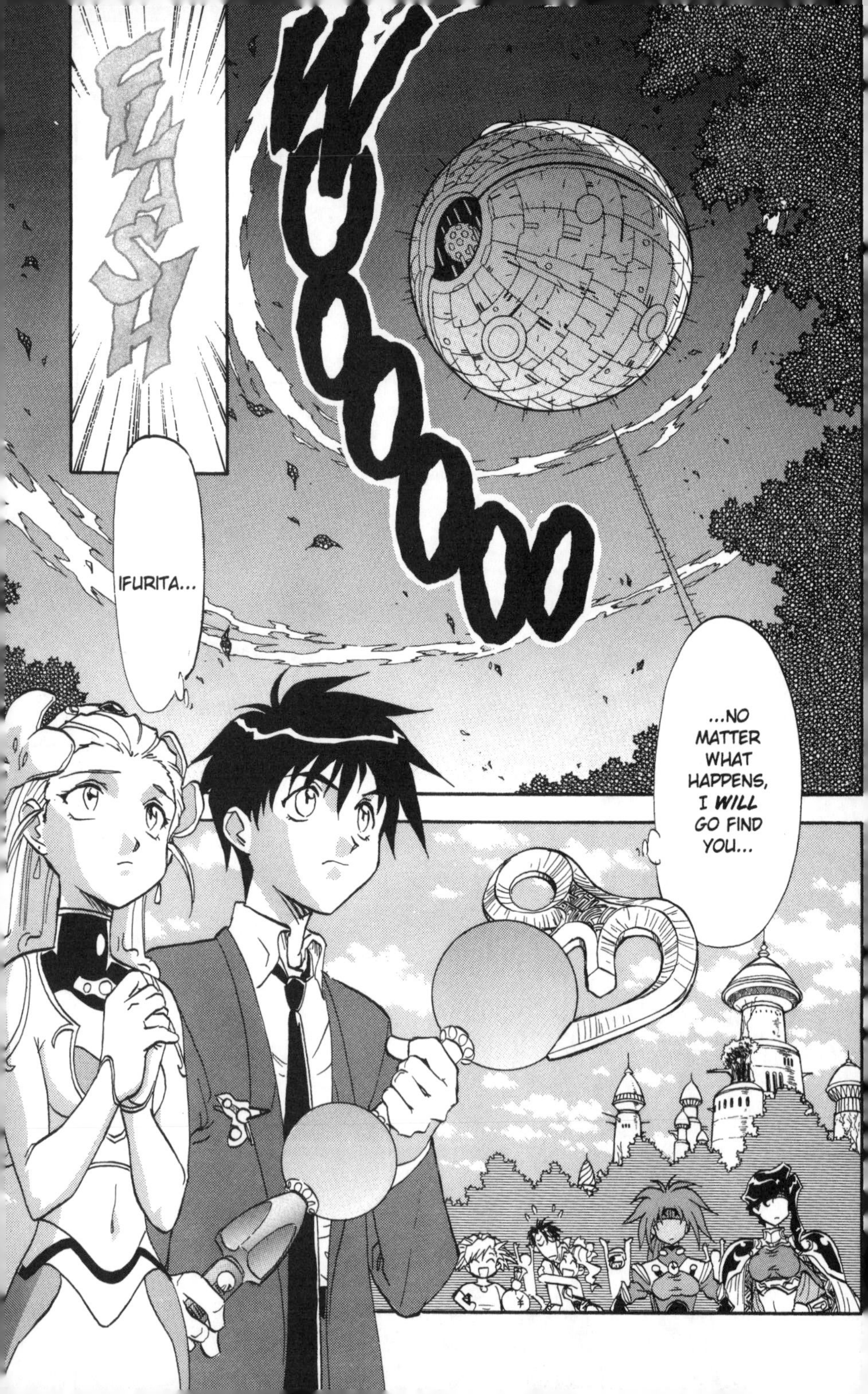
FLASH
WOOOOOOO
IFURITA...
...NO MATTER WHAT HAPPENS, I WILL GO FIND YOU...

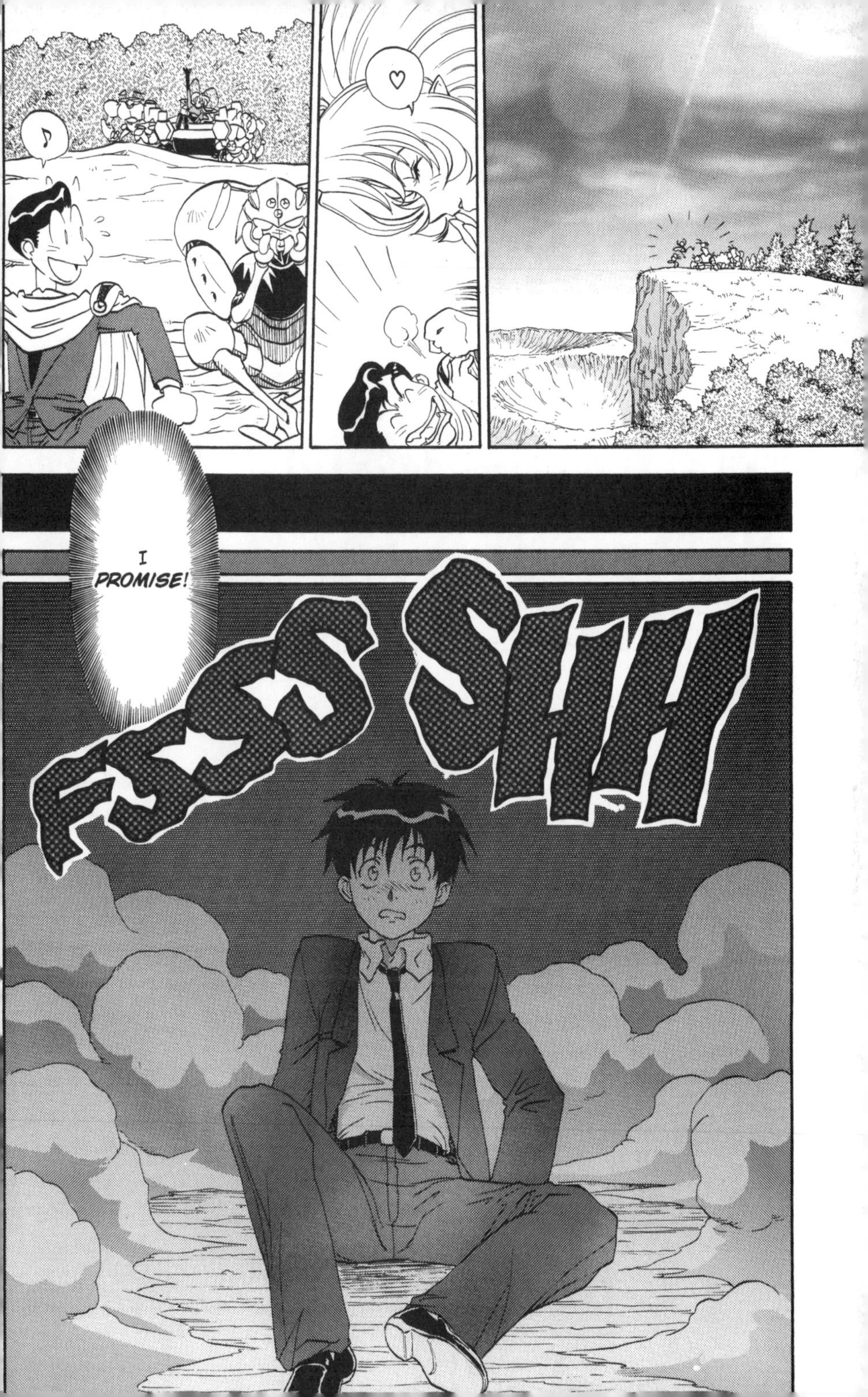
♪
♡
I PROMISE!
FSSS SHH

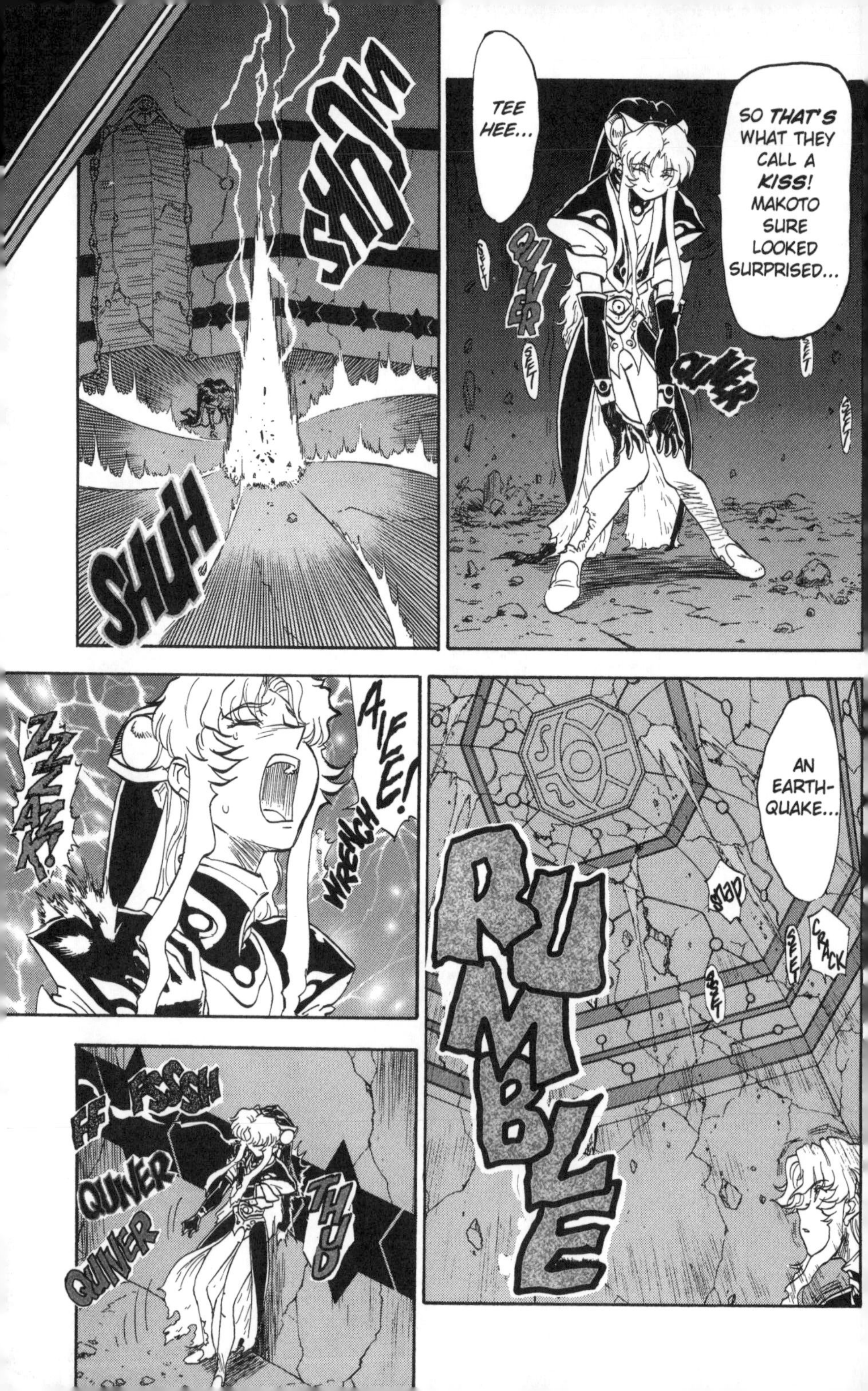
SHOOM
SHUH
TEE HEE...
SO *THAT'S* WHAT THEY CALL A ***KISS***! MAKOTO SURE LOOKED SURPRISED...
QUIVER
SFFT
SFFT
QUIVER
SFFT
SFFT
ZZZAZZK!
AIEEE!
WRENCH
AN EARTH-QUAKE...
RUMBLE
SNAP
SFFT
CRACK
SFFT
FFWOOSH
QUIVER
QUIVER
THUD

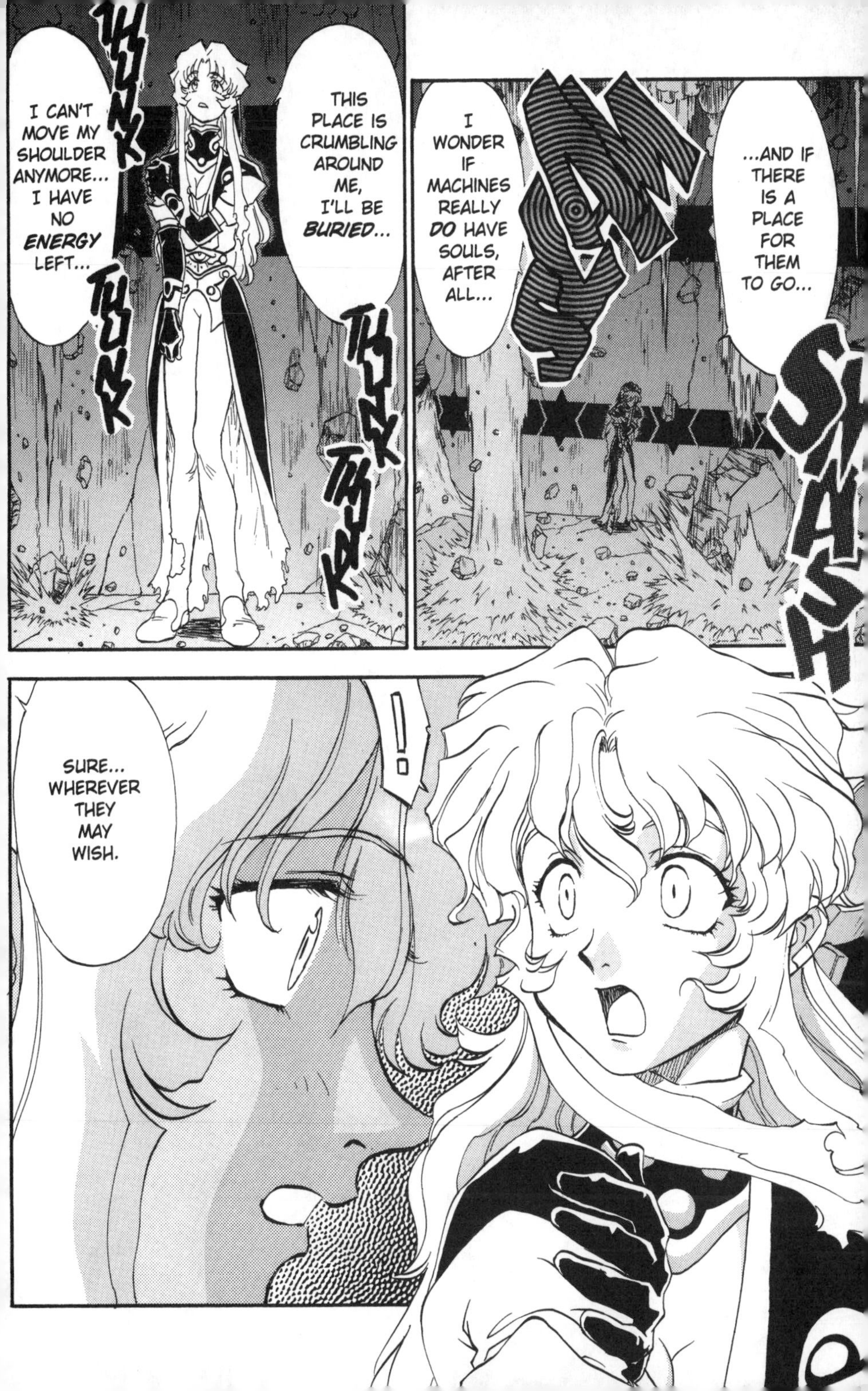

THUNK
I CAN'T MOVE MY SHOULDER ANYMORE... I HAVE NO ENERGY LEFT...
THUNK
THIS PLACE IS CRUMBLING AROUND ME, I'LL BE BURIED...
THUNK
I WONDER IF MACHINES REALLY DO HAVE SOULS, AFTER ALL...
...AND IF THERE IS A PLACE FOR THEM TO GO...
SMASH
SURE... WHEREVER THEY MAY WISH.
!

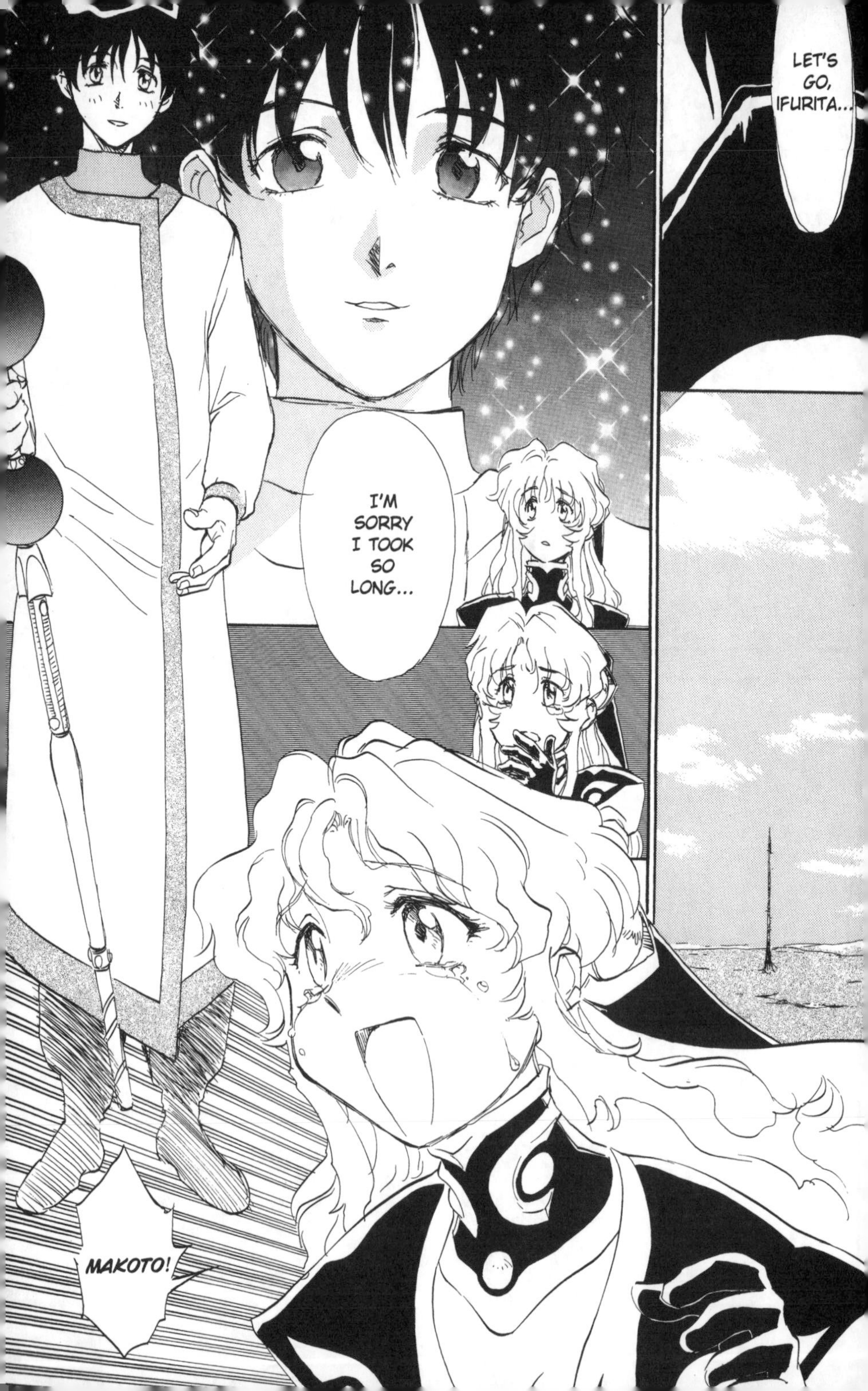
LET'S GO, IFURITA...
I'M SORRY I TOOK SO LONG...
MAKOTO!

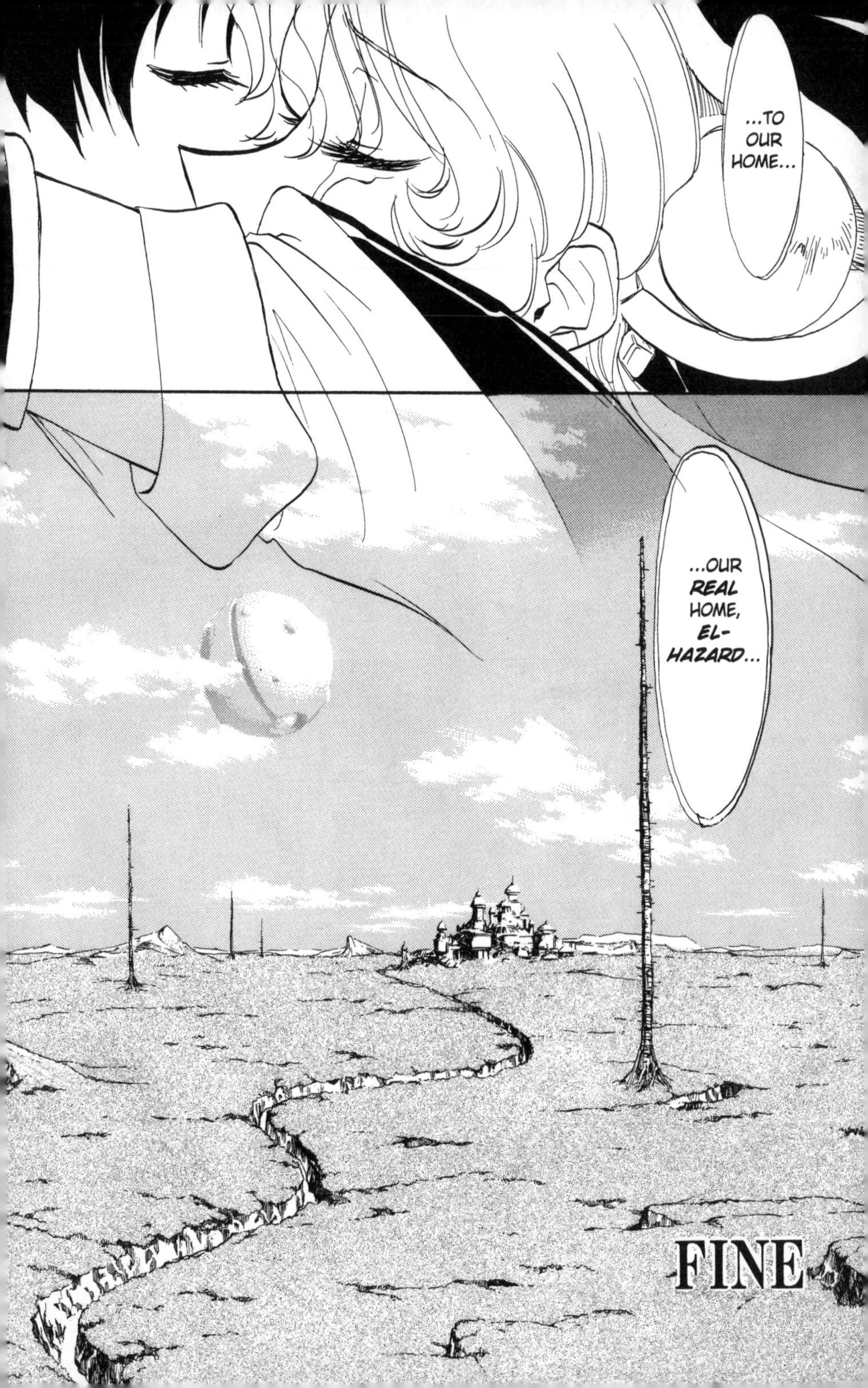
...TO OUR HOME...
...OUR REAL HOME, EL-HAZARD...
FINE

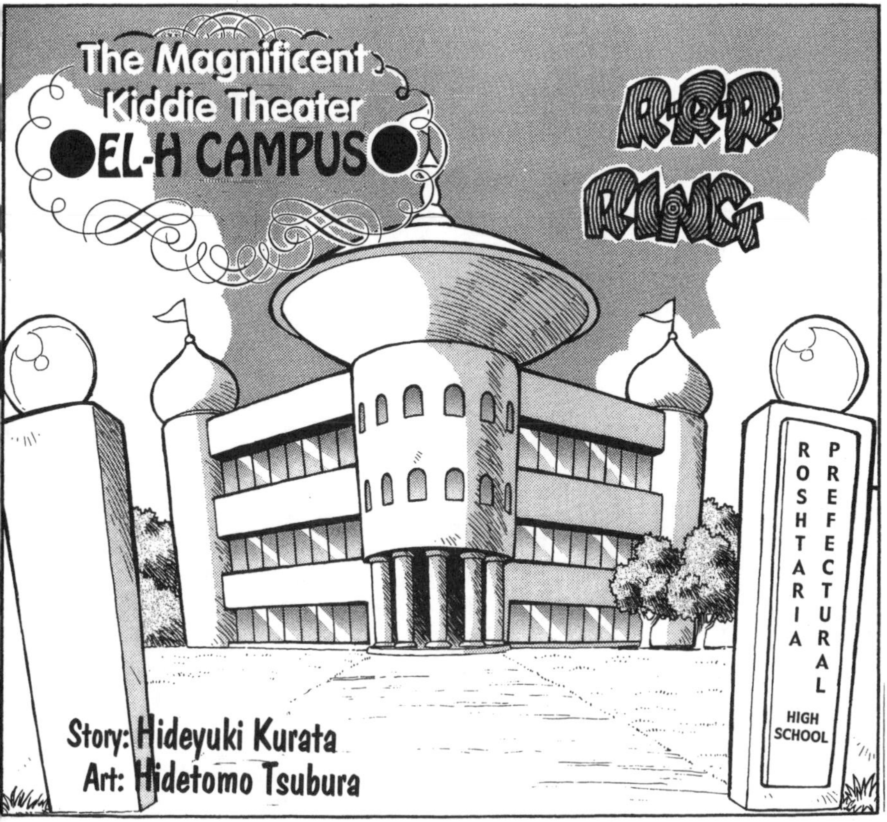
The Magnificent Kiddie Theater
●EL-H CAMPUS●
R-R-R-RING
ROSHTARIA PREFECTURAL HIGH SCHOOL
Story: Hideyuki Kurata
Art: Hidetomo Tsubura

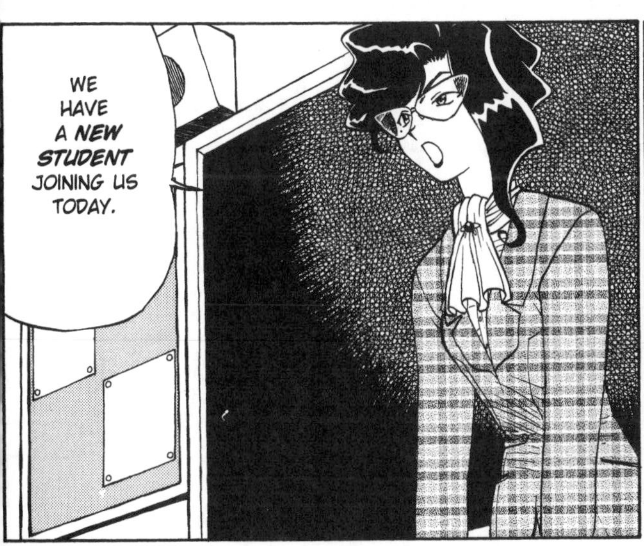
WE HAVE A NEW STUDENT JOINING US TODAY.

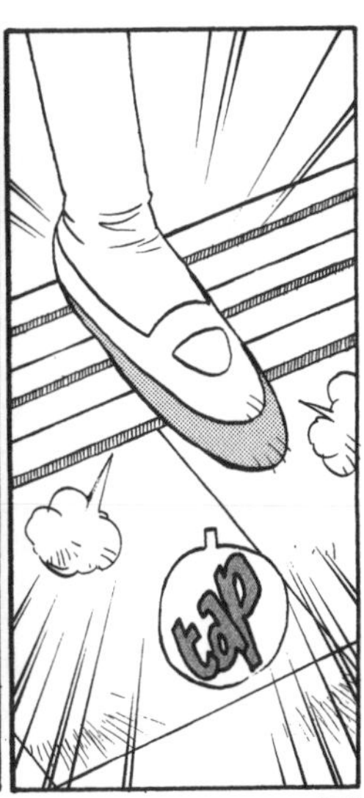
tap

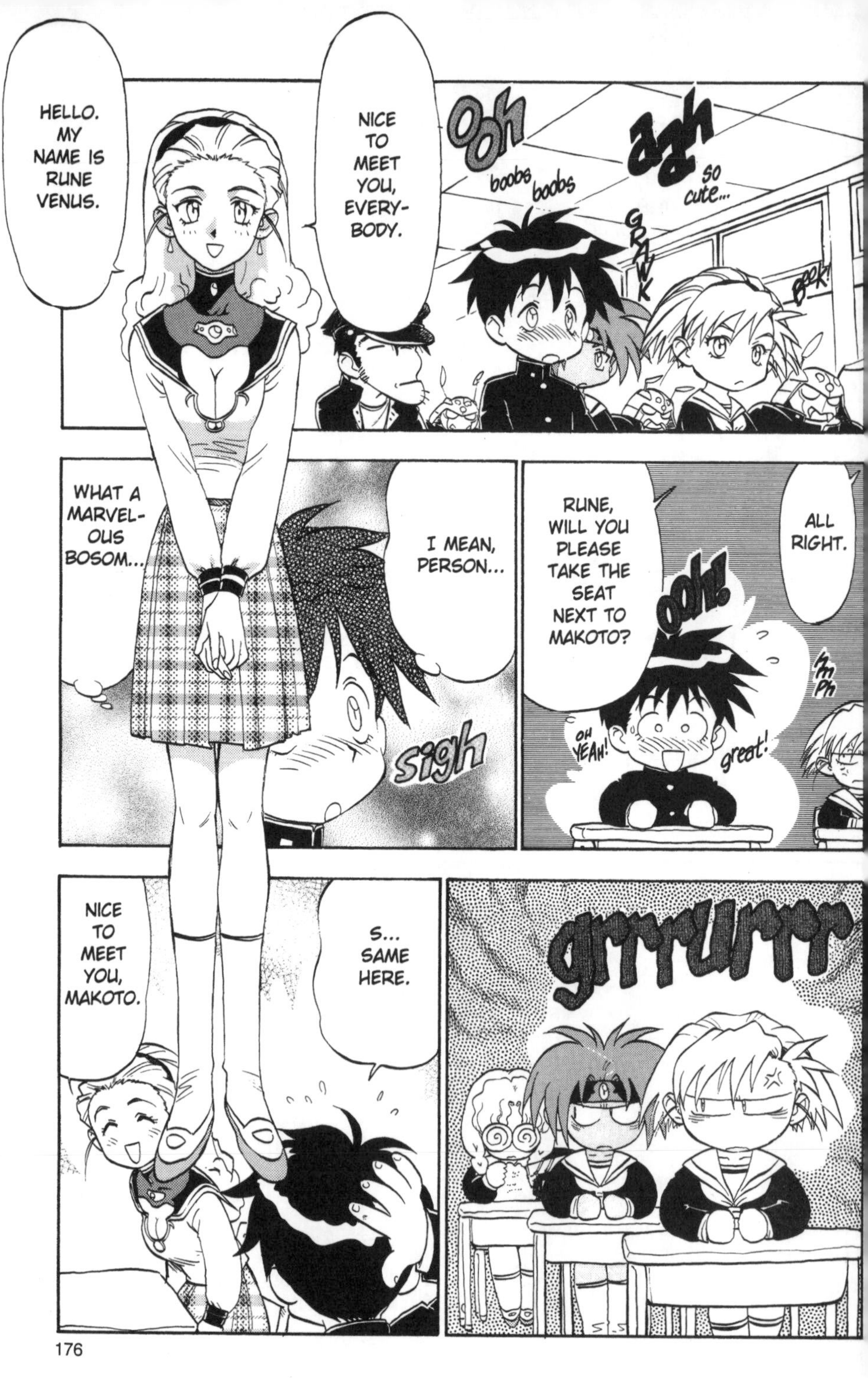
HELLO. MY NAME IS RUNE VENUS.
NICE TO MEET YOU, EVERY-BODY.
oooh
boobs
boobs
aagh
so cute...
GRAWK
BEEK!
WHAT A MARVEL-OUS BOSOM...
I MEAN, PERSON...
sigh
RUNE, WILL YOU PLEASE TAKE THE SEAT NEXT TO MAKOTO?
ALL RIGHT.
OOH!
OH YEAH!
great!
hmph
NICE TO MEET YOU, MAKOTO.
S... SAME HERE.
grrrurrr

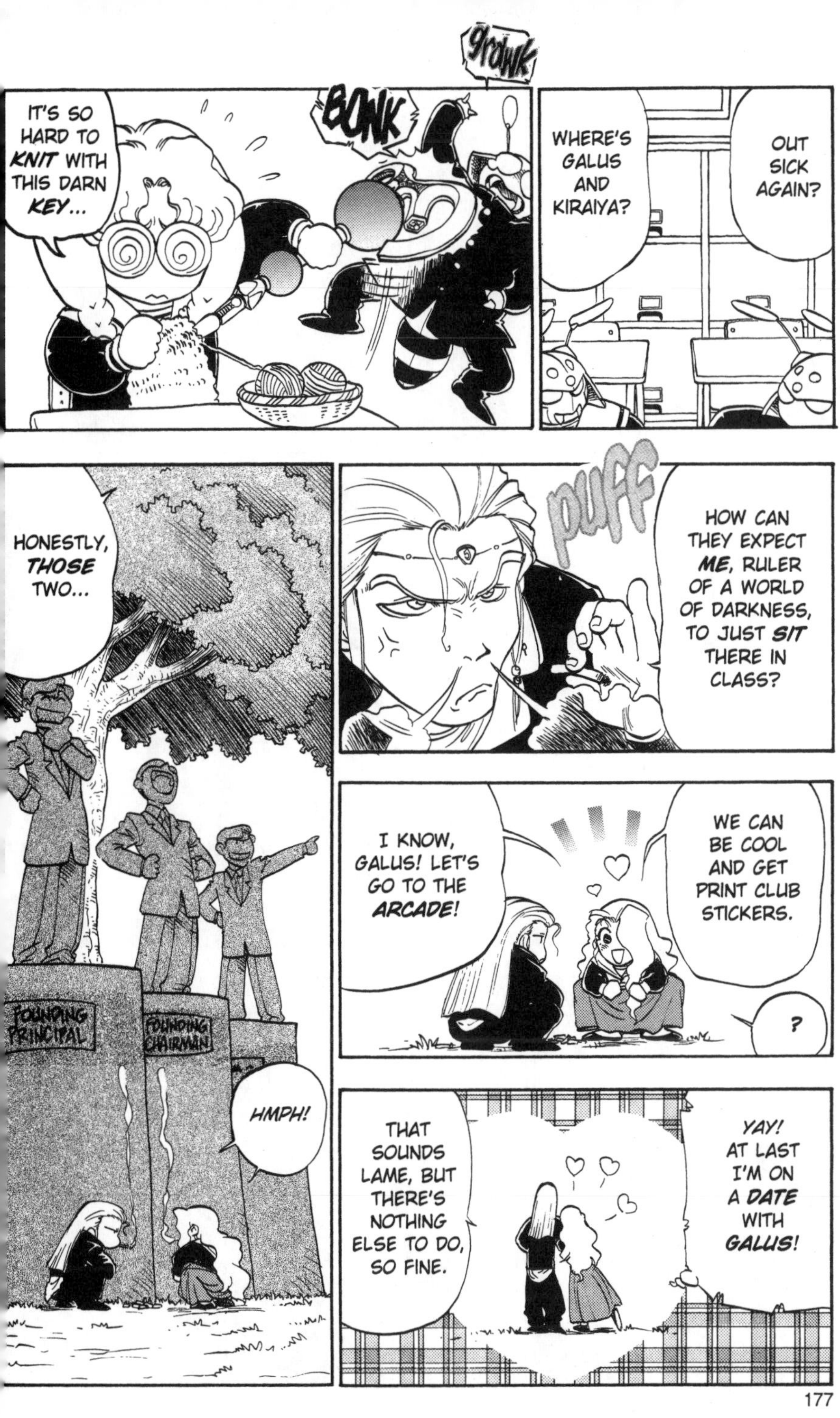
growk
BONK
IT'S SO HARD TO KNIT WITH THIS DARN KEY...
WHERE'S GALUS AND KIRAIYA?
OUT SICK AGAIN?
HONESTLY, THOSE TWO...
FOUNDING PRINCIPAL
FOUNDING CHAIRMAN
HMPH!
PUFF
HOW CAN THEY EXPECT ME, RULER OF A WORLD OF DARKNESS, TO JUST SIT THERE IN CLASS?
I KNOW, GALUS! LET'S GO TO THE ARCADE!
WE CAN BE COOL AND GET PRINT CLUB STICKERS.
?
THAT SOUNDS LAME, BUT THERE'S NOTHING ELSE TO DO, SO FINE.
YAY! AT LAST I'M ON A DATE WITH GALUS!

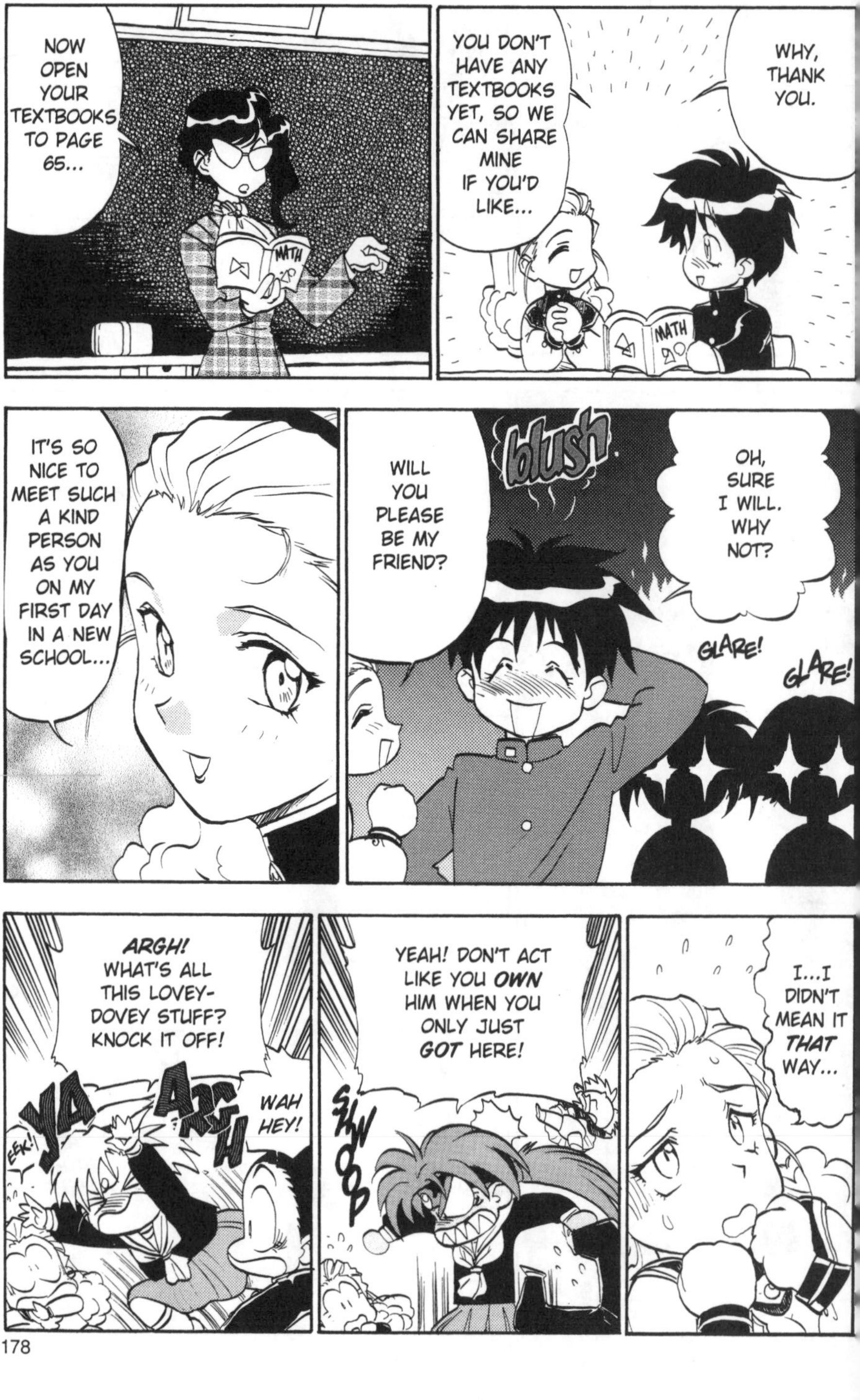
NOW OPEN YOUR TEXTBOOKS TO PAGE 65...
MATH
YOU DON'T HAVE ANY TEXTBOOKS YET, SO WE CAN SHARE MINE IF YOU'D LIKE...
WHY, THANK YOU.
MATH
IT'S SO NICE TO MEET SUCH A KIND PERSON AS YOU ON MY FIRST DAY IN A NEW SCHOOL...
WILL YOU PLEASE BE MY FRIEND?
blush
OH, SURE I WILL. WHY NOT?
GLARE!
GLARE!
ARGH! WHAT'S ALL THIS LOVEY-DOVEY STUFF? KNOCK IT OFF!
YA
ARGH
WAH HEY!
EEK!
YEAH! DON'T ACT LIKE YOU OWN HIM WHEN YOU ONLY JUST GOT HERE!
SWOOP
I...I DIDN'T MEAN IT THAT WAY...

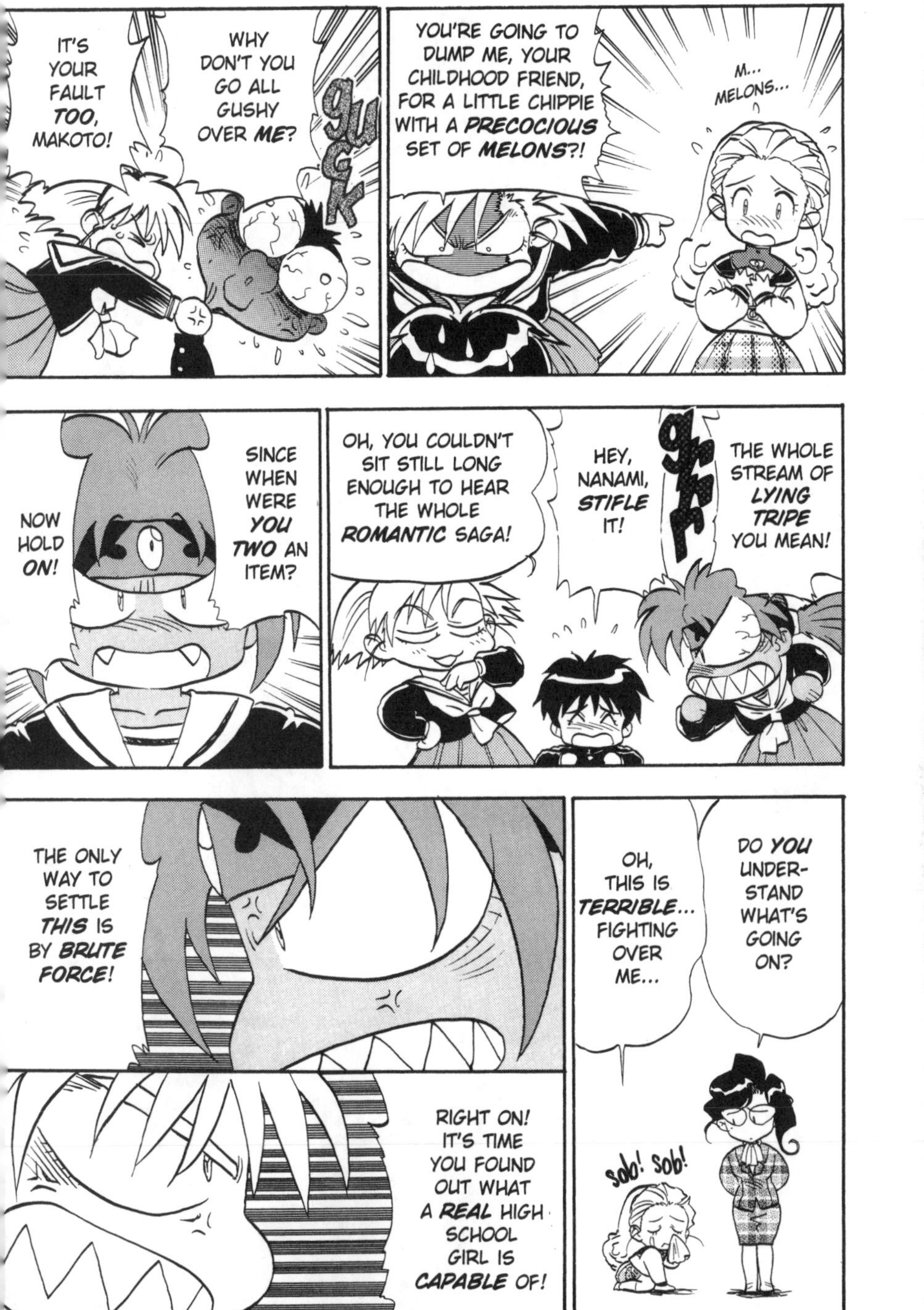

IT'S YOUR FAULT TOO, MAKOTO!
WHY DON'T YOU GO ALL GUSHY OVER ME?
GUCK
YOU'RE GOING TO DUMP ME, YOUR CHILDHOOD FRIEND, FOR A LITTLE CHIPPIE WITH A PRECOCIOUS SET OF MELONS?!
M... MELONS...
NOW HOLD ON!
SINCE WHEN WERE YOU TWO AN ITEM?
OH, YOU COULDN'T SIT STILL LONG ENOUGH TO HEAR THE WHOLE ROMANTIC SAGA!
HEY, NANAMI, STIFLE IT!
THE WHOLE STREAM OF LYING TRIPE YOU MEAN!
THE ONLY WAY TO SETTLE THIS IS BY BRUTE FORCE!
RIGHT ON! IT'S TIME YOU FOUND OUT WHAT A REAL HIGH SCHOOL GIRL IS CAPABLE OF!
OH, THIS IS TERRIBLE... FIGHTING OVER ME...
DO YOU UNDERSTAND WHAT'S GOING ON?
SOB! SOB!

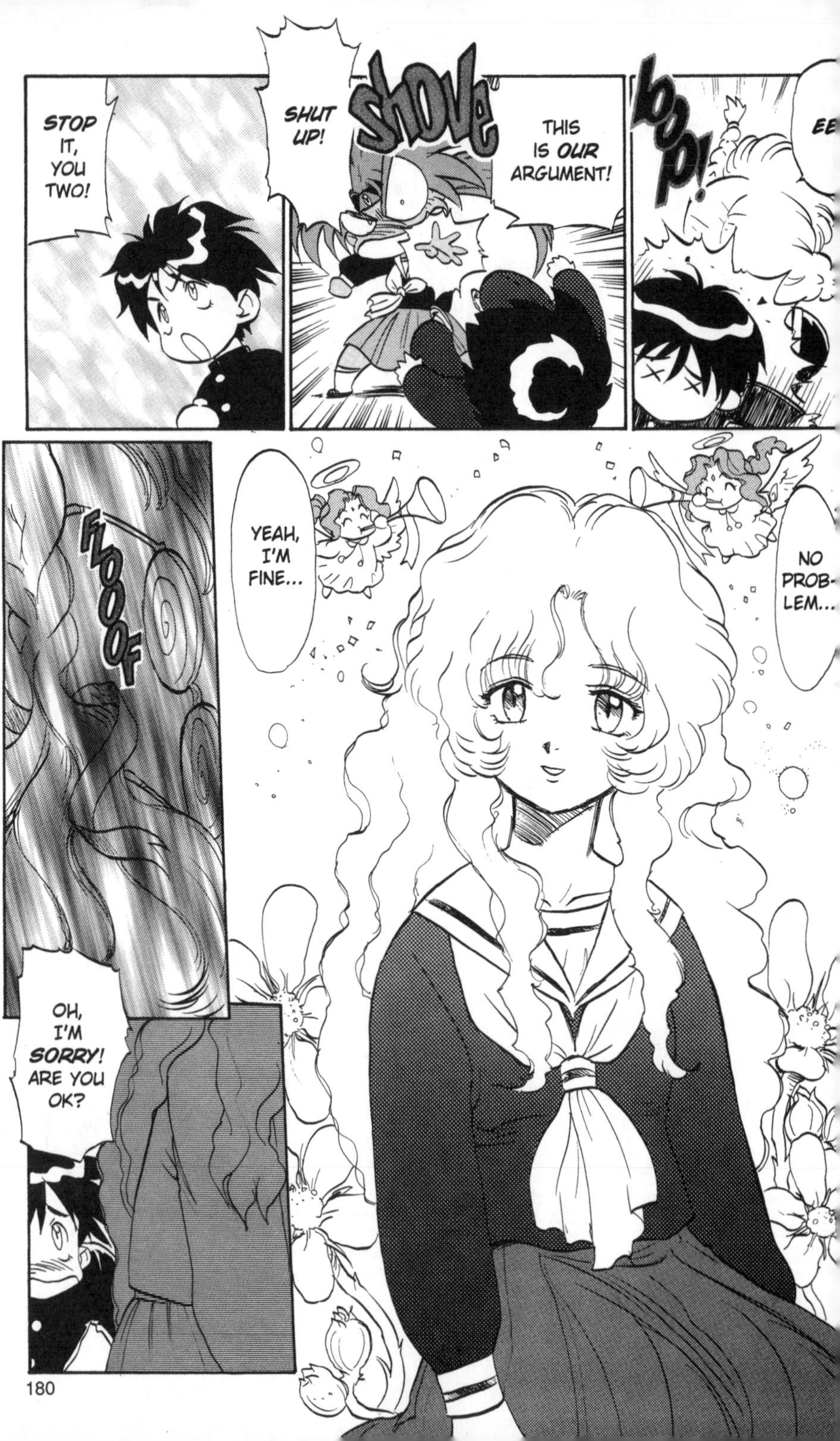
STOP IT, YOU TWO!
SHUT UP!
SHOVE
THIS IS OUR ARGUMENT!
BOOP!
EE
OH, I'M SORRY! ARE YOU OK?
FLOOOF
YEAH, I'M FINE...
NO PROB-LEM...

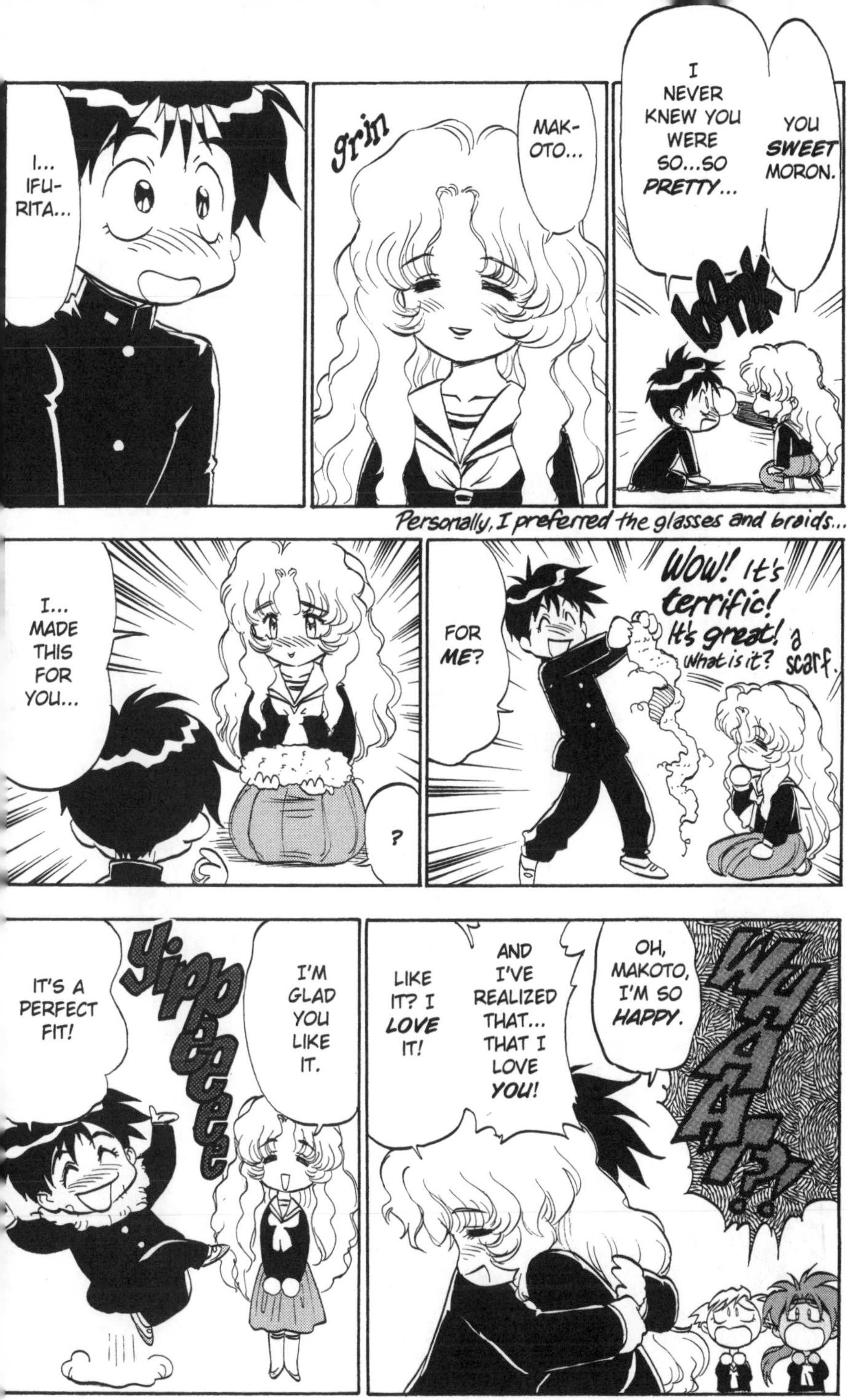

I... IFURITA...
grin
MAKOTO...
I NEVER KNEW YOU WERE SO...SO PRETTY...
bonk
YOU SWEET MORON.
Personally, I preferred the glasses and braids...
I... MADE THIS FOR YOU...
?
FOR ME?
WOW! It's terrific! It's great!
What is it?
a scarf.
IT'S A PERFECT FIT!
yippeeee
I'M GLAD YOU LIKE IT.
LIKE IT? I LOVE IT!
AND I'VE REALIZED THAT... THAT I LOVE YOU!
OH, MAKOTO, I'M SO HAPPY.
WHAAAT!?

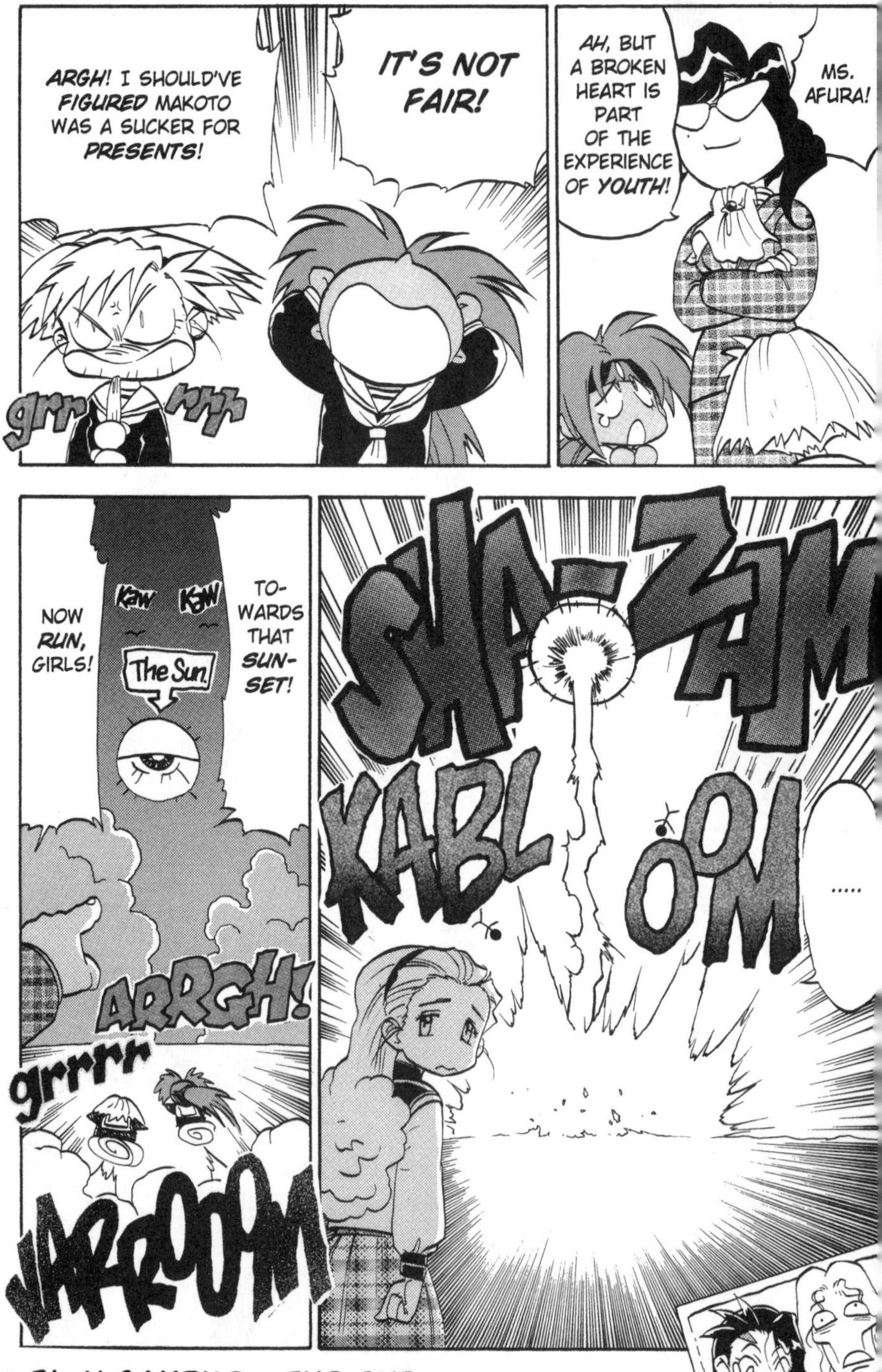
ARGH! I SHOULD'VE FIGURED MAKOTO WAS A SUCKER FOR PRESENTS!
grrr
IT'S NOT FAIR!
AH, BUT A BROKEN HEART IS PART OF THE EXPERIENCE OF YOUTH!
MS. AFURA!
NOW RUN, GIRLS!
Kaw Kaw
The Sun.
TO-WARDS THAT SUN-SET!
ARRGH!
grrrr
VARROOM
SHA-ZAM
KABLOOM
.....

EL-H CAMPUS - THE END.

The following pages showcase the monthly comics covers for ***El-Hazard*** Volume 3 Number 1 to Volume 3 Number 6.

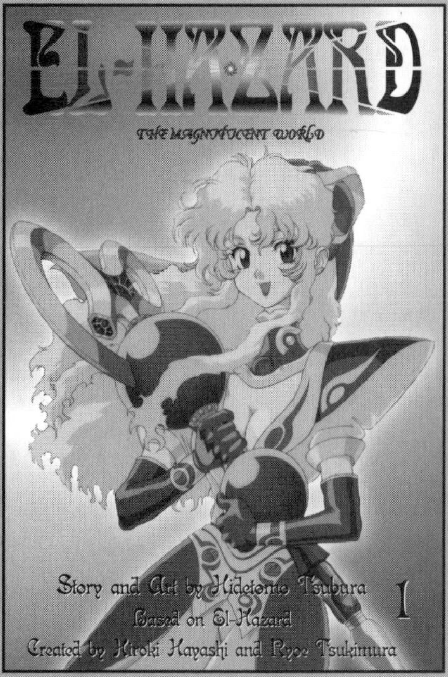
EL-HAZARD
THE MAGNIFICENT WORLD
Story and Art by Hidetomo Tsubura
1
Based on El-Hazard
Created by Hiroki Hayashi and Ryoe Tsukimura

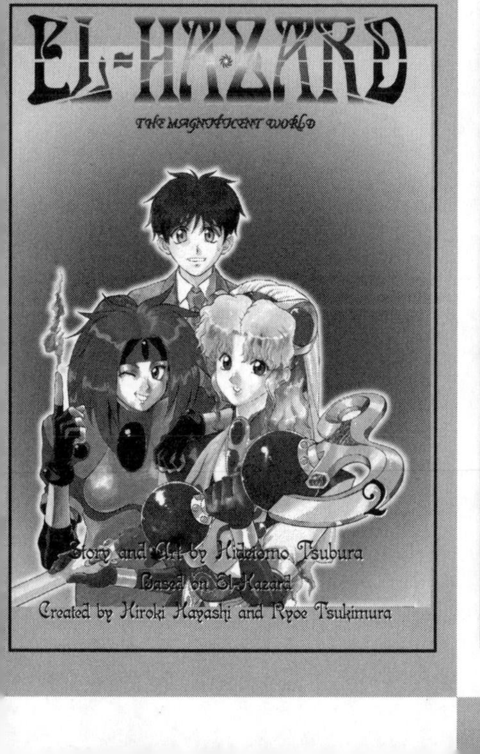
EL-HAZARD
THE MAGNIFICENT WORLD
2
Story and Art by Hidetomo Tsubura
Based on El-Hazard
Created by Hiroki Hayashi and Ryoe Tsukimura

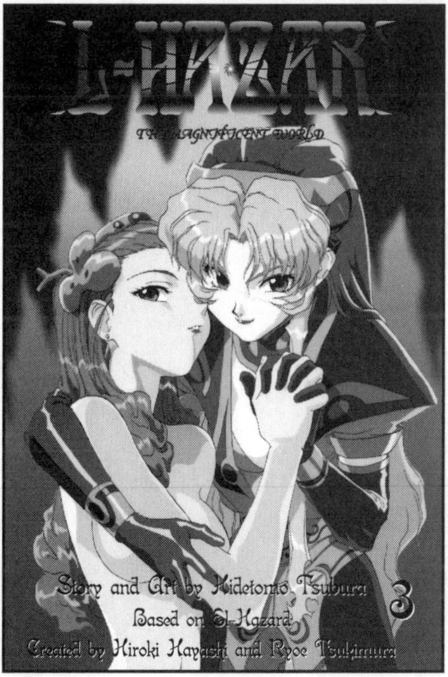
EL-HAZARD
THE MAGNIFICENT WORLD
Story and Art by Hidetomo Tsubura
3
Based on El-Hazard
Created by Hiroki Hayashi and Ryoe Tsukimura

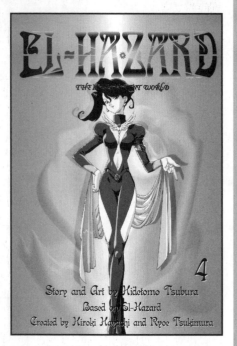

EL-HAZARD
THE MAGNIFICENT WORLD

4

Story and Art by Hidetomo Tsubura
Based on El-Hazard
Created by Hiroki Hayashi and Ryoe Tsukimura

EL-HAZARD
THE MAGNIFICENT WORLD

5

Story and Art by Hidetomo Tsubura
Based on El-Hazard
Created by Hiroki Hayashi and Ryoe Tsukimura

EL-HAZARD
THE MAGNIFICENT WORLD

6

Story and Art by Hidetomo Tsubura
Based on El-Hazard
Created by Hiroki Hayashi and Ryoe Tsukimura